FIREARMS LAWS OF MICHIGAN

2018-2019 Edition

Last Updated: April 2018

Compiled by the Michigan Legislative Service Bureau

Pursuant to Act 381 of the Public Acts of 2000

Michigan Legal Publishing Ltd.
Grand Rapids, Michigan

Academic and bulk discounts available at
www.michlp.com

WE WELCOME YOUR FEEDBACK: info@michlp.com

ISBN-13: 978-1-64002-043-6

TABLE OF CONTENTS

Opinions of the Attorney General

CONSTITUTION OF THE UNITED STATES (EXCERPT)

We the People of the United States, in Order to form a more perfect Union, establish Justice, insure domestic Tranquility, provide for the common defence, promote the general Welfare, and secure the Blessings of Liberty to ourselves and our Posterity, do ordain and establish this Constitution for the United States of America.

AMENDMENT II.

A well regulated Militia, being necessary to the security of a free State, the right of the people to keep and bear Arms, shall not be infringed.

CONSTITUTION OF MICHIGAN OF 1963 (EXCERPT)

Preamble.

We, the people of the State of Michigan, grateful to Almighty God for the blessings of freedom, and earnestly desiring to secure these blessings undiminished to ourselves and our posterity, do ordain and establish this constitution.

ARTICLE I
DECLARATION OF RIGHTS

§ 6 Bearing of arms.

Sec. 6. Every person has a right to keep and bear arms for the defense of himself and the state.

History: Const. 1963, Art. I, § 6, Eff. Jan. 1, 1964.

Former constitution: See Const. 1908, Art. II, § 5.

PURCHASE OF RIFLES AND SHOTGUNS
Act 207 of 1969

AN ACT to permit residents to purchase rifles and shotguns in contiguous states and to provide for reciprocity.

History: 1969, Act 207, Imd. Eff. Aug. 6, 1969.

The People of the State of Michigan enact:

3.111 Rifles and shotguns; purchases by residents.

Sec. 1. Residents of this state may purchase rifles and shotguns in any state if they conform to the federal gun control act of 1968, Public Law 90-618, and the regulations issued under that act, as administered by the secretary of the treasury, and with the laws of the state in which the purchase is made.

History: 1969, Act 207, Imd. Eff. Aug. 6, 1969;—Am. 2012, Act 378, Imd. Eff. Dec. 18, 2012.

3.112 Rifles and shotguns; purchases by nonresidents.

Sec. 2. Residents of another state may purchase rifles and shotguns in this state if they conform to the federal gun control act of 1968, Public Law 90-618, and the regulations issued under that act, as administered by the secretary of the treasury, and with the laws of the state in which the purchaser resides.

History: 1969, Act 207, Imd. Eff. Aug. 6, 1969;—Am. 2012, Act 378, Imd. Eff. Dec. 18, 2012.

REVISED STATUTES OF 1846 (EXCERPT)

History: R.S. 1846, Ch. 1.

Be it enacted by the Senate and House of Representatives of the State of Michigan:

CHAPTER 1
CHAPTER 1. OF THE STATUTES.

8.3t "Firearm" defined.

Sec. 3t. The word "firearm", except as otherwise specifically defined in statute, includes any weapon which will, is designed to, or may readily be converted to expel a projectile by action of an explosive.

History: Add. 1959, Act 189, Imd. Eff. July 22, 1959;—Am. 2015, Act 22, Eff. July 1, 2015.

FIREARMS
Act 372 of 1927

AN ACT to regulate and license the selling, purchasing, possessing, and carrying of certain firearms, gas ejecting devices, and electro-muscular disruption devices; to prohibit the buying, selling, or carrying of certain firearms, gas ejecting devices, and electro-muscular disruption devices without a license or other authorization; to provide for the forfeiture of firearms and electro-muscular disruption devices under certain circumstances; to provide for penalties and remedies; to provide immunity from civil liability under certain circumstances; to prescribe the powers and duties of certain state and local agencies; to prohibit certain conduct against individuals who apply for or receive a license to carry a concealed pistol; to make appropriations; to prescribe certain conditions for the appropriations; and to repeal all acts and parts of acts inconsistent with this act.

History: 1927, Act 372, Eff. Sept. 5, 1927;—Am. 1929, Act 206, Imd. Eff. May 20, 1929;—Am. 1931, Act 333, Imd. Eff. June 16, 1931;—Am. 1980, Act 345, Eff. Mar. 31, 1981;—Am. 1990, Act 320, Eff. Mar. 28, 1991;—Am. 2000, Act 265, Imd. Eff. June 29, 2000;—Am. 2000, Act 381, Eff. July 1, 2001;—Am. 2012, Act 123, Eff. Aug. 6, 2012.

Popular name: CCW

Popular name: Concealed Weapons

Popular name: CPL

Popular name: Right to Carry

Popular name: Shall Issue

The People of the State of Michigan enact:

28.421 Definitions; lawful owning, possessing, carrying, or transporting of pistol greater than 26 inches in length; conditions; firearm not considered as pistol; election.

Sec. 1. (1) As used in this act:

(a) "Corrections officer of the department of corrections" means a state correctional officer as that term is defined in section 2 of the correctional officers' training act of 1982, 1982 PA 415, MCL 791.502.

(b) "Felony" means, except as otherwise provided in this subdivision, that term as defined in section 1 of chapter I of the code of criminal procedure, 1927 PA 175, MCL 761.1, or a violation of a law of the United States or another state that is designated as a felony or that is punishable by death or by imprisonment for more than 1 year. Felony does not include a violation of a penal law of this state that is expressly designated as a misdemeanor.

(c) "Firearm" means any weapon which will, is designed to, or may readily be converted to expel a projectile by action of an explosive.

(d) "Firearms records" means any form, information, or record required for submission to a government agency under sections 2, 2a, 2b, and 5b, or any form, permit, or license issued by a government agency under this act.

(e) "Local corrections officer" means that term as defined in section 2 of the local corrections officers training act, 2003 PA 125, MCL 791.532.

(f) "Misdemeanor" means a violation of a penal law of this state or violation of a local ordinance substantially corresponding to a violation of a penal law of this state that is not a felony or a violation of an order, rule, or regulation of a state agency that is punishable by imprisonment or a fine that is not a civil fine, or both.

(g) "Parole or probation officer of the department of corrections" means any individual employed by the department of corrections to supervise felony probationers or parolees or that individual's immediate supervisor.

(h) "Peace officer" means, except as otherwise provided in this act, an individual who is employed as a law enforcement officer, as that term is defined under section 2 of the Michigan commission on law enforcement standards act, 1965 PA 203, MCL 28.602, by this state or another state, a political subdivision of this state or another state, or the United States, and who is required to carry a firearm in the course of his or her duties as a law enforcement officer.

(i) "Pistol" means a loaded or unloaded firearm that is 26 inches or less in length, or a loaded or unloaded firearm that by its construction and appearance conceals it as a firearm.

(j) "Purchaser" means a person who receives a pistol from another person by purchase or gift.

(k) "Reserve peace officer", "auxiliary officer", or "reserve officer" means, except as otherwise provided in this act, an individual authorized on a voluntary or irregular basis by a duly authorized police agency of this state or a political subdivision of this state to act as a law enforcement officer, who is responsible for the preservation of the peace, the prevention and detection of crime, and the enforcement of the general criminal laws of this state, and who is otherwise eligible to possess a firearm under this act.

(*l*) "Retired corrections officer of the department of corrections" means an individual who was a corrections officer of the department of corrections and who retired in good standing from his or her employment as a corrections officer of the department of corrections.

(m) "Retired federal law enforcement officer" means an individual who was an officer or agent employed by a law enforcement agency of the United States government whose primary responsibility was enforcing laws of the United States, who was required to carry a firearm in the course of his or her duties as a law enforcement officer, and who retired in good standing from his or her employment as a federal law enforcement officer.

(n) "Retired parole or probation officer of the department of corrections" means an individual who was a parole or probation officer of the department of corrections and who retired in good standing from his or her employment as a parole or probation officer of the department of corrections.

(o) "Retired police officer" or "retired law enforcement officer" means an individual who was a police officer or law enforcement officer who was licensed or certified as described in the Michigan commission on law enforcement standards act, 1965 PA 203, MCL 28.601 to 28.615, and retired in good standing from his or her employment as a police officer or law enforcement officer. A police officer or law enforcement officer retired in good standing if he or she receives a pension or other retirement benefit for his or her service as a police officer or law enforcement officer or actively maintained a Michigan commission on law enforcement standards or equivalent state certification or license from this state or another state for not less than 10 consecutive years.

(p) "Seller" means a person who sells or gives a pistol to another person.

(q) "State court judge" means a judge of the district court, circuit court, probate court, or court of appeals or justice of the supreme court of this state who is serving either by election or appointment.

(r) "State court retired judge" means a judge or justice described in subdivision (q) who is retired, or a retired judge of the recorders court.

(2) A person may lawfully own, possess, carry, or transport as a pistol a firearm greater than 26 inches in length if all of the following conditions apply:

(a) The person registered the firearm as a pistol under section 2 or 2a before January 1, 2013.

(b) The person who registered the firearm as described in subdivision (a) has maintained registration of the firearm since January 1, 2013 without lapse.

(c) The person possesses a copy of the license or record issued to him or her under section 2 or 2a.

(3) A person who satisfies all of the conditions listed under subsection (2) nevertheless may elect to have the firearm not be considered to be a pistol. A person who makes the election under this subsection shall notify the department of state police of the election in a manner prescribed by that department.

History: 1927, Act 372, Eff. Sept. 5, 1927;—CL 1929, 16749;—CL 1948, 28.421;—Am. 1964, Act 216, Eff. Aug. 28, 1964;—Am. 1992, Act 219, Imd. Eff. Oct. 13, 1992;—Am. 2000, Act 381, Eff. July 1, 2001;—Am. 2002, Act 719, Eff. July 1, 2003;—Am. 2008, Act 407, Eff. Apr. 6, 2009;—Am. 2012, Act 243, Eff. Jan. 1, 2013;—Am. 2014, Act 203, Eff. Dec. 21, 2014;—Am. 2015, Act 3, Eff. Dec. 1, 2015;—Am. 2015, Act 16, Eff. July 13, 2015;—Am. 2015, Act 25, Eff. July 1, 2015;—Am. 2015, Act 207, Eff. Dec. 1, 2015;—Am. 2016, Act 301, Eff. Jan. 2, 2017;—Am. 2017, Act 95, Eff. Oct. 11, 2017.

Popular name: CCW

Popular name: Concealed Weapons

Popular name: CPL

Popular name: Right to Carry

Popular name: Shall Issue

28.421a Concealed pistol licenses; issuance; creation of standardized system.

Sec. 1a. It is the intent of the legislature to create a standardized system for issuing concealed pistol licenses to prevent criminals and other violent individuals from obtaining a license to carry a concealed pistol, to allow law abiding residents to obtain a license to carry a concealed pistol, and to prescribe the rights and responsibilities of individuals who have obtained a license to carry a concealed pistol. It is also the intent of the legislature to grant an applicant the right to know why his or her application for a concealed pistol license is denied and to create a process by which an applicant may appeal that denial.

History: Add. 2000, Act 381, Eff. July 1, 2001.

Popular name: CCW

Popular name: Concealed Weapons

Popular name: CPL

Popular name: Right to Carry

Popular name: Shall Issue

28.421b Firearms records; confidentiality; disclosure prohibited; exceptions; violation as civil infraction; fine.

Sec. 1b. (1) Firearms records are confidential, are not subject to disclosure under the freedom of information act, 1976 PA 442, MCL 15.231 to 15.246, and shall not be disclosed to any person, except as otherwise provided by this section.

(2) Firearms records may only be accessed and disclosed by a peace officer or authorized system user for the following purposes:

(a) The individual whose firearms records are the subject of disclosure poses a threat to himself or herself or other individuals, including a peace officer.

(b) The individual whose firearms records are the subject of disclosure has committed an offense with a pistol that violates a law of this state, another state, or the United States.

(c) The pistol that is the subject of the firearms records search may have been used during the commission of an offense that violates a law of this state, another state, or the United States.

(d) To ensure the safety of a peace officer.

(e) For purposes of this act.

(f) A peace officer or an authorized user has reason to believe that access to the firearms records is necessary within the commission of his or her lawful duties. The peace officer or authorized system user shall enter and record the specific reason in the system in accordance with the procedures in section 5e.

(3) A person who intentionally violates subsection (2) is responsible for a state civil infraction and may be ordered to pay a civil fine of not more than $500.00.

History: Add. 2014, Act 202, Eff. Dec. 21, 2014.

28.422 License to purchase, carry, possess, or transport pistol; issuance; qualifications; applications; sale of pistol; exemptions; transfer of ownership to heir or devisee; nonresident; active duty status; forging application as felony; implementation during business hours.

Sec. 2. (1) Except as otherwise provided in this act, a person shall not purchase, carry, possess, or transport a pistol in this state without first having obtained a license for the pistol as prescribed in this section.

(2) A person who brings a pistol into this state who is on leave from active duty with the armed forces of the United States or who has been discharged from active duty with the armed forces of the United States shall obtain a license for the pistol within 30 days after his or her arrival in this state.

(3) The commissioner or chief of police of a city, township, or village police department that issues licenses to purchase, carry, possess, or transport pistols, or his or her duly authorized deputy, or the sheriff or his or her duly authorized deputy, in the parts of a county not included within a city, township, or village having an organized police department, in discharging the duty to issue licenses shall with due speed and diligence issue licenses to purchase, carry, possess, or transport pistols to qualified applicants unless he or she has probable cause to believe that the applicant would be a threat to himself or herself or to other individuals, or would commit an offense with the pistol that would violate a law of this or another state or of the United States. An applicant is qualified if all of the following circumstances exist:

(a) The person is not subject to an order or disposition for which he or she has received notice and an opportunity for a hearing, and which was entered into the law enforcement information network under any of the following:

(*i*) Section 464a of the mental health code, 1974 PA 258, MCL 330.1464a.

(*ii*) Section 5107 of the estates and protected individuals code, 1998 PA 386, MCL 700.5107, or section 444a of former 1978 PA 642.

(*iii*) Section 2950 of the revised judicature act of 1961, 1961 PA 236, MCL 600.2950.

(*iv*) Section 2950a of the revised judicature act of 1961, 1961 PA 236, MCL 600.2950a.

(*v*) Section 14 of 1846 RS 84, MCL 552.14.

(*vi*) Section 6b of chapter V of the code of criminal procedure, 1927 PA 175, MCL 765.6b, if the order has a condition imposed under section 6b(3) of chapter V of the code of criminal procedure, 1927 PA 175, MCL 765.6b.

(*vii*) Section 16b of chapter IX of the code of criminal procedure, 1927 PA 175, MCL 769.16b.

(b) The person is 18 years of age or older or, if the seller is licensed under 18 USC 923, is 21 years of age or older.

(c) The person is a citizen of the United States or an alien lawfully admitted into the United States and is a legal resident of this state. For the purposes of this section, a person is considered a legal resident of this state if any of the following apply:

(*i*) The person has a valid, lawfully obtained Michigan driver license issued under the Michigan vehicle code, 1949 PA 300, MCL 257.1 to 257.923, or an official state personal identification card issued under 1972 PA 222, MCL 28.291 to 28.300.

(*ii*) The person is lawfully registered to vote in this state.

(*iii*) The person is on active duty status with the United States armed forces and is stationed outside of this state, but the person's home of record is in this state.

(*iv*) The person is on active duty status with the United States armed forces and is permanently stationed in this state, but the person's home of record is in another state.

(d) A felony charge or a criminal charge listed in section 5b against the person is not pending at the time of application.

(e) The person is not prohibited from possessing, using, transporting, selling, purchasing, carrying, shipping, receiving, or distributing a firearm under section 224f of the Michigan penal code, 1931 PA 328, MCL 750.224f.

(f) The person has not been adjudged insane in this state or elsewhere unless he or she has been adjudged restored to sanity by court order.

(g) The person is not under an order of involuntary commitment in an inpatient or outpatient setting due to mental illness.

(h) The person has not been adjudged legally incapacitated in this state or elsewhere. This subdivision does not apply to a person who has had his or her legal capacity restored by order of the court.

(4) Applications for licenses under this section shall be signed by the applicant under oath upon forms provided by the director of the department of state police. Licenses to purchase, carry, possess, or transport pistols shall be executed in triplicate upon forms provided by the director of the department of state police and shall be signed by the licensing authority. Three copies of the license shall be delivered to the applicant by the licensing authority. A license is void unless used within 30 days after the date it is issued.

(5) If an individual purchases or otherwise acquires a pistol, the seller shall fill out the license forms describing the pistol, together with the date of sale or acquisition, and sign his or her name in ink indicating that the pistol was sold to or otherwise acquired by the purchaser. The purchaser shall also sign his or her name in ink indicating the purchase or other acquisition of

the pistol from the seller. The seller may retain a copy of the license as a record of the transaction. The purchaser shall receive 2 copies of the license. The purchaser shall return 1 copy of the license to the licensing authority within 10 days after the date the pistol is purchased or acquired. The return of the copy to the licensing authority may be made in person or may be made by first-class mail or certified mail sent within the 10-day period to the proper address of the licensing authority. A purchaser who fails to comply with the requirements of this subsection is responsible for a state civil infraction and may be fined not more than $250.00. If a purchaser is found responsible for a state civil infraction under this subsection, the court shall notify the department of state police of that determination.

(6) Within 10 days after receiving the license copy returned under subsection (5), the licensing authority shall electronically enter the information into the pistol entry database as required by the department of state police if it has the ability to electronically enter that information. If the licensing authority does not have that ability, the licensing authority shall provide that information to the department of state police in a manner otherwise required by the department of state police. Any licensing authority that provided pistol descriptions to the department of state police under former section 9 of this act shall continue to provide pistol descriptions to the department of state police under this subsection. Within 48 hours after entering or otherwise providing the information on the license copy returned under subsection (5) to the department of state police, the licensing authority shall forward the copy of the license to the department of state police. The purchaser has the right to obtain a copy of the information placed in the pistol entry database under this subsection to verify the accuracy of that information. The licensing authority may charge a fee not to exceed $1.00 for the cost of providing the copy. The licensee may carry, use, possess, and transport the pistol for 30 days beginning on the date of purchase or acquisition only while he or she is in possession of his or her copy of the license. However, the person is not required to have the license in his or her possession while carrying, using, possessing, or transporting the pistol after this period.

(7) This section does not apply to the purchase of pistols from wholesalers by dealers regularly engaged in the business of selling pistols at retail, or to the sale, barter, or exchange of pistols kept as relics or curios not made for modern ammunition or permanently deactivated.

(8) This section does not prevent the transfer of ownership of pistols to an heir or devisee, whether by testamentary bequest or by the laws of intestacy regardless of whether the pistol is registered with this state. An individual who has inherited a pistol shall obtain a license as required in this section within 30 days of taking physical possession of the pistol. The license may be signed by a next of kin of the decedent or the person authorized to dispose of property under the estates and protected individuals code, 1998 PA 386, MCL 700.1101 to 700.8206, including when the next of kin is the individual inheriting the pistol. If the heir or devisee is not qualified for a license under this section, the heir or devisee may direct the next of kin or person authorized to dispose of property under the estates and protected individuals code, 1998 PA 386, MCL 700.1101 to 700.8206, to dispose of the pistol in any manner that is lawful and the heir or devisee considers appropriate. The person authorized to dispose of property under the estates and protected individuals code, 1998 PA 386, MCL 700.1101 to 700.8206, is not required to obtain a license under this section if he or she takes temporary lawful possession of the pistol in the process of disposing of the pistol pursuant to the decedent's testamentary bequest or the laws of intestacy. A law enforcement agency may not seize or confiscate a pistol being transferred by testamentary bequest or the laws of intestacy unless the heir or devisee does not qualify for obtaining a license under this section and the next of kin or person authorized to dispose of property under the estates and protected individuals code, 1998 PA 386, MCL 700.1101 to 700.8206, is unable to retain his or her temporary possession of the pistol or find alternative lawful storage. If a law enforcement agency seizes or confiscates a pistol under this subsection, the heir or devisee who is not qualified to obtain a license under this section retains ownership interest in the pistol and, within 30 days of being notified of the seizure or confiscation, may file with a court of competent jurisdiction to direct the law enforcement agency to lawfully transfer or otherwise dispose of the pistol. A pistol seized under this subsection shall not be destroyed, sold, or used while in possession of the seizing entity or its agents until 30 days have passed since the heir or devisee has been notified of the seizure and no legal action regarding the lawful possession or ownership of the seized pistol has been filed in any court and is pending. As used in this subsection:

(a) "Devisee" means that term as defined in section 1103 of the estates and protected individuals code, 1998 PA 386, MCL 700.1103.

(b) "Heir" means that term as defined in section 1104 of the estates and protected individuals code, 1998 PA 386, MCL 700.1104.

(9) An individual who is not a resident of this state is not required to obtain a license under this section if all of the following conditions apply:

(a) The individual is licensed in his or her state of residence to purchase, carry, or transport a pistol.

(b) The individual is in possession of the license described in subdivision (a).

(c) The individual is the owner of the pistol he or she possesses, carries, or transports.

(d) The individual possesses the pistol for a lawful purpose.

(e) The individual is in this state for a period of 180 days or less and does not intend to establish residency in this state.

(10) An individual who is a nonresident of this state shall present the license described in subsection (9)(a) upon the demand of a police officer. An individual who violates this subsection is guilty of a misdemeanor punishable by imprisonment for not more than 90 days or a fine of not more than $100.00, or both.

(11) The licensing authority may require a person claiming active duty status with the United States armed forces to provide proof of 1 or both of the following:

(a) The person's home of record.

(b) Permanent active duty assignment in this state.

(12) This section does not apply to a person who is younger than the age required under subsection (3)(b) and who possesses a pistol if all of the following conditions apply:

(a) The person is not otherwise prohibited from possessing that pistol.

(b) The person is at a recognized target range.

(c) The person possesses the pistol for the purpose of target practice or instruction in the safe use of a pistol.

(d) The person is in the physical presence and under the direct supervision of any of the following:

(*i*) The person's parent.

(*ii*) The person's guardian.

(*iii*) An individual who is 21 years of age or older, who is authorized by the person's parent or guardian, and who has successfully completed a pistol safety training course or class that meets the requirements of section 5j(1)(a), (b), or (d), and received a certificate of completion.

(e) The owner of the pistol is physically present.

(13) This section does not apply to a person who possesses a pistol if all of the following conditions apply:

(a) The person is not otherwise prohibited from possessing a pistol.

(b) The person is at a recognized target range or shooting facility.

(c) The person possesses the pistol for the purpose of target practice or instruction in the safe use of a pistol.

(d) The owner of the pistol is physically present and supervising the use of the pistol.

(14) A person who forges any matter on an application for a license under this section is guilty of a felony, punishable by imprisonment for not more than 4 years or a fine of not more than $2,000.00, or both.

(15) A licensing authority shall implement this section during all of the licensing authority's normal business hours and shall set hours for implementation that allow an applicant to use the license within the time period set forth in subsection (4).

History: 1927, Act 372, Eff. Sept. 5, 1927;—CL 1929, 16750;—Am. 1931, Act 333, Imd. Eff. June 16, 1931;—Am. 1941, Act 112, Imd. Eff. May 21, 1941;—Am. 1943, Act 51, Imd. Eff. Mar. 30, 1943;—CL 1948, 28.422;—Am. 1949, Act 170, Eff. Sept. 23, 1949;—Am. 1957, Act 259, Eff. Sept. 27, 1957;—Am. 1964, Act 216, Eff. Aug. 28, 1964;—Am. 1967, Act 158, Eff. Nov. 2, 1967;—Am. 1968, Act 301, Eff. Nov. 15, 1968;—Am. 1972, Act 15, Imd. Eff. Feb. 19, 1972;—Am. 1986, Act 161, Eff. Aug. 1, 1986;—Am. 1990, Act 320, Eff. Mar. 28, 1991;—Am. 1992, Act 219, Imd. Eff. Oct. 13, 1992;—Am. 1992, Act 220, Imd. Eff. Oct. 13, 1992;—Am. 1994, Act 338, Eff. Apr. 1, 1996;—Am. 2004, Act 101, Imd. Eff. May 13, 2004;—Am. 2008, Act 195, Eff. Jan. 7, 2009;—Am. 2008, Act 406, Imd. Eff. Jan. 6, 2009;—Am. 2010, Act 20, Imd. Eff. Mar. 25, 2010;—Am. 2012, Act 377, Imd. Eff. Dec. 18, 2012;—Am. 2014, Act 201, Imd. Eff. June 24, 2014;—Am. 2015, Act 37, Imd. Eff. May 21, 2015;—Am. 2015, Act 200, Eff. Feb. 22, 2016.

Constitutionality: The Michigan Court of Appeals held in *Chan v City of Troy*, 220 Mich App 376; 559 NW2d 374 (1997), that the citizen requirement, now MCL 28.422(3)(c), for a permit to purchase a pistol contained in MCL 28.422(3)(b) violates the Equal Protection Clause of the Fourteenth Amendment to the United States Constitution and is unconstitutional.

Popular name: CCW

Popular name: Concealed Weapons

Popular name: CPL

Popular name: Right to Carry

Popular name: Shall Issue

28.422a Individuals not required to obtain license; completion of record by seller; duties of purchaser; noncompliance as state civil infraction; penalty; entering information into pistol entry database; obtaining copy of information; exemption; material false statement as felony; penalty; rules; verification; definitions.

Sec. 2a. (1) The following individuals are not required to obtain a license under section 2 to purchase, carry, possess, use, or transport a pistol:

(a) An individual licensed under section 5b, except for an individual who has an emergency license issued under section 5a(4) or a receipt serving as a concealed pistol license under section 5b(9) or 5*l*(3).

(b) A federally licensed firearms dealer.

(c) An individual who purchases a pistol from a federally licensed firearms dealer in compliance with 18 USC 922(t).

(d) An individual currently employed as a police officer who is licensed or certified under the Michigan commission on law enforcement standards act, 1965 PA 203, MCL 28.601 to 28.615.

(2) If an individual described in subsection (1) purchases or otherwise acquires a pistol, the seller shall complete a record in triplicate on a form provided by the department of state police. The record shall include the purchaser's concealed weapon license number, the number of the purchaser's license or certificate issued under the Michigan commission on law enforcement standards act, 1965 PA 203, MCL 28.601 to 28.615, or, if the purchaser is a federally licensed firearms dealer, his or her dealer license number. If the purchaser is not licensed under section 5b or does not have a license or certificate issued under the Michigan commission on law enforcement standards act, 1965 PA 203, MCL 28.601 to 28.615, and is not a federally licensed firearms dealer, the record shall include the dealer license number of the federally licensed firearms dealer who is selling the pistol. The purchaser shall sign the record. The seller may retain 1 copy of the record. The purchaser shall receive 2 copies of the record and forward 1 copy to the police department of the city, village, or township in which the purchaser resides, or, if the purchaser does not reside in a city, village, or township having a police department, to the county sheriff, within 10 days following the purchase or acquisition. The return of the copy to the police department or county sheriff may be made in person or may be made by first-class mail or certified mail sent within the 10-day period to the proper address of the police department

or county sheriff. A purchaser who fails to comply with the requirements of this subsection is responsible for a state civil infraction and may be fined not more than $250.00. If a purchaser is found responsible for a state civil infraction under this subsection, the court shall notify the department of state police. If the purchaser is licensed under section 5b, the court shall notify the licensing authority of that determination.

(3) Within 10 days after receiving the record copy returned under subsection (2), the police department or county sheriff shall electronically enter the information into the pistol entry database as required by the department of state police if it has the ability to electronically enter that information. If the police department or county sheriff does not have that ability, the police department or county sheriff shall provide that information to the department of state police in a manner otherwise required by the department of state police. Any police department or county sheriff that provided pistol descriptions to the department of state police under former section 9 of this act shall continue to provide pistol descriptions to the department of state police under this subsection. Within 48 hours after entering or otherwise providing the information on the record copy returned under subsection (2) to the department of state police, the police department or county sheriff shall forward the copy of the record to the department of state police. The purchaser has the right to obtain a copy of the information placed in the pistol entry database under this subsection to verify the accuracy of that information. The police department or county sheriff may charge a fee not to exceed $1.00 for the cost of providing the copy. The purchaser may carry, use, possess, and transport the pistol for 30 days beginning on the date of purchase or acquisition only while he or she is in possession of his or her copy of the record. However, the person is not required to have the record in his or her possession while carrying, using, possessing, or transporting the pistol after this period.

(4) This section does not apply to a person or entity exempt under section 2(7).

(5) An individual who makes a material false statement on a sales record under this section is guilty of a felony punishable by imprisonment for not more than 4 years or a fine of not more than $2,500.00, or both.

(6) The department of state police may promulgate rules to implement this section.

(7) The Michigan commission on law enforcement standards shall provide license or certificate information, as applicable, to the department of state police to verify the requirements of this section.

(8) As used in this section:

(a) "Federally licensed firearms dealer" means a person licensed to sell firearms under 18 USC 923.

(b) "Person" means an individual, partnership, corporation, association, or other legal entity.

History: Add. 2000, Act 381, Eff. July 1, 2001;—Am. 2008, Act 194, Eff. Jan. 7, 2009;—Am. 2010, Act 210, Eff. Feb. 15, 2011; Am. 2012, Act 377, Imd. Eff. Dec. 18, 2012;—Am. 2013, Act 3, Eff. Mar. 12, 2013;—Am. 2015, Act 3, Eff. Dec. 1, 2015;—Am. 2016, Act 6, Eff. May 2, 2016;—Am. 2016, Act 301, Eff. Jan. 2, 2017.

Compiler's note: Former MCL 28.422a, which pertained to a basic pistol safety brochure, was repealed by Act 220 of 1992, Imd. Eff. Oct. 13, 1992.

Popular name: CCW

Popular name: Concealed Weapons

Popular name: CPL

Popular name: Right to Carry

Popular name: Shall Issue

28.422b Entry of order or disposition into law enforcement information network; written notice; person subject of order; request to amend inaccuracy; notice of grant or denial of request; hearing; entry of personal protection order; service required.

Sec. 2b. (1) Except as provided in subsection (5), upon entry of an order or disposition into the law enforcement information network under any provision of law described in section 2(3)(a), the department of state police shall immediately send written notice of that entry to the person who is the subject of the order or disposition. The notice shall be sent by first-class mail to the last known address of the person. The notice shall include at least all of the following:

(a) The name of the person.

(b) The date the order or disposition was entered into the law enforcement information network.

(c) A statement that the person cannot obtain a license to purchase a pistol or obtain a concealed weapon license until the order or disposition is removed from the law enforcement information network.

(d) A statement that the person may request that the state police correct or expunge inaccurate information entered into the law enforcement information network.

(2) A person who is the subject of an order entered into the law enforcement information network under any provision of law described in section 2(3)(a) may request that the department of state police do either of the following:

(a) Amend an inaccuracy in the information entered into the law enforcement information network under any provision of law described in section 2(3)(a).

(b) Expunge the person's name and other information concerning the person from the law enforcement information network regarding 1 or more specific entries in the law enforcement information network under any provision of law described in section 2(3)(a) because 1 or more of the following circumstances exist:

(*i*) The person is not subject to an order of involuntary commitment in an inpatient or outpatient setting due to mental illness.

(*ii*) The person is not subject to an order or disposition determining that the person is legally incapacitated.

(*iii*) The person is not subject to a personal protection order issued under any of the following:
(A) Section 2950 of the revised judicature act of 1961, 1961 PA 236, MCL 600.2950.
(B) Section 2950a of the revised judicature act of 1961, 1961 PA 236, MCL 600.2950a.
(C) Section 14 of 1846 RS 84, MCL 552.14.
(*iv*) The person is not subject to an order for release subject to protective conditions that prohibits the purchase or possession of a firearm by the person issued under section 6b of chapter V of the code of criminal procedure, 1927 PA 175, MCL 765.6b.
(3) Before the expiration of 30 days after a request is made to amend an inaccuracy in the law enforcement information network under subsection (2)(a) or to expunge 1 or more specific entries from the law enforcement information network under subsection (2)(b)(*i*) to (*iv*), the department of state police shall conduct an investigation concerning the accuracy of the information contained in the law enforcement information network, either grant or deny the request and provide the person with written notice of that grant or denial. A notice of denial shall include a statement specifying the basis of the denial, and that a person may appeal the denial pursuant to the administrative procedures act of 1969, 1969 PA 306, MCL 24.201 to 24.328.
(4) If the department of state police refuses a request by a person for amendment or expunction under subsection (2), or fails to act within 30 days after receiving the request under subsection (2), the person may request a hearing before a hearing officer appointed by the department of state police for a determination of whether information entered into the law enforcement information network should be amended or expunged because it is inaccurate or false. The department of state police shall conduct the hearing pursuant to the administrative procedures act of 1969, 1969 PA 306, MCL 24.201 to 24.328.
(5) The department of state police shall not send written notice of an entry of an order or disposition into the law enforcement information network as required for a personal protection order issued under section 2950 or 2950a of the revised judicature act of 1961, 1961 PA 236, MCL 600.2950 and 600.2950a, until that department has received notice that the respondent of the order has been served with or has received notice of the personal protection order.

History: Add. 1994, Act 338, Eff. Apr. 1, 1996;—Am. 2001, Act 199, Eff. Apr. 1, 2002;—Am. 2014, Act 205, Eff. Dec. 21, 2014.

Popular name: CCW

Popular name: Concealed Weapons

Popular name: CPL

Popular name: Right to Carry

Popular name: Shall Issue

28.423 Repealed. 2000, Act 381, Eff. July 1, 2001.

Compiler's note: The repealed section pertained to application fee.

Popular name: CCW

Popular name: Concealed Weapons

Popular name: CPL

Popular name: Right to Carry

Popular name: Shall Issue

28.424 Restoration of rights by circuit court; petition; fee; determination; order; circumstances.

Sec. 4. (1) An individual who is prohibited from possessing, using, transporting, selling, purchasing, carrying, shipping, receiving, or distributing a firearm under section 224f(2) of the Michigan penal code, 1931 PA 328, MCL 750.224f, may petition the circuit court in the county in which he or she resides for restoration of those rights.
(2) An individual who is prohibited from possessing, using, transporting, selling, carrying, shipping, or distributing ammunition under section 224f(4) of the Michigan penal code, 1931 PA 328, MCL 750.224f, may petition the circuit court in the county in which he or she resides for restoration of those rights.
(3) Not more than 1 petition may be submitted under subsection (1) or (2) in any 12-month period. The circuit court shall charge a fee as provided in section 2529 of the revised judicature act of 1961, 1961 PA 236, MCL 600.2529, unless the court waives that fee.
(4) The circuit court shall, by written order, restore the rights of an individual to possess, use, transport, sell, purchase, carry, ship, receive, or distribute a firearm or to possess, use, transport, sell, carry, ship, or distribute ammunition if the circuit court determines, by clear and convincing evidence, that all of the following circumstances exist:
(a) The individual properly submitted a petition for restoration of those rights as provided under this section.
(b) The expiration of 5 years after all of the following circumstances:
(*i*) The individual has paid all fines imposed for the violation resulting in the prohibition.
(*ii*) The individual has served all terms of imprisonment imposed for the violation resulting in the prohibition.
(*iii*) The individual has successfully completed all conditions of probation or parole imposed for the violation resulting in the prohibition.
(c) The individual's record and reputation are such that the individual is not likely to act in a manner dangerous to the safety of other individuals.

History: Add. 1992, Act 219, Imd. Eff. Oct. 13, 1992;—Am. 2014, Act 6, Eff. May 12, 2014;—Am. 2015, Act 3, Eff. Dec. 1, 2015;—Am. 2017, Act 95, Eff. Oct. 11, 2017.

Compiler's note: Former section 4 of this act was not compiled.

Popular name: CCW

Popular name: Concealed Weapons

Popular name: CPL

Popular name: Right to Carry

Popular name: Shall Issue

28.425 Concealed pistol application kits.

Sec. 5. (1) County clerks shall provide concealed pistol application kits during normal business hours and free of charge to individuals who wish to apply for licenses to carry concealed pistols. Each kit shall only contain all of the following:

(a) A concealed pistol license application form provided by the director of the department of state police.

(b) The fingerprint cards under section 5b(10), if required.

(c) Written information regarding the procedures involved in obtaining a license to carry a concealed pistol.

(d) Written information identifying entities that offer the training required under section 5b(7)(c), if maintained by the county clerk.

(2) A county clerk shall not deny an individual the right to receive a concealed pistol application kit under this section.

(3) An individual who is denied an application kit under this section and obtains an order of mandamus directing the county clerk to provide him or her with the application kit shall be awarded his or her actual and reasonable costs and attorney fees for obtaining the order.

(4) The department of state police shall provide the application kits required under this section to county clerks in an electronic format. The department of state police shall not charge a fee for the kits.

History: Add. 2000, Act 381, Eff. July 1, 2001;—Am. 2015, Act 3, Eff. Dec. 1, 2015.

Popular name: CCW

Popular name: Concealed Weapons

Popular name: CPL

Popular name: Right to Carry

Popular name: Shall Issue

28.425a Validity and duration of concealed pistol license issued before December 1, 2015; duties of county clerk; verification by state police; applicant issued personal protection order; emergency license; requirements; notice of statutory disqualification; surrender of emergency license; compilation of firearms laws by legislative service bureau; distribution; statement.

Sec. 5a. (1) A license to carry a concealed pistol issued by a concealed weapon licensing board before December 1, 2015 is valid and remains in effect until the expiration of that license or as otherwise provided by law.

(2) The county clerk is responsible for all of the following:

(a) Storing and maintaining all records related to issuing a license or notice of statutory disqualification in that county.

(b) Issuing licenses to carry a concealed pistol.

(c) Issuing notices of statutory disqualification, notices of suspensions, and notices of revocations.

(3) The department of state police shall verify under section 5b(6) whether an applicant for a license to carry a concealed pistol is eligible to receive a license to carry a concealed pistol.

(4) A county clerk shall issue an emergency license to carry a concealed pistol to an individual if the individual has obtained a personal protection order issued under section 2950 or 2950a of the revised judicature act of 1961, 1961 PA 236, MCL 600.2950 and 600.2950a, or to that individual if a county sheriff determines that there is clear and convincing evidence to believe the safety of the individual or the safety of a member of the individual's family or household is endangered by the individual's inability to immediately obtain a license to carry a concealed pistol. Clear and convincing evidence includes, but is not limited to, an application for a personal protection order, police reports and other law enforcement records, or written, audio, or visual evidence of threats to the individual or member of the individual's family or household. A county clerk shall only issue an emergency license to carry a concealed pistol to an individual who has obtained a personal protection order if the individual is eligible under section 5b(7)(d), (e), (f), (h), (i), (j), (k), and (m) to receive a license based on a criminal record check through the law enforcement information network conducted by the department of state police. The county sheriff shall only issue a determination under this subsection to an individual who is eligible under section 5b(7)(d), (e), (f), (h), (i), (j), (k), and (m) to receive a license based on a criminal record check through the law enforcement information network and only after the county sheriff has taken the individual's fingerprints in compliance with section 5b(9). A county sheriff shall notify the county clerk if the county sheriff determines that an individual is not eligible under section 5b(7)(d), (e), (f), (h), (i), (j), (k), or (m) to receive a license. An emergency license must be on a form provided by the department of state police. An individual who applies for an emergency license shall, within 10 business days after applying for an emergency license, complete a pistol training course under section 5j and apply for a license under section 5b. If an individual who applies for an emergency license does not complete a pistol training course under section 5j and apply for a license under section 5b within 10 business days after applying for an emergency license, that individual's emergency license is no longer valid. A county sheriff who makes a

determination under this section, performs a criminal record check, and takes the applicant's fingerprints may charge a fee not to exceed $15.00. A county clerk may charge a fee not to exceed $10.00 for printing an emergency license. A county clerk shall deposit a fee collected by the county clerk under this subsection in the concealed pistol licensing fund of that county created in section 5x. Except as otherwise provided in this subsection, an emergency license is valid for 45 days or until the county clerk issues a notice of statutory disqualification, whichever occurs first. Except as otherwise provided in this act, an emergency license is, for all other purposes of this act, a license to carry a concealed pistol. The county clerk shall include an indication on the license if an individual is exempt from the prohibitions against carrying a concealed pistol on premises described in section 5o if the applicant provides acceptable proof that he or she qualifies for that exemption. An individual shall not obtain more than 1 emergency license in any 5-year period. If a county clerk issues a notice of statutory disqualification to an applicant who received an emergency license under this section, the applicant shall immediately surrender the emergency license to the county clerk by mail or in person if that emergency license has not expired. An individual who fails to surrender a license as required by this subsection after he or she is notified of a statutory disqualification is guilty of a misdemeanor punishable by imprisonment for not more than 93 days or a fine of not more than $500.00, or both.

(5) The legislative service bureau shall compile the firearms laws of this state, including laws that apply to carrying a concealed pistol, and shall provide copies of the compilation in an electronic format to the department of state police. The department of state police shall provide a copy of the compiled laws to each county clerk in this state. The department of state police shall also provide forms to appeal any notice of statutory disqualification, or suspension or revocation of a license under this act. The department of state police shall distribute copies of the compilation and forms required under this subsection in an electronic format to each county clerk. The county clerk shall distribute a copy of the compilation and forms at no charge to each individual who applies for a license to carry a concealed pistol at the time the application is submitted. The county clerk may distribute copies of the compilation and forms required under this subsection in an electronic format. The county clerk shall require the applicant to sign a written statement acknowledging that he or she has received a copy of the compilation and forms provided under this subsection. An individual is not eligible to receive a license to carry a concealed pistol until he or she has signed the statement.

History: Add. 2000, Act 381, Eff. July 1, 2001;—Am. 2015, Act 3, Eff. Dec. 1, 2015;—Am. 2017, Act 95, Eff. Oct. 11, 2017.

Popular name: CCW

Popular name: Concealed Weapons

Popular name: CPL

Popular name: Right to Carry

Popular name: Shall Issue

28.425b License application; form; contents; material false statement as felony; record; fee; verification of requirements; determination; circumstances for issuance; information of court order or conviction; fingerprints; issuance or denial; individual moving to different county; replacement license; suspension or revocation of license; furnishing copy of application to individual; list of certified instructors; delivery of license by first-class mail; liability for civil damages; voluntary surrender of license; definitions.

Sec. 5b. (1) To obtain a license to carry a concealed pistol, an individual shall apply to the county clerk in the county in which the individual resides. The applicant shall file the application with the county clerk in the county in which the applicant resides during the county clerk's normal business hours. The application must be on a form provided by the director of the department of state police and allow the applicant to designate whether the applicant seeks an emergency license. The applicant shall sign the application under oath. The county clerk or his or her representative shall administer the oath. An application under this subsection is not considered complete until an applicant submits all of the required information and fees and has fingerprints taken under subsection (9). An application under this subsection is considered withdrawn if an applicant does not have fingerprints taken under subsection (9) within 45 days of the date an application is filed under this subsection. A completed application and all receipts issued under this section expire 1 year from the date of application. The county clerk shall issue the applicant a receipt for his or her application at the time the application is submitted containing the name of the applicant, the applicant's state-issued driver license or personal identification card number, the date and time the receipt is issued, the amount paid, the name of the county in which the receipt is issued, an impression of the county seal, and the statement, "This receipt was issued for the purpose of applying for a concealed pistol license and for obtaining fingerprints related to that application. This receipt does not authorize an individual to carry a concealed pistol in this state.". The application must contain all of the following:

(a) The applicant's legal name, date of birth, the address of his or her primary residence, and his or her state-issued driver license or personal identification card number.

(b) A statement by the applicant that the applicant meets the criteria for a license under this act to carry a concealed pistol.

(c) A statement by the applicant authorizing the department of state police to access any record needed to perform the verification in subsection (6).

(d) A statement by the applicant regarding whether he or she has a history of mental illness that would disqualify him or her under subsection (7)(j) to (*l*) from receiving a license to carry a concealed pistol.

(e) A statement by the applicant regarding whether he or she has ever been convicted in this state or elsewhere for any of the following:

(*i*) Any felony.

(*ii*) A misdemeanor listed under subsection (7)(h) if the applicant was convicted of that misdemeanor in the 8 years immediately preceding the date of the application, or a misdemeanor listed under subsection (7)(i) if the applicant was convicted of that misdemeanor in the 3 years immediately preceding the date of the application.

(f) A statement by the applicant whether he or she has been dishonorably discharged from the United States Armed Forces.

(g) If an applicant does not have a digitized photograph on file with the secretary of state, a passport-quality photograph of the applicant provided by the applicant at the time of application.

(h) A certificate stating that the applicant has completed the training course prescribed by this act.

(2) The county clerk shall not require the applicant to submit any additional forms, documents, letters, or other evidence of eligibility for obtaining a license to carry a concealed pistol except as set forth in subsection (1) or as otherwise provided for in this act. The application form must contain a conspicuous warning that the application is executed under oath and that intentionally making a material false statement on the application is a felony punishable by imprisonment for not more than 4 years or a fine of not more than $2,500.00, or both.

(3) An individual who intentionally makes a material false statement on an application under subsection (1) is guilty of a felony punishable by imprisonment for not more than 4 years or a fine of not more than $2,500.00, or both.

(4) The county clerk shall retain a copy of each application for a license to carry a concealed pistol as an official record. One year after the expiration of a concealed pistol license, the county clerk may destroy the record and a name index of the record shall be maintained in the database created in section 5e.

(5) Each applicant shall pay a nonrefundable application and licensing fee of $100.00 by any method of payment accepted by that county for payments of other fees and penalties. Except as provided in subsection (9), no other charge, fee, cost, or assessment, including any local charge, fee, cost, or assessment, is required of the applicant except as specifically authorized in this act. The applicant shall pay the application and licensing fee to the county. The county treasurer shall deposit $26.00 of each application and licensing fee collected under this section in the concealed pistol licensing fund of that county created in section 5x. The county treasurer shall forward the balance remaining to the state treasurer. The state treasurer shall deposit the balance of the fee in the general fund to the credit of the department of state police. The department of state police shall use the money received under this act to process the fingerprints and to reimburse the Federal Bureau of Investigation for the costs associated with processing fingerprints submitted under this act. The balance of the money received under this act must be credited to the department of state police.

(6) The department of state police shall verify the requirements of subsection (7)(d), (e), (f), (h), (i), (j), (k), and (m) through the law enforcement information network and the national instant criminal background check system and shall report to the county clerk all statutory disqualifications, if any, under this act that apply to an applicant.

(7) The county clerk shall issue and shall send by first-class mail a license to an applicant to carry a concealed pistol within the period required under this act if the county clerk determines that all of the following circumstances exist:

(a) The applicant is 21 years of age or older.

(b) The applicant is a citizen of the United States or is an alien lawfully admitted into the United States, is a legal resident of this state, and has resided in this state for not less than the 6 months immediately preceding the date of application. The county clerk shall waive the 6-month residency requirement for an emergency license under section 5a(4) if the applicant is a petitioner for a personal protection order issued under section 2950 or 2950a of the revised judicature act of 1961, 1961 PA 236, MCL 600.2950 and 600.2950a, or if the county sheriff determines that there is clear and convincing evidence to believe that the safety of the applicant or the safety of a member of the applicant's family or household is endangered by the applicant's inability to immediately obtain a license to carry a concealed pistol. If the applicant holds a valid concealed pistol license issued by another state at the time the applicant's residency in this state is established, the county clerk shall waive the 6-month residency requirement and the applicant may apply for a concealed pistol license at the time the applicant's residency in this state is established. For the purposes of this section, an individual is considered a legal resident of this state if any of the following apply:

(*i*) The individual has a valid, lawfully obtained driver license issued under the Michigan vehicle code, 1949 PA 300, MCL 257.1 to 257.923, or official state personal identification card issued under 1972 PA 222, MCL 28.291 to 28.300.

(*ii*) The individual is lawfully registered to vote in this state.

(*iii*) The individual is on active duty status with the United States Armed Forces and is stationed outside of this state, but the individual's home of record is in this state.

(*iv*) The individual is on active duty status with the United States Armed Forces and is permanently stationed in this state, but the individual's home of record is in another state.

(c) The applicant has knowledge and has had training in the safe use and handling of a pistol by the successful completion of a pistol safety training course or class that meets the requirements of section 5j.

(d) Based solely on the report received from the department of state police under subsection (6), the applicant is not the subject of an order or disposition under any of the following:

(*i*) Section 464a of the mental health code, 1974 PA 258, MCL 330.1464a.

(*ii*) Section 5107 of the estates and protected individuals code, 1998 PA 386, MCL 700.5107.

(*iii*) Sections 2950 and 2950a of the revised judicature act of 1961, 1961 PA 236, MCL 600.2950 and 600.2950a.

(*iv*) Section 6b of chapter V of the code of criminal procedure, 1927 PA 175, MCL 765.6b, if the order has a condition imposed under section 6b(3) of chapter V of the code of criminal procedure, 1927 PA 175, MCL 765.6b.

(*v*) Section 16b of chapter IX of the code of criminal procedure, 1927 PA 175, MCL 769.16b.

(e) Based solely on the report received from the department of state police under subsection (6), the applicant is not prohibited from possessing, using, transporting, selling, purchasing, carrying, shipping, receiving, or distributing a firearm under section 224f of the Michigan penal code, 1931 PA 328, MCL 750.224f.

(f) Based solely on the report received from the department of state police under subsection (6), the applicant has never been convicted of a felony in this state or elsewhere, and a felony charge against the applicant is not pending in this state or elsewhere at the time he or she applies for a license described in this section.

(g) The applicant has not been dishonorably discharged from the United States Armed Forces.

(h) Based solely on the report received from the department of state police under subsection (6), the applicant has not been convicted of a misdemeanor violation of any of the following in the 8 years immediately preceding the date of application and a charge for a misdemeanor violation of any of the following is not pending against the applicant in this state or elsewhere at the time he or she applies for a license described in this section:

(*i*) Section 617a (failing to stop when involved in a personal injury accident), section 625 as punishable under subsection (9)(b) of that section (operating while intoxicated, second offense), section 625m as punishable under subsection (4) of that section (operating a commercial vehicle with alcohol content, second offense), section 626 (reckless driving), or a violation of section 904(1) (operating while license suspended or revoked, second or subsequent offense) of the Michigan vehicle code, 1949 PA 300, MCL 257.617a, 257.625, 257.625m, 257.626, and 257.904.

(*ii*) Section 185(7) of the aeronautics code of the state of Michigan, 1945 PA 327, MCL 259.185 (operating aircraft while under the influence of intoxicating liquor or a controlled substance with prior conviction).

(*iii*) Section 29 of the weights and measures act, 1964 PA 283, MCL 290.629 (hindering or obstructing certain persons performing official weights and measures duties).

(*iv*) Section 10 of the motor fuels quality act, 1984 PA 44, MCL 290.650 (hindering, obstructing, assaulting, or committing bodily injury upon director or authorized representative).

(*v*) Section 80176 as punishable under section 80177(1)(b) (operating vessel under the influence of intoxicating liquor or a controlled substance, second offense), section 81134 as punishable under subsection (8)(b) of that section (operating ORV under the influence of intoxicating liquor or a controlled substance, second or subsequent offense), or section 82127 as punishable under section 82128(1)(b) (operating snowmobile under the influence of intoxicating liquor or a controlled substance, second offense) of the natural resources and environmental protection act, 1994 PA 451, MCL 324.80176, 324.80177, 324.81134, 324.82127, and 324.82128.

(*vi*) Section 7403 of the public health code, 1978 PA 368, MCL 333.7403 (possession of controlled substance, controlled substance analogue, or prescription form).

(*vii*) Section 353 of the railroad code of 1993, 1993 PA 354, MCL 462.353, punishable under subsection (4) of that section (operating locomotive under the influence of intoxicating liquor or a controlled substance, or while visibly impaired, second offense).

(*viii*) Section 7 of 1978 PA 33, MCL 722.677 (displaying sexually explicit matter to minors).

(*ix*) Section 81 (assault or domestic assault), section 81a(1) or (2) (aggravated assault or aggravated domestic assault), section 115 (breaking and entering or entering without breaking), section 136b(7) (fourth degree child abuse), section 145n (vulnerable adult abuse), section 157b(3)(b) (solicitation to commit a felony), section 215 (impersonating peace officer or medical examiner), section 223 (illegal sale of a firearm or ammunition), section 224d (illegal use or sale of a self-defense spray), section 226a (sale or possession of a switchblade), section 227c (improper transportation of a loaded firearm), section 229 (accepting a pistol in pawn), section 232a (improperly obtaining a pistol, making a false statement on an application to purchase a pistol, or using false identification to purchase a pistol), section 233 (intentionally aiming a firearm without malice), section 234 (intentionally discharging a firearm aimed without malice), section 234d (possessing a firearm on prohibited premises), section 234e (brandishing a firearm in public), section 234f (possession of a firearm by an individual less than 18 years of age), section 235 (intentionally discharging a firearm aimed without malice causing injury), section 235a (parent of a minor who possessed a firearm in a weapon free school zone), section 236 (setting a spring gun or other device), section 237 (possessing a firearm while under the influence of intoxicating liquor or a controlled substance), section 237a (weapon free school zone violation), section 335a (indecent exposure), section 411h (stalking), or section 520e (fourth degree criminal sexual conduct) of the Michigan penal code, 1931 PA 328, MCL 750.81, 750.81a, 750.115, 750.136b, 750.145n, 750.157b, 750.215, 750.223, 750.224d, 750.226a, 750.227c, 750.229, 750.232a, 750.233, 750.234, 750.234d, 750.234e, 750.234f, 750.235, 750.235a, 750.236, 750.237, 750.237a, 750.335a, 750.411h, and 750.520e.

(*x*) Former section 228 of the Michigan penal code, 1931 PA 328.

(*xi*) Section 1 (reckless, careless, or negligent use of a firearm resulting in injury or death), section 2 (careless, reckless, or negligent use of a firearm resulting in property damage), or section 3a (reckless discharge of a firearm) of 1952 PA 45, MCL 752.861, 752.862, and 752.863a.

(*xii*) A violation of a law of the United States, another state, or a local unit of government of this state or another state substantially corresponding to a violation described in subparagraphs (*i*) to (*xi*).

(i) Based solely on the report received from the department of state police under subsection (6), the applicant has not been convicted of a misdemeanor violation of any of the following in the 3 years immediately preceding the date of application unless the misdemeanor violation is listed under subdivision (h) and a charge for a misdemeanor violation of any of the following is not pending against the applicant in this state or elsewhere at the time he or she applies for a license described in this section:

(*i*) Section 625 (operating under the influence), section 625a (refusal of commercial vehicle operator to submit to a chemical test), section 625k (ignition interlock device reporting violation), section 625*l* (circumventing an ignition interlock device), or section 625m punishable under subsection (3) of that section (operating a commercial vehicle with alcohol content) of the Michigan vehicle code, 1949 PA 300, MCL 257.625, 257.625a, 257.625k, 257.625*l*, and 257.625m.

(*ii*) Section 185 of the aeronautics code of the state of Michigan, 1945 PA 327, MCL 259.185 (operating aircraft under the influence).

(*iii*) Section 81134 (operating ORV under the influence or operating ORV while visibly impaired), or section 82127 (operating a snowmobile under the influence) of the natural resources and environmental protection act, 1994 PA 451, MCL 324.81134 and 324.82127.

(*iv*) Part 74 of the public health code, 1978 PA 368, MCL 333.7401 to 333.7461 (controlled substance violation).

(*v*) Section 353 of the railroad code of 1993, 1993 PA 354, MCL 462.353, punishable under subsection (3) of that section (operating locomotive under the influence).

(*vi*) Section 167 (disorderly person), section 174 (embezzlement), section 218 (false pretenses with intent to defraud), section 356 (larceny), section 356d (second degree retail fraud), section 359 (larceny from a vacant building or structure), section 362 (larceny by conversion), section 362a (larceny – defrauding lessor), section 377a (malicious destruction of property), section 380 (malicious destruction of real property), section 535 (receiving or concealing stolen property), or section 540e (malicious use of telecommunications service or device) of the Michigan penal code, 1931 PA 328, MCL 750.167, 750.174, 750.218, 750.356, 750.356d, 750.359, 750.362, 750.362a, 750.377a, 750.380, 750.535, and 750.540e.

(*vii*) A violation of a law of the United States, another state, or a local unit of government of this state or another state substantially corresponding to a violation described in subparagraphs (*i*) to (*vi*).

(j) Based solely on the report received from the department of state police under subsection (6), the applicant has not been found guilty but mentally ill of any crime and has not offered a plea of not guilty of, or been acquitted of, any crime by reason of insanity.

(k) Based solely on the report received from the department of state police under subsection (6), the applicant is not currently and has never been subject to an order of involuntary commitment in an inpatient or outpatient setting due to mental illness.

(*l*) The applicant has filed a statement under subsection (1)(d) that the applicant does not have a diagnosis of mental illness that includes an assessment that the individual presents a danger to himself or herself or to another at the time the application is made, regardless of whether he or she is receiving treatment for that illness.

(m) Based solely on the report received from the department of state police under subsection (6), the applicant is not under a court order of legal incapacity in this state or elsewhere.

(n) The applicant has a valid state-issued driver license or personal identification card.

(8) Upon entry of a court order or conviction of 1 of the enumerated prohibitions for using, transporting, selling, purchasing, carrying, shipping, receiving, or distributing a firearm in this section the department of state police shall immediately enter the order or conviction into the law enforcement information network. For purposes of this act, information of the court order or conviction must not be removed from the law enforcement information network, but may be moved to a separate file intended for the use of the department of state police, the courts, and other government entities as necessary and exclusively to determine eligibility to be licensed under this act.

(9) An individual, after submitting an application and paying the fee prescribed under subsection (5), shall request that classifiable fingerprints be taken by a county clerk, the department of state police, a county sheriff, a local police agency, or other entity, if the county clerk, department of state police, county sheriff, local police agency, or other entity provides fingerprinting capability for the purposes of this act. An individual who has had classifiable fingerprints taken under section 5a(4) does not need additional fingerprints taken under this subsection. If the individual requests that classifiable fingerprints be taken by the county clerk, department of state police, county sheriff, a local police agency, or other entity, the individual shall also pay a fee of $15.00 by any method of payment accepted for payments of other fees and penalties. A county clerk shall deposit any fee it accepts under this subsection in the concealed pistol licensing fund of that county created in section 5x. The county clerk, department of state police, county sheriff, local police agency, or other entity shall take the fingerprints within 5 business days after the request. County clerks, the department of state police, county sheriffs, local police agencies, and other entities shall provide reasonable access to fingerprinting services during normal business hours as is necessary to comply with the requirements of this act if the county clerk, department of state police, county sheriff, local police agency, or other entity provides fingerprinting capability for the purposes of this act. The entity providing fingerprinting services shall issue the individual a receipt at the time his or her fingerprints are taken. The county clerk, department of state police, county sheriff, local police agency, or other entity shall not provide a receipt under this subsection unless the individual requesting the fingerprints provides an application receipt received under subsection (1). A receipt under this subsection must contain all of the following:

(a) The name of the individual.

(b) The date and time the receipt is issued.

(c) The amount paid.
(d) The name of the entity providing the fingerprint services.
(e) The individual's state-issued driver license or personal identification card number.
(f) The statement "This receipt was issued for the purpose of applying for a concealed pistol license. As provided in section 5b of 1927 PA 372, MCL 28.425b, if a license or notice of statutory disqualification is not issued within 45 days after the date this receipt was issued, this receipt shall serve as a concealed pistol license for the individual named in the receipt when carried with an official state-issued driver license or personal identification card. The receipt is valid as a license until a license or notice of statutory disqualification is issued by the county clerk. This receipt does not exempt the individual named in the receipt from complying with all applicable laws for the purchase of firearms.".

(10) The fingerprints must be taken, under subsection (9), in a manner prescribed by the department of state police. The county clerk, county sheriff, local police agency, or other entity shall immediately forward the fingerprints taken by that entity to the department of state police for comparison with fingerprints already on file with the department of state police. The department of state police shall immediately forward the fingerprints to the Federal Bureau of Investigation. Within 5 business days after completing the verification under subsection (6), the department shall send the county clerk a list of an individual's statutory disqualifications under this act. Except as provided in section 5a(4), the county clerk shall not issue a concealed pistol license until he or she receives the report of statutory disqualifications prescribed in this subsection. If an individual's fingerprints are not classifiable, the department of state police shall, at no charge, take the individual's fingerprints again or provide for the comparisons under this subsection to be conducted through alternative means. The county clerk shall not issue a notice of statutory disqualification because an individual's fingerprints are not classifiable by the Federal Bureau of Investigation.

(11) The county clerk shall send by first-class mail a notice of statutory disqualification for a license under this act to an individual if the individual is not qualified under subsection (7) to receive that license.

(12) A license to carry a concealed pistol that is issued based upon an application that contains a material false statement is void from the date the license is issued.

(13) Subject to subsection (10), the department of state police shall complete the verification required under subsection (6) and the county clerk shall issue a license or a notice of statutory disqualification within 45 days after the date the individual has classifiable fingerprints taken under subsection (9). The county clerk shall include an indication on the license if an individual is exempt from the prohibitions against carrying a concealed pistol on premises described in section 5o if the applicant provides acceptable proof that he or she qualifies for that exemption. If the county clerk receives notice from a county sheriff or chief law enforcement officer that a licensee is no longer a member of a sheriff's posse, an auxiliary officer, or a reserve officer, the county clerk shall notify the licensee that he or she shall surrender the concealed pistol license indicating that the individual is exempt from the prohibitions against carrying a concealed pistol on premises described in section 5o. The licensee shall, within 30 days after receiving notice from the county clerk, surrender the license indicating that the individual is exempt from the prohibitions against carrying a concealed pistol on premises described in section 5o and obtain a replacement license after paying the fee required under subsection (15). If the county clerk issues a notice of statutory disqualification, the county clerk shall within 5 business days do all of the following:

(a) Inform the individual in writing of the reasons for the denial or disqualification. Information under this subdivision shall include all of the following:
(*i*) A statement of each statutory disqualification identified.
(*ii*) The source of the record for each statutory disqualification identified.
(*iii*) The contact information for the source of the record for each statutory disqualification identified.
(b) Inform the individual in writing of his or her right to appeal the denial or notice of statutory disqualification to the circuit court as provided in section 5d.
(c) Inform the individual that he or she should contact the source of the record for any statutory disqualification to correct any errors in the record resulting in the statutory disqualification.

(14) If a license or notice of statutory disqualification is not issued under subsection (13) within 45 days after the date the individual has classifiable fingerprints taken under subsection (9), the receipt issued under subsection (9) serves as a concealed pistol license for purposes of this act when carried with a state-issued driver license or personal identification card and is valid until a license or notice of statutory disqualification is issued by the county clerk.

(15) If an individual licensed under this act to carry a concealed pistol moves to a different county within this state, his or her license remains valid until it expires or is otherwise suspended or revoked under this act. An individual may notify a county clerk that he or she has moved to a different address within this state for the purpose of receiving the notice under section 5*l*(1). A license to carry a concealed pistol that is lost, stolen, defaced, or replaced for any other reason may be replaced by the issuing county clerk for a replacement fee of $10.00. A county clerk shall deposit a replacement fee under this subsection in the concealed pistol licensing fund of that county created in section 5x.

(16) If a license issued under this act is suspended or revoked, the license is forfeited and the individual shall return the license to the county clerk forthwith by mail or in person. The county clerk shall retain a suspended or revoked license as an official record 1 year after the expiration of the license, unless the license is reinstated or a new license is issued. The county clerk shall notify the department of state police if a license is suspended or revoked. The department of state police shall enter that suspension or revocation into the law enforcement information network. An individual who fails to return a license

as required under this subsection after he or she was notified that his or her license was suspended or revoked is guilty of a misdemeanor punishable by imprisonment for not more than 93 days or a fine of not more than $500.00, or both.

(17) An applicant or an individual licensed under this act to carry a concealed pistol may be furnished a copy of his or her application under this section upon request and the payment of a reasonable fee not to exceed $1.00. The county clerk shall deposit any fee collected under this subsection in the concealed pistol licensing fund of that county created in section 5x.

(18) This section does not prohibit the county clerk from making public and distributing to the public at no cost lists of individuals who are certified as qualified instructors as prescribed under section 5j.

(19) A county clerk issuing an initial license or renewal license under this act shall mail the license to the licensee by first-class mail in a sealed envelope. Upon payment of the fee under subsection (15), a county clerk shall issue a replacement license in person at the time of application for a replacement license. A county clerk may also deliver a replacement license by first-class mail if the individual submits to the clerk a written request and a copy of the individual's state-issued driver license or personal identification card.

(20) A county clerk, county sheriff, county prosecuting attorney, police department, or the department of state police is not liable for civil damages as a result of issuing a license under this act to an individual who later commits a crime or a negligent act.

(21) An individual licensed under this act to carry a concealed pistol may voluntarily surrender that license without explanation. A county clerk shall retain a surrendered license as an official record for 1 year after the license is surrendered. If an individual voluntarily surrenders a license under this subsection, the county clerk shall notify the department of state police. The department of state police shall enter into the law enforcement information network that the license was voluntarily surrendered and the date the license was voluntarily surrendered.

(22) As used in this section:

(a) "Acceptable proof" means any of the following:

(*i*) For a retired police officer or retired law enforcement officer, the officer's retired identification or a letter from a law enforcement agency stating that the retired police officer or law enforcement officer retired in good standing.

(*ii*) For an individual who is employed or contracted by an entity described under section 5o(1) to provide security services, a letter from that entity stating that the employee is required by his or her employer or the terms of a contract to carry a concealed firearm on the premises of the employing or contracting entity and his or her employee identification.

(*iii*) For an individual who is licensed as a private investigator or private detective under the professional investigator licensure act, 1965 PA 285, MCL 338.821 to 338.851, his or her license.

(*iv*) For an individual who is a corrections officer of a county sheriff's department, his or her employee identification and a letter stating that the individual has received county sheriff approved weapons training.

(*v*) For an individual who is a retired corrections officer of a county sheriff's department, a letter from the county sheriff's office stating that the retired corrections officer retired in good standing and that the individual has received county sheriff approved weapons training.

(*vi*) For an individual who is a motor carrier officer or capitol security officer of the department of state police, his or her employee identification.

(*vii*) For an individual who is a member of a sheriff's posse, his or her identification.

(*viii*) For an individual who is an auxiliary officer or reserve officer of a police or sheriff's department, his or her employee identification.

(*ix*) For an individual who is a parole, probation, or corrections officer, or absconder recovery unit member, of the department of corrections, his or her employee identification and proof that the individual obtained a Michigan department of corrections weapons permit.

(*x*) For an individual who is a retired parole, probation, or corrections officer, or retired absconder recovery unit member, of the department of corrections, a letter from the department of corrections stating that the retired parole, probation, or corrections officer, or retired absconder recovery unit member, retired in good standing and proof that the individual obtained a Michigan department of corrections weapons permit.

(*xi*) For a state court judge or state court retired judge, a letter from the judicial tenure commission stating that the state court judge or state court retired judge is in good standing.

(*xii*) For an individual who is a court officer, his or her employee identification.

(*xiii*) For a retired federal law enforcement officer, the identification required under the law enforcement officers safety act or a letter from a law enforcement agency stating that the retired federal law enforcement officer retired in good standing.

(*xiv*) For an individual who is a peace officer, his or her employee identification.

(b) "Convicted" means a final conviction, the payment of a fine, a plea of guilty or nolo contendere if accepted by the court, or a finding of guilt for a criminal law violation or a juvenile adjudication or disposition by the juvenile division of probate court or family division of circuit court for a violation that if committed by an adult would be a crime.

(c) "Felony" means, except as otherwise provided in this subdivision, that term as defined in section 1 of chapter I of the code of criminal procedure, 1927 PA 175, MCL 761.1, or a violation of a law of the United States or another state that is designated as a felony or that is punishable by death or by imprisonment for more than 1 year. Felony does not include a violation of a penal law of this state that is expressly designated as a misdemeanor.

(d) "Mental illness" means a substantial disorder of thought or mood that significantly impairs judgment, behavior, capacity to recognize reality, or ability to cope with the ordinary demands of life, and includes, but is not limited to, clinical depression.

(e) "Misdemeanor" means a violation of a penal law of this state or violation of a local ordinance substantially corresponding to a violation of a penal law of this state that is not a felony or a violation of an order, rule, or regulation of a state agency that is punishable by imprisonment or a fine that is not a civil fine, or both.

(f) "Treatment" means care or any therapeutic service, including, but not limited to, the administration of a drug, and any other service for the treatment of a mental illness.

History: Add. 2000, Act 381, Eff. July 1, 2001;—Am. 2002, Act 719, Eff. July 1, 2003;—Am. 2003, Act 31, Imd. Eff. July 1, 2003;—Am. 2006, Act 350, Imd. Eff. Sept. 18, 2006;—Am. 2008, Act 406, Imd. Eff. Jan. 6, 2009;—Am. 2014, Act 207, Eff. Dec. 21, 2014;—Am. 2015, Act 3, Eff. June 2, 2015;—Am. 2015, Act 16, Eff. July 13, 2015;—Am. 2015, Act 207, Eff. Dec. 1, 2015;—Am. 2017, Act 95, Eff. Oct. 11, 2017.

Popular name: CCW

Popular name: Concealed Weapons

Popular name: CPL

Popular name: Right to Carry

Popular name: Shall Issue

28.425c License; form; contents; authorized conduct; photograph.

Sec. 5c. (1) A license to carry a concealed pistol shall be in a form, with the same dimensions as a Michigan operator license, prescribed by the department of state police. Beginning December 1, 2015, the license shall be constructed of plastic laminated paper or hard plastic. No additional fee shall be charged for the license unless otherwise prescribed in this act. A fee not to exceed $10.00 may be charged for an optional hard plastic license only if the county clerk also provides the option of obtaining a plastic laminated paper license at no charge. A county clerk shall deposit a fee collected under this subsection in the concealed pistol licensing fund of that county created in section 5x. The license shall contain all of the following:

(a) The licensee's full name and date of birth.

(b) A photograph and a physical description of the licensee.

(c) A statement of the effective dates of the license.

(d) An indication of exceptions authorized by this act applicable to the licensee.

(e) The licensee's state-issued driver license or personal identification card number.

(f) The premises on which carrying a concealed pistol is prohibited under section 5o.

(g) The peace officer disclosure required under section 5f(3).

(h) An indication whether the license is a duplicate or an emergency license.

(i) If the license is an emergency license, an indication that the emergency license does not exempt the individual from complying with all applicable laws for the purchase of firearms.

(2) The department of state police or a county clerk shall not require a licensee's signature to appear on a license to carry a concealed pistol.

(3) Subject to section 5o and except as otherwise provided by law, a license to carry a concealed pistol issued by the county clerk authorizes the licensee to do all of the following:

(a) Carry a pistol concealed on or about his or her person anywhere in this state.

(b) Carry a pistol in a vehicle, whether concealed or not concealed, anywhere in this state.

(4) The secretary of state shall make a digitized photograph taken of the applicant for a driver license or personal identification card available to the department for use under this act. The department shall provide the photograph of the applicant received from the secretary of state to the county clerk who shall use the photograph on the individual's license unless the applicant does not have a digitized photograph on file with the secretary of state. If an applicant does not have a digitized photograph on file with the secretary of state, the applicant shall provide a passport-quality photograph of the applicant as provided under section 5b(1).

History: Add. 2000, Act 381, Eff. July 1, 2001;—Am. 2002, Act 719, Eff. July 1, 2003;—Am. 2015, Act 3, Eff. Dec. 1, 2015.

Popular name: CCW

Popular name: Concealed Weapons

Popular name: CPL

Popular name: Right to Carry

Popular name: Shall Issue

28.425d Denial or failure to issue notice of statutory disqualification, receipt, or license; appeal.

Sec. 5d. (1) If the county clerk issues a notice of statutory disqualification, fails to provide a receipt that complies with section 5b(1) or 5*l*(3), or fails to issue a license to carry a concealed pistol as provided in this act, the department of state police fails to provide a receipt that complies with section 5*l*(3), or the county clerk, department of state police, county sheriff, local police agency, or other entity fails to provide a receipt that complies with section 5b(9), the applicant may appeal the notice of statutory disqualification, the failure to provide a receipt, or the failure to issue the license to the circuit court in the judicial circuit in which he or she resides. The appeal of the notice of statutory disqualification, failure to provide a receipt, or failure to issue a license shall be determined by a review of the record for error.

(2) If the court determines that the notice of statutory disqualification, failure to provide a receipt that complies with section 5b(1) or (9) or 5*l*(3), or failure to issue a license was clearly erroneous or was arbitrary and capricious, the court shall order the county clerk to issue a license or receipt as required by this act. For applications submitted after November 30, 2015, if the court determines that the notice of statutory disqualification, failure to provide a receipt that complies with section 5b(1) or (9) or 5*l*(3), or failure to issue a license was clearly erroneous, the court may order an entity to refund any filing fees the applicant incurred in filing the appeal, according to the degree of responsibility of that entity.

(3) For applications submitted before December 1, 2015, if the court determines that the decision of the concealed weapon licensing board to deny issuance of a license to an applicant was arbitrary and capricious, the court shall order this state to pay 1/3 and the county in which the concealed weapon licensing board is located to pay 2/3 of the actual costs and actual attorney fees of the applicant in appealing the denial. For applications submitted on or after December 1, 2015, if the court under subsection (2) determines that the notice of statutory disqualification, failure to provide a receipt that complies with section 5b(1) or (9) or 5*l*(3), or failure to issue a license to an applicant was arbitrary and capricious, the court shall order the county clerk, the entity taking the fingerprints, or the state to pay the actual costs and actual attorney fees of the applicant in appealing the notice of statutory disqualification, failure to provide a receipt that complies with section 5b(1) or (9) or 5*l*(3), or failure to issue a license, according to the degree of responsibility of the county clerk, the entity taking the fingerprints, or the state.

(4) If the court determines that an applicant's appeal was frivolous, the court shall order the applicant to pay the actual costs and actual attorney fees of the county clerk, entity taking the fingerprints, or the state in responding to the appeal.

History: Add. 2000, Act 381, Eff. July 1, 2001;—Am. 2002, Act 719, Eff. July 1, 2003;—Am. 2015, Act 3, Eff. Dec. 1, 2015.

Popular name: CCW

Popular name: Concealed Weapons

Popular name: CPL

Popular name: Right to Carry

Popular name: Shall Issue

28.425e Database; annual report.

Sec. 5e. (1) The department of state police shall create and maintain a computerized database of individuals who apply under this act for a license to carry a concealed pistol. The database shall contain only the following information as to each individual:

(a) The individual's name, date of birth, address, county of residence, and state-issued driver license or personal identification card number.

(b) If the individual is licensed to carry a concealed pistol in this state, the license number and date of expiration.

(c) Except as provided in subsection (2), if the individual was denied a license to carry a concealed pistol after July 1, 2001 or issued a notice of statutory disqualification, a statement of the reasons for that denial or notice of statutory disqualification.

(d) A statement of all criminal charges pending and criminal convictions obtained against the individual during the license period.

(e) A statement of all determinations of responsibility for civil infractions of this act pending or obtained against the individual during the license period.

(f) The status of the individual's application or license.

(2) If an individual who was denied a license to carry a concealed pistol after July 1, 2001 or issued a notice of statutory disqualification is subsequently issued a license to carry a concealed pistol, the department of state police shall delete from the computerized database the previous reasons for the denial or notice of statutory disqualification.

(3) The department of state police shall enter the information described in subsection (1)(a), (b), and (f) into the law enforcement information network.

(4) Information in the database shall only be accessed and disclosed according to an access protocol that includes the following requirements:

(a) That the requestor of the firearms records uses the law enforcement information network or another system that maintains a record of the requestor's identity, time, and date that the request was made.

(b) Requires the requestor in an intentional query by name of the firearms records to attest that the firearms records were sought under 1 of the lawful purposes provided in section 1b(2).

(5) The department of state police shall by January 1 of each year file with the secretary of the senate and the clerk of the house of representatives, and post on the department of state police's internet website, an annual report setting forth all of the following information for the state for the previous fiscal year:

(a) The number of concealed pistol applications received.

(b) The number of concealed pistol licenses issued.

(c) The number of statutorily disqualified applicants.

(d) Categories for statutory disqualification under subdivision (c).

(e) The number of concealed pistol licenses suspended or revoked.

(f) Categories for suspension or revocation under subdivision (e).

(g) The number of applications pending at the time the report is made.

(h) The mean and median amount of time and the longest and shortest amount of time used by the Federal Bureau of Investigation to supply the fingerprint comparison report required in section 5b(10). The department may use a statistically significant sample to comply with this subdivision.

(i) The total number of individuals licensed to carry a concealed pistol found responsible for a civil violation of this act, the total number of civil violations of this act categorized by offense, the total number of individuals licensed to carry a concealed pistol convicted of a crime, and the total number of those criminal convictions categorized by offense.

(j) The number of suicides by individuals licensed to carry a concealed pistol.

(k) The total amount of revenue the department of state police has received under this act.

(*l*) Actual costs incurred per initial and renewal license by the department of state police under this act, itemized by each statutory section of this act.

(m) A list of expenditures made by the department of state police from money received under this act, regardless of purpose.

(n) Actual costs incurred per permit for each county clerk.

(o) The number of times the database was accessed, categorized by the purpose for which the database was accessed.

History: Add. 2000, Act 381, Eff. July 1, 2001;—Am. 2014, Act 204, Eff. Dec. 21, 2014;—Am. 2015, Act 3, Eff. Dec. 1, 2015.

Popular name: CCW

Popular name: Concealed Weapons

Popular name: CPL

Popular name: Right to Carry

Popular name: Shall Issue

28.425f Concealed pistol license; possession; disclosure to peace officer; violation; fine; notice to department; suspension or revocation by county clerk; entry into law enforcement information network; seizure by peace officer; forfeiture; "peace officer" defined.

Sec. 5f. (1) An individual who is licensed to carry a concealed pistol shall have his or her license to carry that pistol and his or her state-issued driver license or personal identification card in his or her possession at all times he or she is carrying a concealed pistol or a portable device that uses electro-muscular disruption technology.

(2) An individual who is licensed to carry a concealed pistol and who is carrying a concealed pistol or a portable device that uses electro-muscular disruption technology shall show both of the following to a peace officer upon request by that peace officer:

(a) His or her license to carry a concealed pistol.

(b) His or her state-issued driver license or personal identification card.

(3) An individual licensed under this act to carry a concealed pistol and who is carrying a concealed pistol or a portable device that uses electro-muscular disruption technology and who is stopped by a peace officer shall immediately disclose to the peace officer that he or she is carrying a pistol or a portable device that uses electro-muscular disruption technology concealed upon his or her person or in his or her vehicle.

(4) An individual who violates subsection (1) or (2) is responsible for a state civil infraction and shall be fined $100.00.

(5) An individual who violates subsection (3) is responsible for a state civil infraction and shall be fined as follows:

(a) For a first offense, by a fine of $500.00 and by the individual's license to carry a concealed pistol being suspended for 6 months.

(b) For a subsequent offense within 3 years of a prior offense, by a fine of $1,000.00 and by the individual's license to carry a concealed pistol being revoked.

(6) If an individual is found responsible for a state civil infraction under subsection (5), the peace officer shall notify the department of state police of that civil infraction. The department of state police shall notify the county clerk who issued the license, who shall suspend or revoke that license. The county clerk shall send notice by first-class mail of that suspension or revocation to the individual's last known address as indicated in the records of the county clerk. The department of state police shall immediately enter that suspension or revocation into the law enforcement information network.

(7) A pistol or portable device that uses electro-muscular disruption technology carried in violation of this section is subject to immediate seizure by a peace officer. If a peace officer seizes a pistol or portable device that uses electro-muscular disruption technology under this subsection, the individual has 45 days in which to display his or her license or documentation to an authorized employee of the law enforcement entity that employs the peace officer. If the individual displays his or her license or documentation to an authorized employee of the law enforcement entity that employs the peace officer within the 45-day period, the authorized employee of that law enforcement entity shall return the pistol or portable device that uses electro-muscular disruption technology to the individual unless the individual is prohibited by law from possessing a firearm or portable device that uses electro-muscular disruption technology. If the individual does not display his or her license or documentation within the 45-day period, the pistol or portable device that uses electro-muscular disruption technology is subject to forfeiture as provided in section 5g. A pistol or portable device that uses electro-muscular disruption technology is not subject to immediate seizure under this subsection if both of the following circumstances exist:

(a) The individual has his or her state-issued driver license or personal identification card in his or her possession when the violation occurs.

(b) The peace officer verifies through the law enforcement information network that the individual is licensed to carry a concealed pistol.
(8) As used in this section, "peace officer" includes a motor carrier officer appointed under section 6d of 1935 PA 59, MCL 28.6d, and security personnel employed by the state under section 6c of 1935 PA 59, MCL 28.6c.

History: Add. 2000, Act 381, Eff. July 1, 2001;—Am. 2002, Act 719, Eff. July 1, 2003;—Am. 2008, Act 194, Eff. Jan. 7, 2009;—Am. 2012, Act 123, Eff. Aug. 6, 2012;—Am. 2015, Act 3, Eff. Dec. 1, 2015.

Popular name: CCW

Popular name: Concealed Weapons

Popular name: CPL

Popular name: Right to Carry

Popular name: Shall Issue

28.425g Pistol or portable device that uses electro-muscular disruption technology; subject to seizure and forfeiture; exception.

Sec. 5g. A pistol or portable device that uses electro-muscular disruption technology carried in violation of this act is subject to seizure and forfeiture in the same manner that property is subject to seizure and forfeiture under sections 4701 to 4709 of the revised judicature act of 1961, 1961 PA 236, MCL 600.4701 to 600.4709. This section does not apply if the violation is a state civil infraction under section 5f unless the individual fails to present his or her license within the 45-day period described in that section.

History: Add. 2000, Act 381, Eff. July 1, 2001;—Am. 2012, Act 123, Eff. Aug. 6, 2012.

Popular name: CCW

Popular name: Concealed Weapons

Popular name: CPL

Popular name: Right to Carry

Popular name: Shall Issue

28.425h Expiration of license issued under former law; renewal license.

Sec. 5h. (1) An individual who is licensed to carry a concealed pistol on the effective date of the amendatory act that added this section may carry a concealed pistol under that license until the license expires or the individual's authority to carry a concealed pistol under that license is otherwise terminated, whichever occurs first.
(2) An individual who is licensed under this act to carry a concealed pistol on the effective date of the amendatory act that added this section may apply for a renewal license upon the expiration of that license as provided in section 5*l*.

History: Add. 2000, Act 381, Eff. July 1, 2001.

Popular name: CCW

Popular name: Concealed Weapons

Popular name: CPL

Popular name: Right to Carry

Popular name: Shall Issue

28.425i Instruction or training; liability.

Sec. 5i. (1) A person or entity that provides instruction or training to another person under section 5b is immune from civil liability for damages to any person or property caused by the person who was trained.
(2) This section does not apply if the person or entity providing the instruction or training was grossly negligent.
(3) This section is in addition to and not in lieu of immunity otherwise provided by law.

History: Add. 2000, Act 381, Eff. July 1, 2001.

Popular name: CCW

Popular name: Concealed Weapons

Popular name: CPL

Popular name: Right to Carry

Popular name: Shall Issue

28.425j Pistol training or safety program; conditions; prohibited conduct; violation of subsection (3) as felony; certificate of completion.

Sec. 5j. (1) A pistol training or safety program described in section 5b(7)(c) meets the requirements for knowledge or training in the safe use and handling of a pistol only if the training was provided within 5 years preceding the date of application and consisted of not less than 8 hours of instruction and all of the following conditions are met:
(a) The program is certified by this state or a national or state firearms training organization and provides 5 hours of instruction in, but is not limited to providing instruction in, all of the following:
(*i*) The safe storage, use, and handling of a pistol including, but not limited to, safe storage, use, and handling to protect child safety.

(*ii*) Ammunition knowledge, and the fundamentals of pistol shooting.

(*iii*) Pistol shooting positions.

(*iv*) Firearms and the law, including civil liability issues and the use of deadly force. This portion must be taught by an attorney or an individual trained in the use of deadly force.

(*v*) Avoiding criminal attack and controlling a violent confrontation.

(*vi*) All laws that apply to carrying a concealed pistol in this state.

(b) The program provides at least 3 hours of instruction on a firing range and requires firing at least 30 rounds of ammunition.

(c) The program provides a certificate of completion that states the program complies with the requirements of this section and that the individual successfully completed the course, and that contains the printed name and original handwritten signature of the course instructor. The certificate of completion must contain the statement, "This course complies with section 5j of 1927 PA 372.". For certificates issued on or after December 1, 2015, each certificate must also contain both of the following, which must be printed on the face of the certificate or attached in a separate document:

(*i*) The instructor's name and telephone number.

(*ii*) The name and telephone number of the state agency or a state or national firearms training organization that has certified the individual as an instructor for purposes of this section, his or her instructor certification number, if any, and the expiration date of that certification.

(d) The instructor of the course is certified by this state or a state or national firearms training organization to teach the pistol safety training courses described in this section. The county clerk shall not require any other certification or require an instructor to register with the county or county clerk.

(2) A training certificate that does not meet the requirements under state law applicable at the time the certification was issued may otherwise meet the requirements of subsection (1)(c) if the applicant provides information that reasonably demonstrates that the certificate or the training meets the applicable requirements.

(3) A person shall not do either of the following:

(a) Grant a certificate of completion described under subsection (1)(c) to an individual knowing the individual did not satisfactorily complete the course.

(b) Present a certificate of completion described under subsection (1)(c) to a county clerk knowing that the individual did not satisfactorily complete the course.

(4) A person who violates subsection (3) is guilty of a felony punishable by imprisonment for not more than 4 years or a fine of not more than $2,500.00, or both.

(5) A county clerk shall not require that a specific form, color, wording, or other content appear on a certificate of completion, except as otherwise required under this act.

History: Add. 2000, Act 381, Eff. July 1, 2001;—Am. 2002, Act 719, Eff. July 1, 2003;—Am. 2004, Act 254, Imd. Eff. July 23, 2004;—Am. 2015, Act 3, Eff. Dec. 1, 2015;—Am. 2017, Act 95, Eff. Oct. 11, 2017.

Popular name: CCW

Popular name: Concealed Weapons

Popular name: CPL

Popular name: Right to Carry

Popular name: Shall Issue

28.425k Acceptance of license as implied consent to submit to chemical analysis of breath, blood, or urine; collection and testing; refusal to take chemical test; definitions.

Sec. 5k. (1) Acceptance of a license issued under this act to carry a concealed pistol constitutes implied consent to submit to a chemical analysis under this section. This section also applies to individuals listed in section 12a.

(2) An individual shall not carry a concealed pistol or portable device that uses electro-muscular disruption technology while he or she is under the influence of alcoholic liquor or a controlled substance or while having a bodily alcohol content prohibited under this section. An individual who violates this section is responsible for a state civil infraction or guilty of a crime as follows:

(a) If the person was under the influence of alcoholic liquor or a controlled substance or a combination of alcoholic liquor and a controlled substance, or had a bodily alcohol content of .10 or more grams per 100 milliliters of blood, per 210 liters of breath, or per 67 milliliters of urine, the individual is guilty of a misdemeanor punishable by imprisonment for not more than 93 days or $100.00, or both. The court shall order the county clerk in the county in which the individual was issued a license to carry a concealed pistol to revoke the license. The county clerk shall notify the department of state police of the revocation in a manner prescribed by the department of state police. The department of state police shall immediately enter that revocation into the law enforcement information network.

(b) If the person had a bodily alcohol content of .08 or more but less than .10 grams per 100 milliliters of blood, per 210 liters of breath, or per 67 milliliters of urine, the individual is guilty of a misdemeanor punishable by imprisonment for not more than 93 days or $100.00, or both. The court shall order the county clerk in the county in which the individual was issued a license to carry a concealed pistol to suspend the license for 3 years. The county clerk shall notify the department of state police of that suspension in a manner prescribed by the department of state police. The department of state police shall immediately enter that suspension into the law enforcement information network.

(c) If the person had a bodily alcohol content of .02 or more but less than .08 grams per 100 milliliters of blood, per 210 liters of breath, or per 67 milliliters of urine, the individual is responsible for a state civil infraction and shall be fined $100.00. The peace officer shall notify the department of state police of a civil infraction under this subdivision. The department of state police shall notify the county clerk in the county in which the individual was issued the license, who shall suspend the license for 1 year. The department of state police shall immediately enter that suspension into the law enforcement information network.

(3) This section does not prohibit an individual licensed under this act to carry a concealed pistol who has any bodily alcohol content from doing any of the following:

(a) Transporting that pistol in the locked trunk of his or her motor vehicle or another motor vehicle in which he or she is a passenger or, if the vehicle does not have a trunk, from transporting that pistol unloaded in a locked compartment or container that is separated from the ammunition for that pistol.

(b) Transporting that pistol on a vessel if the pistol is transported unloaded in a locked compartment or container that is separated from the ammunition for that pistol.

(c) Transporting a portable device using electro-muscular disruption technology in the locked trunk of his or her motor vehicle or another motor vehicle in which he or she is a passenger, or, if the vehicle does not have a trunk, from transporting that portable device in a locked compartment or container.

(d) Transporting a portable device using electro-muscular disruption technology on a vessel if the portable device is transported in a locked compartment or container.

(4) A peace officer who has probable cause to believe an individual is carrying a concealed pistol or a portable device using electro-muscular disruption technology in violation of this section may require the individual to submit to a chemical analysis of his or her breath, blood, or urine.

(5) Before an individual is required to submit to a chemical analysis under subsection (4), the peace officer shall inform the individual of all of the following:

(a) The individual may refuse to submit to the chemical analysis, but if he or she chooses to do so, all of the following apply:

(*i*) The officer may obtain a court order requiring the individual to submit to a chemical analysis.

(*ii*) The refusal shall result in his or her license to carry a concealed pistol being suspended for 6 months.

(b) If the individual submits to the chemical analysis, he or she may obtain a chemical analysis described in subsection (4) from a person of his or her own choosing.

(6) The collection and testing of breath, blood, and urine specimens under this section shall be conducted in the same manner that breath, blood, and urine specimens are collected and tested for alcohol- and controlled-substance-related driving violations under the Michigan vehicle code, 1949 PA 300, MCL 257.1 to 257.923.

(7) If a person refuses to take a chemical test authorized under this section, the person is responsible for a state civil infraction and shall be fined $100.00. A peace officer shall promptly report the refusal in writing to the department of state police. The department of state police shall notify the county clerk in the county in which the license was issued, who shall suspend the license for 6 months. The department of state police shall immediately enter that suspension into the law enforcement information network.

(8) As used in this section:

(a) "Alcoholic liquor" means that term as defined in section 105 of the Michigan liquor control code of 1998, 1998 PA 58, MCL 436.1105.

(b) "Controlled substance" means that term as defined in section 7104 of the public health code, 1978 PA 368, MCL 333.7104.

(c) "Under the influence of alcoholic liquor or a controlled substance" means that the individual's ability to properly handle a pistol or to exercise clear judgment regarding the use of that pistol was substantially and materially affected by the consumption of alcoholic liquor or a controlled substance.

History: Add. 2000, Act 381, Eff. July 1, 2001;—Am. 2012, Act 123, Eff. Aug. 6, 2012;—Am. 2015, Act 3, Eff. Dec. 1, 2015.

Popular name: CCW

Popular name: Concealed Weapons

Popular name: CPL

Popular name: Right to Carry

Popular name: Shall Issue

28.425*l* License; validity; duration; renewal; waiver of educational requirements; fingerprints.

Sec. 5*l*. (1) A license to carry a concealed pistol, including a renewal license, is valid until the applicant's date of birth that falls not less than 4 years or more than 5 years after the license is issued or renewed, as applicable. The county clerk shall notify the licensee that his or her license is about to expire and may be renewed as provided in this section. The notification must be sent by the county clerk to the last known address of the licensee as shown on the records of the county clerk. The notification must be sent in a sealed envelope by first-class mail not less than 3 months or more than 6 months before the expiration date of the current license. Except as provided in this section, a renewal of a license under section 5b must be issued in the same manner as an original license issued under section 5b. An applicant is eligible for a renewal of a license under this section if his or her license is not expired, or expired within a 1-year period before the date of application under this section. Each applicant who submits an application for a renewal license to a county clerk under this section shall pay an application and licensing fee of $115.00 by any method of payment accepted by that county for payments of other fees and penalties. No other charge, fee, cost, or assessment, including any local charge, fee, cost, or assessment, is required of the applicant except as specifically authorized in this act. The applicant shall pay the application and licensing fee to the county. The county treasurer shall deposit $36.00 of each fee collected under this subsection in the concealed pistol licensing fund of that county created in section 5x. The county treasurer shall forward the balance remaining to the state treasurer. The state treasurer shall deposit the balance of the fee in the general fund to the credit of the department of state police.

(2) Subject to subsections (9) and (10), an application to renew a license to carry a concealed pistol may be submitted not more than 6 months before the expiration of the current license. No later than December 1, 2018, the department of state police shall provide a system for an applicant to submit his or her application to renew a license to carry a concealed pistol online or by first-class mail and shall accept those applications on behalf of the county clerk as required under this act at no additional charge. Each applicant who submits a renewal license online or by first-class mail to the department of state police under this section shall pay an application and licensing fee of $115.00 by any method of payment accepted by the department of state police. No other charge, fee, cost, or assessment is required of the applicant except as specifically authorized in this act. The applicant shall pay the application and licensing fee to the state. The state treasurer shall forward $36.00 of each fee collected under this subsection to the county treasurer who shall deposit the $36.00 in the concealed pistol licensing fund of that county created in section 5x. The state treasurer shall deposit the balance of the fee in the general fund to the credit of the department of state police. The department of state police shall notify the county clerk of the county in which the applicant resides of a properly submitted online application or application by first-class mail received by the department. If the county clerk issues a renewal license under this section, the county clerk shall send the license to the licensee by first-class mail in a sealed envelope. If the county clerk issues the renewal, the effective date of the renewal license is the date of expiration of the current license or the date of approval or issue of the renewal, whichever is later, and the date of expiration is the applicant's date of birth which is not less than 4 years or more than 5 years from the effective date of the license.

(3) The department of state police shall complete the verification required under section 5b(6) and the county clerk shall issue a renewal license or a notice of statutory disqualification within 30 days after the date the renewal application was received. Beginning on the date the department of state police establishes a system under subsection (2), the department of state police shall provide an applicant a digital receipt, or a receipt by first-class mail if requested, for his or her renewal application submitted online at the time the application is received by the department of state police. Beginning on the date the department of state police establishes a system under subsection (2), the department of state police shall mail an applicant a receipt by first-class mail for his or her renewal application submitted by first-class mail at the time the application is received by the department of state police. The receipt issued under this subsection to an individual applying for a renewal license whose current license is not expired at the time of application must contain all of the following:

(a) The name of the applicant.

(b) The date and time the receipt is issued.

(c) The amount paid.

(d) The applicant's state-issued driver license or personal identification card number.

(e) The statement "This receipt was issued for the purpose of renewal of a concealed pistol license. As provided in section 5*l* of 1927 PA 372, MCL 28.425*l*, this receipt shall serve as a concealed pistol license for the individual named in the receipt when carried with the expired license and is valid until a license or notice of statutory disqualification is issued by the county clerk. This receipt does not exempt the individual named in the receipt from complying with all applicable laws for the purchase of firearms.".

(f) The name of the county in which the receipt is issued, if applicable.

(g) An impression of the county seal, if applicable.

(4) The receipt issued under subsection (3) to an individual applying for a renewal license whose license is expired must contain all of the following:

(a) The name of the applicant.

(b) The date and time the receipt is issued.

(c) The amount paid.

(d) The applicant's state-issued driver license or personal identification card number.

(e) The statement "This receipt was issued for the purpose of renewal of a concealed pistol license. As provided in section 5*l* of 1927 PA 372, MCL 28.425*l*, if a license or notice of statutory disqualification is not issued within 30 days after the date this receipt was issued, this receipt shall serve as a concealed pistol license for the individual named in the receipt when carried with an official state-issued driver license or personal identification card. The receipt is valid as a license until a license or a notice of statutory disqualification is issued by the county clerk. This receipt does not exempt the individual named in the receipt from complying with all applicable laws for the purchase of firearms.".

(5) Until November 30, 2018, a member of the United States Armed Forces, the United States Armed Forces Reserve, or the Michigan National Guard who is on orders to a duty station outside of this state may submit his or her application to renew a license to carry a concealed pistol by first-class mail, containing the required fee, a notarized application, the licensee's address of record within the state, the licensee's orders to report to a duty station outside of this state, and if the licensee desires to have his or her application receipt, renewal license, or any other notices mailed to his or her address of assignment or deployment, a letter requesting that action including the address of assignment or deployment. If the county clerk issues a renewal license

under this section, the county clerk shall send the license to the licensee by first-class mail in a sealed envelope. If the licensee is a member of the United States Armed Forces, the United States Armed Forces Reserve, or the Michigan National Guard who is on orders to a duty station outside of this state and requests that his or her license be sent to the address of assignment or deployment, the county clerk shall mail the license to the licensee at the address of assignment or deployment provided in the renewal application. Until November 30, 2018, if a renewal application is submitted by a member of the United States Armed Forces, the United States Armed Forces Reserve, or the Michigan National Guard who is on orders to a duty station outside of this state, the county clerk shall mail a receipt to the licensee by first-class mail.

(6) If an individual applies for a renewal license before the expiration of his or her license, the expiration date of the current license is extended until the renewal license or notice of statutory disqualification is issued. The county clerk shall notify the department of state police in a manner prescribed by the department of state police after he or she receives an application for renewal. The department of state police shall immediately enter into the law enforcement information network the date that application for renewal was submitted and that the renewal application is pending.

(7) A person carrying a concealed pistol after the expiration date of his or her license under an extension under subsection (6) shall keep the receipt issued by the county clerk under subsection (3) and his or her expired license in his or her possession at all times that he or she is carrying the pistol. For the purposes of this act, the receipt is considered to be part of the license to carry a concealed pistol until a renewal license is issued or denied or a notice of statutory disqualification is issued.

(8) The educational requirements under section 5b(7)(c) are waived for an applicant who is a retired police officer or retired law enforcement officer.

(9) The educational requirements under section 5b(7)(c) for an applicant who is applying for a renewal of a license under this act are waived except that the applicant shall certify that he or she has completed at least 3 hours' review of the training described under section 5b(7)(c) and has had at least 1 hour of firing range time in the 6 months immediately preceding the subsequent application. The educational and firing range requirements of this subsection are met if the applicant certifies on the renewal application form that he or she has complied with the requirements of this subsection. An applicant is not required to verify the statements made under this subsection and is not required to obtain a certificate or undergo training other than as required by this subsection.

(10) An applicant who is applying for a renewal of a license issued under section 5b is not required to have fingerprints taken again under section 5b(9) if all of the following conditions have been met:

(a) There has been established a system for the department of state police to save and maintain in its automated fingerprint identification system (AFIS) database all fingerprints that are submitted to the department of state police under section 5b.

(b) The applicant's fingerprints have been submitted to and maintained by the department of state police as described in subdivision (a) for ongoing comparison with the automated fingerprint identification system (AFIS) database.

History: Add. 2000, Act 381, Eff. July 1, 2001;—Am. 2002, Act 719, Eff. July 1, 2003;—Am. 2005, Act 262, Eff. July 1, 2006;—Am. 2006, Act 92, Eff. July 1, 2006;—Am. 2006, Act 184, Imd. Eff. June 19, 2006;—Am. 2006, Act 456, Imd. Eff. Dec. 20, 2006;—Am. 2008, Act 406, Imd. Eff. Jan. 6, 2009;—Am. 2012, Act 32, Imd. Eff. Feb. 28, 2012;—Am. 2015, Act 3, Eff. June 2, 2015;—Am. 2017, Act 95, Eff. Oct. 11, 2017.

Popular name: CCW

Popular name: Concealed Weapons

Popular name: CPL

Popular name: Right to Carry

Popular name: Shall Issue

28.425m Repealed. 2015, Act 3, Eff. June 2, 2015.

Compiler's note: The repealed section pertained to notification to county concealed weapon licensing board of criminal charge against license holder.

Popular name: CCW

Popular name: Concealed Weapons

Popular name: CPL

Popular name: Right to Carry

Popular name: Shall Issue

28.425n Other license or permit; limitations by employer prohibited.

Sec. 5n. (1) This state or a local unit of government of this state shall not prohibit an individual from doing either of the following as a condition for receiving or maintaining any other license or permit authorized by law:

(a) Applying for or receiving a license to carry a concealed pistol under this act.

(b) Carrying a concealed pistol in compliance with a license issued under this act.

(2) Except as provided in subsection (3), an employer shall not prohibit an employee from doing either of the following:

(a) Applying for or receiving a license to carry a concealed pistol under this act.

(b) Carrying a concealed pistol in compliance with a license issued under this act. This subdivision does not prohibit an employer from prohibiting an employee from carrying a concealed pistol in the course of his or her employment with that employer.

(3) A police agency may prohibit an employee of that police agency from carrying a concealed pistol if carrying a concealed pistol would result in increased insurance premiums or a loss or reduction of insurance coverage for that employer.

History: Add. 2000, Act 381, Eff. July 1, 2001.

Popular name: CCW

Popular name: Concealed Weapons

Popular name: CPL

Popular name: Right to Carry

Popular name: Shall Issue

28.425o Premises on which carrying concealed weapon or portable device that uses electro-muscular disruption technology prohibited; "premises" defined; exceptions to subsections (1) and (2); violation; penalties.

Sec. 5o. (1) Subject to subsection (5), an individual licensed under this act to carry a concealed pistol, or who is exempt from licensure under section 12a(h), shall not carry a concealed pistol on the premises of any of the following:

(a) A school or school property except that a parent or legal guardian of a student of the school is not precluded from carrying a concealed pistol while in a vehicle on school property, if he or she is dropping the student off at the school or picking up the student from the school. As used in this section, "school" and "school property" mean those terms as defined in section 237a of the Michigan penal code, 1931 PA 328, MCL 750.237a.

(b) A public or private child care center or day care center, public or private child caring institution, or public or private child placing agency.

(c) A sports arena or stadium.

(d) A bar or tavern licensed under the Michigan liquor control code of 1998, 1998 PA 58, MCL 436.1101 to 436.2303, where the primary source of income of the business is the sale of alcoholic liquor by the glass and consumed on the premises. This subdivision does not apply to an owner or employee of the business. The Michigan liquor control commission shall develop and make available to holders of licenses under the Michigan liquor control code of 1998, 1998 PA 58, MCL 436.1101 to 436.2303, an appropriate sign stating that "This establishment prohibits patrons from carrying concealed weapons". The owner or operator of an establishment licensed under the Michigan liquor control code of 1998, 1998 PA 58, MCL 436.1101 to 436.2303, may post the sign developed under this subdivision.

(e) Any property or facility owned or operated by a church, synagogue, mosque, temple, or other place of worship, unless the presiding official or officials of the church, synagogue, mosque, temple, or other place of worship permit the carrying of concealed pistol on that property or facility.

(f) An entertainment facility with a seating capacity of 2,500 or more individuals that the individual knows or should know has a seating capacity of 2,500 or more individuals or that has a sign above each public entrance stating in letters not less than 1-inch high a seating capacity of 2,500 or more individuals.

(g) A hospital.

(h) A dormitory or classroom of a community college, college, or university.

(2) Subject to subsection (5), an individual shall not carry a portable device that uses electro-muscular disruption technology on any of the premises described in subsection (1).

(3) An individual licensed under this act to carry a concealed pistol, or who is exempt from licensure under section 12a(h), shall not carry a concealed pistol in violation of R 432.1212 of the Michigan Administrative Code promulgated under the Michigan gaming control and revenue act, 1996 IL 1, MCL 432.201 to 432.226.

(4) As used in subsection (1), "premises" does not include parking areas of the places identified under subsection (1).

(5) Subsections (1) and (2) do not apply to any of the following:

(a) An individual licensed under this act who is a retired police officer, retired law enforcement officer, or retired federal law enforcement officer.

(b) An individual who is licensed under this act and who is employed or contracted by an entity described under subsection (1) to provide security services and is required by his or her employer or the terms of a contract to carry a concealed firearm on the premises of the employing or contracting entity.

(c) An individual who is licensed as a private investigator or private detective under the professional investigator licensure act, 1965 PA 285, MCL 338.821 to 338.851.

(d) An individual who is licensed under this act and who is a corrections officer of a county sheriff's department or who is licensed under this act and is a retired corrections officer of a county sheriff's department, if that individual has received county sheriff approved weapons training.

(e) An individual who is licensed under this act and who is a motor carrier officer or capitol security officer of the department of state police.

(f) An individual who is licensed under this act and who is a member of a sheriff's posse.

(g) An individual who is licensed under this act and who is an auxiliary officer or reserve officer of a police or sheriff's department.

(h) An individual who is licensed under this act and who is any of the following:

(*i*) A parole, probation, or corrections officer, or absconder recovery unit member, of the department of corrections, if that individual has obtained a Michigan department of corrections weapons permit.

(*ii*) A retired parole, probation, or corrections officer, or retired absconder recovery unit member, of the department of corrections, if that individual has obtained a Michigan department of corrections weapons permit.

(i) A state court judge or state court retired judge who is licensed under this act.
(j) An individual who is licensed under this act and who is a court officer.
(k) An individual who is licensed under this act and who is a peace officer.
(6) An individual who violates this section is responsible for a state civil infraction or guilty of a crime as follows:
(a) Except as provided in subdivisions (b) and (c), the individual is responsible for a state civil infraction and may be fined not more than $500.00. The court shall order the individual's license to carry a concealed pistol suspended for 6 months.
(b) For a second violation, the individual is guilty of a misdemeanor punishable by a fine of not more than $1,000.00. The court shall order the individual's license to carry a concealed pistol revoked.
(c) For a third or subsequent violation, the individual is guilty of a felony punishable by imprisonment for not more than 4 years or a fine of not more than $5,000.00, or both. The court shall order the individual's license to carry a concealed pistol revoked.

History: Add. 2000, Act 381, Eff. July 1, 2001;—Am. 2002, Act 719, Eff. July 1, 2003;—Am. 2008, Act 194, Eff. Jan. 7, 2009;—Am. 2008, Act 406, Imd. Eff. Jan. 6, 2009;—Am. 2008, Act 407, Eff. Apr. 6, 2009;—Am. 2012, Act 123, Eff. Aug. 6, 2012;—Am. 2014, Act 206, Eff. Dec. 21, 2014;—Am. 2015, Act 3, Eff. Dec. 1, 2015;—Am. 2015, Act 16, Eff. July 13, 2015;—Am. 2015, Act 206, Eff. Dec. 1, 2015;—Am. 2017, Act 95, Eff. Oct. 11, 2017.

Popular name: CCW

Popular name: Concealed Weapons

Popular name: CPL

Popular name: Right to Carry

Popular name: Shall Issue

28.425v Concealed weapon enforcement fund; creation; disposition of funds; lapse; expenditures.

Sec. 5v. (1) The concealed weapon enforcement fund is created in the state treasury.
(2) The state treasurer may receive money or other assets from any source for deposit into the fund. The state treasurer shall direct the investment of the fund. The state treasurer shall credit to the fund interest and earnings from fund investments.
(3) Money in the fund at the close of the fiscal year shall remain in the fund and shall not lapse to the general fund.
(4) The department of state police shall expend money from the fund only to provide training to law enforcement personnel regarding the rights and responsibilities of individuals who are licensed to carry concealed pistols in this state and proper enforcement techniques in light of those rights and responsibilities.

History: Add. 2000, Act 381, Eff. July 1, 2001.

Popular name: CCW

Popular name: Concealed Weapons

Popular name: CPL

Popular name: Right to Carry

Popular name: Shall Issue

28.425w Appropriation; amount; purpose; total state spending; appropriations and expenditures subject to MCL 18.1101 to 18.1594.

Sec. 5w. (1) One million dollars is appropriated from the general fund to the department of state police for the fiscal year ending September 30, 2001 for all of the following:
(a) Distributing trigger locks or other safety devices for firearms to the public free of charge.
(b) Providing concealed pistol application kits to county sheriffs, local police agencies, and county clerks for distribution under section 5.
(c) The fingerprint analysis and comparison reports required under section 5b(11).
(d) Photographs required under section 5c.
(e) Creating and maintaining the database required under section 5e.
(f) Creating and maintaining a database of firearms that have been reported lost or stolen. Information in the database shall be made available to law enforcement through the law enforcement information network.
(g) Grants to county concealed weapon licensing boards for expenditure only to implement this act.
(h) Training under section 5v(4).
(i) Creating and distributing the reporting forms required under section 5m.
(j) A public safety campaign regarding the requirements of this act.
(2) Pursuant to section 30 of article IX of the state constitution of 1963, total state spending under subsection (1) for the fiscal year ending September 30, 2001 is $1,000,000.00.
(3) The appropriations made and the expenditures authorized under this section and the departments, agencies, commissions, boards, offices, and programs for which an appropriation is made under this section are subject to the management and budget act, 1984 PA 431, MCL 18.1101 to 18.1594.

History: Add. 2000, Act 381, Eff. July 1, 2001.

Popular name: CCW

Popular name: Concealed Weapons

Popular name: CPL

Popular name: Right to Carry

Popular name: Shall Issue

28.425x Concealed pistol licensing fund.

Sec. 5x. (1) Each county shall establish a concealed pistol licensing fund for the deposit of fees collected for the county clerk under this act. The county treasurer shall direct investment of the concealed pistol licensing fund and shall credit to the fund interest and earnings from fund investments.

(2) Money credited to the county concealed pistol licensing fund shall be expended in compliance with the uniform budgeting and accounting act, 1968 PA 2, MCL 141.421 to 141.440a, subject to an appropriation. Expenditures from the county concealed pistol licensing fund shall be used by the county clerk only for the cost of administering this act. Allowable expenditures include, but are not limited to, any of the following costs of the county clerk:

(a) Staffing requirements directly attributable to performing functions required under this act.

(b) Technology upgrades, including technology to take fingerprints by electronic means.

(c) Office supplies.

(d) Document storage and retrieval systems and system upgrades.

History: Add. 2015, Act 3, Eff. June 2, 2015.

Popular name: CCW

Popular name: Concealed Weapons

Popular name: CPL

Popular name: Right to Carry

Popular name: Shall Issue

28.426 Issuance of license; conditions.

Sec. 6. (1) An issuing agency shall not issue a license to an applicant under section 2 unless both of the following apply:

(a) The issuing agency has determined through the federal national instant criminal background check system that the applicant is not prohibited under federal law from possessing or transporting a firearm.

(b) If the applicant is not a United States citizen, the issuing agency has verified through the United States Immigration and Customs Enforcement databases that the applicant is not an illegal alien or a nonimmigrant alien.

(2) A county clerk shall not issue a license to an applicant under section 5b unless both of the following apply:

(a) The department of state police, or the county sheriff under section 5a(4), has determined through the federal national instant criminal background check system that the applicant is not prohibited under federal law from possessing or transporting a firearm.

(b) If the applicant is not a United States citizen, the department of state police has verified through the United States Immigration and Customs Enforcement databases that the applicant is not an illegal alien or a nonimmigrant alien.

History: Add. 2005, Act 242, Imd. Eff. Nov. 22, 2005;—Am. 2017, Act 95, Eff. Oct. 11, 2017.

Compiler's note: Former MCL 28.426, which pertained to concealed weapon licensing board, was repealed by Act 381 of 200, Eff. July 1, 2001.

Popular name: CCW

Popular name: Concealed Weapons

Popular name: CPL

Popular name: Right to Carry

Popular name: Shall Issue

28.426a Repealed. 2015, Act 3, Eff. June 2, 2015.

Compiler's note: The repealed section pertained to license to equip premises or vehicle with gas ejecting device or authorize manufacture or sale of gas ejecting device.

Popular name: CCW

Popular name: Concealed Weapons

Popular name: CPL

Popular name: Right to Carry

Popular name: Shall Issue

Popular name: R 28.91 and R 28.92 of the Michigan Administrative Code

28.428 Suspension, revocation, or reinstatement of license; notice; surrender of license; order or amended order; entry into law enforcement information network; effect of suspension or revocation order; failure to receive notice.

Sec. 8. (1) The county clerk in the county in which a license was issued to an individual to carry a concealed pistol shall suspend, revoke, or reinstate a license as required under this act if ordered by a court or if the county clerk is notified by a law enforcement agency, prosecuting official, or court of a change in the licensee's eligibility to carry a concealed pistol under this act.

(2) If a county clerk is notified by a law enforcement agency, prosecuting official, or court that an individual licensed to carry a concealed pistol is charged with a felony or charged with a misdemeanor listed in section 5b(7)(h) or (i), the county clerk shall immediately suspend the individual's license until there is a final disposition of the charge for that offense. The county clerk shall send notice by first-class mail in a sealed envelope of that suspension to the individual's last known address as indicated in the records of the county clerk. The notice must include the statutory reason for the suspension, the source of the record supporting that suspension, the length of the suspension, and whom to contact for reinstating the license on expiration of the suspension, correcting errors in the record, or appealing the suspension. If a county clerk suspended a license under this subsection and the individual is acquitted of the charge or the charge is dismissed, the individual shall notify the county clerk who shall automatically reinstate the license if the license is not expired and the individual is otherwise qualified to receive a license to carry a concealed pistol, as verified by the department of state police. A county clerk shall not charge a fee for the reinstatement of a license under this subsection.

(3) The department of state police shall notify the county clerk in the county in which a license was issued to an individual to carry a concealed pistol if the department of state police determines that there has been a change in the individual's eligibility under this act to receive a license to carry a concealed pistol. The county clerk shall suspend, revoke, or reinstate the license as required under this act and immediately send notice of the suspension, revocation, or reinstatement under this subsection by first-class mail in a sealed envelope to the individual's last known address as indicated on the records of the county clerk. The notice must include the statutory reason for the suspension, revocation, or reinstatement, the source of the record supporting the suspension, revocation, or reinstatement, the length of the suspension or revocation, and whom to contact for correcting errors in the record, appealing the suspension or revocation, and reapplying for that individual's license. The department of state police shall immediately enter that suspension, revocation, or reinstatement into the law enforcement information network.

(4) If a suspension is imposed under this section, the suspension must be for a period stated in years, months, or days, or until the final disposition of the charge, and state the date the suspension will end, if applicable. The licensee shall promptly surrender his or her license to the county clerk after being notified that his or her license has been revoked or suspended. An individual who fails to surrender a license as required under this subsection after he or she was notified that his or her license was suspended or revoked is guilty of a misdemeanor punishable by imprisonment for not more than 93 days or a fine of not more than $500.00, or both.

(5) Except as otherwise provided in subsections (2) and (6), if a license is suspended under this section and that license was surrendered by the licensee, upon expiration of the suspension period, the applicant may apply for a renewal license in the same manner as provided under section 5*l*. The county clerk or department of state police, as applicable, shall issue the applicant a receipt for his or her application at the time the application is submitted. The receipt must contain all of the following:

(a) The name of the applicant.

(b) The date and time the receipt is issued.

(c) The amount paid.

(d) The applicant's state-issued driver license or personal identification card number.

(e) The statement, "This receipt was issued for the purpose of applying for a renewal of a concealed pistol license following a period of suspension or revocation. This receipt does not authorize an individual to carry a concealed pistol in this state.".

(f) The name of the county in which the receipt is issued, if applicable.

(g) An impression of the county seal, if applicable.

(6) If a license is suspended because of an order under section 5b(7)(d)(*iii*) and that license was surrendered by the licensee, upon expiration of the order and notification to the county clerk, the county clerk shall automatically reinstate the license if the license is not expired and the department of state police has completed the verification required under section 5b(6). The county clerk shall not charge a fee for the reinstatement of a license under this subsection.

(7) If the court orders a county clerk to suspend, revoke, or reinstate a license under this section or amends a suspension, revocation, or reinstatement order, the county clerk shall immediately notify the department of state police in a manner prescribed by the department of state police. The department of state police shall enter the order or amended order into the law enforcement information network.

(8) A suspension or revocation order or amended order issued under this section is immediately effective. However, an individual is not criminally liable for violating the order or amended order unless he or she has received notice of the order or amended order.

(9) If an individual is carrying a pistol in violation of a suspension or revocation order or amended order issued under this section but has not previously received notice of the order or amended order, the individual must be informed of the order or amended order and be given an opportunity to properly store the pistol or otherwise comply with the order or amended order before an arrest is made for carrying the pistol in violation of this act.

(10) If a law enforcement agency or officer notifies an individual of a suspension or revocation order or amended order issued under this section who has not previously received notice of the order or amended order, the law enforcement agency or officer shall enter a statement into the law enforcement information network that the individual has received notice of the order or amended order under this section.

History: 1927, Act 372, Eff. Sept. 5, 1927;—CL 1929, 16757;—CL 1948, 28.428;—Am. 2000, Act 381, Eff. July 1, 2001;—Am. 2008, Act 406, Imd. Eff. Jan. 6, 2009;—Am. 2015, Act 3, Eff. Dec. 1, 2015;—Am. 2015, Act 207, Eff. Dec. 1, 2015;—Am. 2017, Act 95, Eff. Oct. 11, 2017.

Popular name: CCW

Popular name: Concealed Weapons

Popular name: CPL

Popular name: Right to Carry

Popular name: Shall Issue

28.429 Repealed. 2008, Act 195, Eff. Jan. 7, 2009.

Compiler's note: The repealed section pertained to safety inspection requirements for pistols.

Popular name: CCW

Popular name: Concealed Weapons

Popular name: CPL

Popular name: Right to Carry

Popular name: Shall Issue

28.429a Repealed. 2012, Act 377, Imd. Eff. Dec. 18, 2012.

Compiler's note: The repealed section pertained to approval of basic pistol safety pamphlet and questionnaire by department of state police.

Popular name: CCW

Popular name: Concealed Weapons

Popular name: CPL

Popular name: Right to Carry

Popular name: Shall Issue

28.429b Repealed. 2012, Act 377, Imd. Eff. Dec. 18, 2012.

Compiler's note: The repealed section pertained to printing and distribution of basic pistol safety pamphlet and questionnaire by department of state police.

Popular name: CCW

Popular name: Concealed Weapons

Popular name: CPL

Popular name: Right to Carry

Popular name: Shall Issue

28.429c Repealed. 2012, Act 377, Imd. Eff. Dec. 18, 2012.

Compiler's note: The repealed section pertained to distribution of basic pistol safety pamphlet and questionnaire.

Popular name: CCW

Popular name: Concealed Weapons

Popular name: CPL

Popular name: Right to Carry

Popular name: Shall Issue

28.429d Repealed. 2000, Act 381, Eff. July 1, 2001.

Compiler's note: The repealed section pertained to forfeiture of firearm.

Popular name: CCW

Popular name: Concealed Weapons

Popular name: CPL

Popular name: Right to Carry

Popular name: Shall Issue

28.430 Theft of firearm; report required; failure to report theft as civil violation; penalty.

Sec. 10. (1) A person who owns a firearm shall, within 5 days after he or she knows his or her firearm is stolen, report the theft to a police agency having jurisdiction over that theft.

(2) A person who fails to report the theft of a firearm as required under subsection (1) is responsible for a civil violation and may be fined not more than $500.00.

History: Add. 1990, Act 320, Eff. Mar. 28, 1991.

Compiler's note: Former sections 10 and 11 were not compiled.

Popular name: CCW

Popular name: Concealed Weapons

Popular name: CPL

Popular name: Right to Carry

Popular name: Shall Issue

28.431 Repealed. 2012, Act 377, Imd. Eff. Dec. 18, 2012.

Compiler's note: The repealed section pertained to system for review of criminal histories of individuals purchasing firearms.

Popular name: CCW

Popular name: Concealed Weapons

Popular name: CPL

Popular name: Right to Carry

Popular name: Shall Issue

28.432 Inapplicability of MCL 28.422; amendatory act as "Janet Kukuk act".

Sec. 12. (1) Section 2 does not apply to any of the following:

(a) A police or correctional agency of the United States or of this state or any subdivision of this state.

(b) The United States army, air force, navy, or marine corps.

(c) An organization authorized by law to purchase or receive weapons from the United States or from this state.

(d) The national guard, armed forces reserves, or other duly authorized military organization.

(e) A member of an entity or organization described in subdivisions (a) through (d) for a pistol while engaged in the course of his or her duties with that entity or while going to or returning from those duties.

(f) A United States citizen holding a license to carry a pistol concealed upon his or her person issued by another state.

(g) The regular and ordinary possession and transportation of a pistol as merchandise by an authorized agent of a person licensed to manufacture firearms or a licensed dealer.

(h) Purchasing, owning, carrying, possessing, using, or transporting an antique firearm. As used in this subdivision, "antique firearm" means that term as defined in section 231a of the Michigan penal code, 1931 PA 328, MCL 750.231a.

(i) An individual carrying, possessing, using, or transporting a pistol belonging to another individual, if the other individual's possession of the pistol is authorized by law and the individual carrying, possessing, using, or transporting the pistol has obtained a license under section 5b to carry a concealed pistol or is exempt from licensure as provided in section 12a.

(2) The amendatory act that added subsection (1)(h) shall be known and may be cited as the "Janet Kukuk act".

History: 1927, Act 372, Eff. Sept. 5, 1927;—CL 1929, 16761;—CL 1948, 28.432;—Am. 1964, Act 216, Eff. Aug. 28, 1964;—Am. 2000, Act 381, Eff. July 1, 2001;—Am. 2004, Act 99, Imd. Eff. May 13, 2004;—Am. 2006, Act 75, Eff. July 1, 2006;—Am. 2008, Act 195, Eff. Jan. 7, 2009;—Am. 2010, Act 209, Eff. Feb. 15, 2011.

Popular name: CCW

Popular name: Concealed Weapons

Popular name: CPL

Popular name: Right to Carry

Popular name: Shall Issue

28.432a Exceptions.

Sec. 12a. The requirements of this act for obtaining a license to carry a concealed pistol do not apply to any of the following:

(a) A peace officer of a duly authorized police agency of the United States or of this state or a political subdivision of this state, who is regularly employed and paid by the United States or this state or a subdivision of this state, except a township constable.

(b) A constable who is trained and licensed or certified under the Michigan commission on law enforcement standards act, 1965 PA 203, MCL 28.601 to 28.615, while engaged in his or her official duties or going to or coming from his or her official duties, and who is regularly employed and paid by a political subdivision of this state.

(c) An individual regularly employed by the department of corrections and authorized in writing by the director of the department of corrections to carry a concealed pistol during the performance of his or her duties or while going to or returning from his or her duties.

(d) An individual regularly employed as a local corrections officer by a county sheriff, who is trained in the use of force and is authorized in writing by the county sheriff to carry a concealed pistol during the performance of his or her duties.

(e) An individual regularly employed in a city jail or lockup who has custody of individuals detained or incarcerated in the jail or lockup, is trained in the use of force, and is authorized in writing by the chief of police or the county sheriff to carry a concealed pistol during the performance of his or her duties.

(f) A member of the United States Army, Air Force, Navy, or Marine Corps while carrying a concealed pistol in the line of duty.

(g) A member of the National Guard, armed forces reserves, or other duly authorized military organization while on duty or drill or while going to or returning from his or her place of assembly or practice or while carrying a concealed pistol for purposes of that military organization.

(h) A resident of another state who is licensed by that state to carry a concealed pistol.

(i) The regular and ordinary transportation of a pistol as merchandise by an authorized agent of a person licensed to manufacture firearms.

(j) An individual while carrying a pistol unloaded in a wrapper or container in the trunk of his or her vehicle or, if the vehicle does not have a trunk, from transporting that pistol unloaded in a locked compartment or container that is separated from the ammunition for that pistol from the place of purchase to his or her home or place of business or to a place of repair or back to his or her home or place of business, or in moving goods from 1 place of abode or business to another place of abode or business.

(k) A peace officer or law enforcement officer from Canada.

History: Add. 1964, Act 216, Eff. Aug. 28, 1964;—Am. 1976, Act 102, Imd. Eff. Apr. 27, 1976;—Am. 1978, Act 282, Imd. Eff. July 6, 1978;—Am. 1978, Act 519, Imd. Eff. Dec. 19, 1978;—Am. 2000, Act 381, Eff. July 1, 2001;—Am. 2002, Act 719, Eff. July 1, 2003;—Am. 2006, Act 559, Imd. Eff. Dec. 29, 2006;—Am. 2015, Act 207, Eff. Dec. 1, 2015;—Am. 2016, Act 301, Eff. Jan. 2, 2017.

Popular name: CCW

Popular name: Concealed Weapons

Popular name: CPL

Popular name: Right to Carry

Popular name: Shall Issue

28.432b Signaling devices to which MCL 28.422 inapplicable.

Sec. 12b. Section 2 does not apply to a signaling device that is approved by the United States coast guard pursuant to regulations issued under 46 USC 481, or under 46 USC 1454.

History: Add. 1982, Act 182, Eff. July 1, 1982;—Am. 2008, Act 195, Eff. Jan. 7, 2009.

Popular name: CCW

Popular name: Concealed Weapons

Popular name: CPL

Popular name: Right to Carry

Popular name: Shall Issue

28.432c Repealed. 2000, Act 381, Eff. July 1, 2001.

Compiler's note: The repealed section pertained to license renewal.

Popular name: CCW

Popular name: Concealed Weapons

Popular name: CPL

Popular name: Right to Carry

Popular name: Shall Issue

28.433 Unlawful possession of weapon; complaint, search warrant, seizure.

Sec. 13. When complaint shall be made on oath to any magistrate authorized to issue warrants in criminal cases that any pistol or other weapon or device mentioned in this act is unlawfully possessed or carried by any person, such magistrate shall, if he be satisfied that there is reasonable cause to believe the matters in said complaint be true, issue his warrant directed to any peace officer, commanding him to search the person or place described in such complaint, and if such pistol, weapon or device be there found, to seize and hold the same as evidence of a violation of this act.

History: 1927, Act 372, Eff. Sept. 5, 1927;—CL 1929, 16762;—CL 1948, 28.433.

Popular name: CCW

Popular name: Concealed Weapons

Popular name: CPL

Popular name: Right to Carry

Popular name: Shall Issue

28.434 Unlawful possession; weapon forfeited to state; disposal; immunity.

Sec. 14. (1) Subject to sections 5g and 14a, all pistols, weapons, or devices carried or possessed contrary to this act are declared forfeited to the state, and shall be turned over to the director of the department of state police or his or her designated representative, for disposal under this section.

(2) The director of the department of state police shall dispose of firearms under this section by 1 of the following methods:

(a) By conducting a public auction in which firearms received under this section may be purchased at a sale conducted in compliance with section 4708 of the revised judicature act of 1961, 1961 PA 236, MCL 600.4708, by individuals authorized by law to possess those firearms.

(b) By destroying them.

(c) By any other lawful manner prescribed by the director of the department of state police.

(3) Before disposing of a firearm under this section, the director of the department of state police shall do both of the following:

(a) Determine through the law enforcement information network whether the firearm has been reported lost or stolen. If the firearm has been reported lost or stolen and the name and address of the owner can be determined, the director of the department of state police shall provide 30 days' written notice of his or her intent to dispose of the firearm under this section to the owner, and allow the owner to claim the firearm within that 30-day period if he or she is authorized to possess the firearm.

(b) Provide 30 days' notice to the public on the department of state police website of his or her intent to dispose of the firearm under this section. The notice shall include a description of the firearm and shall state the firearm's serial number, if the serial number can be determined. The department of state police shall allow the owner of the firearm to claim the firearm within that 30-day period if he or she is authorized to possess the firearm. The 30-day period required under this subdivision is in addition to the 30-day period required under subdivision (a).

(4) The department of state police is immune from civil liability for disposing of a firearm in compliance with this section.

History: 1927, Act 372, Eff. Sept. 5, 1927;—CL 1929, 16763;—Am. 1943, Act 113, Eff. July 30, 1943;—CL 1948, 28.434;—Am. 2000, Act 381, Eff. July 1, 2001;—Am. 2010, Act 295, Imd. Eff. Dec. 16, 2010.

Popular name: CCW

Popular name: Concealed Weapons

Popular name: CPL

Popular name: Right to Carry

Popular name: Shall Issue

28.434a Disposition of firearm; immunity from civil liability; "law enforcement agency" defined.

Sec. 14a. (1) A law enforcement agency that seizes or otherwise comes into possession of a firearm or a part of a firearm subject to disposal under section 14 may, instead of forwarding the firearm or part of a firearm to the director of the department of state police or his or her designated representative for disposal under that section, retain that firearm or part of a firearm for the following purposes:

(a) For legal sale or trade to a federally licensed firearm dealer. The proceeds from any sale or trade under this subdivision shall be used by the law enforcement agency only for law enforcement purposes. The law enforcement agency shall not sell or trade a firearm or part of a firearm under this subdivision to any individual who is a member of that law enforcement agency unless the individual is a federally licensed firearms dealer and the sale is made pursuant to a public auction.

(b) For official use by members of the seizing law enforcement agency who are employed as peace officers. A firearm or part of a firearm shall not be sold under this subdivision.

(2) A law enforcement agency that sells or trades any pistol to a licensed dealer under subsection (1)(a) or retains any pistol under subsection (1)(b) shall complete a record of the transaction under section 2 or section 2a, as applicable.

(3) A law enforcement agency that sells or trades a firearm or part of a firearm under this section shall retain a receipt of the sale or trade for a period of not less than 7 years. The law enforcement agency shall make all receipts retained under this subsection available for inspection by the department of state police upon demand and for auditing purposes by the state and the local unit of government of which the agency is a part.

(4) Before disposing of a firearm under this section, the law enforcement agency shall do both of the following:

(a) Determine through the law enforcement information network whether the firearm has been reported lost or stolen. If the firearm has been reported lost or stolen and the name and address of the owner can be determined, the law enforcement agency shall provide 30 days' written notice of its intent to dispose of the firearm under this section to the owner, and allow the owner to claim the firearm within that 30-day period if he or she is authorized to possess the firearm. If the police agency determines that a serial number has been altered or has been removed or obliterated from the firearm, the police agency shall submit the firearm to the department of state police or a forensic laboratory for serial number verification or restoration to determine legal ownership.

(b) Provide 30 days' notice to the public on a website maintained by the law enforcement agency of its intent to dispose of the firearm under this section. The notice shall include a description of the firearm and shall state the firearm's serial number, if the serial number can be determined. The law enforcement agency shall allow the owner of the firearm to claim the firearm within that 30-day period if he or she is authorized to possess the firearm. The 30-day period required under this subdivision is in addition to the 30-day period required under subdivision (a).

(5) The law enforcement agency is immune from civil liability for disposing of a firearm in compliance with this section.

(6) As used in this section, "law enforcement agency" means any agency that employs peace officers.

History: Add. 2010, Act 295, Imd. Eff. Dec. 16, 2010.

Popular name: CCW

Popular name: Concealed Weapons

Popular name: CPL

Constitutionality: Right to Carry

Compiler's note: Shall Issue

28.435 Sale of firearms by federally licensed firearms dealer; sale of trigger lock or secured container; exceptions; brochure or pamphlet; statement of compliance; notice of liability; action by political subdivision against firearm or ammunition producer prohibited; rights of state attorney general; exceptions; effect of subsections (9) through (11); violation; penalties; definitions.

Sec. 15. (1) Except as provided in subsection (2), a federally licensed firearms dealer shall not sell a firearm in this state unless the sale includes 1 of the following:

(a) A commercially available trigger lock or other device designed to disable the firearm and prevent the discharge of the firearm.

(b) A commercially available gun case or storage container that can be secured to prevent unauthorized access to the firearm.

(2) This section does not apply to any of the following:

(a) The sale of a firearm to a police officer or a police agency.

(b) The sale of a firearm to a person who presents to the federally licensed firearms dealer 1 of the following:

(*i*) A trigger lock or other device designed to disable the firearm and prevent the discharge of the firearm together with a copy of the purchase receipt for the federally licensed firearms dealer to keep. A separate trigger lock or device and a separate purchase receipt shall be required for each firearm purchased.

(*ii*) A gun case or storage container that can be secured to prevent unauthorized access to the firearm together with a copy of the purchase receipt for the federally licensed firearms dealer to keep. A separate gun case or storage container and a separate purchase receipt shall be required for each firearm purchased.

(c) The sale of an antique firearm. As used in this subdivision, "antique firearm" means that term as defined in section 231a of the Michigan penal code, 1931 PA 328, MCL 750.231a.

(d) The sale or transfer of a firearm if the seller is not a federally licensed firearms dealer.

(3) A federally licensed firearms dealer shall not sell a firearm in this state unless the firearm is accompanied with, free of charge, a brochure or pamphlet that includes safety information on the use and storage of the firearm in a home environment.

(4) Upon the sale of a firearm, a federally licensed firearms dealer shall sign a statement and require the purchaser to sign a statement stating that the sale is in compliance with subsections (1), (2), and (3).

(5) A federally licensed firearms dealer shall retain a copy of the signed statements prescribed in subsection (4) and, if applicable, a copy of the receipt prescribed in subsection (2)(b), for at least 6 years.

(6) A federally licensed firearms dealer in this state shall post in a conspicuous manner at the entrances, exits, and all points of sale on the premises where firearms are sold a notice that says the following: "You may be criminally and civilly liable for any harm caused by a person less than 18 years of age who lawfully gains unsupervised access to your firearm if unlawfully stored.".

(7) A federally licensed firearms dealer is not liable for damages arising from the use or misuse of a firearm if the sale complies with this section, any other applicable law of this state, and applicable federal law.

(8) This section does not create a civil action or liability for damages arising from the use or misuse of a firearm or ammunition for a person, other than a federally licensed firearms dealer, who produces a firearm or ammunition.

(9) Subject to subsections (10) to (12), a political subdivision shall not bring a civil action against any person who produces a firearm or ammunition. The authority to bring a civil action under this section is reserved exclusively to the state and can be brought only by the attorney general. The court shall award costs and reasonable attorney fees to each defendant named in a civil action filed in violation of this subsection.

(10) Subject to subsection (11), subsection (9) does not prohibit a civil action by a political subdivision based on 1 or more of the following, which the court shall narrowly construe:

(a) A breach of contract, other contract issue, or an action based on a provision of the uniform commercial code, 1962 PA 174, MCL 440.1101 to 440.11102, in which the political subdivision is the purchaser and owner of the firearm or ammunition.

(b) Expressed or implied warranties arising from the purchase of a firearm or ammunition by the political subdivision or the use of a firearm or ammunition by an employee or agent of the political subdivision.

(c) A product liability, personal injury, or wrongful death action when an employee or agent or property of the political subdivision has been injured or damaged as a result of a defect in the design or manufacture of the firearm or ammunition purchased and owned by the political subdivision.

(11) Subsection (10) does not allow an action based on any of the following:

(a) A firearm's or ammunition's inherent potential to cause injury, damage, or death.

(b) Failure to warn the purchaser, transferee, or user of the firearm's or ammunition's inherent potential to cause injury, damage, or death.

(c) Failure to sell with or incorporate into the product a device or mechanism to prevent a firearm or ammunition from being discharged by an unauthorized person unless specifically provided for by contract.

(12) Subsections (9) through (11) do not create a civil action.

(13) Subsections (9) through (11) are intended only to clarify the current status of the law in this state, are remedial in nature, and, therefore, apply to a civil action pending on the effective date of this act.

(14) Beginning September 1, 2000, a person who violates this section is guilty of a crime as follows:

(a) Except as provided in subdivision (b) or (c), the person is guilty of a misdemeanor punishable by imprisonment for not more than 93 days or a fine of not more than $500.00, or both.

(b) For a second conviction, the person is guilty of a misdemeanor punishable by imprisonment for not more than 1 year or a fine of not more than $1,000.00, or both.

(c) For a third or subsequent conviction, the person is guilty of a felony punishable by imprisonment for not more than 2 years or a fine of not more than $5,000.00, or both.

(15) As used in this section:

(a) "Federally licensed firearms dealer" means a person licensed under section 923 of title 18 of the United States Code, 18 U.S.C. 923.

(b) "Firearm or ammunition" includes a component of a firearm or ammunition.

(c) "Person" means an individual, partnership, corporation, association, or other legal entity.

(d) "Political subdivision" means a county, city, village, township, charter township, school district, community college, or public university or college.

(e) "Produce" means to manufacture, construct, design, formulate, develop standards for, prepare, process, assemble, inspect, test, list, certify, give a warning or instructions regarding, market, sell, advertise, package, label, distribute, or transfer.

History: Add. 2000, Act 265, Imd. Eff. June 29, 2000.

Popular name: CCW

Popular name: Concealed Weapons

Popular name: CPL

Popular name: Right to Carry

Popular name: Shall Issue

MICHIGAN RETIRED LAW ENFORCEMENT OFFICER'S FIREARM CARRY ACT
Act 537 of 2008

AN ACT to authorize a process for retired law enforcement officers to carry concealed firearms in this state; to prescribe certain powers and duties of the department of state police, the commission on law enforcement standards, and certain other state officers and agencies; to impose certain civil and criminal penalties; to impose certain requirements on certain persons issued certificates to carry concealed firearms; to provide for certain civil immunity; to allow for the collection of certain fees; to create certain funds; to provide for the forfeiture of firearms under certain circumstances; and to provide for the promulgation of rules.

History: 2008, Act 537, Eff. Mar. 31, 2009.

The People of the State of Michigan enact:

28.511 Short title.

Sec. 1. This act shall be known and may be cited as the "Michigan retired law enforcement officer's firearm carry act".

History: 2008, Act 537, Eff. Mar. 31, 2009.

28.512 Definitions.

Sec. 2. As used in this act:

(a) "Active duty firearms standard" means the in-service standard for the training and qualification of active duty law enforcement officers as mandated by the commission under the commission on law enforcement standards act, 1965 PA 203, MCL 28.601 to 28.616.

(b) "Alcoholic liquor" means that term as defined in section 105 of the Michigan liquor control code of 1998, 1998 PA 58, MCL 436.1105.

(c) "Certification" or "certified" means official recognition by the commission that a retired law enforcement officer has met the active duty firearms standard in this state and is eligible to carry a concealed firearm under 18 USC 926C.

(d) "Certificate" means a commission-issued document that identifies a qualified retired law enforcement officer who is certified under 18 USC 926C and this act.

(e) "Controlled substance" means that term as defined in section 7104 of the public health code, 1978 PA 368, MCL 333.7104.

(f) "Certificate holder" means a qualified retired law enforcement officer who is issued a certificate by the commission.

(g) "Commission" means the commission on law enforcement standards established under section 3 of the commission on law enforcement standards act, 1965 PA 203, MCL 28.603.

(h) "Firearm" means that term as defined in section 1 of 1927 PA 372, MCL 28.421.

(i) "Peace officer" means an officer of a law enforcement agency of the state, the federal government, or a county, township, city, or village who is responsible for the prevention and detection of crime and enforcement of the criminal laws of this state, and includes a motor carrier officer appointed under section 6d of 1935 PA 59, MCL 28.6d, and security personnel employed by the department of state police under section 6c of 1935 PA 59, MCL 28.6c. Peace officer does not include a qualified retired law enforcement officer.

(j) "Qualified retired law enforcement officer" means that term as defined in 18 USC 926C(c).

History: 2008, Act 537, Eff. Mar. 31, 2009.

28.513 Certification of qualified retired law enforcement officer to carry concealed firearm; establishment of requirements and procedures by commission; rules.

Sec. 3. The commission shall establish requirements and procedures through which a qualified retired law enforcement officer may be certified to carry a concealed firearm under 18 USC 926C and this act. The commission shall establish requirements and procedures through which certification under 18 USC 926C and this act may be denied or revoked. The commission may promulgate rules to implement this act in accordance with the administrative procedures act of 1969, 1969 PA 306, MCL 24.201 to 24.328.

History: 2008, Act 537, Eff. Mar. 31, 2009.

28.514 Eligibility to carry concealed firearm.

Sec. 4. (1) In order to be eligible to carry a concealed firearm under 18 USC 926C and this act, a qualified retired law enforcement officer must meet the requirements of 18 USC 926C and be a legal resident of this state.

(2) A retired law enforcement officer is not eligible for certification by the commission under 18 USC 926C and this act if he or she is prohibited under federal law from being certified under 18 USC 926C.

History: 2008, Act 537, Eff. Mar. 31, 2009.

28.515 Application requirements and procedures to verify identity; conduct criminal history, and conduct background investigation; establishment by commission.

Sec. 5. (1) The commission shall establish application requirements and procedures in order to verify the identity of an applicant, to conduct a complete criminal history, and to conduct a background investigation into an applicant's fitness to carry a concealed firearm under 18 USC 926C and this act.

(2) The commission shall request the department of state police to conduct a criminal records check through the state of Michigan and the federal bureau of investigation. The commission shall require the individual to submit his or her fingerprints to the department of state police in a manner prescribed by the department of state police for that purpose. The department of state police may charge a fee for conducting the criminal records check. If a criminal arrest fingerprint card is subsequently submitted to the department of state police and matches against a fingerprint that was submitted under this section and stored in the AFIS database, the department of state police shall notify the commission. Once the department of state police has a set of fingerprints on file as a result of being fingerprinted for purposes of this act, the individual is not required to have fingerprints taken for subsequent renewal applications.

History: 2008, Act 537, Eff. Mar. 31, 2009.

28.516 Application form; signature; providing false or misleading information as felony; penalty.

Sec. 6. (1) The commission shall create an application form for certification under this act. The applicant shall sign the application acknowledging that all information contained in the application is true and accurate.

(2) An applicant who knowingly provides false or misleading information on the application, in whole or in part, is guilty of a felony, punishable by imprisonment for not more than 4 years or a fine of not more than $2,000.00, or both.

History: 2008, Act 537, Eff. Mar. 31, 2009.

28.517 Issuance of certificate; carrying certificate and driver license or Michigan personal identification card; disclosure to peace officer; forfeiture upon notice of revocation; violation; penalties.

Sec. 7. (1) The commission or its agent shall issue a certificate to a qualified retired law enforcement officer who has complied with the active duty firearms standard and is eligible to carry a concealed firearm under 18 USC 926C and this act.

(2) A certificate holder shall carry the certificate and a valid driver license or Michigan personal identification card on his or her person at all times while in possession of a concealed firearm and shall produce the documents upon demand by a peace officer.

(3) A certificate holder who is carrying a concealed firearm and who is stopped by a peace officer shall immediately disclose to the peace officer that he or she is carrying a concealed firearm on his or her person or is transporting a firearm in his or her vehicle.

(4) Upon notice of revocation, a certificate holder is required to forfeit his or her certificate to the commission by returning the certificate in person to the commission or returning the certificate by certified mail.

(5) A violation of this section subjects the certificate holder to the penalties provided in section 5f of 1927 PA 372, MCL 28.425f, including forfeiture of the firearm.

History: 2008, Act 537, Eff. Mar. 31, 2009.

28.518 Circumstances requiring report to commission; failure to file report as misdemeanor; penalty.

Sec. 8. (1) A certificate holder shall immediately report to the commission in writing the circumstances of any of the following:

(a) An arrest or a conviction for a violation of any state or federal criminal law.

(b) Becoming the subject of an order or disposition in any jurisdiction that does 1 or more of the following:

(*i*) Restrains the certificate holder from harassing, stalking, or threatening an intimate partner of the person or a child of the intimate partner or person, or engaging in other conduct that would place an intimate partner in reasonable fear of bodily injury to the partner or child.

(*ii*) Prohibits or limits the transport, possession, carrying, or use of firearms or ammunition.

(*iii*) Involves an adjudication of mental illness, a finding of insanity, a finding of legal incapacity, or an order for involuntary commitment in an inpatient or outpatient setting.

(c) A laboratory result reflecting the unauthorized presence of controlled substances following a drug test administered to the certificate holder.

(2) A certificate holder who fails to file a written report as required under subsection (1) is guilty of a misdemeanor punishable by imprisonment for not more than 1 year or a fine of not more than $5,000.00, or both.

History: 2008, Act 537, Eff. Mar. 31, 2009.

28.519 Implied consent to submit to chemical analysis; certificate holder under influence of alcoholic liquor or controlled substance; violation; penalty; exception; collection and testing of breath, blood, and urine specimens; refusal to take chemical test; report of violation to commission.

Sec. 9. (1) Acceptance of a certificate issued under this act constitutes implied consent to submit to a chemical analysis under this section.

(2) A certificate holder shall not carry a concealed firearm while he or she is under the influence of alcoholic liquor or a controlled substance or while having a bodily alcohol content prohibited under this section. A person who violates this section is responsible for a state civil infraction or is guilty of a crime as follows:

(a) If the person was under the influence of alcoholic liquor or a controlled substance or a combination of alcoholic liquor and a controlled substance, or had a bodily alcohol content of .10 or more grams per 100 milliliters of blood, per 210 liters of breath, or per 67 milliliters of urine, the individual is guilty of a misdemeanor punishable by imprisonment for not more than 93 days or a fine of not more than $100.00, or both. The court shall order the commission to permanently revoke the certificate. The commission shall permanently revoke the certificate as ordered by the court.

(b) If the person had a bodily alcohol content of .08 or more but less than .10 grams per 100 milliliters of blood, per 210 liters of breath, or per 67 milliliters of urine, the individual is guilty of a misdemeanor punishable by imprisonment for not more than 93 days or a fine of not more than $100.00, or both. The court may order the commission to revoke the certificate for not more than 3 years. The commission shall revoke the certificate as ordered by the court.

(c) If the person had a bodily alcohol content of .02 or more, but less than .08 grams per 100 milliliters of blood, per 210 liters of breath, or per 67 milliliters of urine, the individual is responsible for a state civil infraction and may be fined not more than $100.00. The court may order the commission to revoke the certificate for 1 year. The commission shall revoke certification if an individual is found responsible for a subsequent violation of this subdivision.

(3) This section does not prohibit an individual certified under this act to carry a concealed firearm who has any bodily alcohol content from transporting that firearm in the locked trunk of his or her motor vehicle or another motor vehicle in which he or she is a passenger or, if the vehicle does not have a trunk, from transporting that firearm unloaded in a locked compartment or container that is separated from the ammunition for that firearm or on a vessel if the firearm is transported unloaded in a locked compartment or container that is separated from the ammunition for that firearm.

(4) A peace officer who has probable cause to believe a certificate holder is carrying a concealed firearm in violation of this section may require the certificate holder to submit to a chemical analysis of his or her breath, blood, or urine.

(5) Before a certificate holder is required to submit to a chemical analysis under subsection (4), the peace officer shall inform the certificate holder of all of the following:

(a) The certificate holder may refuse to submit to the chemical analysis, but if he or she chooses to do so, all of the following apply:

(*i*) The officer may obtain a court order requiring the certificate holder to submit to a chemical analysis.

(*ii*) The refusal may result in his or her certificate being revoked.

(b) If the certificate holder submits to the chemical analysis, he or she may obtain a chemical analysis described in subsection (4) from a person of his or her own choosing.

(6) The collection and testing of breath, blood, and urine specimens under this section shall be conducted in the same manner that breath, blood, and urine specimens are collected and tested for alcohol-related and controlled-substance-related motor vehicle operation violations under the Michigan vehicle code, 1949 PA 300, MCL 257.1 to 257.923.

(7) If a certificate holder refuses to take a chemical test authorized under this section, the peace officer shall promptly report the refusal in writing to the commission.

(8) If a certificate holder takes a chemical test authorized under this section and the test results indicate that the individual had any bodily alcohol content while carrying a concealed firearm, the peace officer shall promptly report the violation in writing to the commission.

History: 2008, Act 537, Eff. Mar. 31, 2009.

28.520 Computerized database; creation and maintenance by commission; information to be contained; deletion; dissemination; confidentiality.

Sec. 10. (1) The commission shall create and maintain a computerized database of individuals who apply for a certificate under this act. The database shall contain only the following information as to each individual:

(a) The individual's name, date of birth, address, and county of residence.

(b) If the individual is issued a certificate, the certificate number and date of expiration.

(c) Except as provided in subsection (2), if the individual was denied a certificate, a statement of the reasons for that denial.

(d) A statement of all criminal charges pending and criminal convictions obtained against the individual during the certificate period.

(e) A statement of all determinations of responsibility for civil infractions of this act pending or obtained against the individual during the certificate period.

(2) If an individual who was denied a certificate is subsequently issued a certificate, the commission shall delete from the computerized database the previous reasons for the denial.

(3) The commission shall provide the information described in subsection (1)(a) and (b) to the department of state police in a manner prescribed by the department of state police for dissemination through the law enforcement information network.

(4) Information in the database, compiled under subsections (1) through (3), is confidential, is not subject to disclosure under the freedom of information act, 1976 PA 442, MCL 15.231 to 15.246, and shall not be disclosed to any person except for purposes of this act or for law enforcement purposes.

History: 2008, Act 537, Eff. Mar. 31, 2009.

28.521 Administration of active duty firearm standard; identification of eligible public entities.

Sec. 11. The commission shall identify public entities eligible to administer the active duty firearm standard to qualified retired law enforcement officers for purposes of carrying out 18 USC 926C and this act.

History: 2008, Act 537, Eff. Mar. 31, 2009.

28.522 Firearm subject to seizure and forfeiture.

Sec. 12. A firearm that is carried in violation of this act is subject to seizure and forfeiture in the same manner that property is subject to seizure and forfeiture under sections 4701 to 4709 of the revised judicature act of 1961, 1961 PA 236, MCL 600.4701 to 600.4709. This section does not apply if the violation is a state civil infraction under section 5f of 1927 PA 372, MCL 28.425f, unless the individual fails to present his or her certificate within the 45-day period described in that section.

History: 2008, Act 537, Eff. Mar. 31, 2009.

28.523 Retired law enforcement officer safety fund; creation in state treasury; credit of funds; balance remaining at end of fiscal year; administration for auditing purposes; expenditures.

Sec. 13. (1) The retired law enforcement officer safety fund is created in the state treasury.

(2) The state treasurer shall credit to the fund deposits from the collection of application fees as provided in section 14. The state treasurer shall direct the investment of the fund. The state treasurer shall credit to the fund interest and earnings from fund investments.

(3) The unencumbered balance remaining in the fund at the end of a fiscal year shall remain in the fund and shall not revert to the general fund.

(4) The department of state police is the administrator of the fund for auditing purposes.

(5) The commission shall expend money from the fund, upon appropriation, only for the purposes of this act.

History: 2008, Act 537, Eff. Mar. 31, 2009.

28.524 Fees.

Sec. 14. The commission may set and collect a fee for actual costs associated with administration under 18 USC 926C and this act by any method of payment accepted by the commission. The fees shall be deposited in the retired law enforcement officer safety fund.

History: 2008, Act 537, Eff. Mar. 31, 2009.

28.525 Immunity from liability.

Sec. 15. The commission or any law enforcement agency, governmental entity, agent, employee, volunteer, designee, or individual who is acting in good faith in discharging his or her responsibilities under this act is immune from civil liability for any damages resulting from the ownership, possession, carrying, use, or discharge of a firearm by any qualified retired law enforcement officer who has been certified under this act or whose certification has been denied. The immunity provided under this section is in addition to any immunity otherwise provided by law.

History: 2008, Act 537, Eff. Mar. 31, 2009.

28.526 Preemption.

Sec. 16. This act does not preempt any existing state or federal statute, regulation, or other authority governing the use, possession, carrying, or receiving of firearms or ammunition in this state, including application by a qualified retired law enforcement officer to carry a concealed firearm under 18 USC 926C.

History: 2008, Act 537, Eff. Mar. 31, 2009.

28.527 Expiration of commission's authority to issue certificates.

Sec. 17. The commission's authority to issue certificates under this act expires immediately upon the repeal of 18 USC 926C.

History: 2008, Act 537, Eff. Mar. 31, 2009.

THE FOURTH CLASS CITY ACT (EXCERPT)
Act 215 of 1895

AN ACT to provide for the incorporation of cities of the fourth class; to provide for the vacation of the incorporation thereof; to define the powers and duties of such cities and the powers and duties of the municipal finance commission or its successor agency and of the department of treasury with regard thereto; to provide for the levy and collection of taxes, borrowing of money, and issuance of bonds and other evidences of indebtedness by cities; to define the application of this act and provide for its amendment by cities subject thereto; to validate such prior amendments and certain prior actions taken and bonds issued by such cities; and to prescribe penalties and provide remedies.

History: 1895, Act 215, Eff. Aug. 30, 1895;—Am. 1931, Act 223, Eff. Sept. 18, 1931;—Am. 1954, Act 110, Eff. Aug. 13, 1954;—Am. 1962, Act 161, Imd. Eff. May 10, 1962;—Am. 1974, Act 345, Imd. Eff. Dec. 21, 1974;—Am. 1983, Act 45, Imd. Eff. May 12, 1983;—Am. 1998, Act 149, Eff. Mar. 23, 1999.

The People of the State of Michigan enact:

CHAPTER XI
GENERAL POWERS OF CITY CORPORATIONS.

91.1 General powers.

Sec. 1. (1) A city incorporated under the provisions of this act has, and the council may pass ordinances relating to, the following general powers:

(a) To restrain and prevent vice and immorality, gambling, noise and disturbance, and indecent or disorderly conduct or assemblages; to prevent and quell riots; to preserve peace and good order; and to protect the property of the city or of persons in the city.

(b) To prohibit vagrancy, truancy, begging, public drunkenness, disorderly conduct, or prostitution.

(c) To prevent injury or annoyance from anything dangerous, offensive, or unhealthy; to prohibit and remove anything tending to cause or promote disease; and to prevent and abate nuisances.

(d) To prohibit and suppress places of disorderly conduct, immorality, or vice.

(e) To regulate or license the use of places of entertainment.

(f) To prohibit and suppress gambling and to authorize the seizure and destruction of instruments and devices used for gambling.

(g) To prohibit and prevent the selling or giving of alcoholic liquor, as defined in section 2 of the Michigan liquor control act, Act No. 8 of the Public Acts of the Extra Session of 1933, being section 436.2 of the Michigan Compiled Laws.

(h) To regulate, restrain, or prohibit sports, exhibitions, caravans, and shows for which money or other reward is demanded or received, except lectures on historic, literary, or scientific subjects.

(i) To prevent the violation of the Sabbath day, or the disturbance of a religious meeting, congregation, or society or other public meeting assembled for a lawful purpose; and to require businesses to be closed on the Sabbath day.

(j) To license, regulate, or prohibit auctioneers, auctions, and sales by public bids or offers by buyers or sellers in the manner of auctions; and to regulate the fees to be paid by and to auctioneers. However, a license shall not be required in case of sales required by law to be made at auction.

(k) To license, regulate, or prohibit hawking and peddling and to license pawnbroking.

(*l*) To license and regulate wharf boats and to regulate the use of boats in and about the harbor, if any, and within the jurisdiction of the city.

(m) To establish, authorize, license, and regulate ferries to and from the city or a place in the city; and to regulate and prescribe the charges and prices for the transportation of persons and property by ferry.

(n) To regulate and license taverns, houses of public entertainment, saloons, restaurants, and eating houses; and to regulate and prescribe the location of saloons. This subdivision does not authorize the licensing of the sale of alcoholic liquor, as defined in section 2 of Act No. 8 of the Public Acts of the Extra Session of 1933.

(o) To license and regulate vehicles used for the transportation of persons or property for hire in the city; and to regulate or fix their stands on the streets and public places and at wharves, boat landings, railroad station grounds, and other places.

(p) To regulate and license toll bridges within the city and to prescribe the rates and charges for passage over the bridges.

(q) To provide for and regulate the inspection of food.

(r) To regulate the inspection, weighing, and measuring of brick, lumber, firewood, coal, hay, and any article of merchandise.

(s) To provide for the inspection and sealing of weights and measures and to enforce the keeping and use of proper weights and measures by venders.

(t) To regulate the construction, repair, and use of vaults, cisterns, areas, hydrants, pumps, sewers, and gutters.

(u) To prohibit and prevent indecent exposure of the person; the show, sale, or exhibition for sale of indecent or obscene pictures, drawings, engravings, paintings, books, or pamphlets; and indecent or obscene exhibitions and shows.

(v) To regulate or prohibit bathing in the city's bodies of water.

(w) To provide for the clearing of driftwood and noxious matter from the city's bodies of water; and to prohibit and prevent the depositing in the city's bodies of water of matter tending to render the water impure, unwholesome, or offensive.

(x) To compel the owner or occupant of any grocery, tallow chandler shop, soap or candy factory, butcher shop or stall, slaughter house, stable, barn, privy, sewer, or other offensive, nauseous, or unwholesome place to cleanse, remove, or abate it when the council considers it necessary for the health, comfort, or convenience of the inhabitants of the city.

(y) To regulate the keeping, selling, and using of dynamite, gunpowder, firecrackers and fireworks, and other explosive or combustible materials; to regulate the exhibition of fireworks and the discharge of firearms; and to restrain the making of fires in the streets and other open spaces in the city.

(z) To direct and regulate the construction of cellars, slips, barns, private drains, sinks, and privies.

(aa) To prohibit, prevent, and suppress mock auctions and fraudulent games, devices, and practices. Persons managing, using, or practicing; attempting to manage, use, or practice; or aiding in the management or practice of a mock auction or fraudulent game, device, or practice may be subject to the provisions of an ordinance under this subdivision.

(bb) To prohibit, prevent, and suppress lotteries for the drawing or disposing of money or other property. Persons maintaining, directing, or managing such lotteries or aiding in the maintenance, directing, or managing of such lotteries may be subject to the provisions of an ordinance under this subdivision.

(cc) To license and regulate solicitors for passengers or for baggage to and from a hotel, tavern, public house, boat, or railroad and to provide the places where they may be admitted to solicit or receive patronage; and to license and regulate porters, runners, and drivers of vehicles used and employed for hire, to provide the places where they be admitted to solicit or receive patronage, and to fix and regulate the amounts and rates of their compensation.

(dd) To provide for the protection and care of paupers.

(ee) To provide for taking a census of the inhabitants of the city, whenever the council sees fit, and to direct and regulate the census.

(ff) To provide for the issuing of licenses to the owners and keepers of dogs and to require the owners and keepers of dogs to pay for and obtain such licenses; and to regulate and prevent the running at large of dogs, to require dogs to be muzzled, and to authorize the killing of dogs running at large or not licensed in violation of an ordinance of the city.

(gg) To prohibit the possession or use of toy pistols, slingshots, and other dangerous toys or implements within the city.

(hh) To require horses, mules, or other animals attached to vehicles or standing in the streets, lanes, or alleys in the city to be securely fastened, hitched, watched, or held and to regulate the placing and provide for the preservation of hitching posts.

(ii) To provide for and regulate the numbering of buildings upon the streets and alleys; to require the owners or occupants of buildings to affix numbers on the buildings; and to designate and change the names of public streets, alleys, and parks.

(jj) To provide for, establish, regulate, and preserve public fountains and reservoirs within the city, and troughs and basins for watering animals.

(kk) To prevent or provide for the construction and operation of street railways, to regulate street railways, and to determine and designate the route and grade of any street railway to be laid or constructed in the city.

(*ll*) To establish and maintain a public library, to provide a suitable building for that public library, and to aid in maintaining such other public libraries as may be established within the city by private beneficence as the council considers to be for the public good.

(mm) To license transient traders. In the case of transient traders who engage in the business of selling goods or merchandise after the commencement of the fiscal year, the license fee may be apportioned with relation to the part of the fiscal year that has expired. If such traders continue in the same business after the commencement of the next fiscal year, and their goods or merchandise are assessed for taxes for the next fiscal year, the traders shall not be required to take out a second license upon the commencement of the next fiscal year.

(2) The council may enact ordinances and make regulations, consistent with the laws and constitution of the state as they may consider necessary for the safety, order, and good government of the city and the general welfare of the inhabitants of the city, but exclusive rights, privileges, or permits shall not be granted by the council.

History: 1895, Act 215, Eff. Aug. 30, 1895;—CL 1897, 3107;—CL 1915, 3021;—CL 1929, 1945;—CL 1948, 91.1;—Am. 1994, Act 19, Eff. May 1, 1994.

FIREARMS AND AMMUNITION
Act 319 of 1990

AN ACT to prohibit local units of government from imposing certain restrictions on the ownership, registration, purchase, sale, transfer, transportation, or possession of pistols, other firearms, or pneumatic guns, ammunition for pistols or other firearms, or components of pistols or other firearms.

History: 1990, Act 319, Eff. Mar. 28, 1991;—Am. 2015, Act 29, Eff. Aug. 10, 2015.

The People of the State of Michigan enact:

123.1101 Definitions.

Sec. 1. As used in this act:

(a) "Firearm" means any weapon which will, is designed to, or may readily be converted to expel a projectile by action of an explosive.

(b) "Local unit of government" means a city, village, township, or county.

(c) "Pistol" means that term as defined in section 222 of the Michigan penal code, 1931 PA 328, MCL 750.222.

(d) "Pneumatic gun" means any implement, designed as a gun, that will expel a BB or pellet by spring, gas, or air. Pneumatic gun includes a paintball gun that expels by pneumatic pressure plastic balls filled with paint for the purpose of marking the point of impact.

History: 1990, Act 319, Eff. Mar. 28, 1991;—Am. 2015, Act 29, Eff. Aug. 10, 2015.

123.1102 Regulation of pistols, other firearms, pneumatic guns, or ammunition.

Sec. 2. A local unit of government shall not impose special taxation on, enact or enforce any ordinance or regulation pertaining to, or regulate in any other manner the ownership, registration, purchase, sale, transfer, transportation, or possession of pistols, other firearms, or pneumatic guns, ammunition for pistols or other firearms, or components of pistols or other firearms, except as otherwise provided by federal law or a law of this state.

History: 1990, Act 319, Eff. Mar. 28, 1991;—Am. 2015, Act 29, Eff. Aug. 10, 2015.

123.1103 Local unit of government; permissible prohibitions or regulation.

Sec. 3. This act does not prohibit a local unit of government from doing any of the following:

(a) Prohibiting or regulating conduct with a pistol, other firearm, or pneumatic gun that is a criminal offense under state law.

(b) Prohibiting or regulating the transportation, carrying, or possession of pistols, other firearms, or pneumatic guns by employees of that local unit of government in the course of their employment with that local unit of government.

(c) Regulating the possession of pneumatic guns within the local unit of government by requiring that an individual below the age of 16 who is in possession of a pneumatic gun be under the supervision of a parent, a guardian, or an individual 18 years of age or older, except that an ordinance shall not regulate possession of a pneumatic gun on or within private property if the individual below the age of 16 is authorized by a parent or guardian and the property owner or legal possessor to possess the pneumatic gun.

(d) Prohibiting an individual from pointing, waving about, or displaying a pneumatic gun in a threatening manner with the intent to induce fear in another individual.

History: 1990, Act 319, Eff. Mar. 28, 1991;—Am. 2015, Act 29, Eff. Aug. 10, 2015.

123.1104 City or charter township; permissible prohibitions or regulation.

Sec. 4. This act does not prohibit a city or a charter township from doing any of the following:

(a) Prohibiting the discharge of a pistol or other firearm within the jurisdiction of that city or charter township.

(b) Prohibiting the discharge of pneumatic guns in any area within the jurisdiction of the city or charter township that is so heavily populated as to make that conduct dangerous to the inhabitants of that area, except that an ordinance shall not prohibit the discharge of pneumatic guns at authorized target ranges, on other property where firearms may be discharged, or on or within private property with the permission of the owner or possessor of that property if conducted with reasonable care to prevent a projectile from crossing the bounds of the property.

History: 1990, Act 319, Eff. Mar. 28, 1991;—Am. 2015, Act 29, Eff. Aug. 10, 2015.

MICHIGAN VEHICLE CODE
Act 300 of 1949

AN ACT to provide for the registration, titling, sale, transfer, and regulation of certain vehicles operated upon the public highways of this state or any other place open to the general public or generally accessible to motor vehicles and distressed vehicles; to provide for the licensing of dealers; to provide for the examination, licensing, and control of operators and chauffeurs; to provide for the giving of proof of financial responsibility and security by owners and operators of vehicles; to provide for the imposition, levy, and collection of specific taxes on vehicles, and the levy and collection of sales and use taxes, license fees, and permit fees; to provide for the regulation and use of streets and highways; to create certain funds; to provide penalties and sanctions for a violation of this act; to provide for civil liability of manufacturers, the manufacturers of certain devices, the manufacturers of automated technology, upfitters, owners, and operators of vehicles and service of process on residents and nonresidents; to regulate the introduction and use of certain evidence; to regulate and certify the manufacturers of certain devices; to provide for approval and certification of installers and servicers of certain devices; to provide for the levy of certain assessments; to provide for the enforcement of this act; to provide for the creation of and to prescribe the powers and duties of certain state and local agencies; to impose liability upon the state or local agencies; to provide appropriations for certain purposes; to repeal all other acts or parts of acts inconsistent with this act or contrary to this act; and to repeal certain parts of this act on a specific date.

History: 1949, Act 300, Eff. Sept. 23, 1949;—Am. 1957, Act 281, Eff. Sept. 27, 1957;—Am. 1978, Act 507, Eff. July 1, 1979;—Am. 1979, Act 66, Eff. Aug. 1, 1979;—Am. 1980, Act 137, Imd. Eff. May 29, 1980;—Am. 1980, Act 518, Eff. Mar. 31, 1981;—Am. 1982, Act 310, Eff. Mar. 30, 1983;—Am. 1987, Act 154, Eff. Dec. 1, 1987;—Am. 1988, Act 255, Eff. Oct. 1, 1989;—Am. 1991, Act 98, Imd. Eff. Aug. 9, 1991;—Am. 2000, Act 282, Imd. Eff. July 10, 2000;—Am. 2000, Act 408, Eff. Mar. 28, 2001;—Am. 2002, Act 554, Eff. Oct. 1, 2002;—Am. 2010, Act 10, Imd. Eff. Mar. 8, 2010;—Am. 2013, Act 231, Eff. Mar. 27, 2014;—Am. 2016, Act 32, Eff. June 6, 2016.

Compiler's note: In OAG 6480, issued November 23, 1987, the Attorney General stated: "It is my opinion, therefore, that 1987 PA 154, which fixes maximum speed limit on certain state highways, becomes effective November 29, 1987."

The People of the State of Michigan enact:

CHAPTER VI
OBEDIENCE TO AND EFFECT OF TRAFFIC LAWS ACCIDENTS

257.623 Accidents; reports by garagekeepers or repairmen.

Sec. 623. The person in charge of any garage or repair shop to which is brought any motor vehicle which shows evidence of having been involved in an accident or having been struck by any bullet shall report the same to the nearest police station or sheriff's office immediately after such motor vehicle is received, giving the engine number, registration number and the name and address of the owner, and/or operator of such vehicle.

History: 1949, Act 300, Eff. Sept. 23, 1949.

SIZE, WEIGHT AND LOAD

257.726c Duly authorized agent of county road commission; shoulder patch required; firearm.

Sec. 726c. (1) A duly authorized agent of a county road commission when enforcing sections 215, 255, 631(1), 717, 719, 719a, 720, 722, 724, 725, and 726 shall wear a shoulder patch that is clearly visible and identifies the branch of government represented.

(2) A duly authorized agent of a county road commission shall not carry a firearm while enforcing sections 215, 255, 631(1), 717, 719, 719a, 720, 722, 724, 725, and 726 unless he or she is licensed or certified as a police officer under the Michigan commission on law enforcement standards act, 1965 PA 203, MCL 28.601 to 28.615.

History: Add. 1984, Act 74, Imd. Eff. Apr. 18, 1984;—Am. 1989, Act 173, Imd. Eff. Aug. 22, 1989;—Am. 2012, Act 529, Eff. Mar. 28, 2013;—Am. 2016, Act 304, Eff. Jan. 2, 2017.

AERONAUTICS CODE OF THE STATE OF MICHIGAN (EXCERPT)
Act 327 of 1945

AN ACT relating to aeronautics in this state; providing for the development and regulation of aeronautics; creating a state aeronautics commission; prescribing powers and duties; providing for the licensing, registration, and supervision and control of all aircraft, airports and landing fields, schools of aviation, flying clubs, airmen, aviation instructors, airport managers, manufacturers, dealers, and commercial operation in intrastate commerce; providing for rules pertaining thereto; prescribing a privilege tax for the use of the aeronautical facilities on the lands and waters of this state; providing for the acquisition, development, and operation of airports, landing fields, and other aeronautical facilities by this state, by political subdivisions, or by airport authorities; providing for the incorporation of airport authorities and providing for the powers, duties, and obligations of airport authorities; providing for the transfer of airport management to airport authorities, including the transfer of airport liabilities, employees, and operational jurisdiction; providing jurisdiction of crimes, torts, and contracts; providing police powers for those entrusted to enforce this act; providing for civil liability of owners, operators, and others; making hunting from aircraft unlawful; providing for a repair station operators lien; providing for appeals from rules or orders issued by the commission; providing for the transfer from the Michigan board of aeronautics to the aeronautics commission all properties and funds held by the board of aeronautics; providing for a state aeronautics fund and making an appropriation therefor; prescribing penalties; and making uniform the law with reference to state development and regulation of aeronautics.

History: 1945, Act 327, Imd. Eff. May 28, 1945;—Am. 1958, Act 114, Eff. Sept. 13, 1958;—Am. 1976, Act 191, Imd. Eff. July 8, 1976;—Am. 2002, Act 90, Imd. Eff. Mar. 26, 2002;—Am. 2015, Act 95, Imd. Eff. June 30, 2015.

The People of the State of Michigan enact:

CHAPTER V
REGULATION OF AIRCRAFT, AIRMEN, AIRPORTS AND AIR INSTRUCTION.

259.80f Possessing, carrying, or attempting to possess certain items in sterile area of airport; prohibitions; violations; penalties; exceptions; other violations; consecutive terms of imprisonment; definitions.

Sec. 80f. (1) An individual shall not possess, carry, or attempt to possess or carry any of the following in a sterile area of a commercial airport:

(a) Firearm.

(b) Explosive.

(c) Knife with a blade of any length.

(d) Razor, box cutter, or item with a similar blade.

(e) Dangerous weapon.

(2) Except as provided in subsection (3), an individual who violates subsection (1) is guilty of a misdemeanor punishable by imprisonment for not more than 1 year or a fine of not more than $1,000.00, or both.

(3) An individual who violates subsection (1) while doing any of the following is guilty of a felony punishable by imprisonment for not more than 10 years or a fine of not more than $10,000.00, or both:

(a) Getting on or attempting to get on an aircraft.

(b) Placing, attempting to place, or attempting to have placed on an aircraft an item listed in subsection (1).

(c) Committing or attempting to commit a felony.

(4) This section does not apply to any of the following:

(a) A peace officer of a duly authorized police agency of this state, a political subdivision of this state, another state, a political subdivision of another state, or the United States.

(b) An individual regularly employed by the department of corrections and authorized in writing by the director of the department of corrections to possess or carry an item listed in subsection (1) during the performance of his or her duties or while going to or returning from his or her duties.

(c) A member of the United States army, air force, navy, marine corps, or coast guard while possessing or carrying an item listed in subsection (1) in the line of duty.

(d) A member of the national guard, armed forces reserves, or other duly authorized military organization while on duty or drill or while possessing or carrying an item listed in subsection (1) for purposes of that military organization.

(e) Security personnel employed to enforce federal regulations for access to a sterile area.

(f) A court officer while engaged in his or her duties as a court officer as authorized by a court.

(g) An airline or airport employee as authorized by his or her employer.

(5) This section does not prohibit the individual from being charged with, convicted of, or punished for any other violation of law committed by that individual while violating this section.

(6) A term of imprisonment imposed under this section may be served consecutively to any other term of imprisonment imposed for a violation of law arising out of the same transaction.

(7) As used in this section:

(a) "Commercial airport" means an airport that has regularly scheduled commercial flights to and from other destinations.

(b) "Felony" means that term as defined in section 1 of chapter I of the code of criminal procedure, 1927 PA 175, MCL 761.1, or a violation of a law of the United States that is designated as a felony or that is punishable by death or by imprisonment for more than 1 year.

(c) "Sterile area" means that term as defined in 14 C.F.R. 107.1.

History: Add. 2001, Act 225, Eff. Apr. 1, 2002.

WILD LIFE SANCTUARIES (EXCERPT)
Act 184 of 1929

AN ACT to provide for the protection and increase of desirable forms of wild life; for the establishment of wild life sanctuaries; for the maintenance and regulation thereof; to provide penalties for the violation of this act and the rules and regulations issued thereunder; and to repeal Act No. 360 of the Public Acts of 1913.

History: 1929, Act 184, Eff. Aug. 28, 1929.

The People of the State of Michigan enact:

317.204 Wild life sanctuaries; unlawful acts; predatory animals, birds; experiments.

Sec. 4. When lands have been so dedicated and posted as a state wild life sanctuary, the possession or carrying of firearms thereon, hunting or trapping thereon, or the killing or molestation of wild life on such lands by any person or by the owners or lessees thereof, or their agents, shall be unlawful during the period of such dedication: Provided, That the director of conservation may issue permits for the taking on any dedicated lands of predatory animals and birds and such other birds and animals as may require control or as may be appropriate in connection with experiments in wild life management or for other purposes not inconsistent with the original intent of the dedication.

History: 1929, Act 184, Eff. Aug. 28, 1929;—CL 1929, 6116;—CL 1948, 317.204.

NATURAL RESOURCES AND ENVIRONMENTAL PROTECTION ACT (EXCERPT)
Act 451 of 1994

AN ACT to protect the environment and natural resources of the state; to codify, revise, consolidate, and classify laws relating to the environment and natural resources of the state; to regulate the discharge of certain substances into the environment; to regulate the use of certain lands, waters, and other natural resources of the state; to protect the people's right to hunt and fish; to prescribe the powers and duties of certain state and local agencies and officials; to provide for certain charges, fees, assessments, and donations; to provide certain appropriations; to prescribe penalties and provide remedies; and to repeal acts and parts of acts.

History: 1994, Act 451, Eff. Mar. 30, 1995;—Am. 1996, Act 434, Imd. Eff. Dec. 2, 1996;—Am. 2005, Act 116, Imd. Eff. Sept. 22, 2005;—Am. 2013, Act 22, Imd. Eff. May 8, 2013.

Popular name: Act 451

Popular name: NREPA

The People of the State of Michigan enact:

ARTICLE I GENERAL PROVISIONS

PART 5
DEPARTMENT OF NATURAL RESOURCES

324.504 Department of natural resources; rules for protection and preservation of lands and property; duties of department; report; applicability of subsections (2) and (3) to commercial forestland; certain rules prohibited; orders; violation as civil infraction; fine.

Sec. 504. (1) The department shall promulgate rules to protect and preserve lands and other property under its control from depredation, damage, or destruction or wrongful or improper use or occupancy.

(2) Subject to subsection (4), the department shall do all of the following:

(a) Keep land under its control open to hunting unless the department determines that the land should be closed to hunting because of public safety, fish or wildlife management, or homeland security concerns or as otherwise required by law.

(b) Manage land under its control to support and promote hunting opportunities to the extent authorized by law.

(c) Manage land under its control to prevent any net decrease in the acreage of such land that is open to hunting.

(3) Subject to subsection (4), by April 1, 2010 and each year thereafter, the department shall submit to the legislature a report that includes all of the following:

(a) The location and acreage of land under its control previously open to hunting that the department closed to hunting during the 1-year period ending the preceding March 1, together with the reasons for the closure.

(b) The location and acreage of land under its control previously closed to hunting that the department opened to hunting during the 1-year period ending the preceding March 1 to compensate for land closed to hunting under subdivision (a).

(4) Subsections (2) and (3) do not apply to commercial forestland as defined in section 51101.

(5) This section does not authorize the department to promulgate a rule that applies to commercial fishing except as otherwise provided by law.

(6) The department shall not promulgate or enforce a rule that prohibits an individual who is licensed or exempt from licensure under 1927 PA 372, MCL 28.421 to 28.435, from carrying a pistol in compliance with that act, whether concealed or otherwise, on property under the control of the department.

(7) The department shall issue orders necessary to implement rules promulgated under this section. These orders shall be effective upon posting.

(8) A person who violates a rule promulgated under this section or an order issued under this section is responsible for a state civil infraction and may be ordered to pay a civil fine of not more than $500.00.

History: 1994, Act 451, Eff. Mar. 30, 1995;—Am. 1996, Act 171, Imd. Eff. Apr. 18, 1996;—Am. 2004, Act 130, Imd. Eff. June 3, 2004;—Am. 2009, Act 47, Imd. Eff. June 18, 2009.

Popular name: Act 451

Popular name: NREPA

Administrative rules: R 299.291a et seq. and R 299.921 et seq. of the Michigan Administrative Code.

ARTICLE III
NATURAL RESOURCES MANAGEMENT

CHAPTER 2
MANAGEMENT OF RENEWABLE RESOURCES

SUBCHAPTER 1
WILDLIFE PART 401
WILDLIFE CONSERVATION

324.40102 Definitions; A to F.

Sec. 40102. (1) "Animals" means wild birds and wild mammals.

(2) "Bag limit" means the number of animals that may be taken and possessed as determined by the department.

(3) "Bow" means a device for propelling an arrow from a string drawn, held, and released by hand where the force used to hold the string in the drawn position is provided by the archer's muscles.

(4) "Buy" or "sell" means an exchange or attempt or offer to exchange for money, barter, or anything of value.

(5) "Chase" means to follow animals with dogs or other wild or domestic animals trained for that purpose.

(6) "Cormorant damage" means adverse impacts of double-crested cormorants on fish, fish hatchery stock, wildlife, plants, and their habitats and on man-made structures.

(7) "Cormorant depredation order" means the depredation order for double-crested cormorants to protect public resources, 50 CFR 21.48, issued by the United States Department of the Interior, Fish and Wildlife Service.

(8) "Crossbow" means a weapon consisting of a bow mounted transversely on a stock or frame and designed to fire an arrow, bolt, or quarrel by the release of a bow string that is controlled by a mechanical or electric trigger and has a working safety and a draw weight of 100 pounds or greater.

(9) "Deer or elk feeding" means the depositing, distributing, or tending of feed in an area frequented by wild, free-ranging white-tailed deer or elk. Deer or elk feeding does not include any of the following:

(a) Feeding wild birds or other wildlife if done in such a manner as to exclude wild, free-ranging white-tailed deer and elk from gaining access to the feed.

(b) The scattering of feed solely as the result of normal logging practices or normal agricultural practices.

(c) The storage or use of feed for agricultural purposes if 1 or more of the following apply:

(*i*) The area is occupied by livestock actively consuming the feed on a daily basis.

(*ii*) The feed is covered to deter wild, free-ranging white-tailed deer or elk from gaining access to the feed.

(*iii*) The feed is in a storage facility that is consistent with normal agricultural practices.

(d) Baiting to take game as provided by an order of the commission under section 40113a.

(10) "Disability" means a determinable physical characteristic of an individual that may result from disease, injury, congenital condition of birth, or functional disorder.

(11) "Feed" means a substance composed of grain, mineral, salt, fruit, vegetable, hay, or any other food material or combination of these materials, whether natural or manufactured, that may attract white-tailed deer or elk. Feed does not include any of the following:

(a) Plantings for wildlife.

(b) Standing farm crops under normal agricultural practices.

(c) Agricultural commodities scattered solely as the result of normal agricultural practices.

(12) "Firearm" means any weapon which will, is designed to, or may readily be converted to expel a projectile by action of an explosive. A pneumatic gun, as defined in section 1 of 1990 PA 319, MCL 123.1101, other than a paintball gun that expels by pneumatic pressure plastic balls filled with paint for the purpose of marking the point of impact, is also considered a firearm for the purpose of this act.

History: Add. 1995, Act 57, Imd. Eff. May 24, 1995;—Am. 1998, Act 86, Imd. Eff. May 13, 1998;—Am. 1999, Act 66, Imd. Eff. June 25, 1999;—Am. 2000, Act 347, Imd. Eff. Dec. 28, 2000;—Am. 2007, Act 48, Imd. Eff. Aug. 3, 2007;—Am. 2015, Act 24, Eff. July 1, 2015.

Popular name: Act 451

Popular name: NREPA

324.40111 Taking animal from in or upon vehicle; transporting or possessing firearm in or upon vehicle; person with disability; transporting or possessing unloaded firearm in or upon vehicle on sporting clays range; individual holding permit to hunt from standing vehicle; possessing and discharging firearm to take game from personal assistive mobility device; transporting or possessing bow or crossbow in or upon vehicle while on public land or highway, road, or street; written permission to hunt or discharge firearm within certain distance of property; definitions.

Sec. 40111. (1) Except as otherwise provided in subsection (3) or (5), this part, or in a department order authorized under section 40107, an individual shall not take an animal from in or upon a vehicle.

(2) Except as otherwise provided in subsection (3), (4), or (5), this part, or in a department order authorized under section 40107, an individual shall not transport or possess a firearm in or upon a vehicle, unless the firearm is unloaded and enclosed in a case, unloaded and carried in the trunk of a vehicle, or unloaded in a motorized boat.

(3) A person with a disability may transport or possess a firearm in or upon a vehicle, except for a car or truck, on a state licensed game bird hunting preserve if the firearm is unloaded and the vehicle is operated at a speed of not greater than 10 miles per hour. A person with a disability may possess a loaded firearm and may discharge that firearm to take an animal from in or upon a vehicle, except for a car or truck, on a state licensed game bird hunting preserve if the vehicle is not moving. The department may demand proof of eligibility under this subsection. An individual shall possess proof of his or her eligibility under this subsection and furnish the proof upon the request of a peace officer.

(4) An individual may transport or possess an unloaded firearm in or upon a vehicle on a sporting clays range.

(5) An individual holding a valid permit to hunt from a standing vehicle under section 40114 may transport or possess an uncased firearm with a loaded magazine on a personal assistive mobility device if the action is open. An individual holding a valid permit to hunt from a standing vehicle under section 40114 may possess a loaded firearm and may discharge that firearm to take game from a personal assistive mobility device if each of the following applies:

(a) The personal assistive mobility device is not moving.

(b) The individual holds a valid base license under section 43523a, holds any other necessary license under part 435, and complies with all other laws and rules for the taking of game.

(6) Except as otherwise provided in this part, an individual shall not transport or possess a bow or crossbow in or upon a vehicle while that vehicle is operated on public land or on a highway, road, or street in this state, unless the bow or crossbow is unstrung, enclosed in a case, or carried in the trunk of a vehicle.

(7) An individual shall not hunt with a firearm within 150 yards of an occupied building, dwelling, house, residence, or cabin, or any barn or other building used in connection with a farm operation, without obtaining the written permission of the owner, renter, or occupant of the property.

(8) As used in this section:

(a) "Person with a disability" means a disabled person as that term is defined in section 19a of the Michigan vehicle code, 1949 PA 300, MCL 257.19a, and who is in possession of 1 of the following:

(*i*) A certificate of identification or windshield placard issued to a disabled person under section 675 of the Michigan vehicle code, 1949 PA 300, MCL 257.675.

(*ii*) A special registration plate issued to a disabled person under section 803d of the Michigan vehicle code, 1949 PA 300, MCL 257.803d.

(b) "Personal assistive mobility device" means any device, including, but not limited to, one that is battery-powered, that is designed solely for use by an individual with mobility impairment for locomotion and is considered an extension of the individual.

(c) "Unloaded" means that the firearm does not have ammunition in the barrel, chamber, cylinder, clip, or magazine when the barrel, chamber, cylinder, clip, or magazine is part of or attached to the firearm.

History: Add. 1995, Act 57, Imd. Eff. May 24, 1995;—Am. 2012, Act 246, Imd. Eff. July 2, 2012;—Am. 2012, Act 340, Imd. Eff. Oct. 16, 2012;—Am. 2015, Act 24, Eff. July 1, 2015;—Am. 2015, Act 185, Eff. Jan. 1, 2016.

Popular name: Act 451

Popular name: NREPA

324.40111c Use of tranquilizer propelled from bow or firearm; use of unmanned vehicle or device; prohibitions.

Sec. 40111c. (1) A person other than the department shall not take game using a tranquilizer propelled from a bow or firearm.

(2) An individual shall not take game or fish using an unmanned vehicle or unmanned device that uses aerodynamic forces to achieve flight or using an unmanned vehicle or unmanned device that operates on the surface of water or underwater.

History: Add. 2008, Act 301, Imd. Eff. Nov. 13, 2008;—Am. 2015, Act 13, Eff. July 13, 2015.

Popular name: Act 451

Popular name: NREPA

324.40113 Artificial light.

Sec. 40113. (1) Except as otherwise provided in a department order authorized under section 40107 for a specified animal, a person shall not use an artificial light in taking game or in an area frequented by animals; throw or cast the rays of a spotlight, headlight, or other artificial light in a field, woodland, or forest while having a bow or firearm or other weapon capable of shooting a projectile in the person's possession or under the person's control unless otherwise permitted by law. A licensed hunter may use an artificial light 1 hour before and 1 hour after shooting hours while in possession of any unloaded firearm or bow and traveling afoot to and from the licensed hunter's hunting location.

(2) Except as otherwise provided in a department order authorized under section 40107, a person shall not throw, cast, or cause to be thrown or cast, the rays of an artificial light from December 1 to October 31 between the hours of 11 p.m. and 6 a.m. for the purpose of locating animals. Except as otherwise permitted by law or an order of the department, from November 1 to

November 30, a person shall not throw, cast, or cause to be thrown or cast, the rays of a spotlight, headlight, or other artificial light for the purpose of locating animals. This subsection does not apply to any of the following:

(a) A peace officer while in the performance of the officer's duties.

(b) A person operating an emergency vehicle in an emergency.

(c) An employee of a public or private utility while working in the scope of his or her employment.

(d) A person operating a vehicle with headlights in a lawful manner upon a street, highway, or roadway.

(e) A person using an artificial light to identify a house or mailbox number.

(f) The use of artificial lights used to conduct a census by the department.

(g) A person using an artificial light from November 1 to November 30 on property that is owned by that person or by a member of that person's immediate family.

(3) The operator of a vehicle from which the rays of an artificial light have been cast in a clear attempt to locate game shall immediately stop the vehicle upon the request of a uniformed peace officer or when signaled by a peace officer with a flashing signal light or siren from a marked patrol vehicle.

History: Add. 1995, Act 57, Imd. Eff. May 24, 1995.

Popular name: Act 451

Popular name: NREPA

PART 419
HUNTING AREA CONTROL

324.41901 Regulation and prohibitions in certain areas; powers of department; area closures; hearings, investigations, studies, and statement of facts; regulations.

Sec. 41901. (1) In addition to all of the department powers, in the interest of public safety and the general welfare, the department may regulate and prohibit hunting, and the discharge of firearms and bow and arrow, as provided in this part, on those areas established under this part where hunting or the discharge of firearms or bow and arrow may or is likely to kill, injure, or disturb persons who can reasonably be expected to be present in the areas or to destroy or damage buildings or personal property situated or customarily situated in the areas or will impair the general safety and welfare. In addition, the department may determine and define the boundaries of the areas. Areas or parts of areas may be closed throughout the year. The department, in furtherance of safety, may designate areas where hunting is permitted only by prescribed methods and weapons that are not inconsistent with law. Whenever the governing body of any political subdivision determines that the safety and well-being of persons or property are endangered by hunters or discharge of firearms or bow and arrows, by resolution it may request the department to recommend closure of the area as may be required to relieve the problem. Upon receipt of a certified resolution, the department shall establish a date for a public hearing in the political subdivision, and the requesting political authority shall arrange for suitable quarters for the hearing. The department shall receive testimony on the nature of the problems resulting from hunting activities and firearms use from all interested parties on the type, extent, and nature of the closure, regulations, or controls desired locally to remedy these problems.

(2) Upon completion of the public hearing, the department shall cause such investigations and studies to be made of the area as it considers appropriate and shall then make a statement of the facts of the situation as found at the hearing and as a result of its investigations. The department shall then prescribe regulations as are necessary to alleviate or correct the problems found.

History: Add. 1995, Act 57, Imd. Eff. May 24, 1995.

Popular name: Act 451

Popular name: NREPA

324.41902 Submission of findings and recommendations; approval or disapproval of prescribed controls; ordinance; certified copy; repeal of ordinance; enforcement; rules.

Sec. 41902. (1) The department shall submit its findings and recommendations to the governing body of the political subdivision concerned. By majority vote, the governing body shall advise the department by certified resolution that it approves or disapproves the prescribed hunting or firearms controls. If the governing body disapproves the prescribed controls, further action shall not be taken. If the governing body approves the prescribed controls, a local ordinance shall be enacted in accordance with the provisions of law pertaining to the enactment of ordinances, which ordinance shall be identical in all respects to the regulations prescribed by the department. A certified copy of the ordinance shall be forwarded to the department. The governing body of the political subdivision, having established such an ordinance, by majority vote, may repeal the ordinance at any time. The department shall be informed of such action by certified resolution.

(2) State, local, and county law enforcement officers shall enforce ordinances enacted in accordance with this part.

(3) All rules promulgated under this section and section 41901 before March 17, 1986 shall remain in effect unless rescinded pursuant to the administrative procedures act of 1969, Act No. 306 of the Public Acts of 1969, being sections 24.201 to 24.328 of the Michigan Compiled Laws.

History: Add. 1995, Act 57, Imd. Eff. May 24, 1995.

Popular name: Act 451

Popular name: NREPA

324.41904 Prohibitions against discharge of firearms; exceptions.

Sec. 41904. Any prohibition against discharge of firearms made under authority of this part does not apply to peace officers or members of any branch of the armed forces in the discharge of their proper duties. The department may authorize the use of firearms to prevent or control the depredations of birds or animals in situations where significant damages are being caused by wildlife.

History: Add. 1995, Act 57, Imd. Eff. May 24, 1995.

Popular name: Act 451

Popular name: NREPA

PART 421
DOG TRAINING AREAS

324.42102 Training dogs; conditions; rules; prohibitions.

Sec. 42102. Permit holders may at any time during the year train their own dogs or the dogs of other persons on land described in section 42101 or permit others to do so under conditions that are mutually agreed upon and under rules as may be considered expedient by the department. Hunting or the carrying or possession of firearms other than a pistol or revolver with blank cartridges at any time of year on lands described in section 42101 is unlawful.

History: Add. 1995, Act 57, Imd. Eff. May 24, 1995.

Popular name: Act 451

Popular name: NREPA

SUBCHAPTER 2
HUNTING AND FISHING LICENSES

PART 435
HUNTING AND FISHING LICENSING

324.43503 Definitions; F.

Sec. 43503. (1) "Fish" means all species of fish.

(2) "Fishing" means the pursuing, capturing, catching, killing, or taking of fish, and includes attempting to pursue, capture, catch, kill, or take fish.

(3) "Firearm" means any weapon which will, is designed to, or may readily be converted to expel a projectile by action of an explosive. A pneumatic gun, as defined in section 1 of 1990 PA 319, MCL 123.1101, other than a paintball gun that expels by pneumatic pressure plastic balls filled with paint for the purpose of marking the point of impact, is also considered a firearm for the purpose of this act.

(4) "Firearm deer season" means any period in which deer may be lawfully hunted with a firearm.

(5) "Fur-bearing animals" includes badger, beaver, bobcat, coyote, fisher, fox, lynx, marten, mink, muskrat, opossum, otter, raccoon, skunk, and weasel.

History: Add. 1995, Act 57, Imd. Eff. May 24, 1995;—Am. 2012, Act 520, Imd. Eff. Dec. 28, 2012;—Am. 2015, Act 24, Eff. July 1, 2015.

Popular name: Act 451

Popular name: NREPA

324.43510 Carrying or transporting firearm, slingshot, bow and arrow, crossbow, or trap; license required; exception; applicability to taking of wild animal.

Sec. 43510. (1) Subject to subsection (2), except as provided in section 43513, and except for an individual hunting on a game bird hunting preserve licensed under part 417, an individual shall not carry or transport a firearm, slingshot, bow and arrow, crossbow, or a trap while in any area frequented by wild animals unless that individual has in his or her possession a license as required under this part.

(2) This act or a rule promulgated or order issued by the department or the commission under this act shall not be construed to prohibit an individual from transporting a pistol or carrying a loaded pistol, whether concealed or not, if either of the following applies:

(a) The individual has in his or her possession a license to carry a concealed pistol under 1927 PA 372, MCL 28.421 to 28.435.

(b) The individual is authorized under the circumstances to carry a concealed pistol without obtaining a license to carry a concealed pistol under 1927 PA 372, MCL 28.421 to 28.435, as provided for under any of the following:

(*i*) Section 12a of 1927 PA 372, MCL 28.432a.

(*ii*) Section 227, 227a, 231, or 231a of the Michigan penal code, 1931 PA 328, MCL 750.227, 750.227a, 750.231, and 750.231a.

(3) Subsection (2) does not authorize an individual to take or attempt to take a wild animal except as provided by law.

History: Add. 1995, Act 57, Imd. Eff. May 24, 1995;—Am. 1996, Act 585, Eff. Mar. 1, 1997;—Am. 2004, Act 129, Imd. Eff. June 3, 2004;—Am. 2006, Act 433, Imd. Eff. Oct. 5, 2006;—Am. 2013, Act 108, Imd. Eff. Sept. 17, 2013.

Popular name: Act 451

Popular name: NREPA

324.43511 Deer or elk season; transporting or possessing shotgun or rifle; license required; exception.

Sec. 43511. (1) Subject to subsection (2), and except as provided in section 43513, during the open season for the taking of deer or elk with a firearm, a person shall not transport or possess a shotgun with buckshot, slug load, ball load, or cut shell or a rifle other than a .22 caliber rim fire, unless the person has in his or her possession a license to hunt deer or elk with a firearm.

(2) Subsection (1) does not apply during muzzle-loading deer season.

History: Add. 1995, Act 57, Imd. Eff. May 24, 1995;—Am. 2006, Act 433, Imd. Eff. Oct. 5, 2006.

Popular name: Act 451

Popular name: NREPA

324.43512 Repealed. 1998, Act 104, Eff. Mar. 23, 1999.

Compiler's note: The repealed section pertained to possession of valid turkey license in order to carry firearm or bow and arrow.

Popular name: Act 451

Popular name: NREPA

324.43513 Carrying, transporting, or possessing firearm, slingshot, bow and arrow, or crossbow; hunting license not required; hunting on game bird hunting preserve; carrying or possessing unloaded weapon.

Sec. 43513. (1) An individual may carry, transport, or possess a firearm without a hunting license if the firearm is unloaded in both barrel and magazine and either enclosed in a case or carried in a vehicle in a location that is not readily accessible to any occupant of the vehicle. An individual may carry, transport, or possess a slingshot, bow and arrow, or crossbow without a hunting license if the slingshot, bow, or crossbow is unstrung, enclosed in a case, or carried in a vehicle in a location that is not readily accessible to any occupant of the vehicle.

(2) Regardless of whether the individual has a license or it is open season for the taking of game, an individual may carry, transport, possess or discharge a firearm, a bow and arrow, or a crossbow if all of the following apply:

(a) The individual is not taking or attempting to take game but is engaged in 1 or more of the following activities:

(*i*) Target practice using an identifiable, artificially constructed target or targets.

(*ii*) Practice with silhouettes, plinking, skeet, or trap.

(*iii*) Sighting-in the firearm, bow and arrow, or crossbow.

(b) The individual is, or is accompanied by or has the permission of, either of the following:

(*i*) The owner of the property on which the activity under subdivision (a) is taking place.

(*ii*) The lessee of that property for a term of not less than 1 year.

(c) The owner or lessee of the property does not receive remuneration for the activity under subdivision (a).

(3) An individual may carry, transport, or possess a firearm, slingshot, bow and arrow, or crossbow without a hunting license if the individual is hunting on a game bird hunting preserve licensed under part 417.

(4) An individual may carry or possess an unloaded weapon at any time if the individual is traveling to or from or participating in a historical reenactment.

History: Add. 1995, Act 57, Imd. Eff. May 24, 1995;—Am. 1996, Act 585, Eff. Mar. 1, 1997;—Am. 1998, Act 129, Eff. Mar. 23, 1999;—Am. 2006, Act 433, Imd. Eff. Oct. 5, 2006;—Am. 2013, Act 108, Imd. Eff. Sept. 17, 2013.

Popular name: Act 451

Popular name: NREPA

324.43516 Hunting, fur harvester, or fishing license; carrying license; exhibiting license upon demand; deer license with unused kill tag; exhibiting tag on request; electronic copy; consent to search electronic device not presumed; expanded use of electronic technology; tribal conservation officer; definition.

Sec. 43516. (1) Until March 1, 2018, an individual who has been issued a hunting, fur harvester's, or fishing license shall carry the license and shall exhibit the license upon the demand of a conservation officer, a law enforcement officer, a tribal conservation officer who complies with subsection (6), or the owner or occupant of the land if either or both of the following apply:

(a) The individual is hunting, trapping, or fishing.

(b) Subject to section 43510(2) and except as provided in section 43513, the individual is in possession of a firearm or other hunting or trapping apparatus or fishing apparatus in an area frequented by wild animals or fish, respectively.

(2) Subject to section 43510(2) and except as provided in section 43513, an individual shall not carry or possess afield a shotgun with buckshot, slug loads, or ball loads; a bow and arrow; a muzzle-loading rifle or black powder handgun; or a centerfire handgun or centerfire rifle during firearm deer season unless that individual has a valid deer license, with an unused

kill tag, if issued, issued in his or her name. The individual shall exhibit an unused kill tag, if issued, upon the request of a conservation officer, a law enforcement officer, or the owner or occupant of the land.

(3) Beginning March 1, 2018, an individual who has been issued a hunting, fur harvester's, or fishing license shall carry the license or, if applicable, an electronic copy of the license and shall exhibit the license or, if applicable, an electronic copy of the license upon the demand of a conservation officer, a law enforcement officer, a tribal conservation officer who complies with subsection (6), or the owner or occupant of the land if either or both of the following apply:

(a) The individual is hunting, trapping, or fishing.

(b) Subject to section 43510(2) and except as provided in section 43513, the individual is in possession of a firearm or other hunting or trapping apparatus or fishing apparatus in an area frequented by wild animals or fish, respectively.

(4) An individual who displays an electronic copy of his or her license using an electronic device as provided in subsection (3) is not presumed to have consented to a search of the electronic device. This state, a law enforcement agency, a tribal conservation officer who complies with subsection (6), an employee of this state or a law enforcement agency, or the owner or occupant of the land is not liable for damage to or loss of an electronic device that occurs as a result of a conservation officer, a tribal conservation officer who complies with subsection (6), a law enforcement officer, or the owner or occupant of the land viewing an electronic copy of a license in the manner provided in this section, regardless of whether the conservation officer, tribal conservation officer who complies with subsection (6), law enforcement officer, or owner or occupant of the land was in possession of the electronic device at the time the damage or loss occurred.

(5) The department shall continue to explore the expanded use of electronic technology to provide additional services that will enhance hunting and fishing experiences for individuals in this state.

(6) A tribal conservation officer under subsection (1), (3), or (4) must be in uniform, display proper credentials, and be on official duty within the ceded territory of the treaty of March 28, 1836, 7 Stat 491.

(7) As used in this section, "tribal conservation officer" means a conservation officer employed by the Great Lakes Indian fish and wildlife commission, the Bay Mills Indian Community, the Sault Ste. Marie Tribe of Chippewa Indians, the Little Traverse Bay Bands of Odawa Indians, the Grand Traverse Band of Ottawa and Chippewa Indians, or the Little River Band of Ottawa Indians.

History: Add. 1995, Act 57, Imd. Eff. May 24, 1995;—Am. 2004, Act 129, Imd. Eff. June 3, 2004;—Am. 2006, Act 433, Imd. Eff. Oct. 5, 2006;—Am. 2013, Act 108, Imd. Eff. Sept. 17, 2013;—Am. 2016, Act 36, Eff. June 6, 2016;—Am. 2016, Act 461, Eff. Mar. 29, 2017.

Popular name: Act 451

Popular name: NREPA

324.43517 Hunting by minor child; order establishing mentored youth hunting program.

Sec. 43517. (1) A parent or legal guardian of a minor child shall not permit or allow the minor child to hunt game under the authority of a license issued under this part except under 1 of the following conditions:

(a) The minor child hunts only on land upon which a parent or guardian is regularly domiciled or a parent or guardian, or another individual at least 18 years old authorized by a parent or guardian, accompanies the minor child. This subdivision does not apply under any 1 of the following circumstances:

(*i*) The license is an apprentice license.

(*ii*) The minor child is less than 14 years old and the license is a license to hunt deer, bear, or elk with a firearm.

(*iii*) The minor child is less than 10 years old.

(b) If the license is an apprentice license, a parent or guardian, or another individual at least 21 years old authorized by a parent or guardian, who is licensed to hunt that game under a license other than an apprentice license accompanies the minor child. In addition, if the minor child is less than 14 years old and the apprentice license is a license to hunt deer, bear, or elk with a firearm, the minor child shall hunt only on private property.

(c) If the minor child is less than 14 years old and the license is a license to hunt deer, bear, or elk with a firearm, the minor child hunts only on private property and a parent or guardian, or another individual authorized by a parent or guardian who is at least 18 years old, accompanies the minor child. This subdivision does not apply if the license is an apprentice license or if the minor child is less than 10 years old.

(d) If the minor child is less than 10 years old, the minor hunts only with a mentor in compliance with the mentored youth hunting program established by the commission under subsection (2).

(2) Within 1 year after the effective date of the amendatory act that added this subsection, the commission shall issue an order under section 40113a establishing a mentored youth hunting program. The order shall provide for at least all of the following:

(a) A mentor shall be at least 21 years of age before participating in the mentored youth hunting program.

(b) A mentor shall possess a valid license to hunt, other than an apprentice license, before engaging in any mentored youth hunting program.

(c) An individual shall not be a mentor unless he or she presents proof of previous hunting experience in the form of a previous hunting license, other than an apprentice license, or certification of completion of training in hunter safety issued to the individual by this state, another state, a province of Canada, or another country.

History: Add. 1995, Act 57, Imd. Eff. May 24, 1995;—Am. 2006, Act 280, Imd. Eff. July 10, 2006;—Am. 2006, Act 282, Imd. Eff. July 10, 2006;—Am. 2011, Act 109, Eff. Sept. 1, 2011.

Popular name: Act 451

Popular name: NREPA

324.43520 Hunting license; issuance to minor child; requirements; duties of issuing agent; proof of previous hunting experience or certification of completion of training in hunter safety; affidavit; information to be recorded; apprentice license; mentored youth hunting license; fee; report.

Sec. 43520. (1) Subject to other requirements of this part, the department may issue a hunting license to a minor child if all of the following requirements are met:

(a) A parent or legal guardian of the minor child applies for the license on behalf of the minor child.

(b) The parent or guardian represents that the requirements of section 43517, as applicable, will be complied with.

(c) The license fee is paid.

(2) A person authorized to sell hunting licenses shall not issue a hunting license to an individual born after January 1, 1960, unless the individual presents proof of previous hunting experience in the form of a hunting license issued by this state, another state, a province of Canada, or another country or presents a certification of completion of training in hunter safety issued to the individual by this state, another state, a province of Canada, or another country. If an applicant for a hunting license does not have proof of such a previous license or a certification of completion of training in hunter safety, a person authorized to sell hunting licenses may issue a hunting license if the applicant submits a signed affidavit stating that the applicant has completed a course in hunter safety or that the applicant possessed such a hunting license previously. The person selling a hunting license shall record as specified by the department the form of proof of the previous hunting experience or certification of completion of hunter safety training presented by the applicant. This subsection does not apply to the issuance of an apprentice license. An apprentice license or the equivalent does not satisfy the requirements of this subsection concerning proof of previous hunting experience.

(3) An individual who does not meet the requirements of subsection (2) may obtain an apprentice license for the same price as the corresponding regular license that the individual would otherwise be qualified to obtain. An individual 17 years old or older shall not hunt game under an apprentice license unless another individual at least 21 years old who possesses a license, other than an apprentice license, to hunt that game accompanies that apprentice licensee and does not accompany more than 1 other apprentice licensee. For the purposes of this subsection and section 43517(1)(b), an individual shall not go along with more than 2 apprentice licensees of any age for the purpose of accompanying those apprentice licensees while those apprentice licensees are hunting. If an individual has represented to an apprentice licensee or, if the apprentice licensee is a minor child, to the apprentice licensee's parent or legal guardian that the individual would accompany the apprentice licensee for the purposes of this subsection, the individual shall not go along with the apprentice licensee while the apprentice licensee is hunting unless the individual actually accompanies the apprentice licensee and possesses a license, other than an apprentice license, to hunt the same game as the apprentice licensee. An individual is not eligible to obtain a specific type of apprentice license, such as a firearm deer license, an archery deer license, a combination deer license, a small game license, or a turkey license, for more than 2 license years. An apprentice license shall be distinguished from a license other than an apprentice license by a notation or other means.

(4) Beginning March 1, 2014, an individual who does not meet the requirements of subsection (2) may obtain an apprentice license for the same price as the corresponding regular license that the individual would otherwise be qualified to obtain. An individual 17 years old or older shall not hunt game under an apprentice license unless another individual at least 21 years old who possesses a license, other than an apprentice license, to hunt that game accompanies that apprentice licensee and does not accompany more than 1 other apprentice licensee. For the purposes of this subsection and section 43517(1)(b), an individual shall not go along with more than 2 apprentice licensees of any age for the purpose of accompanying those apprentice licensees while those apprentice licensees are hunting. If an individual has represented to an apprentice licensee or, if the apprentice licensee is a minor child, to the apprentice licensee's parent or legal guardian that the individual would accompany the apprentice licensee for the purposes of this subsection, the individual shall not go along with the apprentice licensee while the apprentice licensee is hunting unless the individual actually accompanies the apprentice licensee and possesses a license, other than an apprentice license, to hunt the same game as the apprentice licensee. An individual is not eligible to obtain a specific type of apprentice license, such as a deer license, a base license, or a turkey license, for more than 2 license years. An apprentice license shall be distinguished from a license other than an apprentice license by a notation or other means.

(5) Only a minor who is less than 10 years old may obtain a mentored youth hunting license. A minor who is less than 10 years old shall not hunt game under a mentored youth hunting license unless that minor complies with all requirements of the mentored youth hunting program established by the commission under section 43517. The fee for a mentored youth hunting license is $7.50 and shall include all of the privileges conferred by all of the following:

(a) Resident small game license.

(b) Combination deer license.

(c) All species fishing license.

(d) Spring turkey hunting license and fall turkey hunting license.

(e) Resident fur harvester's license.

(6) Beginning March 1, 2014, the fee for a mentored youth hunting license is $7.50 and shall include all of the privileges conferred by all of the following:

(a) Base license.

(b) Deer license.

(c) All-species fishing license.

(d) Spring wild turkey hunting license and fall wild turkey hunting license.
(e) Fur harvester's license.
(7) By September 1, 2015 and every 4 years after that date, the department shall submit a report to the standing committees of the senate and house of representatives with primary responsibility for conservation and outdoor recreation issues evaluating whether the fee revenue received by the department from mentored youth hunting licenses under subsection (6) is adequate to administer the mentored youth hunting program.

History: Add. 1995, Act 57, Imd. Eff. May 24, 1995;—Am. 2006, Act 280, Imd. Eff. July 10, 2006;—Am. 2006, Act 280, Imd. Eff. July 10, 2006;—Am. 2006, Act 282, Imd. Eff. July 10, 2006;—Am. 2011, Act 120, Eff. Sept. 1, 2011;—Am. 2013, Act 108, Imd. Eff. Sept. 17, 2013.

Popular name: Act 451

Popular name: NREPA

324.43523 Repealed. 2013, Act 108, Eff. Mar. 1, 2014.

Compiler's note: The repealed section pertained to small game license and fees.

Popular name: Act 451

Popular name: NREPA

324.43523a Base license; hunting fur-bearing animals; fee; hours void; limited nonresident small game license; development and display of electronic license.

Sec. 43523a. (1) Except as otherwise provided in this part, an individual shall not hunt small game, unless the individual possesses a current base license. A base license authorizes the individual named in the license to hunt for small game, except for animals or birds that require a special license.
(2) If authorized in an order issued under part 401, an individual who possesses a current base license may take specified fur-bearing animals by means other than trapping during the open season for hunting these fur-bearing animals. However, an individual who goes on a bobcat hunt with a licensed hunter is not required to possess a base license if the individual does not carry a firearm, bow, or crossbow and does not own dogs used to chase or locate a bobcat during the hunt.
(3) The fee for a base license is as follows:
(a) Subject to subdivision (b), for a resident, $10.00.
(b) For a resident minor child or nonresident minor child, $5.00.
(c) Subject to subdivision (b), for a nonresident, $150.00.
(4) A base license is void between the hours of 1/2 hour after sunset and 1/2 hour before sunrise with the exception of coyote hunting.
(5) A nonresident may purchase a limited nonresident small game license entitling that individual to hunt for a 7-day period all species of small game that are available to hunt under a nonresident base license. The fee for a limited nonresident small game license is $80.00. The purchase of a 7-day limited nonresident small game license does not entitle the holder to purchase any additional licenses.
(6) Not later than March 1, 2018, the department shall develop an electronic license that allows an individual to display an electronic copy of his or her base license using an electronic device.

History: Add. 2013, Act 108, Imd. Eff. Sept. 17, 2013;—Am. 2016, Act 461, Eff. Mar. 29, 2017.

Popular name: Act 451

Popular name: NREPA

324.43525 Repealed. 2013, Act 108, Eff. Mar. 1, 2014.

Compiler's note: The repealed section pertained to waterfowl hunting license and fees.

Popular name: Act 451

Popular name: NREPA

324.43525a Repealed. 2013, Act 108, Eff. Mar. 1, 2014.

Compiler's note: The repealed section pertained to combination deer license.

Popular name: Act 451

Popular name: NREPA

324.43526 Repealed. 2013, Act 108, Eff. Mar. 1, 2014.

Compiler's note: The repealed section pertained to firearm deer license and fees.

Compiler's note: Act 451

Compiler's note: NREPA

324.43528 Bear hunting license; exception; eligibility beginning March 1, 2014; fees; kill tag; application fee; bear participation license.

Sec. 43528. (1) An individual shall not hunt bear unless the individual possesses a bear hunting license. However, an individual who goes on a bear hunt with a licensed hunter is not required to possess a bear hunting license if the individual does not carry a firearm, bow, or crossbow and does not own dogs used to chase or locate bear during the hunt. Beginning March 1, 2014, only an individual holding a valid base license is eligible to purchase a bear hunting license, pursuant to current regulations.

(2) The fee for a resident bear hunting license is $15.00. The fee for a nonresident bear hunting license is $150.00. Beginning March 1, 2014, the fee for a bear hunting license is $25.00.

(3) The department may issue a kill tag with, or as a part of, a bear hunting license. The kill tag shall bear the license number. The kill tag may also include space for other pertinent information required by the department. The kill tag, if issued, is part of the license.

(4) In addition to the license fees in subsection (2), the department shall charge a nonrefundable application fee not to exceed $4.00 for each individual who applies for a bear hunting license. Beginning March 1, 2014, in addition to the license fees in subsection (2), the department shall charge a nonrefundable application fee not to exceed $5.00 for each individual who applies for a bear hunting license.

(5) Beginning March 1, 2014, the following individuals chasing or locating bear with dogs during the open season for that game and who hold a valid base license are eligible for the purchase of a bear participation license for a fee of $15.00:

(a) Any individual possessing a firearm, crossbow, or bow and arrow.

(b) The owner, when present, of any dog chasing or locating bear.

History: Add. 1995, Act 57, Imd. Eff. May 24, 1995;—Am. 1996, Act 103, Imd. Eff. Mar. 5, 1996;—Am. 1996, Act 585, Eff. Mar. 1, 1997;—Am. 2008, Act 347, Imd. Eff. Dec. 23, 2008;—Am. 2009, Act 70, Imd. Eff. July 9, 2009;—Am. 2013, Act 108, Imd. Eff. Sept. 17, 2013.

Popular name: Act 451

Popular name: NREPA

324.43530 Repealed. 2013, Act 108, Eff. Mar. 1, 2014.

Compiler's note: The repealed section pertained to hunting small game on game bird hunting preserves.

Popular name: Act 451

Popular name: NREPA

324.43531 Fur harvester's license; exception; fees; conditions to issuance of nonresident fur harvester's license; rights of licensee; eligibility beginning March 1, 2014; validity of license.

Sec. 43531. (1) Except as otherwise provided in section 43523(2) or section 43523a(2), an individual shall not trap or hunt fur-bearing animals unless the individual possesses a fur harvester's license. However, an individual who goes on a bobcat hunt with a licensed hunter is not required to possess a fur harvester's license if the individual does not carry a firearm, bow, or crossbow and does not own dogs used to chase or locate a bobcat during the hunt.

(2) The fee for a resident fur harvester's license is $15.00. The fee for a fur harvester's license for a resident or nonresident minor child 10 years old or older shall be discounted 50% from the cost of the resident fur harvester's license.

(3) Until March 1, 2014, the department may issue a nonresident fur harvester's license to a nonresident of this state if the state, province, or country in which the nonresident applicant resides allows residents of this state to obtain equivalent hunting and trapping privileges in that state, province, or country. The fee for an eligible nonresident fur harvester's license is $150.00. Nonresident fur harvester's licenses shall not be sold or purchased before November 15 of each year.

(4) An individual who holds a fur harvester's license may hunt fur-bearing animals during the season open to taking fur-bearing animals with firearms and may trap fur-bearing animals during the season open to trapping fur-bearing animals.

(5) Beginning March 1, 2014, only an individual holding a valid base license is eligible to purchase a fur harvester's license, pursuant to current regulations. The fee for a fur harvester's license is $15.00.

(6) Beginning March 1, 2014, for a nonresident holding a valid base license and a valid fur harvester's license, the fur harvester's license is not valid for fur-bearing species for which a bag limit has been established.

History: Add. 1995, Act 57, Imd. Eff. May 24, 1995;—Am. 1996, Act 585, Eff. Mar. 1, 1997;—Am. 2008, Act 347, Imd. Eff. Dec. 23, 2008;—Am. 2009, Act 70, Imd. Eff. July 9, 2009;—Am. 2011, Act 120, Eff. Sept. 1, 2011;—Am. 2013, Act 108, Imd. Eff. Sept. 17, 2013.

Popular name: Act 451

Popular name: NREPA

324.43535 Senior license; discounted fees.

Sec. 43535. (1) Until March 1, 2014, a resident of this state who is 65 years of age or older may obtain a senior small game license, a senior firearm deer license, a senior bow and arrow deer license, a senior bear hunting license, a senior wild turkey hunting license, or a senior fur harvester's license. The fee for each senior license shall be discounted 60% from the fee for the resident license.

(2) Beginning March 1, 2014, a resident of this state who is 65 years of age or older may obtain a senior base license, a senior deer license, a senior wild turkey hunting license, or a senior fur harvester's license. The fee for each senior license shall be discounted 60% from the fee for the resident license.

History: Add. 1995, Act 57, Imd. Eff. May 24, 1995;—Am. 1996, Act 585, Eff. Mar. 1, 1997;—Am. 2013, Act 108, Imd. Eff. Sept. 17, 2013.

Popular name: Act 451

Popular name: NREPA

324.43543 Course of instruction in safe handling of firearms; instructors; registration; certificate of competency.

Sec. 43543. The department shall provide for a course of instruction in the safe handling of firearms and shall designate persons, without compensation, to serve as instructors and to award certificates. A person desiring to take the course of instruction shall register with an instructor certified by the department. Upon successful completion of the course, the person shall be issued a certificate of competency.

History: Add. 1995, Act 57, Imd. Eff. May 24, 1995.

Popular name: Act 451

Popular name: NREPA

324.43558 Prohibited conduct; misdemeanor; penalties; carrying firearm under influence of controlled substance or alcohol; effect of prior conviction; violation of subsection (1)(d) as misdemeanor.

Sec. 43558. (1) A person is guilty of a misdemeanor if the person does any of the following:

(a) Makes a false statement as to material facts for the purpose of obtaining a license or uses or attempts to use a license obtained by making a false statement.

(b) Affixes to a license a date or time other than the date or time issued.

(c) Issues a license without receiving and remitting the fee to the department.

(d) Without a license, takes or possesses a wild animal, wild bird, or aquatic species, except aquatic insects. This subdivision does not apply to a person less than 17 years of age who without a license takes or possesses aquatic species.

(e) Sells, loans, or permits in any manner another person to use the person's license or uses or attempts to use another person's license.

(f) Falsely makes, alters, forges, or counterfeits a sportcard or a hunting, fishing, or fur harvester's license or possesses an altered, forged, or counterfeited hunting, fishing, or fur harvester's license.

(g) Uses a tag furnished with a deer license, bear hunting license, elk hunting license, or wild turkey hunting license more than 1 time, or attaches or allows a tag to be attached to a deer, bear, elk, or turkey other than a deer, bear, elk, or turkey lawfully killed by the person.

(h) Except as provided by law, makes an application for, obtains, or purchases more than 1 license for a hunting, fishing, or trapping season, not including a limited fishing license, second deer license, antlerless deer license, or other license specifically authorized by law, or if the applicant's license has been lost or destroyed.

(i) Applies for, obtains, or purchases a license during a time that the person is ineligible to secure a license.

(j) Knowingly obtains, or attempts to obtain, a resident or a senior license if that person is not a resident of this state.

(2) Except as provided in subsection (5), a person who violates subsection (1) shall be punished by imprisonment for not more than 90 days, or a fine of not less than $25.00 or more than $250.00 and the costs of prosecution, or both. In addition, the person shall surrender any license and license tag that was wrongfully obtained.

(3) A person licensed to carry a firearm under this part is prohibited from doing so while under the influence of a controlled substance or alcohol or a combination of a controlled substance and alcohol. A person who violates this subsection is guilty of a misdemeanor, punishable by imprisonment for 90 days, or a fine of $500.00, or both.

(4) An applicant for a license under this part who has previously been convicted of a violation of the game and fish laws of this state may be required to file an application with the department together with other information that the department considers expedient. The license may be issued by the department.

(5) A person who violates subsection (1)(d), upon a showing that the person was ineligible to secure a license under court order or other lawful authority, is guilty of a misdemeanor, punishable by imprisonment for not more than 180 days, or a fine of not less than $500.00 and not more than $2,500.00, or both, and the costs of prosecution.

History: Add. 1995, Act 57, Imd. Eff. May 24, 1995;—Am. 1996, Act 585, Eff. Mar. 1, 1997;—Am. 2013, Act 108, Imd. Eff. Sept. 17, 2013.

Popular name: Act 451

Popular name: NREPA

SUBCHAPTER 4
FORESTS

PART 515
PREVENTION AND SUPPRESSION OF FOREST FIRES

324.51504 Acts prohibited.

Sec. 51504. A person shall not do any of the following:

(a) Dispose of a lighted match, cigarette, cigar, ashes or other flaming or glowing substances, or any other substance or thing that is likely to ignite a forest, brush, grass, or woods fire; or throw or drop from a moving vehicle any such object or substance.

(b) Set fire to, or cause or procure the setting on fire of, any flammable material on or adjacent to forest land without taking reasonable precautions both before and while lighting the fire and at all times after the lighting of the fire to prevent the escape of the fire; or leave the fire before it is extinguished.

(c) Set a backfire or cause a backfire to be set, except under the direct supervision of an established fire control agency or unless it can be established that the setting of the backfire is necessary for the purpose of saving life or valuable property.

(d) Destroy, break down, mutilate, or remove any fire control sign or poster erected by an established fire control agency in the administration of its lawful duties and authorities.

(e) Use or operate on or adjacent to forest land, a welding torch, tar pot, or other device that may cause a fire, without clearing flammable material surrounding the operation or without taking other reasonable precautions necessary to ensure against the starting and spreading of fire.

(f) Operate or cause to be operated any engine, other machinery, or powered vehicle not equipped with spark arresters or other suitable devices to prevent the escape of fire or sparks.

(g) Discharge or cause to be discharged a gun firing incendiary or tracer bullets or tracer charge onto or across any forest land.

History: Add. 1995, Act 57, Imd. Eff. May 24, 1995.

Popular name: Act 451

Popular name: NREPA

CHAPTER 4
RECREATION

SUBCHAPTER 1
RECREATION

PART 731
RECREATIONAL TRESPASS

324.73102 Entering or remaining on property of another; consent; exceptions.

Sec. 73102. (1) Except as provided in subsection (4), a person shall not enter or remain upon the property of another person, other than farm property or a wooded area connected to farm property, to engage in any recreational activity or trapping on that property without the consent of the owner or his or her lessee or agent, if either of the following circumstances exists:

(a) The property is fenced or enclosed and is maintained in such a manner as to exclude intruders.

(b) The property is posted in a conspicuous manner against entry. The minimum letter height on the posting signs shall be 1 inch. Each posting sign shall be not less than 50 square inches, and the signs shall be spaced to enable a person to observe not less than 1 sign at any point of entry upon the property.

(2) Except as provided in subsection (4), a person shall not enter or remain upon farm property or a wooded area connected to farm property for any recreational activity or trapping without the consent of the owner or his or her lessee or agent, whether or not the farm property or wooded area connected to farm property is fenced, enclosed, or posted.

(3) On fenced or posted property or farm property, a fisherman wading or floating a navigable public stream may, without written or oral consent, enter upon property within the clearly defined banks of the stream or, without damaging farm products, walk a route as closely proximate to the clearly defined bank as possible when necessary to avoid a natural or artificial hazard or obstruction, including, but not limited to, a dam, deep hole, or a fence or other exercise of ownership by the riparian owner.

(4) A person other than a person possessing a firearm may, unless previously prohibited in writing or orally by the property owner or his or her lessee or agent, enter on foot upon the property of another person for the sole purpose of retrieving a hunting dog. The person shall not remain on the property beyond the reasonable time necessary to retrieve the dog. In an action under section 73109 or 73110, the burden of showing that the property owner or his or her lessee or agent previously prohibited entry under this subsection is on the plaintiff or prosecuting attorney, respectively.

(5) Consent to enter or remain upon the property of another person pursuant to this section may be given orally or in writing. The consent may establish conditions for entering or remaining upon that property. Unless prohibited in the written consent, a written consent may be amended or revoked orally. If the owner or his or her lessee or agent requires all persons entering or remaining upon the property to have written consent, the presence of the person on the property without written consent is prima facie evidence of unlawful entry.

History: Add. 1995, Act 58, Imd. Eff. May 24, 1995;—Am. 1998, Act 546, Eff. Mar. 23, 1999.

Popular name: Act 451

Popular name: NREPA

Popular name: Recreational Trespass Act

324.73103 Discharging firearm within right-of-way of public highway abutting certain property; consent; "public highway" defined.

Sec. 73103. (1) A person shall not discharge a firearm within the right-of-way of a public highway adjoining or abutting any platted property, fenced, enclosed, or posted property, farm property, or a wooded area connected to farm property without the consent of the owner of the abutting property or his or her lessee or agent.

(2) As used in this section, "public highway" means a road or highway under the jurisdiction of the state transportation department, the road commission of a county, or of a local unit of government.

History: Add. 1995, Act 58, Imd. Eff. May 24, 1995.

Popular name: Act 451

Popular name: NREPA

Popular name: Recreational Trespass Act

SUBCHAPTER 2
PARKS

PART 741
STATE PARKS SYSTEM

324.74105 Volunteers; appointment; immunity from civil liability; carrying of firearm prohibited.

Sec. 74105. The department may appoint persons to serve as volunteers for the purpose of facilitating the responsibilities of the department as provided in this part. While a volunteer is serving in such a capacity, the volunteer has the same immunity from civil liability as a department employee and shall be treated in the same manner as an employee under section 8 of Act No. 170 of the Public Acts of 1964, being section 691.1408 of the Michigan Compiled Laws. A volunteer shall not carry a firearm while functioning as a volunteer.

History: Add. 1995, Act 58, Imd. Eff. May 24, 1995.

Popular name: Act 451

Popular name: NREPA

SUBCHAPTER 6
MOTORIZED RECREATIONAL VEHICLES

PART 811
OFF-ROAD RECREATION VEHICLES

324.81133 Operation of ORV; prohibited acts; crash helmet and protective eyewear required; exception; assumption of risk.

Sec. 81133. (1) An individual shall not operate an ORV:

(a) At a rate of speed greater than is reasonable and proper, or in a careless manner, having due regard for conditions then existing.

(b) During the hours of 1/2 hour after sunset to 1/2 hour before sunrise without displaying a lighted headlight and lighted taillight. The requirements of this subdivision are in addition to any applicable requirements of section 81131(12).

(c) Unless the vehicle is equipped with a braking system that may be operated by hand or foot, capable of producing deceleration at 14 feet per second on level ground at a speed of 20 miles per hour; a brake light, brighter than the taillight, visible from behind the vehicle when the brake is activated, if the vehicle is operated during the hours of 1/2 hour after sunset and 1/2 hour before sunrise; and a throttle so designed that when the pressure used to advance the throttle is removed, the engine speed will immediately and automatically return to idle.

(d) In a state game area or state park or recreation area, except on roads, trails, or areas designated for this purpose, notwithstanding section 72118; on other state-owned lands under the control of the department where the operation would be in violation of rules promulgated by the department; in a forest nursery or planting area; on public lands posted or reasonably identifiable as an area of forest reproduction, and when growing stock may be damaged; in a dedicated natural area of the department; or in any area in such a manner as to create an erosive condition, or to injure, damage, or destroy trees or growing crops. However, the department may permit an owner and guests of the owner to use an ORV within the boundaries of a state forest in order to access the owner's property.

(e) On the frozen surface of public waters within 100 feet of an individual not in or upon a vehicle, or within 100 feet of a fishing shanty or shelter or an area that is cleared of snow for skating purposes, except at the minimum speed required to maintain controlled forward movement of the vehicle, or as may be authorized by permit in special events.

(f) Unless the vehicle is equipped with a spark arrester type United States Forest Service approved muffler, in good working order and in constant operation. Exhaust noise emission shall not exceed 86 Db(A) or 82 Db(A) on a vehicle manufactured after January 1, 1986, when the vehicle is under full throttle, traveling in second gear, and measured 50 feet at right angles from the vehicle path with a sound level meter that meets the requirement of ANSI S1.4 1983, using procedure and ancillary equipment therein described; or 99 Db(A) or 94 Db(A) on a vehicle manufactured after January 1, 1986, or that level comparable to the current sound level as provided for by the United States Environmental Protection Agency when tested according to the provisions of the current SAE J1287, June 86 test procedure for exhaust levels of stationary motorcycles, using sound level meters and ancillary equipment therein described. A vehicle subject to this part, manufactured or assembled after December 31, 1972 and used, sold, or offered for sale in this state, shall conform to the noise emission levels established by the United States Environmental Protection Agency under the noise control act of 1972, 42 USC 4901 to 4918.

(g) Within 100 feet of a dwelling at a speed greater than the minimum required to maintain controlled forward movement of the vehicle, except under any of the following circumstances:

(*i*) On property owned by or under the operator's control or on which the operator is an invited guest.

(*ii*) On a forest road or forest trail if the forest road or forest trail is maintained by or under the jurisdiction of the department.

(*iii*) On a street, county road, or highway on which ORV use is authorized pursuant to section 81131(2), (3), (5), or (6).

(h) In or upon the lands of another without the written consent of the owner, the owner's agent, or a lessee, when required by part 731. The operator of the vehicle is liable for damage to private property caused by operation of the vehicle, including, but not limited to, damage to trees, shrubs, or growing crops, injury to other living creatures, or erosive or other ecological damage. The owner of the private property may recover from the individual responsible nominal damages of not less than the amount of damage or injury. Failure to post private property or fence or otherwise enclose in a manner to exclude intruders or of the private property owner or other authorized person to personally communicate against trespass does not imply consent to ORV use.

(i) In an area on which public hunting is permitted during the regular November firearm deer season, from 7 a.m. to 11 a.m. and from 2 p.m. to 5 p.m., except as follows:

(*i*) During an emergency.

(*ii*) For law enforcement purposes.

(*iii*) To go to and from a permanent residence or a hunting camp otherwise inaccessible by a conventional wheeled vehicle.

(*iv*) To remove legally harvested deer, bear, or elk from public land. An individual shall operate an ORV under this subparagraph at a speed not exceeding 5 miles per hour, using the most direct route that complies with subdivision (n).

(*v*) To conduct necessary work functions involving land and timber survey, communication and transmission line patrol, or timber harvest operations.

(*vi*) On property owned or under control of the operator or on which the operator is an invited guest.

(*vii*) While operating a vehicle registered under the code on a private road capable of sustaining automobile traffic or a street, county road, or highway.

(*viii*) If the individual holds a valid permit to hunt from a standing vehicle issued under part 401 or is a person with a disability using an ORV to access public lands for purposes of hunting or fishing through use of a designated trail or forest road. An individual holding a valid permit to hunt from a standing vehicle issued under part 401, or a person with a disability using an ORV to access public lands for purposes of hunting or fishing, may display a flag, the color of which the department shall determine, to identify himself or herself as a person with a disability or an individual holding a permit to hunt from a standing vehicle under part 401.

(j) Except as otherwise provided in section 40111, while transporting on the vehicle a bow unless unstrung or encased, or a firearm unless unloaded and securely encased, or equipped with and made inoperative by a manufactured keylocked trigger housing mechanism.

(k) On or across a cemetery or burial ground, or land used as an airport.

(*l*) Within 100 feet of a slide, ski, or skating area, unless the vehicle is being used for the purpose of servicing the area or is being operated pursuant to section 81131(2), (3), (5), or (6).

(m) On an operating or nonabandoned railroad or railroad right-of-way, or public utility right-of-way, other than for the purpose of crossing at a clearly established site intended for vehicular traffic, except railroad, public utility, or law enforcement personnel while in performance of their duties, and except if the right-of-way is designated as provided for in section 81127.

(n) In or upon the waters of any stream, river, bog, wetland, swamp, marsh, or quagmire except over a bridge, culvert, or similar structure.

(o) To hunt, pursue, worry, kill, or attempt to hunt, pursue, worry, or kill an animal, whether wild or domesticated.

(p) In a manner so as to leave behind litter or other debris.

(q) On public land, in a manner contrary to operating regulations.

(r) While transporting or possessing, in or on the vehicle, alcoholic liquor in a container that is open or uncapped or upon which the seal is broken, except under either of the following circumstances:

(*i*) The container is in a trunk or compartment separate from the passenger compartment of the vehicle.

(*ii*) If the vehicle does not have a trunk or compartment separate from the passenger compartment, the container is encased or enclosed.

(s) While transporting any passenger in or upon an ORV unless the manufacturing standards for the vehicle make provisions for transporting passengers.

(t) On adjacent private land, in an area zoned residential, within 300 feet of a dwelling at a speed greater than the minimum required to maintain controlled forward movement of the vehicle except under any of the following circumstances:

(*i*) On a forest road or forest trail if the forest road or forest trail is maintained by or under the jurisdiction of the department.

(*ii*) On a street, county road, or highway on which ORV use is authorized under section 81131(2), (3), (5), or (6).

(u) On a forest trail if the ORV is greater than 50 inches in width.

(2) An individual who is operating or is a passenger on an ORV shall wear a crash helmet and protective eyewear that are approved by the United States Department of Transportation. This subsection does not apply to any of the following:

(a) An individual who owns the property on which the ORV is operating, is a family member of the owner and resides at that property, or is an invited guest of an individual who owns the property. An exception under this subdivision does not apply to any of the following:

(*i*) An individual less than 16 years of age.

(*ii*) An individual 16 or 17 years of age, unless the individual has consent from his or her parent or guardian to ride without a crash helmet.

(*iii*) An individual participating in an organized ORV riding or racing event if an individual who owns the property receives consideration for use of the property for operating ORVs.

(b) An individual wearing a properly adjusted and fastened safety belt if the ORV is equipped with a roof that meets or exceeds United States Department of Transportation standards for a crash helmet.

(c) An ORV operated on a state-licensed game bird hunting preserve at a speed of not greater than 10 miles per hour.

(3) Each person who participates in the sport of ORV riding accepts the risks associated with that sport insofar as the dangers are inherent. Those risks include, but are not limited to, injuries to persons or property that can result from variations in terrain; defects in traffic lanes; surface or subsurface snow or ice conditions; bare spots; rocks, trees, and other forms of natural growth or debris; and collisions with fill material, decks, bridges, signs, fences, trail maintenance equipment, or other ORVs. Those risks do not include injuries to persons or property that result from the use of an ORV by another person in a careless or negligent manner likely to endanger person or property. When an ORV is operated in the vicinity of a railroad right-of-way, each person who participates in the sport of ORV riding additionally assumes risks including, but not limited to, entanglement with railroad tracks, switches, and ties and collisions with trains and train-related equipment and facilities.

History: Add. 1995, Act 58, Imd. Eff. May 24, 1995;—Am. 1998, Act 86, Imd. Eff. May 13, 1998;—Am. 2008, Act 240, Imd. Eff. July 17, 2008;—Am. 2008, Act 365, Imd. Eff. Dec. 23, 2008;—Am. 2012, Act 246, Imd. Eff. July 2, 2012;—Am. 2012, Act 340, Imd. Eff. Oct. 16, 2012;—Am. 2013, Act 119, Imd. Eff. Sept. 25, 2013;—Am. 2013, Act 249, Imd. Eff. Dec. 26, 2013;—Am. 2014, Act 147, Imd. Eff. June 4, 2014;—Am. 2016, Act 288, Imd. Eff. Sept. 28, 2016.

Popular name: Act 451

Popular name: NREPA

Popular name: Off-Road Vehicle Act

Popular name: ORV

PART 821
SNOWMOBILES

324.82126 Operation of snowmobile; prohibitions; exemption; construction, operation, and maintenance of snowmobile trail; conditions; demarcation of trail by signing; "operate" defined; prohibited conduct; assumption of risk; violation of subsection (2) as civil infraction; fine.

Sec. 82126. (1) A person shall not operate a snowmobile under any of the following circumstances:

(a) At a rate of speed greater than is reasonable and proper having due regard for conditions then existing.

(b) In a forest nursery, planting area, or on public lands posted or reasonably identifiable as an area of forest reproduction when growing stock may be damaged or posted or reasonably identifiable as a natural dedicated area that is in zone 2 or zone 3.

(c) On the frozen surface of public waters as follows:

(*i*) Within 100 feet of a person, including a skater, who is not in or upon a snowmobile.

(*ii*) Within 100 feet of a fishing shanty or shelter except at the minimum speed required to maintain forward movement of the snowmobile.

(*iii*) On an area that has been cleared of snow for skating purposes unless the area is necessary for access to the public water.

(d) Within 100 feet of a dwelling between 12 midnight and 6 a.m., at a speed greater than the minimum required to maintain forward movement of the snowmobile.

(e) In an area on which public hunting is permitted during the regular November firearm deer season from 7 a.m. to 11 a.m. and from 2 p.m. to 5 p.m., except under 1 or more of the following circumstances:

(*i*) During an emergency.

(*ii*) For law enforcement purposes.

(*iii*) To go to and from a permanent residence or a hunting camp otherwise inaccessible by a conventional wheeled vehicle.

(*iv*) For the conduct of necessary work functions involving land and timber survey, communication and transmission line patrol, or timber harvest operations.

(*v*) On the person's own property or property under the person's control or as an invited guest.

(f) While transporting on the snowmobile a bow, unless unstrung or encased, or a firearm, unless unloaded in both barrel and magazine and securely encased.

(g) On or across a cemetery or burial ground.

(h) Within 100 feet of a slide, ski, or skating area except when traveling on a county road right-of-way pursuant to section 82119 or a snowmobile trail that is designated and funded by the department. A snowmobile may enter such an area for the purpose of servicing the area or for medical emergencies.

(i) On a railroad or railroad right-of-way. This prohibition does not apply to railroad personnel, public utility personnel, law enforcement personnel while in the performance of their duties, or persons using a snowmobile trail located on or along a railroad right-of-way, or an at-grade snowmobile trail crossing of a railroad right-of-way, that has been expressly approved in writing by the owner of the right-of-way and each railroad company using the tracks and that meets the conditions imposed in subsections (4) and (5). A snowmobile trail or an at-grade snowmobile trail crossing shall not be constructed on a right-of-way designated by the federal government as a high-speed rail corridor.

(2) Except as provided under subsection (3), a person shall not operate a snowmobile unless the snowmobile is equipped with a muffler in good working order and in constant operation from which noise emission does not exceed either of the following:

(a) For a snowmobile manufactured after July 1, 1977 and sold or offered for sale in this state, 78 decibels at 50 feet, as measured using the 2003 society of automotive engineers standard J192.

(b) For a stationary snowmobile manufactured after July 1, 1980 and sold or offered for sale in this state, 88 decibels, as measured using the 2004 society of automotive engineers standard J2567.

(3) A person is exempt from the requirement of subsection (2) under either of the following circumstances:

(a) While operating a snowmobile during an organized race on a course that is used solely for racing.

(b) While operating a snowmobile on private property, with the permission of the private property owner, in preparation for an organized race, if the operation of the snowmobile is in compliance with applicable local noise ordinances.

(4) A snowmobile trail located on or along a railroad right-of-way shall be constructed, operated, and maintained by a person other than the person owning the railroad right-of-way and the person operating the railroad, except that an at-grade snowmobile trail crossing of a railroad right-of-way shall be constructed and maintained by the person operating the railroad at the sole cost and expense of the person operating the trail connected by the crossing, pursuant to terms of a lease agreement under which the person operating the trail agrees to do all of the following:

(a) Indemnify the person owning the railroad right-of-way and the person operating the railroad against any claims associated with, arising from, or incidental to the construction, maintenance, operation, and use of the trail or at-grade snowmobile trail crossing.

(b) Provide liability insurance in the amount of $2,000,000.00 naming the person owning the railroad right-of-way and the person operating the railroad as named insureds.

(c) Meet any other obligations or provisions considered appropriate by the person owning the railroad right-of-way or the person operating the railroad including, but not limited to, the payment of rent that the person owning the railroad right-of-way or the person operating the railroad is authorized to charge under this part and the meeting of all construction, operating, and maintenance conditions imposed by the person owning the railroad right-of-way and the person operating the railroad regarding the snowmobile trail.

(5) A snowmobile trail shall be clearly demarcated by signing constructed and maintained at the sole cost and expense of the grant program sponsor. The signing shall be placed at the outer edge of the railroad right-of-way, as far from the edge of the railroad tracks as possible, and not closer than 20 feet from the edge of the railroad tracks unless topography or other natural or manmade features require the trail to lie within 20 feet of the edge of the railroad tracks. The at-grade snowmobile trail crossing of a railroad right-of-way shall be aligned at 90 degrees or as close to 90 degrees as possible to the railroad track being crossed, and shall be located where approach grades to the crossing are minimal and where the vision of a person operating a snowmobile will be unobstructed as he or she approaches the railroad tracks. The design of the snowmobile trail, including the location of signing, shall be included upon plan sheets by the person constructing, operating, and maintaining the trail, and shall be approved in writing by the person owning the right-of-way and the person operating the railroad. Signing shall conform to specifications issued by the department to its snowmobile trail grant program sponsors.

(6) Notwithstanding section 82101, as used in this section, "operate" means to cause to function, run, or manage.

(7) A person shall not alter, deface, damage, or remove a snowmobile trail sign or control device.

(8) Each person who participates in the sport of snowmobiling accepts the risks associated with that sport insofar as the dangers are obvious and inherent. Those risks include, but are not limited to, injuries to persons or property that can result from variations in terrain; surface or subsurface snow or ice conditions; bare spots; rocks, trees, and other forms of natural growth or debris; and collisions with signs, fences, or other snowmobiles or snow-grooming equipment. Those risks do not include injuries to persons or property that can result from the use of a snowmobile by another person in a careless or negligent manner likely to endanger person or property. When a snowmobile is operated in the vicinity of a railroad right-of-way, each person who participates in the sport of snowmobiling additionally assumes risks including, but not limited to, entanglement with tracks, switches, and ties and collisions with trains and other equipment and facilities.

(9) A person who violates subsection (2) is responsible for a state civil infraction and shall be ordered to pay a civil fine of not less than $100.00 or more than $250.00.

History: Add. 1995, Act 58, Imd. Eff. May 24, 1995;—Am. 1995, Act 201, Imd. Eff. Nov. 29, 1995;—Am. 1996, Act 500, Imd. Eff. Jan. 9, 1997;—Am. 1998, Act 30, Imd. Eff. Mar. 18, 1998;—Am. 2003, Act 2, Imd. Eff. Apr. 22, 2003;—Am. 2008, Act 27, Imd. Eff. Mar. 13, 2008;—Am. 2008, Act 399, Imd. Eff. Jan. 6, 2009.

Popular name: Act 451

Popular name: NREPA

Popular name: Snowmobiles

SUBCHAPTER 7
FOREST RECREATION

PART 831
STATE FOREST RECREATION

324.83105 Forest recreation activities; volunteers.

Sec. 83105. (1) The department may appoint persons to function as volunteers for the purpose of facilitating forest recreation activities. While a volunteer is serving in such a capacity, the volunteer has the same immunity from civil liability as a department employee and shall be treated in the same manner as an employee under section 8 of 1964 PA 170, MCL 691.1408.

(2) A volunteer under subsection (1) shall not carry a firearm when functioning as a volunteer.

History: Add. 1998, Act 418, Imd. Eff. Dec. 29, 1998.

Popular name: Act 451

Popular name: NREPA

MENTAL HEALTH CODE (EXCERPT)
Act 258 of 1974

AN ACT to codify, revise, consolidate, and classify the laws relating to mental health; to prescribe the powers and duties of certain state and local agencies and officials and certain private agencies and individuals; to regulate certain agencies and facilities providing mental health or substance use disorder services; to provide for certain charges and fees; to establish civil admission procedures for individuals with mental illness, substance use disorder, or developmental disability; to establish guardianship procedures for individuals with developmental disability; to establish procedures regarding individuals with mental illness, substance use disorder, or developmental disability who are in the criminal justice system; to provide for penalties and remedies; and to repeal acts and parts of acts.

History: 1974, Act 258, Eff. Aug. 6, 1975;—Am. 1980, Act 423, Eff. Mar. 31, 1981;—Am. 1990, Act 263, Imd. Eff. Oct. 15, 1990;—Am. 1995, Act 290, Eff. Mar. 28, 1996;—Am. 2014, Act 200, Imd. Eff. June 24, 2014.

The People of the State of Michigan enact:

CHAPTER 1
DEPARTMENT OF MENTAL HEALTH

330.1134a Employing, contracting, or granting clinical privileges to individuals; prohibitions; written consent; criminal history check; conditional employment or granting clinical privileges; false information; use of information obtained under subsection (3) or (4); condition of continued employment; failure to conduct criminal history check; establishment of automated fingerprint identification system database; electronic web-based system; definitions.

Sec. 134a. (1) Except as otherwise provided in subsection (2), a psychiatric facility or other facility defined in 42 USC 1396d(d) shall not employ, independently contract with, or grant clinical privileges to an individual who regularly has direct access to or provides direct services to patients or residents in the psychiatric facility or other facility defined in 42 USC 1396d(d) if the individual satisfies 1 or more of the following:

(a) Has been convicted of a relevant crime described under 42 USC 1320a-7(a).

(b) Has been convicted of any of the following felonies, an attempt or conspiracy to commit any of those felonies, or any other state or federal crime that is similar to the felonies described in this subdivision, other than a felony for a relevant crime described under 42 USC 1320a-7(a), unless 15 years have lapsed since the individual completed all of the terms and conditions of his or her sentencing, parole, and probation for that conviction prior to the date of application for employment or clinical privileges or the date of the execution of the independent contract:

(*i*) A felony that involves the intent to cause death or serious impairment of a body function, that results in death or serious impairment of a body function, that involves the use of force or violence, or that involves the threat of the use of force or violence.

(*ii*) A felony involving cruelty or torture.

(*iii*) A felony under chapter XXA of the Michigan penal code, 1931 PA 328, MCL 750.145m to 750.145r.

(*iv*) A felony involving criminal sexual conduct.

(*v*) A felony involving abuse or neglect.

(*vi*) A felony involving the use of a firearm or dangerous weapon.

(*vii*) A felony involving the diversion or adulteration of a prescription drug or other medications.

(c) Has been convicted of a felony or an attempt or conspiracy to commit a felony, other than a felony for a relevant crime described under 42 USC 1320a-7(a) or a felony described under subdivision (b), unless 10 years have lapsed since the individual completed all of the terms and conditions of his or her sentencing, parole, and probation for that conviction prior to the date of application for employment or clinical privileges or the date of the execution of the independent contract.

(d) Has been convicted of any of the following misdemeanors, other than a misdemeanor for a relevant crime described under 42 USC 1320a-7(a), or a state or federal crime that is substantially similar to the misdemeanors described in this subdivision, within the 10 years immediately preceding the date of application for employment or clinical privileges or the date of the execution of the independent contract:

(*i*) A misdemeanor involving the use of a firearm or dangerous weapon with the intent to injure, the use of a firearm or dangerous weapon that results in a personal injury, or a misdemeanor involving the use of force or violence or the threat of the use of force or violence.

(*ii*) A misdemeanor under chapter XXA of the Michigan penal code, 1931 PA 328, MCL 750.145m to 750.145r.

(*iii*) A misdemeanor involving criminal sexual conduct.

(*iv*) A misdemeanor involving cruelty or torture unless otherwise provided under subdivision (e).

(*v*) A misdemeanor involving abuse or neglect.

(e) Has been convicted of any of the following misdemeanors, other than a misdemeanor for a relevant crime described under 42 USC 1320a-7(a), or a state or federal crime that is substantially similar to the misdemeanors described in this subdivision, within the 5 years immediately preceding the date of application for employment or clinical privileges or the date of the execution of the independent contract:

(*i*) A misdemeanor involving cruelty if committed by an individual who is less than 16 years of age.

(*ii*) A misdemeanor involving home invasion.

(*iii*) A misdemeanor involving embezzlement.

(*iv*) A misdemeanor involving negligent homicide or a violation of section 601d(1) of the Michigan vehicle code, 1940 PA 300, MCL 257.601d.

(*v*) A misdemeanor involving larceny unless otherwise provided under subdivision (g).

(*vi*) A misdemeanor of retail fraud in the second degree unless otherwise provided under subdivision (g).

(*vii*) Any other misdemeanor involving assault, fraud, theft, or the possession or delivery of a controlled substance unless otherwise provided under subdivision (d), (f), or (g).

(f) Has been convicted of any of the following misdemeanors, other than a misdemeanor for a relevant crime described under 42 USC 1320a-7(a), or a state or federal crime that is substantially similar to the misdemeanors described in this subdivision, within the 3 years immediately preceding the date of application for employment or clinical privileges or the date of the execution of the independent contract:

(*i*) A misdemeanor for assault if there was no use of a firearm or dangerous weapon and no intent to commit murder or inflict great bodily injury.

(*ii*) A misdemeanor of retail fraud in the third degree unless otherwise provided under subdivision (g).

(*iii*) A misdemeanor under part 74 of the public health code, 1978 PA 368, MCL 333.7401 to 333.7461, unless otherwise provided under subdivision (g).

(g) Has been convicted of any of the following misdemeanors, other than a misdemeanor for a relevant crime described under 42 USC 1320a-7(a), or a state or federal crime that is substantially similar to the misdemeanors described in this subdivision, within the year immediately preceding the date of application for employment or clinical privileges or the date of the execution of the independent contract:

(*i*) A misdemeanor under part 74 of the public health code, 1978 PA 368, MCL 333.7401 to 333.7461, if the individual, at the time of conviction, is under the age of 18.

(*ii*) A misdemeanor for larceny or retail fraud in the second or third degree if the individual, at the time of conviction, is under the age of 16.

(h) Is the subject of an order or disposition under section 16b of chapter IX of the code of criminal procedure, 1927 PA 175, MCL 769.16b.

(i) Engages in conduct that becomes the subject of a substantiated finding of neglect, abuse, or misappropriation of property by a state or federal agency according to an investigation conducted in accordance with 42 USC 1395i-3 or 1396r.

(2) Except as otherwise provided in this subsection or subsection (5), a psychiatric facility or other facility defined in 42 USC 1396d(d) shall not employ, independently contract with, or grant privileges to an individual who regularly has direct access to or provides direct services to patients or residents in the psychiatric facility or other facility defined in 42 USC 1396d(d) until the psychiatric facility or other facility defined in 42 USC 1396d(d) or staffing agency has conducted a criminal history check in compliance with this section or received criminal history record information in compliance with subsection (3) or (10). This subsection and subsection (1) do not apply to any of the following:

(a) An individual who is employed by, under independent contract to, or granted clinical privileges in a psychiatric facility or other facility defined in 42 USC 1396d(d) before April 1, 2006. On or before April 1, 2011, an individual who is exempt under this subdivision and who has not been the subject of a criminal history check conducted in compliance with this section shall provide the department of state police with a set of fingerprints and the department of state police shall input those fingerprints into the automated fingerprint identification system database established under subsection (13). An individual who is exempt under this subdivision is not limited to working within the psychiatric facility or other facility defined in 42 USC 1396d(d) with which he or she is employed by, under independent contract to, or granted clinical privileges on April 1, 2006 but may transfer to another psychiatric facility or other facility defined in 42 USC 1396d(d), covered health facility, or adult foster care facility. If an individual who is exempt under this subdivision is subsequently convicted of a crime described under subsection (1)(a) through (g) or found to be the subject of a substantiated finding described under subsection (1)(i) or an order or disposition described under subsection (1)(h), or is found to have been convicted of a relevant crime described under subsection (1)(a), then he or she is no longer exempt and shall be terminated from employment or denied employment or clinical privileges.

(b) An individual who is under an independent contract with a psychiatric facility or other facility defined in 42 USC 1396d(d) if he or she is not under the facility's control and the services for which he or she is contracted is not directly related to the provision of services to a patient or resident or if the services for which he or she is contracted allows for direct access to the patients or residents but is not performed on an ongoing basis. This exception includes, but is not limited to, an individual who is under an independent contract with the psychiatric facility or other facility defined in 42 USC 1396d(d) to provide utility, maintenance, construction, or communications services.

(3) An individual who applies for employment either as an employee or as an independent contractor or for clinical privileges with a psychiatric facility or other facility defined in 42 USC 1396d(d) or a staffing agency and who has not been the subject of a criminal history check conducted in compliance with this section shall give written consent at the time of application for the department of state police to conduct a criminal history check under this section, along with identification acceptable to the

department of state police. If the applicant has been the subject of a criminal history check conducted in compliance with this section, the applicant shall give written consent at the time of application for the psychiatric facility or other facility defined in 42 USC 1396d(d) or staffing agency to obtain the criminal history record information as prescribed in subsection (4) from the relevant licensing or regulatory department and for the department of state police to conduct a criminal history check under this section if the requirements of subsection (10) are not met and a request to the federal bureau of investigation to make a determination of the existence of any national criminal history pertaining to the applicant is necessary, along with identification acceptable to the department of state police. Upon receipt of the written consent to obtain the criminal history record information and identification required under this subsection, the psychiatric facility or other facility defined in 42 USC 1396d(d) or staffing agency that has made a good-faith offer of employment or an independent contract or clinical privileges to the applicant shall request the criminal history record information from the relevant licensing or regulatory department and shall make a request regarding that applicant to the relevant licensing or regulatory department to conduct a check of all relevant registries in the manner required in subsection (4). If the requirements of subsection (10) are not met and a request to the federal bureau of investigation to make a subsequent determination of the existence of any national criminal history pertaining to the applicant is necessary, the psychiatric facility or other facility defined in 42 USC 1396d(d) or staffing agency shall proceed in the manner required in subsection (4). A staffing agency that employs an applicant who regularly has direct access to or provides direct services to patients or residents under an independent contract with a psychiatric facility or other facility defined in 42 USC 1396d(d) shall submit information regarding the criminal history check conducted by the staffing agency to the psychiatric facility or other facility defined in 42 USC 1396d(d) that has made a good-faith offer of independent contract to that applicant.

(4) Upon receipt of the written consent to conduct a criminal history check and identification required under subsection (3), a psychiatric facility or other facility defined in 42 USC 1396d(d) or staffing agency that has made a good-faith offer of employment or an independent contract or clinical privileges to the applicant shall make a request to the department of state police to conduct a criminal history check on the applicant, to input the applicant's fingerprints into the automated fingerprint identification system database, and to forward the applicant's fingerprints to the federal bureau of investigation. The department of state police shall request the federal bureau of investigation to make a determination of the existence of any national criminal history pertaining to the applicant. The applicant shall provide the department of state police with a set of fingerprints. The request shall be made in a manner prescribed by the department of state police. The psychiatric facility or other facility defined in 42 USC 1396d(d) or staffing agency shall make the written consent and identification available to the department of state police. The psychiatric facility or other facility defined in 42 USC 1396d(d) or staffing agency shall make a request regarding that applicant to the relevant licensing or regulatory department to conduct a check of all relevant registries established under federal and state law and regulations for any substantiated findings of abuse, neglect, or misappropriation of property. If the department of state police or the federal bureau of investigation charges a fee for conducting the criminal history check, the psychiatric facility or other facility defined in 42 USC 1396d(d) or staffing agency shall pay the cost of the charge. The psychiatric facility or other facility defined in 42 USC 1396d(d) or staffing agency shall not seek reimbursement for a charge imposed by the department of state police or the federal bureau of investigation from the individual who is the subject of the criminal history check. A prospective employee or a prospective independent contractor covered under this section may not be charged for the cost of a criminal history check required under this section. The department of state police shall conduct a criminal history check on the applicant named in the request. The department of state police shall provide the department with a written report of the criminal history check conducted under this subsection. The report shall contain any criminal history record information on the applicant maintained by the department of state police. The department of state police shall provide the results of the federal bureau of investigation determination to the department within 30 days after the request is made. If the requesting psychiatric facility or other facility defined in 42 USC 1396d(d) or staffing agency is not a state department or agency and if criminal history record information is disclosed on the written report of the criminal history check or the federal bureau of investigation determination that resulted in a conviction, the department shall notify the psychiatric facility or other facility defined in 42 USC 1396d(d) or staffing agency and the applicant in writing of the type of crime disclosed on the written report of the criminal history check or the federal bureau of investigation determination without disclosing the details of the crime. Any charges imposed by the department of state police or the federal bureau of investigation for conducting a criminal history check or making a determination under this subsection shall be paid in the manner required under this subsection. The notice shall include a statement that the applicant has a right to appeal the information relied upon by the psychiatric facility or other facility defined in 42 USC 1396d(d) or staffing agency regarding his or her employment eligibility based on the criminal history check. The notice shall also include information regarding where to file and describing the appellate procedures established under section 20173b of the public health code, 1978 PA 368, MCL 333.20173b.

(5) If a psychiatric facility or other facility defined in 42 USC 1396d(d) determines it necessary to employ or grant clinical privileges to an applicant before receiving the results of the applicant's criminal history check or criminal history record information under this section, the psychiatric facility or other facility defined in 42 USC 1396d(d) may conditionally employ or grant conditional clinical privileges to the individual if all of the following apply:

(a) The psychiatric facility or other facility defined in 42 USC 1396d(d) requests the criminal history check or criminal history record information under this section upon conditionally employing or conditionally granting clinical privileges to the individual.

(b) The individual signs a statement in writing that indicates all of the following:

(*i*) That he or she has not been convicted of 1 or more of the crimes that are described in subsection (1)(a) through (g) within the applicable time period prescribed by each subdivision respectively.

(*ii*) That he or she is not the subject of an order or disposition described in subsection (1)(h).

(*iii*) That he or she has not been the subject of a substantiated finding as described in subsection (1)(i).

(*iv*) The individual agrees that, if the information in the criminal history check conducted under this section does not confirm the individual's statements under subparagraphs (*i*) through (*iii*), his or her employment or clinical privileges will be terminated by the psychiatric facility or other facility defined in 42 USC 1396d(d) as required under subsection (1) unless and until the individual appeals and can prove that the information is incorrect.

(*v*) That he or she understands the conditions described in subparagraphs (*i*) through (*iv*) that result in the termination of his or her employment or clinical privileges and that those conditions are good cause for termination.

(c) Except as otherwise provided in this subdivision, the psychiatric facility or other facility defined in 42 USC 1396d(d) does not permit the individual to have regular direct access to or provide direct services to patients or residents in the psychiatric facility or other facility defined in 42 USC 1396d(d) without supervision until the criminal history check or criminal history record information is obtained and the individual is eligible for that employment or clinical privileges. If required under this subdivision, the psychiatric facility or other facility defined in 42 USC 1396d(d) shall provide on-site supervision of an individual in the facility on a conditional basis under this subsection by an individual who has undergone a criminal history check conducted in compliance with this section. A psychiatric facility or other facility defined in 42 USC 1396d(d) may permit an individual in the facility on a conditional basis under this subsection to have regular direct access to or provide direct services to patients or residents in the psychiatric facility or other facility defined in 42 USC 1396d(d) without supervision if all of the following conditions are met:

(*i*) The psychiatric facility or other facility defined in 42 USC 1396d(d), at its own expense and before the individual has direct access to or provides direct services to patients or residents of the psychiatric facility or other facility defined in 42 USC 1396d(d), conducts a search of public records on that individual through the internet criminal history access tool maintained by the department of state police and the results of that search do not uncover any information that would indicate that the individual is not eligible to have regular direct access to or provide direct services to patients or residents under this section.

(*ii*) Before the individual has direct access to or provides direct services to patients or residents of the psychiatric facility or other facility defined in 42 USC 1396d(d), the individual signs a statement in writing that he or she has resided in this state without interruption for at least the immediately preceding 12-month period.

(*iii*) If applicable, the individual provides to the department of state police a set of fingerprints on or before the expiration of 10 business days following the date the individual was conditionally employed or granted conditional clinical privileges under this subsection.

(6) The department shall develop and distribute a model form for the statements required under subsection (5)(b) and (c). The department shall make the model form available to psychiatric facilities or other facility defined in 42 USC 1396d(d) subject to this section upon request at no charge.

(7) If an individual is employed as a conditional employee or is granted conditional clinical privileges under subsection (5), and the information under subsection (3) or report under subsection (4) does not confirm the individual's statement under subsection (5)(b)(*i*) through (*iii*), the psychiatric facility or other facility defined in 42 USC 1396d(d) shall terminate the individual's employment or clinical privileges as required by subsection (1).

(8) An individual who knowingly provides false information regarding his or her identity, criminal convictions, or substantiated findings on a statement described in subsection (5)(b)(*i*) through (*iii*) is guilty of a misdemeanor punishable by imprisonment for not more than 93 days or a fine of not more than $500.00, or both.

(9) A psychiatric facility or other facility defined in 42 USC 1396d(d) or staffing agency shall use criminal history record information obtained under subsection (3) or (4) only for the purpose of evaluating an applicant's qualifications for employment, an independent contract, or clinical privileges in the position for which he or she has applied and for the purposes of subsections (5) and (7). A psychiatric facility or other facility defined in 42 USC 1396d(d) or staffing agency or an employee of the psychiatric facility or other facility defined in 42 USC 1396d(d) or staffing agency shall not disclose criminal history record information obtained under subsection (3) or (4) to a person who is not directly involved in evaluating the applicant's qualifications for employment, an independent contract, or clinical privileges. An individual who knowingly uses or disseminates the criminal history record information obtained under subsection (3) or (4) in violation of this subsection is guilty of a misdemeanor punishable by imprisonment for not more than 93 days or a fine of not more than $1,000.00, or both. Except for a knowing or intentional release of false information, a psychiatric facility or other facility defined in 42 USC 1396d(d) or staffing agency has no liability in connection with a criminal history check conducted in compliance with this section or the release of criminal history record information under this subsection.

(10) Upon consent of an applicant as required in subsection (3) and upon request from a psychiatric facility or other facility defined in 42 USC 1396d(d) or staffing agency that has made a good-faith offer of employment or an independent contract or clinical privileges to the applicant, the relevant licensing or regulatory department shall review the criminal history record information, if any, and notify the requesting psychiatric facility or other facility defined in 42 USC 1396d(d) or staffing agency of the information in the manner prescribed in subsection (4). Until the federal bureau of investigation implements an automatic notification system similar to the system required of the state police under subsection (13) and federal regulations allow the federal criminal record to be used for subsequent authorized uses, as determined in an order issued by the department, a covered health or staffing agency facility may rely on the criminal history record information provided by the relevant licensing

or regulatory department under this subsection and a request to the federal bureau of investigation to make a subsequent determination of the existence of any national criminal history pertaining to the applicant is not necessary if all of the following requirements are met:

(a) The criminal history check was conducted during the immediately preceding 12-month period.

(b) The applicant has been continuously employed by a psychiatric facility or other facility defined in 42 USC 1396d(d), covered health facility, or adult foster care facility or the staffing agency since the criminal history check was conducted in compliance with this section or meets the continuous employment requirement of this subdivision other than being on layoff status for less than 1 year from a psychiatric facility or other facility defined in 42 USC 1396d(d), covered health facility, or adult foster care facility.

(c) The applicant can provide evidence acceptable to the relevant licensing or regulatory department that he or she has been a resident of this state for the immediately preceding 12-month period.

(11) As a condition of continued employment, each employee, independent contractor, or individual granted clinical privileges shall do each of the following:

(a) Agree in writing to report to the psychiatric facility or other facility defined in 42 USC 1396d(d) or staffing agency immediately upon being arraigned for 1 or more of the criminal offenses listed in subsection (1)(a) through (g), upon being convicted of 1 or more of the criminal offenses listed in subsection (1)(a) through (g), upon becoming the subject of an order or disposition described under subsection (1)(h), and upon being the subject of a substantiated finding of neglect, abuse, or misappropriation of property as described in subsection (1)(i). Reporting of an arraignment under this subdivision is not cause for termination or denial of employment.

(b) If a set of fingerprints is not already on file with the department of state police, provide the department of state police with a set of fingerprints.

(12) In addition to sanctions set forth in this act, a licensee, owner, administrator, or operator of a psychiatric facility or other facility defined in 42 USC 1396d(d) or staffing agency who knowingly and willfully fails to conduct the criminal history checks as required under this section is guilty of a misdemeanor punishable by imprisonment for not more than 1 year or a fine of not more than $5,000.00, or both.

(13) In collaboration with the department of state police, the department of technology, management, and budget shall establish and maintain an automated fingerprint identification system database that would allow the department of state police to store and maintain all fingerprints submitted under this section and would provide for an automatic notification if and when a subsequent criminal arrest fingerprint card submitted into the system matches a set of fingerprints previously submitted under this section. Upon notification, the department of state police shall immediately notify the department and the department shall immediately contact each respective psychiatric facility or other facility defined in 42 USC 1396d(d) or staffing agency with which that individual is associated. Information in the database established under this subsection is confidential, is not subject to disclosure under the freedom of information act, 1976 PA 442, MCL 15.231 to 15.246, and shall not be disclosed to any person except for purposes of this act or for law enforcement purposes.

(14) The department shall maintain an electronic web-based system to assist psychiatric facilities or other facility defined in 42 USC 1396d(d) and staffing agencies required to check relevant registries and conduct criminal history checks of its employees and independent contractors, and individuals granted privileges and to provide for an automated notice to those psychiatric facilities or other facility defined in 42 USC 1396d(d) and staffing agencies for those individuals inputted in the system who, since the initial criminal history check, have been convicted of a disqualifying offense or have been the subject of a substantiated finding of abuse, neglect, or misappropriation of property. The department may charge a staffing agency a 1-time set-up fee of up to $100.00 for access to the electronic web-based system under this section.

(15) As used in this section:

(a) "Adult foster care facility" means an adult foster care facility licensed under the adult foster care facility licensing act, 1979 PA 218, MCL 400.701 to 400.737.

(b) "Convicted" means either of the following:

(*i*) For a crime that is not a relevant crime, a final conviction, the payment of a fine, a plea of guilty or nolo contendere if accepted by the court, or a finding of guilt for a criminal law violation or a juvenile adjudication or disposition by the juvenile division of probate court or family division of circuit court for a violation that if committed by an adult would be a crime.

(*ii*) For a relevant crime described under 42 USC 1320a-7(a), convicted means that term as defined in 42 USC 1320a-7.

(c) "Covered health facility" means a nursing home, county medical care facility, hospice, hospital that provides swing bed services, or home for the aged licensed under article 17 of the public health code, 1978 PA 368, MCL 333.20101 to 333.22260, or home health agency.

(d) "Criminal history check conducted in compliance with this section" includes a criminal history check conducted under this section, under section 20173a of the public health code, 1978 PA 3658, MCL 333.20173a, or under section 34b of the adult foster care facility licensing act, 1979 PA 218, MCL 400.734b.

(e) "Direct access" means access to a patient or resident or to a patient's or resident's property, financial information, medical records, treatment information, or any other identifying information.

(f) "Home health agency" means a person certified by medicare whose business is to provide to individuals in their places of residence other than in a hospital, nursing home, or county medical care facility 1 or more of the following services: nursing services, therapeutic services, social work services, homemaker services, home health aide services, or other related services.

(g) "Independent contract" means a contract entered into by a health facility or agency with an individual who provides the contracted services independently or a contract entered into by a health facility or agency with a staffing agency that complies with the requirements of this section to provide the contracted services to the psychiatric facility or other facility defined in 42 USC 1396d(d) on behalf of the staffing agency.

(h) "Medicare" means benefits under the federal medicare program established under title XVIII of the social security act, 42 USC 1395 to 1395kkk-1.

(i) "Staffing agency" means an entity that recruits candidates and provides temporary and permanent qualified staffing for psychiatric facilities or other facility defined in 42 USC 1396d(d), including independent contractors.

(j) "Under the facility's control" means an individual employed by or under independent contract with a psychiatric facility or other facility defined in 42 USC 1396d(d) for whom the psychiatric facility or other facility defined in 42 USC 1396d(d) does both of the following:

(*i*) Determines whether the individual who has access to patients or residents may provide care, treatment, or other similar support service functions to patients or residents served by the psychiatric facility or other facility defined in 42 USC 1396d(d).

(*ii*) Directs or oversees 1 or more of the following:

(A) The policy or procedures the individual must follow in performing his or her duties.

(B) The tasks performed by the individual.

(C) The individual's work schedule.

(D) The supervision or evaluation of the individual's work or job performance, including imposing discipline or granting performance awards.

(E) The compensation the individual receives for performing his or her duties.

(F) The conditions under which the individual performs his or her duties.

History: Add. 2006, Act 27, Eff. Apr. 1, 2006;—Am. 2008, Act 445, Imd. Eff. Jan. 9, 2009;—Am. 2008, Act 446, Eff. Oct. 31, 2010;—Am. 2010, Act 293, Imd. Eff. Dec. 16, 2010;—Am. 2014, Act 72, Imd. Eff. Mar. 28, 2014.

Compiler's note: Enacting section 1 of Act 27 of 2006 provides:

"Enacting section 1. Section 134a of the mental health code, 1974 PA 258, MCL 330.1134a, as added by this amendatory act, takes effect April 1, 2006, since the department has secured the necessary federal approval to utilize federal funds to reimburse those facilities for the costs incurred for requesting a national criminal history check to be conducted by the federal bureau of investigation and the department has filed written notice of that approval with the secretary of state."

In subsection (15)(d), the citation "1978 PA 3658, MCL 333.20173a" evidently should read "1978 PA 368, MCL 333.20173a".

330.1276 Individual taken into protective custody by peace officer; transporting individual to approved service program or emergency medical service; lawful force; arrest record prohibited; inability to complete transfer to program or service; commission of misdemeanor; emergency treatment.

Sec. 276. (1) An individual who appears to be incapacitated in a public place shall be taken into protective custody by a peace officer and taken to an approved service program or to an emergency medical service, or to a transfer facility according to subsection (4) for subsequent transportation to an approved service program or emergency medical service. Except as otherwise provided in this subsection, if requested by a peace officer, an emergency service unit or staff shall provide transportation for the individual to an approved service program or an emergency medical service. This subsection does not apply to the transportation of an individual by an emergency service unit or staff if the peace officer reasonably believes that the individual will attempt escape or will be unreasonably difficult for staff to control.

(2) A peace officer may take an individual into protective custody with that kind and degree of force that is lawful for the officer to arrest that individual for a misdemeanor without a warrant. In taking the individual, a peace officer may take reasonable steps to protect himself or herself. The protective steps may include a pat-down search of the individual in his or her immediate surroundings, but only to the extent necessary to discover and seize any dangerous weapon that may on that occasion be used against the officer or other individuals present. The peace officer shall take these protective steps before an emergency service unit or staff provides transportation of an individual to an approved service program or emergency medical service.

(3) The taking of an individual to an approved service program, emergency medical service, or transfer facility under subsection (1) is not an arrest, but is a taking into protective custody with or without consent of the individual. The peace officer shall inform the individual that he or she is being held in protective custody and is not under arrest. An entry or other record shall not be made to indicate that the individual was arrested or charged with either a crime or being incapacitated. An entry shall be made indicating the date, time, and place of the taking, but the entry shall not be treated for any purpose as an arrest or criminal record.

(4) An individual taken into protective custody under subsection (1) may be taken to a transfer facility for not more than 8 hours, if an approved service program or an emergency medical service is not located in that county and if, due to distance or other circumstances, a peace officer is unable to complete transport of the individual to an approved service program or emergency medical service. The peace officer or agency shall immediately notify and request the nearest approved service program or emergency medical service to provide an emergency service unit or staff as soon as possible to transport the individual to that approved service program or emergency medical service. If an emergency service unit or staff is not available for transportation, a peace officer may transport the individual to an approved service program or emergency medical service. If an emergency service unit or staff is to provide transportation, the designated representative of the transfer facility shall assume custody of the individual and shall take all reasonable steps to ensure the individual's health and safety until custody is transferred to the emergency service unit or staff of an approved service program or emergency medical service.

(5) An individual arrested by a peace officer for the commission of a misdemeanor punishable by imprisonment for not more than 3 months, or by a fine of not more than $500.00, or both, may be taken to an approved service program or an emergency medical service for emergency treatment if the individual appears to be incapacitated at the time of arrest. This treatment is not in lieu of criminal prosecution of the individual for the offense with which the individual is charged and it does not preclude the administration of any tests as provided for by law.

History: Add. 2012, Act 500, Imd. Eff. Dec. 28, 2012;—Am. 2014, Act 200, Imd. Eff. June 24, 2014.

330.1427a Protective custody; use of force; protective steps; individual not under arrest; entry.

Sec. 427a. (1) If a peace officer is taking an individual into protective custody, the peace officer may use that kind and degree of force that would be lawful if the peace officer were effecting an arrest for a misdemeanor without a warrant. In taking the individual into custody, a peace officer may take reasonable steps for self-protection. The protective steps may include a pat down search of the individual in the individual's immediate surroundings, but only to the extent necessary to discover and seize a dangerous weapon that may be used against the officer or other persons present. These protective steps shall be taken by the peace officer before the individual is transported to a preadmission screening unit or a hospital designated by the community mental health services program.

(2) The taking of an individual to a community mental health services program's preadmission screening unit or a hospital under section 427 is not an arrest, but is a taking into protective custody. The peace officer shall inform the individual that he or she is being held in protective custody and is not under arrest. An entry shall be made indicating the date, time, and place of the taking, but the entry shall not be treated for any purpose as an arrest or criminal record.

History: Add. 1978, Act 598, Imd. Eff. Jan. 4, 1979;—Am. 1995, Act 290, Eff. Mar. 28, 1996.

PUBLIC HEALTH CODE (EXCERPT)
Act 368 of 1978

AN ACT to protect and promote the public health; to codify, revise, consolidate, classify, and add to the laws relating to public health; to provide for the prevention and control of diseases and disabilities; to provide for the classification, administration, regulation, financing, and maintenance of personal, environmental, and other health services and activities; to create or continue, and prescribe the powers and duties of, departments, boards, commissions, councils, committees, task forces, and other agencies; to prescribe the powers and duties of governmental entities and officials; to regulate occupations, facilities, and agencies affecting the public health; to regulate health maintenance organizations and certain third party administrators and insurers; to provide for the imposition of a regulatory fee; to provide for the levy of taxes against certain health facilities or agencies; to promote the efficient and economical delivery of health care services, to provide for the appropriate utilization of health care facilities and services, and to provide for the closure of hospitals or consolidation of hospitals or services; to provide for the collection and use of data and information; to provide for the transfer of property; to provide certain immunity from liability; to regulate and prohibit the sale and offering for sale of drug paraphernalia under certain circumstances; to provide for the implementation of federal law; to provide for penalties and remedies; to provide for sanctions for violations of this act and local ordinances; to provide for an appropriation and supplements; to repeal certain acts and parts of acts; to repeal certain parts of this act; and to repeal certain parts of this act on specific dates.

History: 1978, Act 368, Eff. Sept. 30, 1978;—Am. 1985, Act 198, Eff. Mar. 31, 1986;—Am. 1988, Act 60, Eff. Aug. 1, 1989;—Am. 1988, Act 139, Imd. Eff. June 3, 1988;—Am. 1993, Act 361, Eff. Sept. 1, 1994;—Am. 1994, Act 170, Imd. Eff. June 17, 1994;—Am. 1998, Act 332, Imd. Eff. Aug. 10, 1998;—Am. 2002, Act 303, Imd. Eff. May 10, 2002;—Am. 2003, Act 234, Imd. Eff. Dec. 29, 2003.

Compiler's note: For transfer of the Department of Insurance and Office of the Commissioner on Insurance from the Department of Licensing and Regulation to the Department of Commerce, see E.R.O. No. 1991-9, compiled at MCL 338.3501 of the Michigan Compiled Laws.

For transfer of powers and duties of certain health-related functions, boards, and commissions from the Department of Licensing and Regulation to the Department of Commerce, see E.R.O. No. 1991-9, compiled at MCL 338.3501 of the Michigan Compiled Laws.

For transfer of powers and duties of licensing of substance abuse programs and certification of substance abuse workers in the division of program standards, evaluation, and data services of the center for substance abuse services, from the department of public health to the director of the department of commerce, see E.R.O. No. 1996-1, compiled at MCL 330.3101 of the Michigan Compiled Laws.

Popular name: Act 368

The People of the State of Michigan enact:

ARTICLE 7
CONTROLLED SUBSTANCES

PART 74
OFFENSES AND PENALTIES

333.7401c Manufacture of controlled substance; prohibited acts; violation as felony; exceptions; imposition of consecutive terms; court order to pay response activity costs; definitions.

Sec. 7401c. (1) A person shall not do any of the following:

(a) Own, possess, or use a vehicle, building, structure, place, or area that he or she knows or has reason to know is to be used as a location to manufacture a controlled substance in violation of section 7401 or a counterfeit substance or a controlled substance analogue in violation of section 7402.

(b) Own or possess any chemical or any laboratory equipment that he or she knows or has reason to know is to be used for the purpose of manufacturing a controlled substance in violation of section 7401 or a counterfeit substance or a controlled substance analogue in violation of section 7402.

(c) Provide any chemical or laboratory equipment to another person knowing or having reason to know that the other person intends to use that chemical or laboratory equipment for the purpose of manufacturing a controlled substance in violation of section 7401 or a counterfeit substance or a controlled substance analogue in violation of section 7402.

(2) A person who violates this section is guilty of a felony punishable as follows:

(a) Except as provided in subdivisions (b) to (f), by imprisonment for not more than 10 years or a fine of not more than $100,000.00, or both.

(b) If the violation is committed in the presence of a minor, by imprisonment for not more than 20 years or a fine of not more than $100,000.00, or both.

(c) If the violation involves the unlawful generation, treatment, storage, or disposal of a hazardous waste, by imprisonment for not more than 20 years or a fine of not more than $100,000.00, or both.

(d) If the violation occurs within 500 feet of a residence, business establishment, school property, or church or other house of worship, by imprisonment for not more than 20 years or a fine of not more than $100,000.00, or both.

(e) If the violation involves the possession, placement, or use of a firearm or any other device designed or intended to be used to injure another person, by imprisonment for not more than 25 years or a fine of not more than $100,000.00, or both.

(f) If the violation involves or is intended to involve the manufacture of a substance described in section 7214(c)(*ii*), by imprisonment for not more than 20 years or a fine of not more than $25,000.00, or both.

(3) This section does not apply to a violation involving only a substance described in section 7214(a)(*iv*) or marihuana, or both.

(4) This section does not prohibit the person from being charged with, convicted of, or punished for any other violation of law committed by that person while violating or attempting to violate this section.

(5) A term of imprisonment imposed under this section may be served consecutively to any other term of imprisonment imposed for a violation of law arising out of the same transaction.

(6) The court may, as a condition of sentence, order a person convicted of a violation punishable under subsection (2)(c) to pay response activity costs arising out of the violation.

(7) As used in this section:

(a) "Hazardous waste" means that term as defined in section 11103 of the natural resources and environmental protection act, 1994 PA 451, MCL 324.11103.

(b) "Laboratory equipment" means any equipment, device, or container used or intended to be used in the process of manufacturing a controlled substance, counterfeit substance, or controlled substance analogue.

(c) "Manufacture" means the production, preparation, propagation, compounding, conversion, or processing of a controlled substance, directly or indirectly by extraction from substances of natural origin, or independently by means of chemical synthesis, or by a combination of extraction and chemical synthesis. Manufacture does not include any of the following:

(*i*) The packaging or repackaging of the substance or labeling or relabeling of its container.

(*ii*) The preparation or compounding of a controlled substance by any of the following:

(A) A practitioner as an incident to the practitioner's administering or dispensing of a controlled substance in the course of his or her professional practice.

(B) A practitioner, or by the practitioner's authorized agent under his or her supervision, for the purpose of, or as an incident to, research, teaching, or chemical analysis and not for sale.

(d) "Minor" means an individual less than 18 years of age.

(e) "Response activity costs" means that term as defined in section 20101 of the natural resources and environmental protection act, 1994 PA 451, MCL 324.20101.

(f) "School property" means that term as defined in section 7410.

(g) "Vehicle" means that term as defined in section 79 of the Michigan vehicle code, 1949 PA 300, MCL 257.79.

History: Add. 2000, Act 314, Eff. Jan. 1, 2001;—Am. 2003, Act 310, Eff. Apr. 1, 2004.

Popular name: Act 368

ARTICLE 17

FACILITIES AND AGENCIES

PART 201

GENERAL PROVISIONS

333.20173a Covered facility; employees or applicants for employment; prohibitions; criminal history check; procedure; conditional employment; knowingly providing false information as misdemeanor; prohibited use or dissemination of criminal history information as misdemeanor; review by licensing or regulatory department; conditions of continued employment; failure to conduct criminal history checks as misdemeanor; establishment of automated fingerprint identification system database; electronic web-based system; definitions.

Sec. 20173a. (1) Except as otherwise provided in subsection (2), a covered facility shall not employ, independently contract with, or grant clinical privileges to an individual who regularly has direct access to or provides direct services to patients or residents in the covered facility if the individual satisfies 1 or more of the following:

(a) Has been convicted of a relevant crime described under 42 USC 1320a-7(a).

(b) Has been convicted of any of the following felonies, an attempt or conspiracy to commit any of those felonies, or any other state or federal crime that is similar to the felonies described in this subdivision, other than a felony for a relevant crime described under 42 USC 1320a-7(a), unless 15 years have lapsed since the individual completed all of the terms and conditions of his or her sentencing, parole, and probation for that conviction prior to the date of application for employment or clinical privileges or the date of the execution of the independent contract:

(*i*) A felony that involves the intent to cause death or serious impairment of a body function, that results in death or serious impairment of a body function, that involves the use of force or violence, or that involves the threat of the use of force or violence.

(*ii*) A felony involving cruelty or torture.

(*iii*) A felony under chapter XXA of the Michigan penal code, 1931 PA 328, MCL 750.145m to 750.145r.

(*iv*) A felony involving criminal sexual conduct.

(*v*) A felony involving abuse or neglect.

(*vi*) A felony involving the use of a firearm or dangerous weapon.

(*vii*) A felony involving the diversion or adulteration of a prescription drug or other medications.

(c) Has been convicted of a felony or an attempt or conspiracy to commit a felony, other than a felony for a relevant crime described under 42 USC 1320a-7(a) or a felony described under subdivision (b), unless 10 years have lapsed since the individual completed all of the terms and conditions of his or her sentencing, parole, and probation for that conviction prior to the date of application for employment or clinical privileges or the date of the execution of the independent contract.

(d) Has been convicted of any of the following misdemeanors, other than a misdemeanor for a relevant crime described under 42 USC 1320a-7(a), or a state or federal crime that is substantially similar to the misdemeanors described in this subdivision, within the 10 years immediately preceding the date of application for employment or clinical privileges or the date of the execution of the independent contract:

(*i*) A misdemeanor involving the use of a firearm or dangerous weapon with the intent to injure, the use of a firearm or dangerous weapon that results in a personal injury, or a misdemeanor involving the use of force or violence or the threat of the use of force or violence.

(*ii*) A misdemeanor under chapter XXA of the Michigan penal code, 1931 PA 328, MCL 750.145m to 750.145r.

(*iii*) A misdemeanor involving criminal sexual conduct.

(*iv*) A misdemeanor involving cruelty or torture unless otherwise provided under subdivision (e).

(*v*) A misdemeanor involving abuse or neglect.

(e) Has been convicted of any of the following misdemeanors, other than a misdemeanor for a relevant crime described under 42 USC 1320a-7(a), or a state or federal crime that is substantially similar to the misdemeanors described in this subdivision, within the 5 years immediately preceding the date of application for employment or clinical privileges or the date of the execution of the independent contract.

(*i*) A misdemeanor involving cruelty if committed by an individual who is less than 16 years of age

(*ii*) A misdemeanor involving home invasion.

(*iii*) A misdemeanor involving embezzlement.

(*iv*) A misdemeanor involving negligent homicide or a violation of section 601d(1) of the Michigan vehicle code, 1949 PA 300, MCL 257.601d.

(*v*) A misdemeanor involving larceny unless otherwise provided under subdivision (g).

(*vi*) A misdemeanor of retail fraud in the second degree unless otherwise provided under subdivision (g).

(*vii*) Any other misdemeanor involving assault, fraud, theft, or the possession or delivery of a controlled substance unless otherwise provided under subdivision (d), (f), or (g).

(f) Has been convicted of any of the following misdemeanors, other than a misdemeanor for a relevant crime described under 42 USC 1320a-7(a), or a state or federal crime that is substantially similar to the misdemeanors described in this subdivision, within the 3 years immediately preceding the date of application for employment or clinical privileges or the date of the execution of the independent contract:

(*i*) A misdemeanor for assault if there was no use of a firearm or dangerous weapon and no intent to commit murder or inflict great bodily injury.

(*ii*) A misdemeanor of retail fraud in the third degree unless otherwise provided under subdivision (g).

(*iii*) A misdemeanor under part 74 unless otherwise provided under subdivision (g).

(g) Has been convicted of any of the following misdemeanors, other than a misdemeanor for a relevant crime described under 42 USC 1320a-7(a), or a state or federal crime that is substantially similar to the misdemeanors described in this subdivision, within the year immediately preceding the date of application for employment or clinical privileges or the date of the execution of the independent contract:

(*i*) A misdemeanor under part 74 if the individual, at the time of conviction, is under the age of 18.

(*ii*) A misdemeanor for larceny or retail fraud in the second or third degree if the individual, at the time of conviction, is under the age of 16.

(h) Is the subject of an order or disposition under section 16b of chapter IX of the code of criminal procedure, 1927 PA 175, MCL 769.16b.

(i) Engages in conduct that becomes the subject of a substantiated finding of neglect, abuse, or misappropriation of property by a state or federal agency pursuant to an investigation conducted in accordance with 42 USC 1395i-3 or 1396r.

(2) Except as otherwise provided in this subsection or subsection (5), a covered facility shall not employ, independently contract with, or grant privileges to an individual who regularly has direct access to or provides direct services to patients or residents in the covered facility until the covered facility or staffing agency has a criminal history check conducted in compliance with this section or has received criminal history record information in compliance with subsections (3) and (10). This subsection and subsection (1) do not apply to any of the following:

(a) An individual who is employed by, under independent contract to, or granted clinical privileges in a covered facility before April 1, 2006. On or before April 1, 2011, an individual who is exempt under this subdivision and who has not been the subject of a criminal history check conducted in compliance with this section shall provide the department of state police with a set of fingerprints and the department of state police shall input those fingerprints into the automated fingerprint identification system database established under subsection (13). An individual who is exempt under this subdivision is not limited to working within the covered facility with which he or she is employed by, under independent contract to, or granted clinical privileges on April 1, 2006 but may transfer to another covered facility, adult foster care facility, or mental health facility. If an individual who is exempt under this subdivision is subsequently convicted of a crime described under subsection (1)(a) to (g) or found to be the subject of a substantiated finding described under subsection (1)(i) or an order or disposition described under subsection (1)(h), or is found to have been convicted of a relevant crime described under 42 USC 1320a-7(a), then he or she is no longer exempt and shall be terminated from employment or denied employment or clinical privileges.

(b) An individual who is under an independent contract with a covered facility if he or she is not under the facility's control and the services for which he or she is contracted are not directly related to the provision of services to a patient or resident or if the services for which he or she is contracted allow for direct access to the patients or residents but are not performed on an ongoing basis. This exception includes, but is not limited to, an individual who is under an independent contract with the covered facility to provide utility, maintenance, construction, or communications services.

(3) An individual who applies for employment either as an employee or as an independent contractor or for clinical privileges with a staffing agency or covered facility and who has not been the subject of a criminal history check conducted in compliance with this section shall give written consent at the time of application for the department of state police to conduct a criminal history check under this section, along with identification acceptable to the department of state police. If the applicant has been the subject of a criminal history check conducted in compliance with this section, the applicant shall give written consent at the time of application for the covered facility or staffing agency to obtain the criminal history record information as prescribed in subsection (4) from the relevant licensing or regulatory department and for the department of state police to conduct a criminal history check under this section if the requirements of subsection (10) are not met and a request to the federal bureau of investigation to make a determination of the existence of any national criminal history pertaining to the applicant is necessary, along with identification acceptable to the department of state police. Upon receipt of the written consent to obtain the criminal history record information and identification required under this subsection, the staffing agency or covered facility that has made a good faith offer of employment or an independent contract or clinical privileges to the applicant shall request the criminal history record information from the relevant licensing or regulatory department and shall make a request regarding that applicant to the relevant licensing or regulatory department to conduct a check of all relevant registries in the manner required in subsection (4). If the requirements of subsection (10) are not met and a request to the federal bureau of investigation to make a subsequent determination of the existence of any national criminal history pertaining to the applicant is necessary, the covered facility or staffing agency shall proceed in the manner required in subsection (4). A staffing agency that employs an individual who regularly has direct access to or provides direct services to patients or residents under an independent contract with a covered facility shall submit information regarding the criminal history check conducted by the staffing agency to the covered facility that has made a good faith offer of independent contract to that applicant.

(4) Upon receipt of the written consent to conduct a criminal history check and identification required under subsection (3), a staffing agency or covered facility that has made a good faith offer of employment or an independent contract or clinical privileges to the applicant shall make a request to the department of state police to conduct a criminal history check on the applicant, to input the applicant's fingerprints into the automated fingerprint identification system database, and to forward the applicant's fingerprints to the federal bureau of investigation. The department of state police shall request the federal bureau of investigation to make a determination of the existence of any national criminal history pertaining to the applicant. The applicant shall provide the department of state police with a set of fingerprints. The request shall be made in a manner prescribed by the department of state police. The staffing agency or covered facility shall make the written consent and identification available to the department of state police. The staffing agency or covered facility shall make a request regarding that applicant to the relevant licensing or regulatory department to conduct a check of all relevant registries established pursuant to federal and state law and regulations for any substantiated findings of abuse, neglect, or misappropriation of property. If the department of state police or the federal bureau of investigation charges a fee for conducting the criminal history check, the staffing agency or covered facility shall pay the cost of the charge. If the department of state police or the federal bureau of investigation charges a fee for conducting the criminal history check, the department shall pay the cost of or reimburse the charge for a covered facility that is a home for the aged. The staffing agency or covered facility shall not seek reimbursement for a charge imposed by the department of state police or the federal bureau of investigation from the individual who is the subject of the criminal history check. A prospective employee or a prospective independent contractor covered under this section may not be charged for the cost of a criminal history check required under this section. The department of state police shall conduct a criminal history check on the applicant named in the request. The department of state police shall provide the department with a written report of the criminal history check conducted under this subsection. The report shall contain any criminal history record information on the applicant maintained by the department of state police. The department of state police shall provide the results of the federal bureau of investigation determination to the department within 30 days after the request is made. If the requesting staffing agency or covered facility is not a state department or agency and if criminal history record information is disclosed on the written report of the criminal history check or the federal bureau of investigation determination that resulted in a conviction, the department shall notify the staffing agency or covered facility and the applicant in writing of the type of crime disclosed on the written report of the criminal history check or the federal bureau of investigation determination without disclosing the details of the crime. Any charges imposed by the department of state police or the federal bureau of investigation for conducting a criminal history check or making a determination under this subsection shall be paid in the manner required under this subsection. The notice shall include a statement that the applicant has a right to appeal the information relied upon

by the staffing agency or covered facility in making its decision regarding his or her employment eligibility based on the criminal history check. The notice shall also include information regarding where to file and describing the appellate procedures established under section 20173b.

(5) If a covered facility determines it necessary to employ or grant clinical privileges to an applicant before receiving the results of the applicant's criminal history check or criminal history record information under this section, the covered facility may conditionally employ or grant conditional clinical privileges to the individual if all of the following apply:

(a) The covered facility requests the criminal history check or criminal history record information under this section upon conditionally employing or conditionally granting clinical privileges to the individual.

(b) The individual signs a statement in writing that indicates all of the following:

(*i*) That he or she has not been convicted of 1 or more of the crimes that are described in subsection (1)(a) to (g) within the applicable time period prescribed by each subdivision respectively.

(*ii*) That he or she is not the subject of an order or disposition described in subsection (1)(h).

(*iii*) That he or she has not been the subject of a substantiated finding as described in subsection (1)(i).

(*iv*) That he or she agrees that, if the information in the criminal history check conducted under this section does not confirm the individual's statements under subparagraphs (*i*) to (*iii*), his or her employment or clinical privileges will be terminated by the covered facility as required under subsection (1) unless and until the individual appeals and can prove that the information is incorrect.

(*v*) That he or she understands that the conditions described in subparagraphs (*i*) to (*iv*) may result in the termination of his or her employment or clinical privileges and that those conditions are good cause for termination.

(c) Except as otherwise provided in this subdivision, the covered facility does not permit the individual to have regular direct access to or provide direct services to patients or residents in the covered facility without supervision until the criminal history check or criminal history record information is obtained and the individual is eligible for that employment or clinical privileges. If required under this subdivision, the covered facility shall provide on-site supervision of an individual in the covered facility on a conditional basis under this subsection by an individual who has undergone a criminal history check conducted in compliance with this section. A covered facility may permit an individual in the covered facility on a conditional basis under this subsection to have regular direct access to or provide direct services to patients or residents in the covered facility without supervision if all of the following conditions are met:

(*i*) The covered facility, at its own expense and before the individual has direct access to or provides direct services to patients or residents of the covered facility, conducts a search of public records on that individual through the internet criminal history access tool maintained by the department of state police and the results of that search do not uncover any information that would indicate that the individual is not eligible to have regular direct access to or provide direct services to patients or residents under this section.

(*ii*) Before the individual has direct access to or provides direct services to patients or residents of the covered facility, the individual signs a statement in writing that he or she has resided in this state without interruption for at least the immediately preceding 12-month period.

(*iii*) If applicable, the individual provides to the department of state police a set of fingerprints on or before the expiration of 10 business days following the date the individual was conditionally employed or granted conditional clinical privileges under this subsection.

(6) The department shall develop and distribute a model form for the statements required under subsection (5)(b) and (c). The department shall make the model form available to covered facilities upon request at no charge.

(7) If an individual is employed as a conditional employee or is granted conditional clinical privileges under subsection (5), and the information under subsection (3) or report under subsection (4) does not confirm the individual's statement under subsection (5)(b)(*i*) to (*iii*), the covered facility shall terminate the individual's employment or clinical privileges as required by subsection (1).

(8) An individual who knowingly provides false information regarding his or her identity, criminal convictions, or substantiated findings on a statement described in subsection (5)(b)(*i*) to (*iii*) is guilty of a misdemeanor punishable by imprisonment for not more than 93 days or a fine of not more than $500.00, or both.

(9) A staffing agency or covered facility shall use criminal history record information obtained under subsection (3) or (4) only for the purpose of evaluating an applicant's qualifications for employment, an independent contract, or clinical privileges in the position for which he or she has applied and for the purposes of subsections (5) and (7). A staffing agency or covered facility or an employee of the staffing agency or covered facility shall not disclose criminal history record information obtained under subsection (3) or (4) to a person who is not directly involved in evaluating the applicant's qualifications for employment, an independent contract, or clinical privileges. An individual who knowingly uses or disseminates the criminal history record information obtained under subsection (3) or (4) in violation of this subsection is guilty of a misdemeanor punishable by imprisonment for not more than 93 days or a fine of not more than $1,000.00, or both. Except for a knowing or intentional release of false information, a staffing agency or covered facility has no liability in connection with a criminal history check conducted in compliance with this section or the release of criminal history record information under this subsection.

(10) Upon consent of an applicant as required in subsection (3) and upon request from a staffing agency or covered facility that has made a good faith offer of employment or an independent contract or clinical privileges to the applicant, the relevant licensing or regulatory department shall review the criminal history record information, if any, and notify the requesting staffing

agency or covered facility of the information in the manner prescribed in subsection (4). Until the federal bureau of investigation implements an automatic notification system similar to the system required of the state police under subsection (13) and federal regulations allow the federal criminal record to be used for subsequent authorized uses, as determined in an order issued by the department, a staffing agency or covered facility may rely on the criminal history record information provided by the relevant licensing or regulatory department under this subsection and a request to the federal bureau of investigation to make a subsequent determination of the existence of any national criminal history pertaining to the applicant is not necessary if all of the following requirements are met:

(a) The criminal history check was conducted during the immediately preceding 12-month period.

(b) The applicant has been continuously employed by the staffing agency or a covered facility, adult foster care facility, or mental health facility since the criminal history check was conducted in compliance with this section or meets the continuous employment requirement of this subdivision other than being on layoff status for less than 1 year from a covered facility, adult foster care facility, or mental health facility.

(c) The applicant can provide evidence acceptable to the relevant licensing or regulatory department that he or she has been a resident of this state for the immediately preceding 12-month period.

(11) As a condition of continued employment, each employee, independent contractor, or individual granted clinical privileges shall do each of the following:

(a) Agree in writing to report to the staffing agency or covered facility immediately upon being arraigned for 1 or more of the criminal offenses listed in subsection (1)(a) to (g), upon being convicted of 1 or more of the criminal offenses listed in subsection (1)(a) to (g), upon becoming the subject of an order or disposition described under subsection (1)(h), and upon being the subject of a substantiated finding of neglect, abuse, or misappropriation of property as described in subsection (1)(i). Reporting of an arraignment under this subdivision is not cause for termination or denial of employment.

(b) If a set of fingerprints is not already on file with the department of state police, provide the department of state police with a set of fingerprints.

(12) In addition to sanctions set forth in section 20165, a licensee, owner, administrator, or operator of a staffing agency or covered facility who knowingly and willfully fails to conduct the criminal history checks as required under this section is guilty of a misdemeanor punishable by imprisonment for not more than 1 year or a fine of not more than $5,000.00, or both.

(13) In collaboration with the department of state police, the department of technology, management, and budget shall establish and maintain an automated fingerprint identification system database that would allow the department of state police to store and maintain all fingerprints submitted under this section and would provide for an automatic notification if and when a subsequent criminal arrest fingerprint card submitted into the system matches a set of fingerprints previously submitted under this section. Upon such notification, the department of state police shall immediately notify the department and the department shall immediately contact each respective staffing agency or covered facility with which that individual is associated. Information in the database established under this subsection is confidential, is not subject to disclosure under the freedom of information act, 1976 PA 442, MCL 15.231 to 15.246, and shall not be disclosed to any person except for purposes of this act or for law enforcement purposes.

(14) The department shall maintain an electronic web-based system to assist staffing agencies and covered facilities required to check relevant registries and conduct criminal history checks of its employees, independent contractors, and individuals granted privileges and to provide for an automated notice to those staffing agencies and covered facilities for those individuals inputted in the system who, since the initial criminal history check, have been convicted of a disqualifying offense or have been the subject of a substantiated finding of abuse, neglect, or misappropriation of property. The department may charge a staffing agency a 1-time set-up fee of up to $100.00 for access to the electronic web-based system under this section.

(15) As used in this section:

(a) "Adult foster care facility" means an adult foster care facility licensed under the adult foster care facility licensing act, 1979 PA 218, MCL 400.701 to 400.737.

(b) "Convicted" means either of the following:

(*i*) For a crime that is not a relevant crime, a final conviction, the payment of a fine, a plea of guilty or nolo contendere if accepted by the court, or a finding of guilt for a criminal law violation or a juvenile adjudication or disposition by the juvenile division of probate court or family division of circuit court for a violation that if committed by an adult would be a crime.

(*ii*) For a relevant crime described under 42 USC 1320a-7(a), convicted means that term as defined in 42 USC 1320a-7.

(c) "Covered facility" means a health facility or agency that is a nursing home, county medical care facility, hospice, hospital that provides swing bed services, home for the aged, or home health agency.

(d) "Criminal history check conducted in compliance with this section" includes a criminal history check conducted under this section, under section 134a of the mental health code, 1974 PA 258, MCL 330.1134a, or under section 34b of the adult foster care facility licensing act, 1979 PA 218, MCL 400.734b.

(e) "Direct access" means access to a patient or resident or to a patient's or resident's property, financial information, medical records, treatment information, or any other identifying information.

(f) "Home health agency" means a person certified by medicare whose business is to provide to individuals in their places of residence other than in a hospital, nursing home, or county medical care facility 1 or more of the following services: nursing services, therapeutic services, social work services, homemaker services, home health aide services, or other related services.

(g) "Independent contract" means a contract entered into by a covered facility with an individual who provides the contracted services independently or a contract entered into by a covered facility with a staffing agency that complies with the requirements of this section to provide the contracted services to the covered facility on behalf of the staffing agency.

(h) "Medicare" means benefits under the federal medicare program established under title XVIII of the social security act, 42 USC 1395 to 1395kkk-1.

(i) "Mental health facility" means a psychiatric facility or other facility defined in 42 USC 1396d(d) as described under the mental health code, 1974 PA 258, MCL 330.1001 to 330.2106.

(j) "Staffing agency" means an entity that recruits candidates and provides temporary and permanent qualified staffing for covered facilities, including independent contractors.

(k) "Under the facility's control" means an individual employed by or under independent contract with a covered facility for whom the covered facility does both of the following:

(*i*) Determines whether the individual who has access to patients or residents may provide care, treatment, or other similar support service functions to patients or residents served by the covered facility.

(*ii*) Directs or oversees 1 or more of the following:

(A) The policy or procedures the individual must follow in performing his or her duties.

(B) The tasks performed by the individual.

(C) The individual's work schedule.

(D) The supervision or evaluation of the individual's work or job performance, including imposing discipline or granting performance awards.

(E) The compensation the individual receives for performing his or her duties.

(F) The conditions under which the individual performs his or her duties.

History: Add. 2006, Act 28, Eff. Apr. 1, 2006;—Am. 2008, Act 123, Imd. Eff. May 9, 2008;—Am. 2008, Act 443, Imd. Eff. Jan. 9, 2009;—Am. 2008, Act 444, Eff. Oct. 31, 2010;—Am. 2010, Act 291, Imd. Eff. Dec. 16, 2010;—Am. 2014, Act 66, Imd. Eff. Mar. 28, 2014.

Compiler's note: Enacting section 1 of Act 28 of 2006 provides:

"Enacting section 1. (1) Section 20173 of the public health code, 1978 PA 368, MCL 333.20173, is repealed effective April 1, 2006.

"(2) Section 20173a of the public health code, 1978 PA 368, MCL 333.20173a, as added by this amendatory act, takes effect April 1, 2006, since the department has secured the necessary federal approval to utilize federal funds to reimburse those facilities for the costs incurred for requesting a national criminal history check to be conducted by the federal bureau of investigation and the department has filed written notice of that approval with the secretary of state. The department shall issue a medicaid policy bulletin regarding the payment and reimbursement for the criminal history checks by April 1, 2006.

"(3) Section 20173b of the public health code, 1978 PA 368, MCL 333.20173b, as added by this amendatory act, takes effect the date this amendatory act is enacted."

PROFESSIONAL INVESTIGATOR LICENSURE ACT (EXCERPT)
Act 285 of 1965

AN ACT to license and regulate professional investigators; to provide for certain powers and duties for certain state agencies and local officials; to provide for the imposition for certain fees; to protect the general public against unauthorized, unlicensed and unethical operations by professional investigators; to provide for immunity for certain persons under certain circumstances; to provide for penalties and remedies; and to repeal acts and parts of acts.

History: 1965, Act 285, Imd. Eff. July 22, 1965;—Am. 2002, Act 474, Eff. Oct. 1, 2002;—Am. 2008, Act 146, Imd. Eff. May 28, 2008.

The People of the State of Michigan enact:

338.826 License; qualifications; reciprocal agreements.

Sec. 6. (1) The department shall issue a license to conduct business as a professional investigator if satisfied that the applicant is a person, or if a firm, partnership, company, limited liability company, or corporation, the sole or principal license holder is a person who meets all of the following qualifications:

(a) Is a citizen of the United States.

(b) Is not less than 25 years of age.

(c) Has a high school education or its equivalent.

(d) Has not been convicted of a felony, or a misdemeanor involving any of the following:

(*i*) Dishonesty or fraud.

(*ii*) Unauthorized divulging or selling of information or evidence.

(*iii*) Impersonation of a law enforcement officer or employee of the United States or a state, or a political subdivision of the United States or a state.

(*iv*) Illegally using, carrying, or possessing a dangerous weapon.

(*v*) Two or more alcohol related offenses.

(*vi*) Controlled substances under the public health code, 1978 PA 368, MCL 333.1101 to 333.25211.

(*vii*) An assault.

(e) Has not been dishonorably discharged from a branch of the United States military service.

(f) For a period of not less than 3 years has been or is any of the following on a full-time basis:

(*i*) Lawfully engaged in the professional investigation business as a licensee, registrant, or investigative employee in another state.

(*ii*) Lawfully engaged in the investigation business as an investigative employee of the holder of a license to conduct a professional investigation agency.

(*iii*) An investigator, detective, special agent, intelligence specialist, parole agent, probation officer, or certified police officer employed by any government executive, military, judicial, or legislative agency, or other public authority engaged in investigative or intelligence activities. This subdivision does not include individuals employed by educational or charitable institutions who are solely engaged in academic, consulting, educational, instructional, or research activities. In the case of the experience requirement under this subparagraph for an applicant demonstrating experience as a probation officer or parole agent, the department shall consider any application filed on or after January 1, 2005 for eligibility regarding that experience.

(*iv*) A graduate of an accredited institution of higher education with a baccalaureate or postgraduate degree in the field of police administration, security management, investigation, law, criminal justice, or computer forensics or other computer forensic industry certificated study that is acceptable to the department.

(*v*) Lawfully engaged in the investigation business as a full-time proprietary or in-house investigator employed by a business or attorney, or as an investigative reporter employed by a recognized media outlet, acceptable to the department. This subdivision does not include individuals employed by educational or charitable institutions who are solely engaged in academic, consulting, educational, instructional, or research activities.

(g) Has posted with the department a bond or insurance policy provided for in this act.

(2) In the case of a person, firm, partnership, company, limited liability company, or corporation now doing or seeking to do business in this state, the manager shall comply with the qualifications of this section.

(3) Beginning July 1, 2010, a law enforcement officer, as that term is defined in section 2 of the commission of law enforcement standards act, 1965 PA 203, MCL 28.602, shall not be issued a new or renewal license and shall not be employed and working in an investigative capacity by, or authorized to operate in a capacity as, a professional investigator unless the law enforcement officer obtains and produces, in a manner acceptable to the department, any 1 of the following:

(a) Written permission to act as a professional investigator from the current chief of police, county sheriff, or other official having executive authority and responsibility over the law enforcement matters in that jurisdiction if the law enforcement officer does not work under the authority of a chief of police or county sheriff.

(b) A copy of the law enforcement officer's jurisdiction's published policies and procedures allowing off-duty employment, which policies and procedures include the prohibition of the off-duty use of investigative tools or equipment, or both, provided exclusively for law enforcement and indicate that the off-duty employment as a professional investigator is not considered in conflict with employment as a law enforcement officer.

(c) A copy of the collective bargaining agreement of the law enforcement officer's jurisdiction.

(4) This act does not prevent a licensee from acting as a professional investigator outside of this state to the extent allowed by that other state under the laws of that state.

(5) The department may enter into reciprocal agreements with other states that have professional investigator qualification laws to allow a professional investigator license or registration to be used by that licensee or registrant within the jurisdiction of either this state or another state. The reciprocal agreement shall be limited to only allow professional investigators to continue investigations that originate in the investigator's home state and that require investigation in another state. The department may enter into a reciprocal agreement if the other state meets all of the following conditions:

(a) Issues a professional investigator identification card with an expiration date printed on the card.

(b) Is available to verify the license or registration status for law enforcement purposes.

(c) Has disqualification, suspension, and revocation standards for licenses and registrations.

(d) Requires the applicant for a license or registration as a professional investigator to submit to a criminal history records check pursuant to applicable state and federal law.

(6) Each reciprocal agreement shall, at a minimum, include the following provisions:

(a) A requirement that the professional investigator possess a professional investigator license or registration in good standing from his or her home state.

(b) A requirement that the professional investigator shall be time-limited to a maximum of 30 days per case while conducting an investigation in this state, or a lesser amount of time if required to comply with the reciprocity statutes or regulations of the other state.

(c) A requirement that the professional investigator from the other state not solicit any business in this state while conducting investigations in this state.

History: 1965, Act 285, Imd. Eff. July 22, 1965;—Am. 1967, Act 164, Eff. Nov. 2, 1967;—Am. 1978, Act 311, Imd. Eff. July 10, 1978;—Am. 2002, Act 474, Eff. Oct. 1, 2002;—Am. 2008, Act 146, Imd. Eff. May 28, 2008.

338.830 License; suspension or revocation; grounds; additional sanctions; surrendering license and identification card; noncompliance as misdemeanor.

Sec. 10. (1) The department may suspend or revoke a license issued under this act if the department determines that the licensee or licensee's manager, if an individual, or if the licensee is a person other than an individual, that an officer, director, partner, or its manager, has done any of the following:

(a) Made false statements or given false information in connection with an application for a license or a renewal or reinstatement of a license.

(b) Violated this act or any rule promulgated under this act.

(c) Been convicted of a felony or misdemeanor involving dishonesty or fraud, unauthorized divulging or selling of information or evidence.

(d) Been convicted of impersonation of a law enforcement officer or employee of the United States or a state, or a political subdivision of the United States or a state.

(e) Been convicted of illegally using, carrying, or possessing a dangerous weapon.

(f) In the case of a law enforcement officer issued a license under the conditions contained in section 6(3), violated the policies and procedures governing off-duty employment.

(2) In addition to the suspension or revocation provisions available to the department under subsection (1), the department may do 1 or more of the following regarding a licensee or a licensee's manager, if an individual, or if the licensee is a person other than an individual, an officer, director, partner, member, or its manager, who violates this act or a rule or order promulgated or issued under this act:

(a) Place a limitation on a license.

(b) Deny a renewal of a license.

(c) Issue an order of censure.

(d) Issue an order of probation.

(e) Impose a requirement that restitution be made.

(3) Upon notification from the department of the suspension or revocation of the license, the licensee, within 24 hours, shall surrender to the department the license and his or her identification card. Failure to surrender the license in compliance with this subsection is a misdemeanor.

History: 1965, Act 285, Imd. Eff. July 22, 1965;—Am. 1978, Act 311, Imd. Eff. July 10, 1978;—Am. 2002, Act 474, Eff. Oct. 1, 2002;—Am. 2008, Act 146, Imd. Eff. May 28, 2008.

338.838 Hiring of person convicted of certain felonies or misdemeanors prohibited; refusal to surrender license or identification card.

Sec. 18. (1) A licensee shall not knowingly employ any person who has been convicted of a felony, or convicted of a misdemeanor within the preceding 8 years involving any of the following:

(a) Dishonesty or fraud.

(b) Unauthorized divulging or selling of information or evidence.

(c) Impersonation of a law enforcement officer or employee of the United States, this state, or a political subdivision of this state.

(d) Illegally using, carrying, or possessing a dangerous weapon.

(e) Two or more alcohol related offenses.

(f) Controlled substances under the public health code, 1978 PA 368, MCL 333.1101 to 333.25211.

(g) An assault.

(2) Any employee or operator who, upon demand, fails to surrender to the licensee his or her identification card and any other property issued to him or her for use in connection with his or her employer's business is guilty of a misdemeanor.

History: 1965, Act 285, Imd. Eff. July 22, 1965;—Am. 2002, Act 474, Eff. Oct. 1, 2002.

338.839 Carrying deadly weapon; license required.

Sec. 19. Any person licensed as a professional investigator, or in the employ of a professional investigator agency, is not authorized to carry a deadly weapon unless he is so licensed in accordance with the present laws of this state.

History: 1965, Act 285, Imd. Eff. July 22, 1965;—Am. 2008, Act 146, Imd. Eff. May 28, 2008.

PRIVATE SECURITY BUSINESS AND SECURITY ALARM ACT (EXCERPT)
Act 330 of 1968

AN ACT to license and regulate private security guards, private security police, private security guard agencies, private college security forces, and security alarm systems servicing, installing, operating, and monitoring; to provide penalties for violations; to protect the general public against unauthorized, unlicensed and unethical operations by individuals engaged in private security activity or security alarm systems sales, installations, service, maintenance, and operations; to establish minimum qualifications for individuals as well as private agencies engaged in the security business and security alarm systems and operations; to impose certain fees; to create certain funds; and to prescribe certain powers and duties of certain private colleges and certain state departments, agencies, and officers.

History: 1968, Act 330, Imd. Eff. July 12, 1968;—Am. 1975, Act 190, Imd. Eff. Aug. 5, 1975;—Am. 2000, Act 411, Eff. Mar. 28, 2001;—Am. 2002, Act 473, Eff. Oct. 1, 2002;—Am. 2010, Act 68, Imd. Eff. May 13, 2010.

The People of the State of Michigan enact:

338.1060 License; revocation; grounds; failure to pay fines or fees; surrender of license; misdemeanor.

Sec. 10. (1) The department may revoke any license issued under this act if it determines, upon good cause shown, that the licensee or his or her manager, if the licensee is an individual, or if the licensee is not an individual, that any of its officers, directors, partners or its manager, has done any of the following:

(a) Made any false statements or given any false information in connection with an application for a license or a renewal or reinstatement of a license.

(b) Violated any provision of this act.

(c) Been, while licensed or employed by a licensee, convicted of a felony or a misdemeanor involving any of the following:

(*i*) Dishonesty or fraud.

(*ii*) Unauthorized divulging or selling of information or evidence.

(*iii*) Impersonation of a law enforcement officer or employee of the United States, this state, or a political subdivision of this state.

(*iv*) Illegally using, carrying, or possessing a dangerous weapon.

(*v*) Two or more alcohol related offenses.

(*vi*) Controlled substances under the public health code, 1978 PA 368, MCL 333.1101 to 333.25211.

(*vii*) An assault.

(d) Knowingly submitted any of the following:

(*i*) A name other than the true name of a prospective employee.

(*ii*) Fingerprints not belonging to the prospective employee.

(*iii*) False identifying information in connection with the application of a prospective employee.

(2) The department shall not renew a license of a licensee who owes any fine or fee to the department at the time for a renewal.

(3) Within 48 hours after notification from the department of the revocation of a license under this act, the licensee shall surrender the license and the identification card issued under section 14. A person who violates this subsection is guilty of a misdemeanor punishable by imprisonment for not more than 93 days or a fine of not more than $500.00, or both.

History: 1968, Act 330, Imd. Eff. July 12, 1968;—Am. 1994, Act 326, Eff. Mar. 30, 1995;—Am. 2000, Act 411, Eff. Mar. 28, 2001;—Am. 2002, Act 473, Eff. Oct. 1, 2002.

338.1069 Uniform and insignia; shoulder identification patches or emblems; badge or shield; deadly weapons; tactical baton.

Sec. 19. (1) The particular type of uniform and insignia worn by a licensee or his or her employees must be approved by the department and shall not deceive or confuse the public or be identical with that of a law enforcement officer of the federal government, state, or a political subdivision of the state in the community of the license holder. Shoulder identification patches shall be worn on all uniform jackets, coats, and shirts and shall include the name of the licensee or agency. Shoulder identification patches or emblems shall not be less than 3 inches by 5 inches in size.

(2) A badge or shield shall not be worn or carried by a security alarm system agent, private security police officer, private college security force officer, or an employee or licensee of a security alarm system contractor, private security police organization, private college security force, or private security guard agency, unless approved by the director of the department.

(3) A person who is not employed as a security guard shall not display a badge or shield or wear a uniform of a security guard. A person who violates this subsection is guilty of a misdemeanor punishable by imprisonment for not more than 93 days or a fine of not more than $500.00, or both.

(4) A person licensed as a security alarm system contractor, security alarm system agent, or a private security guard or agency is not authorized to carry a deadly weapon unless he or she is licensed to do so in accordance with the laws of this state.

(5) A licensee may authorize his or her employees to carry any commercially available tactical baton.

History: 1968, Act 330, Imd. Eff. July 12, 1968;—Am. 1975, Act 190, Imd. Eff. Aug. 5, 1975;—Am. 2000, Act 411, Eff. Mar. 28, 2001;—Am. 2002, Act 473, Eff. Oct. 1, 2002;—Am. 2010, Act 68, Imd. Eff. May 13, 2010.

338.1079 Licensure of private security police; rules; applicability of act to private security guards and police; use of pistols.

Sec. 29. (1) The licensure of private security police and private college security forces shall be administered by the department of state police. The application, qualification, and enforcement provisions under this act apply to private security police and private college security forces except that the administration of those provisions shall be performed by, and the payment of the appropriate fees shall be paid to, the department of state police. The director of the department may jointly promulgate rules with the department of state police under the administrative procedures act of 1969, 1969 PA 306, MCL 24.201 to 24.328, to facilitate the bifurcation of authority described in this subsection.

(2) This act does not require licensing of any private security guards employed for the purpose of protecting the property and employees of their employer and generally maintaining security for their employer. However, any person, firm, limited liability company, business organization, educational institution, or corporation maintaining a private security police organization or a private college security force may voluntarily apply for licensure under this act. When a private security police employer or private college security force employer as described in this section provides the employee with a pistol for the purpose of protecting the property of the employer, the pistol shall be considered the property of the employer and the employer shall retain custody of the pistol, except during the actual working hours of the employee. All such private security people shall be subject to the provisions of sections 17(1) and 19(1).

History: 1968, Act 330, Imd. Eff. July 12, 1968;—Am. 1969, Act 168, Imd. Eff. Aug. 5, 1969;—Am. 2000, Act 411, Eff. Mar. 28, 2001;—Am. 2002, Act 473, Eff. Oct. 1, 2002;—Am. 2010, Act 68, Imd. Eff. May 13, 2010.

Constitutionality: This act, which requires the licensing of guards, does not demonstrate the requisite degree of state action to bring the activities of guards under color of state law so as to subject their activities to constitutional restraint and to require guards to give suspects warnings of their constitutional rights before eliciting inculpatory statements, and especially does not subject the activities of private police who are employed to protect the property and employees of their employer to constitutional restraint because such guards need not be licensed under the act. Grand Rapids v Impens, 414 Mich 667; 327 NW2d 278 (1982).

Participation by an off-duty deputy sheriff from another county, employed as a private guard, with other guards in the apprehension and detention of a shoplifting suspect did not provide a sufficient relationship so as to bring the activities of the guards under color of state law and require warnings of the suspect's constitutional rights before eliciting inculpatory statements by the suspect where the deputy did not obtain the statements and identified himself to the suspect only as a store employee. Grand Rapids v Impens, 414 Mich 667; 327 NW2d 278 (1982).

THE REVISED SCHOOL CODE (EXCERPT)
Act 451 of 1976

AN ACT to provide a system of public instruction and elementary and secondary schools; to revise, consolidate, and clarify the laws relating to elementary and secondary education; to provide for the organization, regulation, and maintenance of schools, school districts, public school academies, intermediate school districts, and other public school entities; to prescribe rights, powers, duties, and privileges of schools, school districts, public school academies, intermediate school districts, and other public school entities; to provide for the regulation of school teachers and certain other school employees; to provide for school elections and to prescribe powers and duties with respect thereto; to provide for the levy and collection of taxes; to provide for the borrowing of money and issuance of bonds and other evidences of indebtedness; to establish a fund and provide for expenditures from that fund; to make appropriations for certain purposes; to provide for and prescribe the powers and duties of certain state departments, the state board of education, and certain other boards and officials; to provide for licensure of boarding schools; to prescribe penalties; and to repeal acts and parts of acts.

History: 1976, Act 451, Imd. Eff. Jan. 13, 1977;—Am. 1977, Act 43, Imd. Eff. June 29, 1977;—Am. 1988, Act 339, Imd. Eff. Oct. 18, 1988;—Am. 1990, Act 161, Imd. Eff. July 2, 1990;—Am. 1995, Act 289, Eff. July 1, 1996;—Am. 2003, Act 179, Imd. Eff. Oct. 3, 2003;—Am. 2016, Act 192, Imd. Eff. June 21, 2016.

Constitutionality: The Michigan School Reform Act does not violate federal and state constitutional protections, Moore v Detroit School Reform Board, 293 F3d 352 (CA 6 2002).

Compiler's note: Senate Bill 393 (SB 393) was enrolled on August 13, 2003, and presented to the governor for her approval on September 8, 2003, at 5:00 p.m. On September 18, 2003, the senate requested that the bill be returned to the senate. The governor granted the senate's request on that same date and returned the bill to that body (without objections), where a motion was made to vacate the enrollment and the motion prevailed. On September 23, 2003, the house of representatives approved a motion to send a letter to the senate agreeing with the senate's request that the governor return SB 393. Neither the Senate Journal nor the House Journal entries reveal any other action taken by the house of representatives regarding the return of SB 393.

In order to determine whether SB 393 had become law, as requested, the attorney general examined whether SB 393 was recalled by concurrent action of the house of representatives and the senate within the 14-day period afforded the governor for vetoing a bill under the last sentence of Const 1963, art IV, § 33: "SB 393 was presented to the Governor on September 8, 2003, at 5:00 p.m. The 14-day period afforded for consideration, measured in hours and minutes, therefore expired on September 22, 2003 at 5:00 p.m. While the Senate had acted to recall the bill within that 14-day period (on September 18, 2003), the House did not. Its action concurring in the request to recall SB 393 was not taken until September 23, 2003. In the absence of concurrent action by both houses of the Legislature within the 14-day period, SB 393 was not effectively recalled and 'further legislative action thereon' was not authorized." The attorney general declared that "in the absence of a return of the bill with objections, SB 393 therefore became law by operation of the last sentence of Const 1963, art IV, § 33." OAG, 2003, No. 7139 (October 2, 2003).

Popular name: Act 451

The People of the State of Michigan enact:

ARTICLE 2

PART 15
SCHOOL DISTRICTS; POWERS AND DUTIES GENERALLY

380.1163 Gun safety instruction for elementary school pupils; model program.

Sec. 1163. (1) Not later than August 1, 2011, the department shall develop or adopt, and shall make available to schools, 1 or more model programs for gun safety instruction for elementary school pupils. The model program shall adopt or be based on the "Eddie Eagle" gunsafe accident prevention program developed by the national rifle association.

(2) Each school district and public school academy is encouraged to adopt and implement the model gun safety instruction program developed under subsection (1) in at least grade 3 beginning in the 2011-2012 school year.

History: Add. 2010, Act 367, Imd. Eff. Dec. 22, 2010.

Popular name: Act 451

380.1310d Suspension or expulsion of pupil; factors; exercise of discretion; rebuttable presumption; section inapplicable for possession of firearm in weapon free school zone; consideration of factors mandatory; definitions.

Sec. 1310d. (1) Before suspending or expelling a pupil under section 1310, 1311(1), 1311(2), or 1311a, the board of a school district or intermediate school district or board of directors of a public school academy, or a superintendent, school principal, or other designee under section 1311(1), shall consider each of the following factors:

(a) The pupil's age.
(b) The pupil's disciplinary history.
(c) Whether the pupil is a student with a disability.
(d) The seriousness of the violation or behavior committed by the pupil.
(e) Whether the violation or behavior committed by the pupil threatened the safety of any pupil or staff member.
(f) Whether restorative practices will be used to address the violation or behavior committed by the pupil.

(g) Whether a lesser intervention would properly address the violation or behavior committed by the pupil.
(2) Except as provided in subsection (3), this section applies to give the board of a school district or intermediate school district or board of directors of a public school academy, or its designee, discretion over whether or not to suspend or expel a pupil under section 1310, 1311(1), 1311(2), or 1311a. In exercising this discretion with regard to a suspension of more than 10 days or an expulsion, there is a rebuttable presumption that a suspension or expulsion is not justified unless the board or board of directors, or its designee, can demonstrate that it considered each of the factors listed under subsection (1). For a suspension of 10 or fewer days, there is no rebuttable presumption, but the board or board of directors, or its designee, shall consider each of the factors listed under subsection (1).
(3) This section does not apply to a pupil being expelled under section 1311(2) for possessing a firearm in a weapon free school zone.
(4) Except as provided in subsection (3), consideration of the factors listed in subsection (1) is mandatory before suspending or expelling a student under section 1310, 1311(1), 1311(2), or 1311a. The method used for consideration of the factors is at the sole discretion of the board of a school district or intermediate school district or board of directors of a public school academy, or its designee.
(5) As used in this section:
(a) "Expel" means to exclude a pupil from school for disciplinary reasons for a period of 60 or more school days.
(b) "Firearm" means that term as defined in section 1311.
(c) "Suspend" means to exclude a pupil from school for disciplinary reasons for a period of fewer than 60 school days.
(d) "Weapon free school zone" means that term as defined in section 1311.

History: Add. 2016, Act 360, Eff. Aug. 1, 2017.

Popular name: Act 451

PART 16
BOARDS OF EDUCATION; POWERS AND DUTIES GENERALLY

380.1311 Suspension or expulsion of pupil.

Sec. 1311. (1) Subject to subsection (2), the school board, or the school district superintendent, a school building principal, or another school district official if designated by the school board, may authorize or order the suspension or expulsion from school of a pupil guilty of gross misdemeanor or persistent disobedience if, in the judgment of the school board or its designee, as applicable, the interest of the school is served by the authorization or order. If there is reasonable cause to believe that the pupil is a student with a disability, and the school district has not evaluated the pupil in accordance with rules of the superintendent of public instruction to determine if the pupil is a student with a disability, the pupil shall be evaluated immediately by the intermediate school district of which the school district is constituent in accordance with section 1711.
(2) Subject to subsection (3) and section 1310d, if a pupil possesses in a weapon free school zone a weapon that constitutes a dangerous weapon, commits arson in a school building or on school grounds, or commits criminal sexual conduct in a school building or on school grounds, the school board, or the designee of the school board as described in subsection (1) on behalf of the school board, shall expel the pupil from the school district permanently, subject to possible reinstatement under subsection (6). However, a school board is not required to expel a pupil for possessing a weapon if the pupil establishes in a clear and convincing manner at least 1 of the following:
(a) The object or instrument possessed by the pupil was not possessed by the pupil for use as a weapon, or for direct or indirect delivery to another person for use as a weapon.
(b) The weapon was not knowingly possessed by the pupil.
(c) The pupil did not know or have reason to know that the object or instrument possessed by the pupil constituted a dangerous weapon.
(d) The weapon was possessed by the pupil at the suggestion, request, or direction of, or with the express permission of, school or police authorities.
(3) There is a rebuttable presumption that expulsion under subsection (2) for possession of a weapon is not justified if both of the following are met:
(a) The school board or its designee determines in writing that at least 1 of the factors listed in subsection (2)(a) to (d) has been established in a clear and convincing manner.
(b) The pupil has no history of suspension or expulsion.
(4) If an individual is expelled pursuant to subsection (2), the expelling school district shall enter on the individual's permanent record that he or she has been expelled pursuant to subsection (2). Except if a school district operates or participates cooperatively in an alternative education program appropriate for individuals expelled pursuant to subsection (2) and in its discretion admits the individual to that program, and except for a strict discipline academy established under sections 1311b to 1311m, an individual expelled pursuant to subsection (2) is expelled from all public schools in this state and the officials of a school district shall not allow the individual to enroll in the school district unless the individual has been reinstated under subsection (6). Except as otherwise provided by law, a program operated for individuals expelled pursuant to subsection (2) shall ensure that those individuals are physically separated at all times during the school day from the general pupil population. If an individual expelled from a school district pursuant to subsection (2) is not placed in an alternative education program or strict discipline academy, the school district may provide, or may arrange for the intermediate school district to provide,

appropriate instructional services to the individual at home. The type of services provided shall meet the requirements of section 6(4)(u) of the state school aid act of 1979, MCL 388.1606, and the services may be contracted for in the same manner as services for homebound pupils under section 109 of the state school aid act of 1979, MCL 388.1709. This subsection does not require a school district to expend more money for providing services for a pupil expelled pursuant to subsection (2) than the amount of the foundation allowance the school district receives for the pupil as calculated under section 20 of the state school aid act of 1979, MCL 388.1620.

(5) If a school board expels an individual pursuant to subsection (2), the school board shall ensure that, within 3 days after the expulsion, an official of the school district refers the individual to the appropriate county department of social services or county community mental health agency and notifies the individual's parent or legal guardian or, if the individual is at least age 18 or is an emancipated minor, notifies the individual of the referral.

(6) The parent or legal guardian of an individual expelled pursuant to subsection (2) or, if the individual is at least age 18 or is an emancipated minor, the individual may petition the expelling school board for reinstatement of the individual to public education in the school district. If the expelling school board denies a petition for reinstatement, the parent or legal guardian or, if the individual is at least age 18 or is an emancipated minor, the individual may petition another school board for reinstatement of the individual in that other school district. All of the following apply to reinstatement under this subsection:

(a) For an individual who was enrolled in grade 5 or below at the time of the expulsion and who has been expelled for possessing a firearm or threatening another person with a dangerous weapon, the parent or legal guardian or, if the individual is at least age 18 or is an emancipated minor, the individual may initiate a petition for reinstatement at any time after the expiration of 60 school days after the date of expulsion. For an individual who was enrolled in grade 5 or below at the time of the expulsion and who has been expelled pursuant to subsection (2) for a reason other than possessing a firearm or threatening another person with a dangerous weapon, the parent or legal guardian or, if the individual is at least age 18 or is an emancipated minor, the individual may initiate a petition for reinstatement at any time. For an individual who was in grade 6 or above at the time of expulsion, the parent or legal guardian or, if the individual is at least age 18 or is an emancipated minor, the individual may initiate a petition for reinstatement at any time after the expiration of 150 school days after the date of expulsion.

(b) An individual who was in grade 5 or below at the time of the expulsion and who has been expelled for possessing a firearm or threatening another person with a dangerous weapon shall not be reinstated before the expiration of 90 school days after the date of expulsion. An individual who was in grade 5 or below at the time of the expulsion and who has been expelled pursuant to subsection (2) for a reason other than possessing a firearm or threatening another person with a dangerous weapon shall not be reinstated before the expiration of 10 school days after the date of the expulsion. An individual who was in grade 6 or above at the time of the expulsion shall not be reinstated before the expiration of 180 school days after the date of expulsion.

(c) It is the responsibility of the parent or legal guardian or, if the individual is at least age 18 or is an emancipated minor, of the individual to prepare and submit the petition. A school board is not required to provide any assistance in preparing the petition. Upon request by a parent or legal guardian or, if the individual is at least age 18 or is an emancipated minor, by the individual, a school board shall make available a form for a petition.

(d) Not later than 10 school days after receiving a petition for reinstatement under this subsection, a school board shall appoint a committee to review the petition and any supporting information submitted by the parent or legal guardian or, if the individual is at least age 18 or is an emancipated minor, by the individual. The committee shall consist of 2 school board members, 1 school administrator, 1 teacher, and 1 parent of a pupil in the school district. During this time the superintendent of the school district may prepare and submit for consideration by the committee information concerning the circumstances of the expulsion and any factors mitigating for or against reinstatement.

(e) Not later than 10 school days after all members are appointed, the committee described in subdivision (d) shall review the petition and any supporting information and information provided by the school district and shall submit a recommendation to the school board on the issue of reinstatement. The recommendation shall be for unconditional reinstatement, for conditional reinstatement, or against reinstatement, and shall be accompanied by an explanation of the reasons for the recommendation and of any recommended conditions for reinstatement. The recommendation shall be based on consideration of all of the following factors:

(*i*) The extent to which reinstatement of the individual would create a risk of harm to pupils or school personnel.

(*ii*) The extent to which reinstatement of the individual would create a risk of school district liability or individual liability for the school board or school district personnel.

(*iii*) The age and maturity of the individual.

(*iv*) The individual's school record before the incident that caused the expulsion.

(*v*) The individual's attitude concerning the incident that caused the expulsion.

(*vi*) The individual's behavior since the expulsion and the prospects for remediation of the individual.

(*vii*) If the petition was filed by a parent or legal guardian, the degree of cooperation and support that has been provided by the parent or legal guardian and that can be expected if the individual is reinstated, including, but not limited to, receptiveness toward possible conditions placed on the reinstatement.

(f) Not later than the next regularly scheduled board meeting after receiving the recommendation of the committee under subdivision (e), a school board shall make a decision to unconditionally reinstate the individual, conditionally reinstate the individual, or deny reinstatement of the individual. The decision of the school board is final.

(g) A school board may require an individual and, if the petition was filed by a parent or legal guardian, his or her parent or legal guardian to agree in writing to specific conditions before reinstating the individual in a conditional reinstatement. The conditions may include, but are not limited to, agreement to a behavior contract, which may involve the individual, parent or legal guardian, and an outside agency; participation in or completion of an anger management program or other appropriate counseling; periodic progress reviews; and specified immediate consequences for failure to abide by a condition. A parent or legal guardian or, if the individual is at least age 18 or is an emancipated minor, the individual may include proposed conditions in a petition for reinstatement submitted under this subsection.

(7) A school board or school administrator that complies with subsection (2) is not liable for damages for expelling a pupil pursuant to subsection (2), and the authorizing body of a public school academy is not liable for damages for expulsion of a pupil by the public school academy pursuant to subsection (2).

(8) The department shall develop and distribute to all school districts a form for a petition for reinstatement to be used under subsection (6).

(9) This section does not diminish any rights under federal law of a pupil who has been determined to be eligible for special education programs and services.

(10) If a pupil expelled from a public school district pursuant to subsection (2) is enrolled by a public school district sponsored alternative education program or a public school academy during the period of expulsion, the public school academy or alternative education program shall immediately become eligible for the prorated share of either the public school academy or operating school district's foundation allowance or the expelling school district's foundation allowance, whichever is higher.

(11) If an individual is expelled pursuant to subsection (2), it is the responsibility of that individual and of his or her parent or legal guardian to locate a suitable alternative educational program and to enroll the individual in such a program during the expulsion. The office of safe schools in the department shall compile information on and catalog existing alternative education programs or schools and nonpublic schools that may be open to enrollment of individuals expelled pursuant to subsection (2) and pursuant to section 1311a, and shall periodically distribute this information to school districts for distribution to expelled individuals. A school board that establishes an alternative education program or school described in this subsection shall notify the office of safe schools about the program or school and the types of pupils it serves. The office of safe schools also shall work with and provide technical assistance to school districts, authorizing bodies for public school academies, and other interested parties in developing these types of alternative education programs or schools in geographic areas that are not being served.

(12) As used in this section:

(a) "Arson" means a felony violation of chapter X of the Michigan penal code, 1931 PA 328, MCL 750.71 to 750.79.

(b) "Criminal sexual conduct" means a violation of section 520b, 520c, 520d, 520e, or 520g of the Michigan penal code, 1931 PA 328, MCL 750.520b, 750.520c, 750.520d, 750.520e, and 750.520g.

(c) "Dangerous weapon" means that term as defined in section 1313.

(d) "Firearm" means that term as defined in section 921 of title 18 of the United States Code, 18 USC 921.

(e) "School board" means a school board, intermediate school board, or the board of directors of a public school academy.

(f) "School district" means a school district, intermediate school district, or public school academy.

(g) "Weapon free school zone" means that term as defined in section 237a of the Michigan penal code, 1931 PA 328, MCL 750.237a.

History: 1976, Act 451, Imd. Eff. Jan. 13, 1977;—Am. 1993, Act 335, Imd. Eff. Dec. 31, 1993;—Am. 1994, Act 328, Eff. Jan. 1, 1995;—Am. 1995, Act 250, Imd. Eff. Jan. 2, 1996;—Am. 1999, Act 23, Imd. Eff. May 12, 1999;—Am. 2007, Act 138, Imd. Eff. Nov. 13, 2007;—Am. 2008, Act 1, Imd. Eff. Jan. 11, 2008;—Am. 2016, Act 364, Eff. Aug. 1, 2017.

Popular name: Act 451

380.1313 Dangerous weapon found in possession of pupil; report; confiscation by school official; determination of legal owner; "dangerous weapon" defined.

Sec. 1313. (1) If a dangerous weapon is found in the possession of a pupil while the pupil is in attendance at school or a school activity or while the pupil is enroute to or from school on a school bus, the superintendent of the school district or intermediate school district, or his or her designee, immediately shall report that finding to the pupil's parent or legal guardian and the local law enforcement agency.

(2) If a school official finds that a dangerous weapon is in the possession of a pupil as described in subsection (1), the school official may confiscate the dangerous weapon or shall request a law enforcement agency to respond as soon as possible and to confiscate the dangerous weapon. If a school official confiscates a dangerous weapon under this subsection, the school official shall give the dangerous weapon to a law enforcement agency and shall not release the dangerous weapon to any other person, including the legal owner of the dangerous weapon. A school official who complies in good faith with this section is not civilly or criminally liable for that compliance.

(3) A law enforcement agency that takes possession of a dangerous weapon under subsection (2) shall check all available local and state stolen weapon and stolen property files and the national crime information center stolen gun and property files to determine the legal owner of the dangerous weapon. If the dangerous weapon is a pistol, the law enforcement agency also shall check the state pistol registration records to determine the legal owner. If the law enforcement agency is able to determine the legal owner of the dangerous weapon, and if the legal owner did not knowingly provide the dangerous weapon to the pupil or lawfully provided the dangerous weapon to the pupil but did not know or have reason to know that the pupil would possess

the dangerous weapon while in attendance at school or a school activity or while en route to or from school on a school bus, the law enforcement agency shall send by certified mail to the legal owner a notice that the agency is in possession of the dangerous weapon and that the legal owner has 90 days from receipt of the notice to claim the dangerous weapon.

(4) As used in this section, "dangerous weapon" means a firearm, dagger, dirk, stiletto, knife with a blade over 3 inches in length, pocket knife opened by a mechanical device, iron bar, or brass knuckles.

History: Add. 1987, Act 211, Imd. Eff. Dec. 22, 1987;—Am. 1995, Act 76, Eff. Aug. 1, 1995.

Popular name: Act 451

ADULT FOSTER CARE FACILITY LICENSING ACT (EXCERPT)
Act 218 of 1979

AN ACT to provide for the licensing and regulation of adult foster care facilities; to provide for the establishment of standards of care for adult foster care facilities; to prescribe powers and duties of the department of licensing and regulatory affairs and other departments; to prescribe certain fees; to prescribe penalties; and to repeal certain acts and parts of acts.

History: 1979, Act 218, Eff. Mar. 27, 1980;—Am. 1992, Act 176, Imd. Eff. July 23, 1992;—Am. 2016, Act 525, Eff. Apr. 9, 2017.

Compiler's note: For transfer of powers and duties pertaining to adult foster care, adult foster care facility, adult foster care camp, adult camp, adult foster care family home, and adult foster care group home licensing and regulation from department of human services to department of licensing and regulatory affairs, see E.R.O. No. 2015-1, compiled at MCL 400.227.

For transfer of powers and duties pertaining to children's camp, child care center, day care center, family day care home, and group day care home licensing and regulation from department of human services to department of licensing and regulatory affairs, see E.R.O. No. 2015-1, compiled at MCL 400.227.

The People of the State of Michigan enact:

400.734b Employing or contracting with certain individuals providing direct services to residents; prohibitions; criminal history check; exemptions; written consent and identification; conditional employment; use of criminal history record information; disclosure; determination of existence of national criminal history; failure to conduct criminal history check; automated fingerprint identification system database; electronic web-based system; costs; definitions.

Sec. 34b. (1) In addition to the restrictions prescribed in sections 13, 22, and 31, and except as otherwise provided in subsection (2), an adult foster care facility shall not employ or independently contract with an individual who regularly has direct access to or provides direct services to residents of the adult foster care facility if the individual satisfies 1 or more of the following:

(a) Has been convicted of a relevant crime described under 42 USC 1320a-7(a).

(b) Has been convicted of any of the following felonies, an attempt or conspiracy to commit any of those felonies, or any other state or federal crime that is similar to the felonies described in this subdivision, other than a felony for a relevant crime described under 42 USC 1320a-7(a), unless 15 years have lapsed since the individual completed all of the terms and conditions of his or her sentencing, parole, and probation for that conviction prior to the date of application for employment or the date of the execution of the independent contract:

(*i*) A felony that involves the intent to cause death or serious impairment of a body function, that results in death or serious impairment of a body function, that involves the use of force or violence, or that involves the threat of the use of force or violence.

(*ii*) A felony involving cruelty or torture.

(*iii*) A felony under chapter XXA of the Michigan penal code, 1931 PA 328, MCL 750.145m to 750.145r.

(*iv*) A felony involving criminal sexual conduct.

(*v*) A felony involving abuse or neglect.

(*vi*) A felony involving the use of a firearm or dangerous weapon.

(*vii*) A felony involving the diversion or adulteration of a prescription drug or other medications.

(c) Has been convicted of a felony or an attempt or conspiracy to commit a felony, other than a felony for a relevant crime described under 42 USC 1320a-7(a) or a felony described under subdivision (b), unless 10 years have lapsed since the individual completed all of the terms and conditions of his or her sentencing, parole, and probation for that conviction prior to the date of application for employment or the date of the execution of the independent contract.

(d) Has been convicted of any of the following misdemeanors, other than a misdemeanor for a relevant crime described under 42 USC 1320a-7(a), or a state or federal crime that is substantially similar to the misdemeanors described in this subdivision, within the 10 years immediately preceding the date of application for employment or the date of the execution of the independent contract:

(*i*) A misdemeanor involving the use of a firearm or dangerous weapon with the intent to injure, the use of a firearm or dangerous weapon that results in a personal injury, or a misdemeanor involving the use of force or violence or the threat of the use of force or violence.

(*ii*) A misdemeanor under chapter XXA of the Michigan penal code, 1931 PA 328, MCL 750.145m to 750.145r.

(*iii*) A misdemeanor involving criminal sexual conduct.

(*iv*) A misdemeanor involving cruelty or torture unless otherwise provided under subdivision (e).

(*v*) A misdemeanor involving abuse or neglect.

(e) Has been convicted of any of the following misdemeanors, other than a misdemeanor for a relevant crime described under 42 USC 1320a-7(a), or a state or federal crime that is substantially similar to the misdemeanors described in this subdivision, within the 5 years immediately preceding the date of application for employment or the date of the execution of the independent contract:

(*i*) A misdemeanor involving cruelty if committed by an individual who is less than 16 years of age.

(*ii*) A misdemeanor involving home invasion.

(*iii*) A misdemeanor involving embezzlement.

(*iv*) A misdemeanor involving negligent homicide or a violation of section 601d(1) of the Michigan vehicle code, 1949 PA 300, MCL 257.601d.

(*v*) A misdemeanor involving larceny unless otherwise provided under subdivision (g).

(*vi*) A misdemeanor of retail fraud in the second degree unless otherwise provided under subdivision (g).

(*vii*) Any other misdemeanor involving assault, fraud, theft, or the possession or delivery of a controlled substance unless otherwise provided under subdivision (d), (f), or (g).

(f) Has been convicted of any of the following misdemeanors, other than a misdemeanor for a relevant crime described under 42 USC 1320a-7(a), or a state or federal crime that is substantially similar to the misdemeanors described in this subdivision, within the 3 years immediately preceding the date of application for employment or the date of the execution of the independent contract:

(*i*) A misdemeanor for assault if there was no use of a firearm or dangerous weapon and no intent to commit murder or inflict great bodily injury.

(*ii*) A misdemeanor of retail fraud in the third degree unless otherwise provided under subdivision (g).

(*iii*) A misdemeanor under part 74 of the public health code, 1978 PA 368, MCL 333.7401 to 333.7461, unless otherwise provided under subdivision (g).

(g) Has been convicted of any of the following misdemeanors, other than a misdemeanor for a relevant crime described under 42 USC 1320a-7(a), or a state or federal crime that is substantially similar to the misdemeanors described in this subdivision, within the year immediately preceding the date of application for employment or the date of the execution of the independent contract:

(*i*) A misdemeanor under part 74 of the public health code, 1978 PA 368, MCL 333.7401 to 333.7461, if the individual, at the time of conviction, is under the age of 18.

(*ii*) A misdemeanor for larceny or retail fraud in the second or third degree if the individual, at the time of conviction, is under the age of 16.

(h) Is the subject of an order or disposition under section 16b of chapter IX of the code of criminal procedure, 1927 PA 175, MCL 769.16b.

(i) Engages in conduct that becomes the subject of a substantiated finding of neglect, abuse, or misappropriation of property by a state or federal agency according to an investigation conducted in accordance with 42 USC 1395i-3 or 1396r.

(2) Except as otherwise provided in this subsection or subsection (6), an adult foster care facility shall not employ or independently contract with an individual who has direct access to residents until the adult foster care facility or staffing agency has conducted a criminal history check in compliance with this section or has received criminal history record information in compliance with subsections (3) and (11). This subsection and subsection (1) do not apply to an individual who is employed by or under contract to an adult foster care facility before April 1, 2006. On or before April 1, 2011, an individual who is exempt under this subsection and who has not been the subject of a criminal history check conducted in compliance with this section shall provide the department of state police a set of fingerprints and the department of state police shall input those fingerprints into the automated fingerprint identification system database established under subsection (14). An individual who is exempt under this subsection is not limited to working within the adult foster care facility with which he or she is employed by or under independent contract with on April 1, 2006 but may transfer to another adult foster care facility, mental health facility, or covered health facility. If an individual who is exempt under this subsection is subsequently convicted of a crime or offense described under subsection (1)(a) to (g) or found to be the subject of a substantiated finding described under subsection (1)(i) or an order or disposition described under subsection (1)(h), or is found to have been convicted of a relevant crime described under 42 USC 1320a-7(a), he or she is no longer exempt and shall be terminated from employment or denied employment.

(3) An individual who applies for employment either as an employee or as an independent contractor with an adult foster care facility or staffing agency and who has not been the subject of a criminal history check conducted in compliance with this section shall give written consent at the time of application for the department of state police to conduct a criminal history check under this section, along with identification acceptable to the department of state police. If the individual has been the subject of a criminal history check conducted in compliance with this section, the individual shall give written consent at the time of application for the adult foster care facility or staffing agency to obtain the criminal history record information as prescribed in subsection (4) or (5) from the relevant licensing or regulatory department and for the department of state police to conduct a criminal history check under this section if the requirements of subsection (11) are not met and a request to the federal bureau of investigation to make a determination of the existence of any national criminal history pertaining to the individual is necessary, along with identification acceptable to the department of state police. Upon receipt of the written consent to obtain the criminal history record information and identification required under this subsection, the adult foster care facility or staffing agency that has made a good faith offer of employment or an independent contract to the individual shall request the criminal history record information from the relevant licensing or regulatory department and shall make a request regarding that individual to the relevant licensing or regulatory department to conduct a check of all relevant registries in the manner required in subsection (4). If the requirements of subsection (11) are not met and a request to the federal bureau of investigation to make a subsequent determination of the existence of any national criminal history pertaining to the individual is necessary, the adult foster care facility or staffing agency shall proceed in the manner required in subsection (5). A staffing agency that employs an individual who regularly has direct access to or provides direct services to residents under an independent contract with an adult foster care facility shall submit information regarding the criminal history check conducted by the staffing agency to the adult foster care facility that has made a good faith offer of independent contract to that applicant.

(4) Upon receipt of the written consent to conduct a criminal history check and identification required under subsection (3), the adult foster care facility or staffing agency that has made a good faith offer of employment or independent contract to the individual shall make a request to the department of state police to conduct a criminal history check on the individual and

input the individual's fingerprints into the automated fingerprint identification system database, and shall make a request to the relevant licensing or regulatory department to perform a check of all relevant registries established according to federal and state law and regulations for any substantiated findings of abuse, neglect, or misappropriation of property. The request shall be made in a manner prescribed by the department of state police and the relevant licensing or regulatory department or agency. The adult foster care facility or staffing agency shall make the written consent and identification available to the department of state police and the relevant licensing or regulatory department or agency. If the department of state police or the federal bureau of investigation charges a fee for conducting the criminal history check, the charge shall be paid by or reimbursed by the department. The adult foster care facility or staffing agency shall not seek reimbursement for a charge imposed by the department of state police or the federal bureau of investigation from the individual who is the subject of the criminal history check. The department of state police shall conduct a criminal history check on the individual named in the request. The department of state police shall provide the department with a written report of the criminal history check conducted under this subsection. The report shall contain any criminal history record information on the individual maintained by the department of state police.

(5) Upon receipt of the written consent to conduct a criminal history check and identification required under subsection (3), if the individual has applied for employment either as an employee or as an independent contractor with an adult foster care facility or staffing agency, the adult foster care facility or staffing agency that has made a good faith offer of employment or independent contract shall comply with subsection (4) and shall make a request to the department of state police to forward the individual's fingerprints to the federal bureau of investigation. The department of state police shall request the federal bureau of investigation to make a determination of the existence of any national criminal history pertaining to the individual. An individual described in this subsection shall provide the department of state police with a set of fingerprints. The department of state police shall complete the criminal history check under subsection (4) and, except as otherwise provided in this subsection, provide the results of its determination under subsection (4) and the results of the federal bureau of investigation determination to the department within 30 days after the request is made. If the requesting adult foster care facility or staffing agency is not a state department or agency and if criminal history record information is disclosed on the written report of the criminal history check or the federal bureau of investigation determination that resulted in a conviction, the department shall notify the adult foster care facility or staffing agency and the individual in writing of the type of crime disclosed on the written report of the criminal history check or the federal bureau of investigation determination without disclosing the details of the crime. The notification shall inform the adult foster care facility or staffing agency and the applicant regarding the appeal process in section 34c and shall include a statement that the individual has a right to appeal the information relied upon by the adult foster care facility or staffing agency in making its decision regarding his or her employment eligibility based on the criminal history check. Any charges imposed by the department of state police or the federal bureau of investigation for conducting a criminal history check or making a determination under this subsection shall be paid in the manner required under subsection (4).

(6) If an adult foster care facility determines it necessary to employ or independently contract with an individual before receiving the results of the individual's criminal history check or criminal history record information required under this section, the adult foster care facility may conditionally employ the individual if all of the following apply:

(a) The adult foster care facility requests the criminal history check or criminal history record information required under this section, upon conditionally employing the individual.

(b) The individual signs a written statement indicating all of the following:

(*i*) That he or she has not been convicted of 1 or more of the crimes that are described in subsection (1)(a) to (g) within the applicable time period prescribed by subsection (1)(a) to (g).

(*ii*) That he or she is not the subject of an order or disposition described in subsection (1)(h).

(*iii*) That he or she has not been the subject of a substantiated finding as described in subsection (1)(i).

(*iv*) The individual agrees that, if the information in the criminal history check conducted under this section does not confirm the individual's statement under subparagraphs (*i*) to (*iii*), his or her employment will be terminated by the adult foster care facility as required under subsection (1) unless and until the individual can prove that the information is incorrect.

(*v*) That he or she understands the conditions described in subparagraphs (*i*) to (*iv*) that result in the termination of his or her employment and that those conditions are good cause for termination.

(c) Except as otherwise provided in this subdivision, the adult foster care facility does not permit the individual to have regular direct access to or provide direct services to residents in the adult foster care facility without supervision until the criminal history check or criminal history record information is obtained and the individual is eligible for that employment. If required under this subdivision, the adult foster care facility shall provide on-site supervision of an individual in the facility on a conditional basis under this subsection by an individual who has undergone a criminal history check conducted in compliance with this section. An adult foster care facility may permit an individual in the facility on a conditional basis under this subsection to have regular direct access to or provide direct services to residents in the adult foster care facility without supervision if all of the following conditions are met:

(*i*) The adult foster care facility, at its own expense and before the individual has direct access to or provides direct services to residents of the facility, conducts a search of public records on that individual through the internet criminal history access tool maintained by the department of state police and the results of that search do not uncover any information that would indicate that the individual is not eligible to have regular direct access to or provide direct services to residents under this section.

(*ii*) Before the individual has direct access to or provides direct services to residents of the adult foster care facility, the individual signs a statement in writing that he or she has resided in this state without interruption for at least the immediately preceding 12-month period.

(*iii*) If applicable, the individual provides to the department of state police a set of fingerprints on or before the expiration of 10 business days following the date the individual was conditionally employed under this subsection.

(7) The department shall develop and distribute the model form for the statements required under subsection (6)(b) and (c). The department shall make the model form available to adult foster care facilities upon request at no charge.

(8) If an individual is conditionally employed under subsection (6), and the information under subsection (3) or report under subsection (4) or (5), if applicable, does not confirm the individual's statement under subsection (6)(b)(*i*) to (*iii*), the adult foster care facility shall terminate the individual's employment as required by subsection (1).

(9) An individual who knowingly provides false information regarding his or her identity, criminal convictions, or substantiated findings on a statement described in subsection (6)(b)(*i*) to (*iii*) is guilty of a misdemeanor punishable by imprisonment for not more than 93 days or a fine of not more than $500.00, or both.

(10) An adult foster care facility or staffing agency shall use criminal history record information obtained under subsection (3), (4), or (5) only for the purpose of evaluating an individual's qualifications for employment in the position for which he or she has applied and for the purposes of subsections (6) and (8). An adult foster care facility or staffing agency or an employee of the adult foster care facility or staffing agency shall not disclose criminal history record information obtained under this section to a person who is not directly involved in evaluating the individual's qualifications for employment or independent contract. An individual who knowingly uses or disseminates the criminal history record information obtained under subsection (3), (4), or (5) in violation of this subsection is guilty of a misdemeanor punishable by imprisonment for not more than 93 days or a fine of not more than $1,000.00, or both. Except for a knowing or intentional release of false information, an adult foster care facility or staffing agency has no liability in connection with a criminal history check conducted in compliance with this section or the release of criminal history record information under this subsection.

(11) Upon consent of an individual as required in subsection (3) and upon request from an adult foster care facility or staffing agency that has made a good faith offer of employment or an independent contract to the individual, the relevant licensing or regulatory department shall review the criminal history record information, if any, and notify the requesting adult foster care facility or staffing agency of the information in the manner prescribed in subsection (4) or (5). Until the federal bureau of investigation implements an automatic notification system similar to the system required of the state police under subsection (14) and federal regulations allow the federal criminal record to be used for subsequent authorized uses, as determined in an order issued by the department, an adult foster care facility or staffing agency may rely on the criminal history record information provided by the relevant licensing or regulatory department under this subsection and a request to the federal bureau of investigation to make a subsequent determination of the existence of any national criminal history pertaining to the individual is not necessary if all of the following requirements are met:

(a) The criminal history check was conducted during the immediately preceding 12-month period.

(b) The individual has been continuously employed by an adult foster care facility, mental health facility, or covered health facility, or the staffing agency since the criminal history check was conducted in compliance with this section or meets the continuous employment requirement of this subdivision other than being on layoff status for less than 1 year from an adult foster care facility, mental health facility, or covered health facility.

(c) The individual can provide evidence acceptable to the relevant licensing or regulatory department that he or she has been a resident of this state for the immediately preceding 12-month period.

(12) As a condition of continued employment, each employee or independent contractor shall do both of the following:

(a) Agree in writing to report to the adult foster care facility or staffing agency immediately upon being arraigned on 1 or more of the criminal offenses listed in subsection (1)(a) to (g), upon being convicted of 1 or more of the criminal offenses listed in subsection (1)(a) to (g), upon becoming the subject of an order or disposition described under subsection (1)(h), and upon becoming the subject of a substantiated finding described under subsection (1)(i). Reporting of an arraignment under this subdivision is not cause for termination or denial of employment.

(b) If a set of fingerprints is not already on file with the department of state police, provide the department of state police with a set of fingerprints.

(13) In addition to sanctions set forth in this act, a licensee, owner, administrator, or operator of an adult foster care facility or staffing agency who knowingly and willfully fails to conduct the criminal history checks as required under this section is guilty of a misdemeanor punishable by imprisonment for not more than 1 year or a fine of not more than $5,000.00, or both.

(14) In collaboration with the department of state police, the department of technology, management, and budget shall establish and maintain an automated fingerprint identification system database that would allow the department of state police to store and maintain all fingerprints submitted under this section and would provide for an automatic notification at the time a subsequent criminal arrest fingerprint card submitted into the system matches a set of fingerprints previously submitted under this section. Upon such notification, the department of state police shall immediately notify the department and the department shall immediately contact each respective adult foster care facility or staffing agency with which that individual is associated. Information in the database established under this subsection is confidential, is not subject to disclosure under the freedom of information act, 1976 PA 442, MCL 15.231 to 15.246, and shall not be disclosed to any person except for purposes of this act or for law enforcement purposes.

(15) If an individual independently contracts with an adult foster care facility, subsections (1) and (2) do not apply if the individual is not under the adult foster care facility's control and the contractual work performed by the individual is not directly related to the clinical, health care, or personal services delivered by the adult foster care facility or if the individual's duties are

not performed on an ongoing basis with direct access to residents. This exception includes, but is not limited to, an individual who independently contracts with the adult foster care facility to provide utility, maintenance, construction, or communication services.

(16) The department shall maintain an electronic web-based system to assist the adult foster care facilities and staffing agencies required to check relevant registries and conduct criminal history checks of its employees and independent contractors and to provide for an automated notice to the adult foster care facilities and staffing agencies for the individuals entered in the system who, since the initial criminal history check, have been convicted of a disqualifying offense or have been the subject of a substantiated finding of abuse, neglect, or misappropriation of property. The department may charge a staffing agency a 1-time set-up fee of up to $100.00 for access to the electronic web-based system under this section.

(17) An adult foster care facility, staffing agency, or a prospective employee covered under this section may not be charged for the cost of a criminal history check required under this act.

(18) As used in this section:

(a) "Convicted" means either of the following:

(*i*) For a crime that is not a relevant crime, a final conviction, the payment of a fine, a plea of guilty or nolo contendere if accepted by the court, or a finding of guilt for a criminal law violation or a juvenile adjudication or disposition by the juvenile division of probate court or family division of circuit court for a violation that if committed by an adult would be a crime.

(*ii*) For a relevant crime described under 42 USC 1320a-7(a), convicted means that term as defined in 42 USC 1320a-7.

(b) "Covered health facility" means a nursing home, county medical care facility, hospice, hospital that provides swing bed services, home for the aged, or home health agency licensed under article 17 of the public health code, 1978 PA 368, MCL 333.20101 to 333.22260.

(c) "Criminal history check conducted in compliance with this section" includes a criminal history check conducted under this section, under section 134a of the mental health code, 1974 PA 258, MCL 330.1134a, or under section 20173a of the public health code, 1978 PA 368, MCL 333.20173a.

(d) "Direct access" means access to a resident or resident's property, financial information, medical records, treatment information, or any other identifying information.

(e) "Home health agency" means that term as defined in section 20173a of the public health code, 1978 PA 368, MCL 333.20173a.

(f) "Independent contract" means a contract entered into by an adult foster care facility with an individual who provides the contracted services independently or a contract entered into by an adult foster care facility with a staffing agency that complies with the requirements of this section to provide the contracted services to the adult foster care facility on behalf of the staffing agency.

(g) "Mental health facility" means a psychiatric facility or other facility defined in 42 USC 1396d(d) as described under the mental health code, 1974 PA 258, MCL 330.1001 to 330.2106.

(h) "Staffing agency" means an entity that recruits candidates and provides temporary and permanent qualified staffing for adult foster care facilities, including independent contractors.

(i) "Title XIX" means title XIX of the social security act, 42 USC 1396 to 1396w-5.

(j) "Under the adult foster care facility's control" means an individual employed by or under independent contract with an adult foster care facility for whom the adult foster care facility does both of the following:

(*i*) Determines whether the individual who has access to residents may provide care, treatment, or other similar support service functions to residents served by the adult foster care facility.

(*ii*) Directs or oversees 1 or more of the following:

(A) The policy or procedures the individual must follow in performing his or her duties.

(B) The tasks performed by the individual.

(C) The individual's work schedule.

(D) The supervision or evaluation of the individual's work or job performance, including imposing discipline or granting performance awards.

(E) The compensation the individual receives for performing his or her duties.

(F) The conditions under which the individual performs his or her duties.

History: Add. 2006, Act 29, Eff. Apr. 1, 2006;—Am. 2008, Act 135, Imd. Eff. May 21, 2008;—Am. 2008, Act 441, Imd. Eff. Jan. 9, 2009;—Am. 2008, Act 442, Eff. Oct. 31, 2010;—Am. 2010, Act 292, Imd. Eff. Dec. 16, 2010;—Am. 2014, Act 73, Imd. Eff. Mar. 28, 2014.

Compiler's note: Enacting section 2 of Act 29 of 2006 provides:

"Enacting section 2. Sections 34b and 34c of the adult foster care facility licensing act, 1979 PA 218, MCL 400.734b, as added by this amendatory act, take effect April 1, 2006, since the department has secured the necessary federal approval to utilize federal funds to reimburse those facilities for the costs incurred for requesting a national criminal history check to be conducted by the federal bureau of investigation and the department has filed written notice of that approval with the secretary of state. The department shall issue a medicaid policy bulletin regarding the payment and reimbursement for the criminal history checks by April 1, 2006."

For transfer of powers and duties of state fire marshal to department of labor and economic growth, bureau of construction codes and fire safety, by type II transfer, see E.R.O. No. 2003-1, compiled at MCL 445.2011.

For transfer of powers and duties of the bureau of family services from the department of consumer and industry services to the family independence agency by Type II transfer, see E.R.O. No. 2003-1, compiled at MCL 445.2011.

For transfer of powers and duties of adult foster care licensing advisory council to the family independence agency by Type II transfer, see E.R.O. No. 2003-1, compiled at MCL 445.2011.

ANIMALS RUNNING AT LARGE (EXCERPT)
Act 328 of 1976

AN ACT to regulate animals running at large; to provide for compensation for damage done by animals running at large; to prescribe penalties; and to repeal certain acts and parts of acts.

History: 1976, Act 328, Eff. Mar. 31, 1977.

The People of the State of Michigan enact:

433.14a Public nuisance; authority to kill swine running at large; prohibition.

Sec. 4a. (1) Swine running at large on public or private property are a public nuisance.

(2) A local animal control officer appointed under the dog law of 1919, 1919 PA 339, MCL 287.261 to 287.290, or a law enforcement officer may kill a swine running at large on public or private property.

(3) A person who possesses a license to carry a concealed pistol issued under 1927 PA 372, MCL 28.421 to 28.435, or a valid hunting license for any game issued under part 435 of the natural resources and environmental protection act, 1994 PA 451, MCL 324.43501 to 324.43561, may kill a swine running at large on public property. A person may kill swine running at large on private property if the person is, or is accompanied by or has the permission of, the owner or lessee of the property.

(4) Subsection (3) does not authorize the discharge of a bow and arrow, crossbow, or firearm in an area where the discharge of that weapon, or hunting with that weapon, is prohibited by an ordinance adopted pursuant to part 419 of the natural resources and environmental protection act, 1994 PA 451, MCL 324.41901 to 324.41905.

History: Add. 2010, Act 69, Imd. Eff. May 13, 2010.

RURAL CEMETERY CORPORATIONS (EXCERPT)
Act 12 of 1869

AN ACT to authorize and encourage the formation of corporations to establish rural cemeteries; to provide for the care and maintenance thereof; to provide for the revision and codification of the laws relating to cemeteries, mausoleums, crypts, vaults, crematoriums, and other means of disposing of the dead; to make an appropriation therefor; and to impose certain duties upon the department of commerce.

History: 1869, Act 12, Imd. Eff. Feb. 19, 1869;—Am. 1929, Act 215, Eff. Aug. 28, 1929;—Am. 1982, Act 110, Imd. Eff. Apr. 19, 1982.

The People of the State of Michigan enact:

456.114 Use of firearms in cemetery; entering over fence; penalty.

Sec. 14. No person shall use firearms upon the grounds of any cemetery owned and inclosed by any such corporation, nor hunt game therein. No person shall enter into such inclosed cemetery by climbing or leaping over or through any fence or wall around the same, nor direct or cause any animal to enter therein in any such manner. Any person offending against any of the provisions of this section shall be punished by a fine not exceeding 50 dollars or by imprisonment not exceeding 3 months, or by both, in the discretion of the court.

History: 1869, Act 12, Imd. Eff. Feb. 19, 1869;—CL 1871, 3421;—Am. 1875, Act 218, Eff. Aug. 3, 1875;—How. 4776;—CL 1897, 8412;—CL 1915, 11173;—CL 1929, 10453;—CL 1948, 456.114.

REVISED JUDICATURE ACT OF 1961 (EXCERPT)
Act 236 of 1961

AN ACT to revise and consolidate the statutes relating to the organization and jurisdiction of the courts of this state; the powers and duties of the courts, and of the judges and other officers of the courts; the forms and attributes of civil claims and actions; the time within which civil actions and proceedings may be brought in the courts; pleading, evidence, practice, and procedure in civil and criminal actions and proceedings in the courts; to provide for the powers and duties of certain state governmental officers and entities; to provide remedies and penalties for the violation of certain provisions of this act; to repeal all acts and parts of acts inconsistent with or contravening any of the provisions of this act; and to repeal acts and parts of acts.

History: 1961, Act 236, Eff. Jan. 1, 1963;—Am. 1974, Act 52, Imd. Eff. Mar. 26, 1974;—Am. 1999, Act 239, Imd. Eff. Dec. 28, 1999;—Am. 2009, Act 29, Eff. July 5, 2009.

The People of the State of Michigan enact:

CHAPTER 6
JURISDICTION OF THE CIRCUIT COURTS

600.606 Violations by certain juveniles; jurisdiction of circuit court; "specified juvenile violation" defined.

Sec. 606. (1) The circuit court has jurisdiction to hear and determine a specified juvenile violation if committed by a juvenile 14 years of age or older and less than 17 years of age.

(2) As used in this section, "specified juvenile violation" means any of the following:

(a) A violation of section 72, 83, 86, 89, 91, 316, 317, 349, 520b, 529, 529a, or 531 of the Michigan penal code, Act No. 328 of the Public Acts of 1931, being sections 750.72, 750.83, 750.86, 750.89, 750.91, 750.316, 750.317, 750.349, 750.520b, 750.529, 750.529a, and 750.531 of the Michigan Compiled Laws.

(b) A violation of section 84 or 110a(2) of Act No. 328 of the Public Acts of 1931, being sections 750.84 and 750.110a of the Michigan Compiled Laws, if the juvenile is armed with a dangerous weapon. As used in this subdivision, "dangerous weapon" means 1 or more of the following:

(*i*) A loaded or unloaded firearm, whether operable or inoperable.

(*ii*) A knife, stabbing instrument, brass knuckles, blackjack, club, or other object specifically designed or customarily carried or possessed for use as a weapon.

(*iii*) An object that is likely to cause death or bodily injury when used as a weapon and that is used as a weapon or carried or possessed for use as a weapon.

(*iv*) An object or device that is used or fashioned in a manner to lead a person to believe the object or device is an object or device described in subparagraphs (*i*) to (*iii*).

(c) A violation of section 186a of Act No. 328 of the Public Acts of 1931, being section 750.186a of the Michigan Compiled Laws, regarding escape or attempted escape from a juvenile facility, but only if the juvenile facility from which the individual escaped or attempted to escape was 1 of the following:

(*i*) A high-security or medium-security facility operated by the family independence agency.

(*ii*) A high-security facility operated by a private agency under contract with the family independence agency.

(d) A violation of section 7401(2)(a)(*i*) or 7403(2)(a)(*i*) of the public health code, Act No. 368 of the Public Acts of 1978, being sections 333.7401 and 333.7403 of the Michigan Compiled Laws.

(e) An attempt to commit a violation described in subdivisions (a) to (d).

(f) Conspiracy to commit a violation described in subdivisions (a) to (d).

(g) Solicitation to commit a violation described in subdivisions (a) to (d).

(h) Any lesser included offense of a violation described in subdivisions (a) to (g) if the individual is charged with a violation described in subdivisions (a) to (g).

(i) Any other violation arising out of the same transaction as a violation described in subdivisions (a) to (g) if the individual is charged with a violation described in subdivisions (a) to (g).

History: Add. 1988, Act 52, Eff. Oct. 1, 1988;—Am. 1994, Act 193, Eff. Oct. 1, 1994;—Am. 1996, Act 260, Eff. Jan. 1, 1997.

Compiler's note: Section 3 of Act 52 of 1988 provides: "This amendatory act shall take effect June 1, 1988." This section was amended by Act 171 of 1988 to read as follows: "This amendatory act shall take effect October 1, 1988."

CHAPTER 10A.
DRUG TREATMENT COURTS

600.1060 Definitions.

Sec. 1060. As used in this chapter:

(a) "Dating relationship" means that term as defined in section 2950.

(b) "Domestic violence offense" means any crime alleged to have been committed by an individual against his or her spouse or former spouse, an individual with whom he or she has a child in common, an individual with whom he or she has had a dating relationship, or an individual who resides or has resided in the same household.

(c) "Drug treatment court" means a court supervised treatment program for individuals who abuse or are dependent upon any controlled substance or alcohol. A drug treatment court shall comply with the 10 key components promulgated by the national association of drug court professionals, which include all of the following essential characteristics:

(*i*) Integration of alcohol and other drug treatment services with justice system case processing.

(*ii*) Use of a nonadversarial approach by prosecution and defense that promotes public safety while protecting any participant's due process rights.

(*iii*) Identification of eligible participants early with prompt placement in the program.

(*iv*) Access to a continuum of alcohol, drug, and other related treatment and rehabilitation services.

(*v*) Monitoring of participants effectively by frequent alcohol and other drug testing to ensure abstinence from drugs or alcohol.

(*vi*) Use of a coordinated strategy with a regimen of graduated sanctions and rewards to govern the court's responses to participants' compliance.

(*vii*) Ongoing close judicial interaction with each participant and supervision of progress for each participant.

(*viii*) Monitoring and evaluation of the achievement of program goals and the program's effectiveness.

(*ix*) Continued interdisciplinary education in order to promote effective drug court planning, implementation, and operation.

(*x*) The forging of partnerships among other drug courts, public agencies, and community-based organizations to generate local support.

(d) "Participant" means an individual who is admitted into a drug treatment court.

(e) "Prosecutor" means the prosecuting attorney of the county, the city attorney, the village attorney, or the township attorney.

(f) "Traffic offense" means a violation of the Michigan vehicle code, 1949 PA 300, MCL 257.1 to 257.923, or a violation of a local ordinance substantially corresponding to a violation of that act, that involves the operation of a vehicle and, at the time of the violation, is a felony or misdemeanor.

(g) "Violent offender" means an individual who meets either of the following criteria:

(*i*) Is currently charged with or has pled guilty to, or, if a juvenile, is currently alleged to have committed or has admitted responsibility for, an offense involving the death of or a serious bodily injury to any individual, or the carrying, possessing, or use of a firearm or other dangerous weapon by that individual, whether or not any of these circumstances are an element of the offense, or is criminal sexual conduct of any degree.

(*ii*) Has 1 or more prior convictions for, or, if a juvenile, has 1 or more prior findings of responsibility for, a felony involving the use or attempted use of force against another individual with the intent to cause death or serious bodily harm.

History: Add. 2004, Act 224, Eff. Jan. 1, 2005;—Am. 2006, Act 620, Imd. Eff. Jan. 3, 2007.

CHAPTER 29
PROVISIONS CONCERNING SPECIFIC ACTIONS

600.2950 Personal protection order; restraining or enjoining spouse, former spouse, individual with child in common, individual in dating relationship, or person residing or having resided in same household from certain conduct; respondent required to carry concealed weapon; omitting address of residence from documents; issuance, contents, effectiveness, duration, and service of personal protection order; entering order into law enforcement information network; notice; failure to comply with order; false statement to court; enforcement; minor; ownership interest in animal; definitions.

Sec. 2950. (1) Except as provided in subsections (27) and (28), by commencing an independent action to obtain relief under this section, by joining a claim to an action, or by filing a motion in an action in which the petitioner and the individual to be restrained or enjoined are parties, an individual may petition the family division of circuit court to enter a personal protection order to restrain or enjoin a spouse, a former spouse, an individual with whom he or she has had a child in common, an individual with whom he or she has or has had a dating relationship, or an individual residing or having resided in the same household as the petitioner from doing 1 or more of the following:

(a) Entering onto premises.

(b) Assaulting, attacking, beating, molesting, or wounding a named individual.

(c) Threatening to kill or physically injure a named individual.

(d) Removing minor children from the individual having legal custody of the children, except as otherwise authorized by a custody or parenting time order issued by a court of competent jurisdiction.

(e) Purchasing or possessing a firearm.

(f) Interfering with petitioner's efforts to remove petitioner's children or personal property from premises that are solely owned or leased by the individual to be restrained or enjoined.

(g) Interfering with petitioner at petitioner's place of employment or education or engaging in conduct that impairs petitioner's employment or educational relationship or environment.

(h) Having access to information in records concerning a minor child of both petitioner and respondent that will inform respondent about the address or telephone number of petitioner and petitioner's minor child or about petitioner's employment address.

(i) Engaging in conduct that is prohibited under section 411h or 411i of the Michigan penal code, 1931 PA 328, MCL 750.411h and 750.411i.

(j) Any of the following with the intent to cause the petitioner mental distress or to exert control over the petitioner with respect to an animal in which the petitioner has an ownership interest:

(*i*) Injuring, killing, torturing, neglecting, or threatening to injure, kill, torture, or neglect the animal. A restraining order that enjoins conduct under this subparagraph does not prohibit the lawful killing or other use of the animal as described in section 50(11) of the Michigan penal code, 1931 PA 328, MCL 750.50.

(*ii*) Removing the animal from the petitioner's possession.

(*iii*) Retaining or obtaining possession of the animal.

(k) Any other specific act or conduct that imposes upon or interferes with personal liberty or that causes a reasonable apprehension of violence.

(2) If the respondent is a person who is issued a license to carry a concealed weapon and is required to carry a weapon as a condition of his or her employment, a police officer licensed or certified by the Michigan commission on law enforcement standards act, 1965 PA 203, MCL 28.601 to 28.615, a sheriff, a deputy sheriff or a member of the Michigan department of state police, a local corrections officer, department of corrections employee, or a federal law enforcement officer who carries a firearm during the normal course of his or her employment, the petitioner shall notify the court of the respondent's occupation prior to the issuance of the personal protection order. This subsection does not apply to a petitioner who does not know the respondent's occupation.

(3) A petitioner may omit his or her address of residence from documents filed with the court under this section. If a petitioner omits his or her address of residence, the petitioner shall provide the court with a mailing address.

(4) The court shall issue a personal protection order under this section if the court determines that there is reasonable cause to believe that the individual to be restrained or enjoined may commit 1 or more of the acts listed in subsection (1). In determining whether reasonable cause exists, the court shall consider all of the following:

(a) Testimony, documents, or other evidence offered in support of the request for a personal protection order.

(b) Whether the individual to be restrained or enjoined has previously committed or threatened to commit 1 or more of the acts listed in subsection (1).

(5) A court shall not issue a personal protection order that restrains or enjoins conduct described in subsection (1)(a) if all of the following apply:

(a) The individual to be restrained or enjoined is not the spouse of the moving party.

(b) The individual to be restrained or enjoined or the parent, guardian, or custodian of the minor to be restrained or enjoined has a property interest in the premises.

(c) The moving party or the parent, guardian, or custodian of a minor petitioner has no property interest in the premises.

(6) A court shall not refuse to issue a personal protection order solely due to the absence of any of the following:

(a) A police report.

(b) A medical report.

(c) A report or finding of an administrative agency.

(d) Physical signs of abuse or violence.

(7) If the court refuses to grant a personal protection order, it shall state immediately in writing the specific reasons it refused to issue a personal protection order. If a hearing is held, the court shall also immediately state on the record the specific reasons it refuses to issue a personal protection order.

(8) A personal protection order may not be made mutual. Correlative separate personal protection orders are prohibited unless both parties have properly petitioned the court under subsection (1).

(9) A personal protection order is effective and immediately enforceable anywhere in this state when signed by a judge. Upon service, a personal protection order may also be enforced by another state, an Indian tribe, or a territory of the United States.

(10) The court shall designate the law enforcement agency that is responsible for entering the personal protection order into the law enforcement information network as provided by the C.J.I.S. policy council act, 1974 PA 163, MCL 28.211 to 28.215.

(11) A personal protection order must include all of the following, and to the extent practicable the following shall be contained in a single form:

(a) A statement that the personal protection order has been entered to restrain or enjoin conduct listed in the order and that violation of the personal protection order will subject the individual restrained or enjoined to 1 or more of the following:

(*i*) If the respondent is 17 years of age or more, immediate arrest and the civil and criminal contempt powers of the court, and that if he or she is found guilty of criminal contempt, he or she shall be imprisoned for not more than 93 days and may be fined not more than $500.00.

(*ii*) If the respondent is less than 17 years of age, immediate apprehension or being taken into custody, and subject to the dispositional alternatives listed in section 18 of chapter XIIA of the probate code of 1939, 1939 PA 288, MCL 712A.18.

(*iii*) If the respondent violates the personal protection order in a jurisdiction other than this state, the respondent is subject to the enforcement procedures and penalties of the state, Indian tribe, or United States territory under whose jurisdiction the violation occurred.

(b) A statement that the personal protection order is effective and immediately enforceable anywhere in this state when signed by a judge, and that, upon service, a personal protection order also may be enforced by another state, an Indian tribe, or a territory of the United States.

(c) A statement listing the type or types of conduct enjoined.

(d) An expiration date stated clearly on the face of the order.

(e) A statement that the personal protection order is enforceable anywhere in Michigan by any law enforcement agency.

(f) The law enforcement agency designated by the court to enter the personal protection order into the law enforcement information network.

(g) For ex parte orders, a statement that the individual restrained or enjoined may file a motion to modify or rescind the personal protection order and request a hearing within 14 days after the individual restrained or enjoined has been served or has received actual notice of the order and that motion forms and filing instructions are available from the clerk of the court.

(12) A court shall issue an ex parte personal protection order without written or oral notice to the individual restrained or enjoined or his or her attorney if it clearly appears from specific facts shown by verified complaint, written motion, or affidavit that immediate and irreparable injury, loss, or damage will result from the delay required to effectuate notice or that the notice will itself precipitate adverse action before a personal protection order can be issued.

(13) A personal protection order issued under subsection (12) is valid for not less than 182 days. The individual restrained or enjoined may file a motion to modify or rescind the personal protection order and request a hearing under the Michigan court rules. The motion to modify or rescind the personal protection order must be filed within 14 days after the order is served or after the individual restrained or enjoined has received actual notice of the personal protection order unless good cause is shown for filing the motion after the 14 days have elapsed.

(14) Except as otherwise provided in this subsection, the court shall schedule a hearing on the motion to modify or rescind the ex parte personal protection order within 14 days after the filing of the motion to modify or rescind. If the respondent is a person described in subsection (2) and the personal protection order prohibits him or her from purchasing or possessing a firearm, the court shall schedule a hearing on the motion to modify or rescind the ex parte personal protection order within 5 days after the filing of the motion to modify or rescind.

(15) The clerk of the court that issues a personal protection order shall do all of the following immediately upon issuance and without requiring a proof of service on the individual restrained or enjoined:

(a) File a true copy of the personal protection order with the law enforcement agency designated by the court in the personal protection order.

(b) Provide the petitioner with 2 or more true copies of the personal protection order.

(c) If respondent is identified in the pleadings as a law enforcement officer, notify the officer's employing law enforcement agency, if known, about the existence of the personal protection order.

(d) If the personal protection order prohibits respondent from purchasing or possessing a firearm, notify the concealed weapon licensing board in respondent's county of residence about the existence and contents of the personal protection order.

(e) If the respondent is identified in the pleadings as a department of corrections employee, notify the state department of corrections about the existence of the personal protection order.

(f) If the respondent is identified in the pleadings as being a person who may have access to information concerning the petitioner or a child of the petitioner or respondent and that information is contained in friend of the court records, notify the friend of the court for the county in which the information is located about the existence of the personal protection order.

(16) The clerk of the court shall inform the petitioner that he or she may take a true copy of the personal protection order to the law enforcement agency designated by the court under subsection (10) to be immediately entered into the law enforcement information network.

(17) The law enforcement agency that receives a true copy of the personal protection order under subsection (15) or (16) shall immediately and without requiring proof of service enter the personal protection order into the law enforcement information network as provided by the C.J.I.S. policy council act, 1974 PA 163, MCL 28.211 to 28.215.

(18) A personal protection order issued under this section must be served personally or by registered or certified mail, return receipt requested, delivery restricted to the addressee at the last known address or addresses of the individual restrained or enjoined or by any other manner provided in the Michigan court rules. If the individual restrained or enjoined has not been served, a law enforcement officer or clerk of the court who knows that a personal protection order exists may, at any time, serve the individual restrained or enjoined with a true copy of the order or advise the individual restrained or enjoined about the existence of the personal protection order, the specific conduct enjoined, the penalties for violating the order, and where the individual restrained or enjoined may obtain a copy of the order. If the respondent is less than 18 years of age, the parent, guardian, or custodian of that individual must also be served personally or by registered or certified mail, return receipt requested, delivery restricted to the addressee at the last known address or addresses of the parent, guardian, or custodian of the individual restrained or enjoined. A proof of service or proof of oral notice must be filed with the clerk of the court issuing the personal protection order. This subsection does not prohibit the immediate effectiveness of a personal protection order or its immediate enforcement under subsections (21) and (22).

(19) The clerk of the court shall immediately notify the law enforcement agency that received the personal protection order under subsection (15) or (16) if either of the following occurs:

(a) The clerk of the court has received proof that the individual restrained or enjoined has been served.

(b) The personal protection order is rescinded, modified, or extended by court order.

(20) The law enforcement agency that receives information under subsection (19) shall enter the information or cause the information to be entered into the law enforcement information network as provided by the C.J.I.S. policy council act, 1974 PA 163, MCL 28.211 to 28.215.

(21) Subject to subsection (22), a personal protection order is immediately enforceable anywhere in this state by any law enforcement agency that has received a true copy of the order, is shown a copy of it, or has verified its existence on the law enforcement information network as provided by the C.J.I.S. policy council act, 1974 PA 163, MCL 28.211 to 28.215.

(22) If the individual restrained or enjoined has not been served, the law enforcement agency or officer responding to a call alleging a violation of a personal protection order shall serve the individual restrained or enjoined with a true copy of the order or advise the individual restrained or enjoined about the existence of the personal protection order, the specific conduct enjoined, the penalties for violating the order, and where the individual restrained or enjoined may obtain a copy of the order. The law enforcement officer shall enforce the personal protection order and immediately enter or cause to be entered into the law enforcement information network that the individual restrained or enjoined has actual notice of the personal protection order. The law enforcement officer also shall file a proof of service or proof of oral notice with the clerk of the court issuing the personal protection order. If the individual restrained or enjoined has not received notice of the personal protection order, the individual restrained or enjoined shall be given an opportunity to comply with the personal protection order before the law enforcement officer makes a custodial arrest for violation of the personal protection order. The failure to immediately comply with the personal protection order is grounds for an immediate custodial arrest. This subsection does not preclude an arrest under section 15 or 15a of chapter IV of the code of criminal procedure, 1927 PA 175, MCL 764.15 and 764.15a, or a proceeding under section 14 of chapter XIIA of the probate code of 1939, 1939 PA 288, MCL 712A.14.

(23) An individual who is 17 years of age or more and who refuses or fails to comply with a personal protection order under this section is subject to the criminal contempt powers of the court and, if found guilty, shall be imprisoned for not more than 93 days and may be fined not more than $500.00. An individual who is less than 17 years of age and who refuses or fails to comply with a personal protection order issued under this section is subject to the dispositional alternatives listed in section 18 of chapter XIIA of the probate code of 1939, 1939 PA 288, MCL 712A.18. The criminal penalty provided for under this section may be imposed in addition to a penalty that may be imposed for another criminal offense arising from the same conduct.

(24) An individual who knowingly and intentionally makes a false statement to the court in support of his or her petition for a personal protection order is subject to the contempt powers of the court.

(25) A personal protection order issued under this section is also enforceable under chapter XIIA of the probate code of 1939, 1939 PA 288, MCL 712A.1 to 712A.32, and section 15b of chapter IV of the code of criminal procedure, 1927 PA 175, MCL 764.15b.

(26) A personal protection order issued under this section is also enforceable under chapter 17.

(27) A court shall not issue a personal protection order that restrains or enjoins conduct described in subsection (1) if any of the following apply:

(a) The respondent is the unemancipated minor child of the petitioner.

(b) The petitioner is the unemancipated minor child of the respondent.

(c) The respondent is a minor child less than 10 years of age.

(28) If the respondent is less than 18 years of age, issuance of a personal protection order under this section is subject to chapter XIIA of the probate code of 1939, 1939 PA 288, MCL 712A.1 to 712A.32.

(29) A personal protection order that is issued before March 1, 1999 is not invalid on the ground that it does not comply with 1 or more of the requirements added by 1998 PA 477.

(30) For purposes of subsection (1)(j), a petitioner has an ownership interest in an animal if 1 or more of the following are applicable:

(a) The petitioner has a right of property in the animal.

(b) The petitioner keeps or harbors the animal.

(c) The animal is in the petitioner's care.

(d) The petitioner permits the animal to remain on or about premises occupied by the petitioner.

(31) As used in this section:

(a) "Dating relationship" means frequent, intimate associations primarily characterized by the expectation of affectional involvement. Dating relationship does not include a casual relationship or an ordinary fraternization between 2 individuals in a business or social context.

(b) "Federal law enforcement officer" means an officer or agent employed by a law enforcement agency of the United States government whose primary responsibility is the enforcement of laws of the United States.

(c) "Neglect" means that term as defined in section 50 of the Michigan penal code, 1931 PA 328, MCL 750.50.

(d) "Personal protection order" means an injunctive order issued by the circuit court or the family division of circuit court restraining or enjoining activity and individuals listed in subsection (1).

History: Add. 1983, Act 228, Imd. Eff. Nov. 28, 1983;—Am. 1994, Act 58, Eff. July 1, 1994;—Am. 1994, Act 61, Eff. July 1, 1994;—Am. 1994, Act 341, Eff. Apr. 1, 1996;—Am. 1994, Act 402, Eff. Apr. 1, 1995;—Am. 1996, Act 10, Eff. June 1, 1996;—Am. 1997, Act 115, Imd. Eff. Aug. 21, 1997;—Am. 1998, Act 477, Eff. Mar. 1, 1999;—Am. 1999, Act 268, Eff. July 1, 2000;—Am. 2001, Act 200, Eff. Apr. 1, 2002;—Am. 2016, Act 94, Eff. Aug. 1, 2016;—Am. 2016, Act 296, Eff. Jan. 2, 2017.

600.2950a. Personal protection order restraining or enjoining individual from engaging in conduct prohibited under MCL 750.411h, 750.411i, or 750.411s; facts alleging stalking; conduct; respondent required to carry concealed weapon; omitting address of residence from documents; reasons for issuing or refusing to grant order; mutual order prohibited; effectiveness, issuance, contents, and duration of order; duties of court clerk; entering order into L.E.I.N.; service; notice to law enforcement agency; enforcement; refusal or failure to comply; false statement to court; purchase or possession of firearm; minor; issuance to prisoner prohibited; definitions.

Sec. 2950a. (1) Except as provided in subsections (28), (29), and (31), by commencing an independent action to obtain relief under this section, by joining a claim to an action, or by filing a motion in an action in which the petitioner and the individual to be restrained or enjoined are parties, an individual may petition the family division of circuit court to enter a personal protection order to restrain or enjoin an individual from engaging in conduct that is prohibited under section 411h, 411i, or 411s of the Michigan penal code, 1931 PA 328, MCL 750.411h, 750.411i, and 750.411s. Relief under this subsection shall not be granted unless the petition alleges facts that constitute stalking as defined in section 411h or 411i, or conduct that is prohibited under section 411s, of the Michigan penal code, 1931 PA 328, MCL 750.411h, 750.411i, and 750.411s. Relief may be sought and granted under this subsection whether or not the individual to be restrained or enjoined has been charged or convicted under section 411h, 411i, or 411s of the Michigan penal code, 1931 PA 328, MCL 750.411h, 750.411i, and 750.411s, for the alleged violation.

(2) Except as provided in subsections (28), (29), and (31), by commencing an independent action to obtain relief under this section, by joining a claim to an action, or by filing a motion in an action in which the petitioner and the individual to be restrained or enjoined are parties, an individual may petition the family division of circuit court to enter a personal protection order to restrain or enjoin an individual from engaging in any of the following:

(a) One or more of the acts listed in subsection (3), if the respondent has been convicted of a sexual assault of the petitioner, or the respondent has been convicted of furnishing obscene material to the petitioner under section 142 of the Michigan penal code, 1931 PA 328, MCL 750.142, or a substantially similar law of the United States, another state, or a foreign country or tribal or military law. Relief under this subdivision shall be granted if the court determines that the respondent has been convicted of a sexual assault of the petitioner or that the respondent was convicted of furnishing obscene material to the petitioner under section 142 of the Michigan penal code, 1931 PA 328, MCL 750.142, or a substantially similar law of the United States, another state, or a foreign country or tribal or military law.

(b) One or more of the acts listed in subsection (3), if the petitioner has been subjected to, threatened with, or placed in reasonable apprehension of sexual assault by the individual to be enjoined. Relief under this subdivision shall not be granted unless the petition alleges facts that demonstrate that the respondent has perpetrated or threatened sexual assault against the petitioner. Evidence that a respondent has furnished obscene material to a minor petitioner constitutes evidence that the respondent has threatened sexual assault against the petitioner. Relief may be sought and granted under this subdivision regardless of whether the individual to be restrained or enjoined has been charged with or convicted of sexual assault or an offense under section 142 of the Michigan penal code, 1931 PA 328, MCL 750.142, or a substantially similar law of the United States, another state, or a foreign country or tribal or military law.

(3) The court may restrain or enjoin an individual against whom a protection order is sought under subsection (2) from 1 or more of the following:

(a) Entering onto premises.

(b) Threatening to sexually assault, kill, or physically injure petitioner or a named individual.

(c) Purchasing or possessing a firearm.

(d) Interfering with the petitioner's efforts to remove the petitioner's children or personal property from premises that are solely owned or leased by the individual to be restrained or enjoined.

(e) Interfering with the petitioner at the petitioner's place of employment or education or engaging in conduct that impairs the petitioner's employment or educational relationship or environment.

(f) Following or appearing within the sight of the petitioner.

(g) Approaching or confronting the petitioner in a public place or on private property.

(h) Appearing at the petitioner's workplace or residence.

(i) Entering onto or remaining on property owned, leased, or occupied by the petitioner.

(j) Contacting the petitioner by telephone.

(k) Sending mail or electronic communications to the petitioner.

(*l*) Placing an object on, or delivering an object to, property owned, leased, or occupied by the petitioner.

(m) Engaging in conduct that is prohibited under section 411s of the Michigan penal code, 1931 PA 328, MCL 750.411s.

(n) Any other specific act or conduct that imposes upon or interferes with personal liberty or that causes a reasonable apprehension of violence or sexual assault.

(4) Section 520j of the Michigan penal code, 1931 PA 328, MCL 750.520j, applies in any hearing on a petition for, a motion to modify or terminate, or an alleged violation of a personal protection order requested or issued under subsection (2), except as follows:

(a) The written motion and offer of proof shall be filed at least 24 hours before a hearing on a petition to issue a personal protection order or on an alleged violation of a personal protection order.

(b) The written motion and offer of proof shall be filed at the same time that a motion to modify or terminate a personal protection order is filed.

(5) If the respondent to a petition under this section is a person who is issued a license to carry a concealed weapon and is required to carry a weapon as a condition of his or her employment, a police officer licensed or certified by the Michigan commission on law enforcement standards act, 1965 PA 203, MCL 28.601 to 28.615, a sheriff, a deputy sheriff or a member of the Michigan department of state police, a local corrections officer, a department of corrections employee, or a federal law enforcement officer who carries a firearm during the normal course of his or her employment, the petitioner shall notify the court of the respondent's occupation before the personal protection order is issued. This subsection does not apply to a petitioner who does not know the respondent's occupation.

(6) A petitioner may omit his or her address of residence from documents filed with the court under this section. If a petitioner omits his or her address of residence, the petitioner shall provide the court a mailing address.

(7) If a court issues or refuses to issue a personal protection order, the court shall immediately state in writing the specific reasons for issuing or refusing to issue the personal protection order. If a hearing is held, the court shall also immediately state on the record the specific reasons for issuing or refusing to issue a personal protection order.

(8) A personal protection order shall not be made mutual. Correlative separate personal protection orders are prohibited unless both parties have properly petitioned the court under subsection (1) or (2).

(9) A personal protection order is effective and immediately enforceable anywhere in this state when signed by a judge. Upon service, a personal protection order also may be enforced by another state, an Indian tribe, or a territory of the United States.

(10) The court shall designate the law enforcement agency that is responsible for entering the personal protection order into the L.E.I.N.

(11) A personal protection order issued under this section shall include all of the following, to the extent practicable in a single form:

(a) A statement that the personal protection order has been entered to enjoin or restrain conduct listed in the order and that violation of the personal protection order will subject the individual restrained or enjoined to 1 or more of the following:

(*i*) If the respondent is 17 years of age or older, immediate arrest and the civil and criminal contempt powers of the court. If the respondent is found guilty of criminal contempt, he or she shall be imprisoned for not more than 93 days and may be fined not more than $500.00.

(*ii*) If the respondent is less than 17 years of age, immediate apprehension or being taken into custody and the dispositional alternatives listed in section 18 of chapter XIIA of the probate code of 1939, 1939 PA 288, MCL 712A.18.

(*iii*) If the respondent violates the personal protection order in a jurisdiction other than this state, the enforcement procedures and penalties of the state, Indian tribe, or United States territory under whose jurisdiction the violation occurred.

(b) A statement that the personal protection order is effective and immediately enforceable anywhere in this state when signed by a judge, and that upon service, a personal protection order also may be enforced by another state, an Indian tribe, or a territory of the United States.

(c) A statement listing each type of conduct enjoined.

(d) An expiration date stated clearly on the face of the order.

(e) A statement that the personal protection order is enforceable anywhere in Michigan by any law enforcement agency.

(f) The law enforcement agency designated by the court to enter the personal protection order into the L.E.I.N.

(g) For an ex parte order, a statement that the individual restrained or enjoined may file a motion to modify or rescind the personal protection order and request a hearing within 14 days after the individual restrained or enjoined is served or receives actual notice of the personal protection order and that motion forms and filing instructions are available from the clerk of the court.

(12) An ex parte personal protection order shall not be issued and effective without written or oral notice to the individual enjoined or his or her attorney unless it clearly appears from specific facts shown by verified complaint, written motion, or affidavit that immediate and irreparable injury, loss, or damage will result from the delay required to effectuate notice or that the notice will precipitate adverse action before a personal protection order can be issued.

(13) A personal protection order issued under subsection (12) is valid for not less than 182 days. The individual restrained or enjoined may file a motion to modify or rescind the personal protection order and request a hearing under the Michigan court rules. The motion to modify or rescind the personal protection order shall be filed within 14 days after the order is served or after the individual restrained or enjoined receives actual notice of the personal protection order unless good cause is shown for filing the motion after 14 days have elapsed.

(14) Except as otherwise provided in this subsection, the court shall schedule a hearing on the motion to modify or rescind the ex parte personal protection order within 14 days after the motion to modify or rescind is filed. If the respondent is a person described in subsection (5) and the personal protection order prohibits him or her from purchasing or possessing a firearm, the court shall schedule a hearing on the motion to modify or rescind the ex parte personal protection order within 5 days after the motion to modify or rescind is filed.

(15) The clerk of the court that issues a personal protection order shall do all of the following immediately upon issuance without requiring proof of service on the individual restrained or enjoined:

(a) File a true copy of the personal protection order with the law enforcement agency designated by the court in the personal protection order.

(b) Provide the petitioner with 2 or more true copies of the personal protection order.

(c) If the individual restrained or enjoined is identified in the pleadings as a law enforcement officer, notify the officer's employing law enforcement agency of the existence of the personal protection order.

(d) If the personal protection order prohibits the individual restrained or enjoined from purchasing or possessing a firearm, notify the concealed weapon licensing board in the individual's county of residence of the existence and content of the personal protection order.

(e) If the individual restrained or enjoined is identified in the pleadings as a department of corrections employee, notify the department of corrections of the existence of the personal protection order.

(f) If the individual restrained or enjoined is identified in the pleadings as a person who may have access to information concerning the petitioner or a child of the petitioner or individual and that information is contained in friend of the court records, notify the friend of the court for the county in which the information is located of the existence of the personal protection order.

(16) The clerk of a court that issues a personal protection order shall inform the petitioner that he or she may take a true copy of the personal protection order to the law enforcement agency designated by the court under subsection (10) to be immediately entered into the L.E.I.N.

(17) The law enforcement agency that receives a true copy of a personal protection order under subsection (15) or (16) shall immediately, without requiring proof of service, enter the personal protection order into the L.E.I.N.

(18) A personal protection order issued under this section shall be served personally, by registered or certified mail, return receipt requested, delivery restricted to the addressee at the last known address or addresses of the individual restrained or enjoined or by any other method allowed by the Michigan court rules. If the individual restrained or enjoined has not been served, a law enforcement officer or clerk of the court who knows that a personal protection order exists may, at any time, serve the individual restrained or enjoined with a true copy of the order or advise the individual restrained or enjoined of the existence of the personal protection order, the specific conduct enjoined, the penalties for violating the order, and where the individual restrained or enjoined may obtain a copy of the order. If the individual restrained or enjoined is less than 18 years of age, the parent, guardian, or custodian of the individual shall also be served personally or by registered or certified mail, return receipt requested, delivery restricted to the addressee at the last known address or addresses of the parent, guardian, or custodian. A proof of service or proof of oral notice shall be filed with the clerk of the court issuing the personal protection order. This subsection does not prohibit the immediate effectiveness of a personal protection order or immediate enforcement under subsection (21) or (22).

(19) The clerk of the court that issued a personal protection order shall immediately notify the law enforcement agency that received the personal protection order under subsection (15) or (16) if either or both of the following occur:

(a) The clerk of the court receives proof that the individual restrained or enjoined has been served.

(b) The personal protection order is rescinded, modified, or extended by court order.

(20) The law enforcement agency that receives information under subsection (19) shall enter the information or cause the information to be entered into the L.E.I.N.

(21) Subject to subsection (22), a personal protection order is immediately enforceable anywhere in this state by any law enforcement agency that has received a true copy of the order, is shown a copy of it, or has verified its existence on the L.E.I.N.

(22) If the individual restrained or enjoined by a personal protection order has not been served, a law enforcement agency or officer responding to a call alleging a violation of the personal protection order shall serve the individual restrained or enjoined with a true copy of the order or advise the individual restrained or enjoined of the existence of the personal protection order, the specific conduct enjoined, the penalties for violating the order, and where the individual restrained or enjoined may obtain a copy of the order. The law enforcement officer shall enforce the personal protection order and immediately enter or cause to be entered into the L.E.I.N. that the individual restrained or enjoined has actual notice of the personal protection order. The law enforcement officer also shall file a proof of service or proof of oral notice with the clerk of the court that issued the personal protection order. If the individual restrained or enjoined has not received notice of the personal protection order, the individual restrained or enjoined shall be given an opportunity to comply with the personal protection order before the law enforcement officer makes a custodial arrest for violation of the personal protection order. Failure to immediately comply with the personal protection order is grounds for an immediate custodial arrest. This subsection does not preclude an arrest under section 15 or 15a of chapter IV of the code of criminal procedure, 1927 PA 175, MCL 764.15 and 764.15a, or a proceeding under section 14 of chapter XIIA of the probate code of 1939, 1939 PA 288, MCL 712A.14.

(23) An individual 17 years of age or older who refuses or fails to comply with a personal protection order issued under this section is subject to the criminal contempt powers of the court and, if found guilty of criminal contempt, shall be imprisoned for not more than 93 days and may be fined not more than $500.00. An individual less than 17 years of age who refuses or fails to comply with a personal protection order issued under this section is subject to the dispositional alternatives listed in section 18 of chapter XIIA of the probate code of 1939, 1939 PA 288, MCL 712A.18. The criminal penalty under this section may be imposed in addition to any penalty that may be imposed for any other criminal offense arising from the same conduct.

(24) An individual who knowingly and intentionally makes a false statement to a court in support of his or her petition for a personal protection order is subject to the contempt powers of the court.

(25) A personal protection order issued under this section is also enforceable under chapter XIIA of the probate code of 1939, 1939 PA 288, MCL 712A.1 to 712A.32, and section 15b of chapter IV of the code of criminal procedure, 1927 PA 175, MCL 764.15b.

(26) A personal protection order issued under this section may enjoin or restrain an individual from purchasing or possessing a firearm.

(27) A personal protection order issued under this section is also enforceable under chapter 17.

(28) A court shall not issue a personal protection order that restrains or enjoins conduct described in subsection (1) or (3) if any of the following apply:

(a) The respondent is the unemancipated minor child of the petitioner.

(b) The petitioner is the unemancipated minor child of the respondent.

(c) The respondent is a minor child less than 10 years of age.

(29) If the respondent is less than 18 years old, issuance of a personal protection order under this section is subject to chapter XIIA of the probate code of 1939, 1939 PA 288, MCL 712A.1 to 712A.32.

(30) A personal protection order issued before March 1, 1999 is not invalid on the ground that it does not comply with 1 or more of the requirements added by 1998 PA 476.

(31) A court shall not issue a personal protection order under this section if the petitioner is a prisoner. If a personal protection order is issued in violation of this subsection, a court shall rescind the personal protection order upon notification and verification that the petitioner is a prisoner.

(32) As used in this section:

(a) "Convicted" means 1 of the following:

(*i*) The subject of a judgment of conviction or a probation order entered in a court that has jurisdiction over criminal offenses, including a tribal court or a military court.

(*ii*) Assigned to youthful trainee status under sections 11 to 15 of chapter II of the code of criminal procedure, 1927 PA 175, MCL 762.11 to 762.15, if the individual's status of youthful trainee is revoked and an adjudication of guilt is entered.

(*iii*) The subject of an order of disposition entered under section 18 of chapter XIIA of the probate code of 1939, 1939 PA 288, MCL 712A.18, that is open to the general public under section 28 of chapter XIIA of the probate code of 1939, 1939 PA 288, MCL 712A.28.

(*iv*) The subject of an order of disposition or other adjudication in a juvenile matter in another state or country.

(b) "Federal law enforcement officer" means an officer or agent employed by a law enforcement agency of the United States government whose primary responsibility is the enforcement of laws of the United States.

(c) "L.E.I.N." means the law enforcement information network administered under the C.J.I.S. policy council act, 1974 PA 163, MCL 28.211 to 28.215.

(d) "Personal protection order" means an injunctive order issued by the circuit court or the family division of circuit court restraining or enjoining conduct prohibited under subsection (1) or (3).

(e) "Prisoner" means a person subject to incarceration, detention, or admission to a prison who is accused of, convicted of, sentenced for, or adjudicated delinquent for violations of federal, state, or local law or the terms and conditions of parole, probation, pretrial release, or a diversionary program.

(f) "Sexual assault" means an act, attempted act, or conspiracy to engage in an act of criminal conduct as defined in section 520b, 520c, 520d, 520e, or 520g of the Michigan penal code, 1931 PA 328, MCL 750.520b, 750.520c, 750.520d, 750.520e, and 750.520g, or an offense under a law of the United States, another state, or a foreign country or tribal or military law that is substantially similar to an offense listed in this subdivision.

History: Add. 1992, Act 262, Eff. Jan. 1, 1993;—Am. 1994, Act 61, Eff. July 1, 1994;—Am. 1994, Act 341, Eff. Apr. 1, 1996;—Am. 1994, Act 404, Eff. Apr. 1, 1995;—Am. 1997, Act 115, Imd. Eff. Aug. 21, 1997;—Am. 1998, Act 476, Eff. Mar. 1, 1999;—Am. 1999, Act 268, Eff. July 1, 2000;—Am. 2001, Act 196, Eff. Apr. 1, 2002;—Am. 2001, Act 201, Eff. Apr. 1, 2002;—Am. 2010, Act 19, Imd. Eff. Mar. 25, 2010;—Am. 2016, Act 296, Eff. Jan. 2, 2017.

600.2951 "Approved signaling device" and "pistol" defined; use of approved signaling device; strict liability for damages; exception.

Sec. 2951. (1) As used in this section:

(a) "Approved signaling device" means a pistol that is a signaling device approved by the United States coast guard under regulations issued under 46 USC 3306 or under 46 USC 4302, or predecessor statutes, and including, but not limited to, 46 CFR parts 160 and 161.

(b) "Pistol" means a firearm, loaded or unloaded, 26 inches or less in length, or any firearm, loaded or unloaded, that by its construction and appearance conceals it as a firearm.

(2) A person who uses an approved signaling device shall be strictly liable for any damages caused to person or property by that use unless the person reasonably believes that its use is necessary for the safety of himself or herself or of another person on the waters of this state or in an aircraft.

History: Add. 1982, Act 186, Eff. July 1, 1982;—Am. 2012, Act 244, Eff. Jan. 1, 2013.

600.3801 Nuisance; injunction; abatement; guilt; "controlled substance" defined.

Sec. 3801. (1) A building, vehicle, boat, aircraft, or place is a nuisance if 1 or more of the following apply:

(a) It is used for the purpose of lewdness, assignation, prostitution, or gambling.

(b) It is used by, or kept for the use of, prostitutes or other disorderly persons.

(c) It is used for the unlawful manufacture, transporting, sale, keeping for sale, bartering, or furnishing of a controlled substance.

(d) It is used for the unlawful manufacture, transporting, sale, keeping for sale, bartering, or furnishing of vinous, malt, brewed, fermented, spirituous, or intoxicating liquors or mixed liquors or beverages, any part of which is intoxicating.

(e) It is used for conduct prohibited by section 49 of the Michigan penal code, 1931 PA 328, MCL 750.49.

(f) It is used for conduct prohibited by chapter LXVIIA of the Michigan penal code, 1931 PA 328, MCL 750.462a to 750.462h.

(g) It is used to facilitate armed violence in connection with the unlawful use of a firearm or other dangerous weapon.

(2) All furniture, fixtures, and contents of a building, vehicle, boat, aircraft, or place described in subsection (1) and all intoxicating liquors in the building, vehicle, boat, aircraft, or place are also declared a nuisance.

(3) All controlled substances and nuisances shall be enjoined and abated as provided in this act and the court rules.

(4) A person, or a servant, agent, or employee of the person, who owns, leases, conducts, or maintains a building, vehicle, or place described in subsection (1) is guilty of a nuisance.

(5) As used in this section, "controlled substance" means that term as defined in section 7104 of the public health code, 1978 PA 368, MCL 333.7104.

History: 1961, Act 236, Eff. Jan. 1, 1963;—Am. 1988, Act 2, Eff. Apr. 1, 1988;—Am. 2012, Act 352, Imd. Eff. Dec. 13, 2012;—Am. 2014, Act 387, Eff. Mar. 18, 2015.

SPORT SHOOTING RANGES
Act 269 of 1989

AN ACT to provide civil immunity to persons who operate or use certain sport shooting ranges; and to regulate the application of state and local laws, rules, regulations, and ordinances regarding sport shooting ranges.

History: 1989, Act 269, Imd. Eff. Dec. 26, 1989.

The People of the State of Michigan enact:

691.1541 Definitions.

Sec. 1. As used in this act:

(a) "Generally accepted operation practices" means those practices adopted by the commission of natural resources that are established by a nationally recognized nonprofit membership organization that provides voluntary firearm safety programs that include training individuals in the safe handling and use of firearms, which practices are developed with consideration of all information reasonably available regarding the operation of shooting ranges. The generally accepted operation practices shall be reviewed at least every 5 years by the commission of natural resources and revised as the commission considers necessary. The commission shall adopt generally accepted operation practices within 90 days of the effective date of section 2a.

(b) "Local unit of government" means a county, city, township, or village.

(c) "Person" means an individual, proprietorship, partnership, corporation, club, governmental entity, or other legal entity.

(d) "Sport shooting range" or "range" means an area designed and operated for the use of archery, rifles, shotguns, pistols, silhouettes, skeet, trap, black powder, or any other similar sport shooting.

History: 1989, Act 269, Imd. Eff. Dec. 26, 1989;—Am. 1994, Act 250, Imd. Eff. July 5, 1994.

691.1542 Sport shooting ranges; civil liability or criminal prosecution; state rules or regulations.

Sec. 2. (1) Notwithstanding any other provision of law, and in addition to other protections provided in this act, a person who owns or operates or uses a sport shooting range that conforms to generally accepted operation practices in this state is not subject to civil liability or criminal prosecution in any matter relating to noise or noise pollution resulting from the operation or use of the range if the range is in compliance with any noise control laws or ordinances that applied to the range and its operation at the time of construction or initial operation of the range.

(2) In addition to other protections provided in this act, a person who owns, operates, or uses a sport shooting range that conforms to generally accepted operation practices is not subject to an action for nuisance, and a court of the state shall not enjoin or restrain the use or operation of a range on the basis of noise or noise pollution, if the range is in compliance with any noise control laws or ordinances that applied to the range and its operation at the time of construction or initial operation of the range.

(3) Rules or regulations adopted by any state department or agency for limiting levels of noise in terms of decibel level which may occur in the outdoor atmosphere do not apply to a sport shooting range exempted from liability under this act. However, this subsection does not restrict the application of any provision of the generally accepted operation practices.

History: 1989, Act 269, Imd. Eff. Dec. 26, 1989;—Am. 1994, Act 250, Imd. Eff. July 5, 1994.

691.1542a Continuation of preexisting sport shooting ranges.

Sec. 2a. (1) A sport shooting range that is operated and is not in violation of existing law at the time of the enactment of an ordinance shall be permitted to continue in operation even if the operation of the sport shooting range at a later date does not conform to the new ordinance or an amendment to an existing ordinance.

(2) A sport shooting range that is in existence as of the effective date of this section and operates in compliance with generally accepted operation practices, even if not in compliance with an ordinance of a local unit of government, shall be permitted to do all of the following within its preexisting geographic boundaries if in compliance with generally accepted operation practices:

(a) Repair, remodel, or reinforce any conforming or nonconforming building or structure as may be necessary in the interest of public safety or to secure the continued use of the building or structure.

(b) Reconstruct, repair, restore, or resume the use of a nonconforming building damaged by fire, collapse, explosion, act of god, or act of war occurring after the effective date of this section. The reconstruction, repair, or restoration shall be completed within 1 year following the date of the damage or settlement of any property damage claim. If reconstruction, repair, or restoration is not completed within 1 year, continuation of the nonconforming use may be terminated in the discretion of the local unit of government.

(c) Do anything authorized under generally accepted operation practices, including, but not limited to:

(*i*) Expand or increase its membership or opportunities for public participation.

(*ii*) Expand or increase events and activities.

History: Add. 1994, Act 250, Imd. Eff. July 5, 1994.

691.1543 Local regulation.

Sec. 3. Except as otherwise provided in this act, this act does not prohibit a local unit of government from regulating the location, use, operation, safety, and construction of a sport shooting range.

History: 1989, Act 269, Imd. Eff. Dec. 26, 1989;—Am. 1994, Act 250, Imd. Eff. July 5, 1994.

691.1544 Acceptance of risk.

Sec. 4. Each person who participates in sport shooting at a sport shooting range that conforms to generally accepted operation practices accepts the risks associated with the sport to the extent the risks are obvious and inherent. Those risks include, but are not limited to, injuries that may result from noise, discharge of a projectile or shot, malfunction of sport shooting equipment not owned by the shooting range, natural variations in terrain, surface or subsurface snow or ice conditions, bare spots, rocks, trees, and other forms of natural growth or debris.

History: Add. 1994, Act 251, Imd. Eff. July 5, 1994.

PROBATE CODE OF 1939 (EXCERPT)
Act 288 of 1939

AN ACT to revise and consolidate the statutes relating to certain aspects of the family division of circuit court, to the jurisdiction, powers, and duties of the family division of circuit court and its judges and other officers, to the change of name of adults and children, and to the adoption of adults and children; to prescribe certain jurisdiction, powers, and duties of the family division of circuit court and its judges and other officers; to prescribe the manner and time within which certain actions and proceedings may be brought in the family division of the circuit court; to prescribe pleading, evidence, practice, and procedure in certain actions and proceedings in the family division of circuit court; to provide for appeals from certain actions in the family division of circuit court; to prescribe the powers and duties of certain state departments, agencies, and officers; to provide for certain immunity from liability; and to provide remedies and penalties.

History: 1939, Act 288, Eff. Sept. 29, 1939;—Am. 1972, Act 175, Imd. Eff. June 16, 1972;—Am. 1982, Act 72, Imd. Eff. Apr. 14, 1982;—Am. 1982, Act 398, Imd. Eff. Dec. 28, 1982;—Am. 1997, Act 163, Eff. Jan. 1, 1998;—Am. 2000, Act 232, Eff. Jan. 1, 2001.

The People of the State of Michigan enact:

CHAPTER XIIA
JURISDICTION, PROCEDURE, AND DISPOSITION INVOLVING MINORS

712A.2 Authority and jurisdiction of court.

Sec. 2. The court has the following authority and jurisdiction:

(a) Exclusive original jurisdiction superior to and regardless of the jurisdiction of another court in proceedings concerning a juvenile under 17 years of age who is found within the county if 1 or more of the following applies:

(1) Except as otherwise provided in this sub-subdivision, the juvenile has violated any municipal ordinance or law of the state or of the United States. If the court enters into an agreement under section 2e of this chapter, the court has jurisdiction over a juvenile who committed a civil infraction as provided in that section. The court has jurisdiction over a juvenile 14 years of age or older who is charged with a specified juvenile violation only if the prosecuting attorney files a petition in the court instead of authorizing a complaint and warrant. As used in this sub-subdivision, "specified juvenile violation" means 1 or more of the following:

(A) A violation of section 72, 83, 86, 89, 91, 316, 317, 349, 520b, 529, 529a, or 531 of the Michigan penal code, 1931 PA 328, MCL 750.72, 750.83, 750.86, 750.89, 750.91, 750.316, 750.317, 750.349, 750.520b, 750.529, 750.529a, and 750.531.

(B) A violation of section 84 or 110a(2) of the Michigan penal code, 1931 PA 328, MCL 750.84 and 750.110a, if the juvenile is armed with a dangerous weapon. As used in this paragraph, "dangerous weapon" means 1 or more of the following:

(*i*) A loaded or unloaded firearm, whether operable or inoperable.

(*ii*) A knife, stabbing instrument, brass knuckles, blackjack, club, or other object specifically designed or customarily carried or possessed for use as a weapon.

(*iii*) An object that is likely to cause death or bodily injury when used as a weapon and that is used as a weapon or carried or possessed for use as a weapon.

(*iv*) An object or device that is used or fashioned in a manner to lead a person to believe the object or device is an object or device described in subparagraphs (*i*) to (*iii*).

(C) A violation of section 186a of the Michigan penal code, 1931 PA 328, MCL 750.186a, regarding escape or attempted escape from a juvenile facility, but only if the juvenile facility from which the individual escaped or attempted to escape was 1 of the following:

(*i*) A high-security or medium-security facility operated by the department of human services or a county juvenile agency.

(*ii*) A high-security facility operated by a private agency under contract with the department of human services or a county juvenile agency.

(D) A violation of section 7401(2)(a)(*i*) or 7403(2)(a)(*i*) of the public health code, 1978 PA 368, MCL 333.7401 and 333.7403.

(E) An attempt to commit a violation described in paragraphs (A) to (D).

(F) Conspiracy to commit a violation described in paragraphs (A) to (D).

(G) Solicitation to commit a violation described in paragraphs (A) to (D).

(H) A lesser included offense of a violation described in paragraphs (A) to (G) if the individual is charged with a violation described in paragraphs (A) to (G).

(I) Another violation arising out of the same transaction as a violation described in paragraphs (A) to (G) if the individual is charged with a violation described in paragraphs (A) to (G).

(2) The juvenile has deserted his or her home without sufficient cause, and the court finds on the record that the juvenile has been placed or refused alternative placement or the juvenile and the juvenile's parent, guardian, or custodian have exhausted or refused family counseling.

(3) The juvenile is repeatedly disobedient to the reasonable and lawful commands of his or her parents, guardian, or custodian, and the court finds on the record by clear and convincing evidence that court-accessed services are necessary.

(4) The juvenile willfully and repeatedly absents himself or herself from school or other learning program intended to meet the juvenile's educational needs, or repeatedly violates rules and regulations of the school or other learning program, and the court finds on the record that the juvenile, the juvenile's parent, guardian, or custodian, and school officials or learning program personnel have met on the juvenile's educational problems and educational counseling and alternative agency help have been sought. As used in this sub-subdivision only, "learning program" means an organized educational program that is appropriate, given the age, intelligence, ability, and psychological limitations of a juvenile, in the subject areas of reading, spelling, mathematics, science, history, civics, writing, and English grammar.

(b) Jurisdiction in proceedings concerning a juvenile under 18 years of age found within the county:

(1) Whose parent or other person legally responsible for the care and maintenance of the juvenile, when able to do so, neglects or refuses to provide proper or necessary support, education, medical, surgical, or other care necessary for his or her health or morals, who is subject to a substantial risk of harm to his or her mental well-being, who is abandoned by his or her parents, guardian, or other custodian, or who is without proper custody or guardianship. As used in this sub-subdivision:

(A) "Education" means learning based on an organized educational program that is appropriate, given the age, intelligence, ability, and psychological limitations of a juvenile, in the subject areas of reading, spelling, mathematics, science, history, civics, writing, and English grammar.

(B) "Without proper custody or guardianship" does not mean a parent has placed the juvenile with another person who is legally responsible for the care and maintenance of the juvenile and who is able to and does provide the juvenile with proper care and maintenance.

(2) Whose home or environment, by reason of neglect, cruelty, drunkenness, criminality, or depravity on the part of a parent, guardian, nonparent adult, or other custodian, is an unfit place for the juvenile to live in.

(3) If the juvenile is dependent and is in danger of substantial physical or psychological harm. The juvenile may be found to be dependent when any of the following occurs:

(A) The juvenile is homeless or not domiciled with a parent or other legally responsible person.

(B) The juvenile has repeatedly run away from home and is beyond the control of a parent or other legally responsible person.

(C) The juvenile is alleged to have committed a commercial sexual activity as that term is defined in section 462a of the Michigan penal code, 1931 PA 328, MCL 750.462a or a delinquent act that is the result of force, fraud, coercion, or manipulation exercised by a parent or other adult.

(D) The juvenile's custodial parent or legally responsible person has died or has become permanently incapacitated and no appropriate parent or legally responsible person is willing and able to provide care for the juvenile.

(4) Whose parent has substantially failed, without good cause, to comply with a limited guardianship placement plan described in section 5205 of the estates and protected individuals code, 1998 PA 386, MCL 700.5205, regarding the juvenile.

(5) Whose parent has substantially failed, without good cause, to comply with a court-structured plan described in section 5207 or 5209 of the estates and protected individuals code, 1998 PA 386, MCL 700.5207 and 700.5209, regarding the juvenile.

(6) If the juvenile has a guardian under the estates and protected individuals code, 1998 PA 386, MCL 700.1101 to 700.8206, and the juvenile's parent meets both of the following criteria:

(A) The parent, having the ability to support or assist in supporting the juvenile, has failed or neglected, without good cause, to provide regular and substantial support for the juvenile for 2 years or more before the filing of the petition or, if a support order has been entered, has failed to substantially comply with the order for 2 years or more before the filing of the petition.

(B) The parent, having the ability to visit, contact, or communicate with the juvenile, has regularly and substantially failed or neglected, without good cause, to do so for 2 years or more before the filing of the petition.

If a petition is filed in the court alleging that a juvenile is within the provisions of subdivision (b)(1), (2), (3), (4), (5), or (6) and the custody of that juvenile is subject to the prior or continuing order of another court of record of this state, the manner of notice to the other court of record and the authority of the court to proceed is governed by rule of the supreme court.

(c) Jurisdiction over juveniles under 18 years of age, jurisdiction of whom has been waived to the family division of circuit court by a circuit court under a provision in a temporary order for custody of juveniles based upon a complaint for divorce or upon a motion related to a complaint for divorce by the prosecuting attorney, in a divorce judgment dissolving a marriage between the juvenile's parents, or by an amended judgment relative to the juvenile's custody in a divorce.

(d) If the court finds on the record that voluntary services have been exhausted or refused, concurrent jurisdiction in proceedings concerning a juvenile between the ages of 17 and 18 found within the county who is 1 or more of the following:

(1) Repeatedly addicted to the use of drugs or the intemperate use of alcoholic liquors.

(2) Repeatedly associating with criminal, dissolute, or disorderly persons.

(3) Found of his or her own free will and knowledge in a house of prostitution, assignation, or ill-fame.

(4) Repeatedly associating with thieves, prostitutes, pimps, or procurers.

(5) Willfully disobedient to the reasonable and lawful commands of his or her parents, guardian, or other custodian and in danger of becoming morally depraved.

If a juvenile is brought before the court in a county other than that in which the juvenile resides, before a hearing and with the consent of the judge of the court in the county of residence, the court may enter an order transferring jurisdiction of the matter to the court of the county of residence. Consent to transfer jurisdiction is not required if the county of residence is a county juvenile agency and satisfactory proof of residence is furnished to the court of the county of residence. The order does not constitute a legal settlement in this state that is required for the purpose of section 55 of the social welfare act, 1939 PA 280, MCL 400.55. The order and a certified copy of the proceedings in the transferring court shall be delivered to the court of the county of residence. A case designated as a case in which the juvenile shall be tried in the same manner as an adult under section 2d of this chapter may be transferred for venue or for juvenile disposition, but shall not be transferred on grounds of residency. If the case is not transferred, the court having jurisdiction of the offense shall try the case.

(e) Authority to establish or assist in developing a program or programs within the county to prevent delinquency and provide services to act upon reports submitted to the court related to the behavior of a juvenile who does not require formal court jurisdiction but otherwise falls within subdivision (a). These services shall be used only if the juvenile and his or her parents, guardian, or custodian voluntarily accepts them.

(f) If the court operates a detention home for juveniles within the court's jurisdiction under subdivision (a)(1), authority to place a juvenile within that home pending trial if the juvenile is within the circuit court's jurisdiction under section 606 of the revised judicature act of 1961, 1961 PA 236, MCL 600.606, and if the circuit court orders the family division of circuit court in the same county to place the juvenile in that home. The family division of circuit court shall comply with that order.

(g) Authority to place a juvenile in a county jail under section 27a of chapter IV of the code of criminal procedure, 1927 PA 175, MCL 764.27a, if the court designates the case under section 2d of this chapter as a case in which the juvenile is to be tried in the same manner as an adult and the court determines there is probable cause to believe that the offense was committed and probable cause to believe the juvenile committed that offense.

(h) Jurisdiction over a proceeding under section 2950 or 2950a of the revised judicature act of 1961, 1961 PA 236, MCL 600.2950 and 600.2950a, in which a minor less than 18 years of age is the respondent, or a proceeding to enforce a valid foreign protection order issued against a respondent who is a minor less than 18 years of age. A personal protection order shall not be issued against a respondent who is a minor less than 10 years of age. Venue for an initial action under section 2950 or 2950a of the revised judicature act of 1961, 1961 PA 236, MCL 600.2950 and 600.2950a, is proper in the county of residence of either the petitioner or respondent. If the respondent does not live in this state, venue for the initial action is proper in the petitioner's county of residence.

(i) In a proceeding under this chapter concerning a juvenile's care and supervision, the court may issue orders affecting a party as necessary. This subdivision does not apply after May 1, 2018. As used in this subdivision, "party" means 1 of the following:

(*i*) In a delinquency proceeding, the petitioner and juvenile.

(*ii*) In a child protective proceeding, the petitioner, department of human services, child, respondent, parent, guardian, or legal custodian, and any licensed child caring institution or child placing agency under contract with the department of human services to provide for a juvenile's care and supervision.

History: Add. 1944, 1st Ex. Sess., Act 54, Imd. Eff. Mar. 6, 1944;—Am. 1947, Act 68, Imd. Eff. May 2, 1947;—CL 1948, 712A.2;—Am. 1953, Act 193, Eff. Oct. 2, 1953;—Am. 1965, Act 182, Imd. Eff. July 15, 1965;—Am. 1972, Act 175, Imd. Eff. June 16, 1972;—Am. 1984, Act 131, Imd. Eff. June 1, 1984;—Am. 1986, Act 203, Imd. Eff. July 25, 1986;—Am. 1988, Act 53, Eff. Oct. 1, 1988;—Am. 1988, Act 224, Eff. Apr. 1, 1989;—Am. 1990, Act 314, Imd. Eff. Dec. 20, 1990;—Am. 1994, Act 192, Eff. Oct. 1, 1994;—Am. 1996, Act 250, Eff. Jan. 1, 1997;—Am. 1996, Act 409, Eff. Jan. 1, 1998;—Am. 1998, Act 474, Eff. Mar. 1, 1999;—Am. 1998, Act 478, Eff. Jan. 12, 1999;—Am. 1998, Act 530, Eff. July 1, 1999;—Am. 2000, Act 55, Eff. Apr. 1, 2000;—Am. 2001, Act 211, Eff. Apr. 1, 2002;—Am. 2014, Act 342, Eff. Jan. 14, 2015;—Am. 2014, Act 519, Imd. Eff. Jan. 14, 2015.

Compiler's note: Section 3 of Act 53 of 1988 provides: "This amendatory act shall take effect June 1, 1988." This section was amended by Act 172 of 1988 to read as follows: "This amendatory act shall take effect October 1, 1988."

Former law: See sections 2, 3, 4 and 5 of Ch. XII of Act 288 of 1939, and CL 1929, § 12834.

Popular name: Probate Code

Popular name: Juvenile Code

712A.2d Juvenile to be tried as adult; designation by prosecuting attorney or court; factors; probable cause hearing; setting case for trial; proceedings as criminal proceedings; disposition or imposition of sentence; "specified juvenile violation" defined.

Sec. 2d. (1) In a petition or amended petition alleging that a juvenile is within the court's jurisdiction under section 2(a)(1) of this chapter for a specified juvenile violation, the prosecuting attorney may designate the case as a case in which the juvenile is to be tried in the same manner as an adult. An amended petition making a designation under this subsection shall be filed only by leave of the court.

(2) In a petition alleging that a juvenile is within the court's jurisdiction under section 2(a)(1) of this chapter for an offense other than a specified juvenile violation, the prosecuting attorney may request that the court designate the case as a case in which the juvenile is to be tried in the same manner as an adult. The court may designate the case following a hearing if it determines that the best interests of the juvenile and the public would be served by the juvenile being tried in the same manner as an adult. In determining whether the best interests of the juvenile and the public would be served, the court shall consider all of the following factors, giving greater weight to the seriousness of the alleged offense and the juvenile's prior delinquency record than to the other factors:

(a) The seriousness of the alleged offense in terms of community protection, including, but not limited to, the existence of any aggravating factors recognized by the sentencing guidelines, the use of a firearm or other dangerous weapon, and the impact on any victim.

(b) The juvenile's culpability in committing the alleged offense, including, but not limited to, the level of the juvenile's participation in planning and carrying out the offense and the existence of any aggravating or mitigating factors recognized by the sentencing guidelines.

(c) The juvenile's prior record of delinquency including, but not limited to, any record of detention, any police record, any school record, or any other evidence indicating prior delinquent behavior.

(d) The juvenile's programming history, including, but not limited to, the juvenile's past willingness to participate meaningfully in available programming.

(e) The adequacy of the punishment or programming available in the juvenile justice system.

(f) The dispositional options available for the juvenile.

(3) If a case is designated under this section, the case shall be set for trial in the same manner as the trial of an adult in a court of general criminal jurisdiction unless a probable cause hearing is required under subsection (4).

(4) If the petition in a case designated under this section alleges an offense that if committed by an adult would be a felony or punishable by imprisonment for more than 1 year, the court shall conduct a probable cause hearing not later than 14 days after the case is designated to determine whether there is probable cause to believe the offense was committed and whether there is probable cause to believe the juvenile committed the offense. This hearing may be combined with the designation hearing under subsection (2) for an offense other than a specified juvenile offense. A probable cause hearing under this section is the equivalent of the preliminary examination in a court of general criminal jurisdiction and satisfies the requirement for that hearing. A probable cause hearing shall be conducted by a judge other than the judge who will try the case if the juvenile is tried in the same manner as an adult.

(5) If the court determines there is probable cause to believe the offense alleged in the petition was committed and probable cause to believe the juvenile committed the offense, the case shall be set for trial in the same manner as the trial of an adult in a court of general criminal jurisdiction.

(6) If the court determines that an offense did not occur or there is not probable cause to believe the juvenile committed the offense, the court shall dismiss the petition. If the court determines there is probable cause to believe another offense was committed and there is probable cause to believe the juvenile committed that offense, the court may further determine whether the case should be designated as a case in which the juvenile should be tried in the same manner as an adult as provided in subsection (2). If the court designates the case, the case shall be set for trial in the same manner as the trial of an adult in a court of general criminal jurisdiction.

(7) If a case is designated under this section, the proceedings are criminal proceedings and shall afford all procedural protections and guarantees to which the juvenile would be entitled if being tried for the offense in a court of general criminal jurisdiction. A plea of guilty or nolo contendere or a verdict of guilty shall result in entry of a judgment of conviction. The conviction shall have the same effect and liabilities as if it had been obtained in a court of general criminal jurisdiction.

(8) Following a judgment of conviction, the court shall enter a disposition or impose a sentence authorized under section 18(1)(n) of this chapter.

(9) As used in this section, "specified juvenile violation" means any of the following:

(a) A violation of section 72, 83, 86, 89, 91, 316, 317, 349, 520b, 529, 529a, or 531 of the Michigan penal code, 1931 PA 328, MCL 750.72, 750.83, 750.86, 750.89, 750.91, 750.316, 750.317, 750.349, 750.520b, 750.529, 750.529a, and 750.531.

(b) A violation of section 84 or 110a(2) of the Michigan penal code, 1931 PA 328, MCL 750.84 and 750.110a, if the juvenile is armed with a dangerous weapon. As used in this subdivision, "dangerous weapon" means 1 or more of the following:

(*i*) A loaded or unloaded firearm, whether operable or inoperable.

(*ii*) A knife, stabbing instrument, brass knuckles, blackjack, club, or other object specifically designed or customarily carried or possessed for use as a weapon.

(*iii*) An object that is likely to cause death or bodily injury when used as a weapon and that is used as a weapon or carried or possessed for use as a weapon.

(*iv*) An object or device that is used or fashioned in a manner to lead a person to believe the object or device is an object or device described in subparagraphs (*i*) to (*iii*).

(c) A violation of section 186a of the Michigan penal code, 1931 PA 328, MCL 750.186a, regarding escape or attempted escape from a juvenile facility, but only if the juvenile facility from which the juvenile escaped or attempted to escape was 1 of the following:

(*i*) A high-security or medium-security facility operated by the family independence agency or a county juvenile agency.

(*ii*) A high-security facility operated by a private agency under contract with the family independence agency or a county juvenile agency.

(d) A violation of section 7401(2)(a)(*i*) or 7403(2)(a)(*i*) of the public health code, 1978 PA 368, MCL 333.7401 and 333.7403.

(e) An attempt to commit a violation described in subdivisions (a) to (d).

(f) Conspiracy to commit a violation described in subdivisions (a) to (d).

(g) Solicitation to commit a violation described in subdivisions (a) to (d).

(h) Any lesser included offense of an offense described in subdivisions (a) to (g) if the juvenile is alleged in the petition to have committed an offense described in subdivisions (a) to (g).

(i) Any other offense arising out of the same transaction as an offense described in subdivisions (a) to (g) if the juvenile is alleged in the petition to have committed an offense described in subdivisions (a) to (g).

History: Add. 1996, Act 244, Eff. Aug. 1, 1996;—Am. 1998, Act 478, Eff. Jan. 12, 1999.

Popular name: Probate Code

Popular name: Juvenile Code

712A.4 Waiver of jurisdiction when child of 14 or older accused of felony.

Sec. 4. (1) If a juvenile 14 years of age or older is accused of an act that if committed by an adult would be a felony, the judge of the family division of circuit court in the county in which the offense is alleged to have been committed may waive jurisdiction under this section upon motion of the prosecuting attorney. After waiver, the juvenile may be tried in the court having general criminal jurisdiction of the offense.

(2) Before conducting a hearing on the motion to waive jurisdiction, the court shall give notice of the hearing in the manner provided by supreme court rule to the juvenile and the prosecuting attorney and, if addresses are known, to the juvenile's parents or guardians. The notice shall state clearly that a waiver of jurisdiction to a court of general criminal jurisdiction has been requested and that, if granted, the juvenile can be prosecuted for the alleged offense as though he or she were an adult.

(3) Before the court waives jurisdiction, the court shall determine on the record if there is probable cause to believe that an offense has been committed that if committed by an adult would be a felony and if there is probable cause to believe that the juvenile committed the offense. Before a juvenile may waive a probable cause hearing under this subsection, the court shall inform the juvenile that a waiver of this subsection waives the preliminary examination required by chapter VI of the code of criminal procedure, Act No. 175 of the Public Acts of 1927, being sections 766.1 to 766.18 of the Michigan Compiled Laws.

(4) Upon a showing of probable cause under subsection (3), the court shall conduct a hearing to determine if the best interests of the juvenile and the public would be served by granting a waiver of jurisdiction to the court of general criminal jurisdiction. In making its determination, the court shall consider all of the following criteria, giving greater weight to the seriousness of the alleged offense and the juvenile's prior record of delinquency than to the other criteria:

(a) The seriousness of the alleged offense in terms of community protection, including, but not limited to, the existence of any aggravating factors recognized by the sentencing guidelines, the use of a firearm or other dangerous weapon, and the impact on any victim.

(b) The culpability of the juvenile in committing the alleged offense, including, but not limited to, the level of the juvenile's participation in planning and carrying out the offense and the existence of any aggravating or mitigating factors recognized by the sentencing guidelines.

(c) The juvenile's prior record of delinquency including, but not limited to, any record of detention, any police record, any school record, or any other evidence indicating prior delinquent behavior.

(d) The juvenile's programming history, including, but not limited to, the juvenile's past willingness to participate meaningfully in available programming.

(e) The adequacy of the punishment or programming available in the juvenile justice system.

(f) The dispositional options available for the juvenile.

(5) If the court determines that there is probable cause to believe that an offense has been committed that if committed by an adult would be a felony and that the juvenile committed the offense, the court shall waive jurisdiction of the juvenile if the court finds that the juvenile has previously been subject to the jurisdiction of the circuit court under this section or section 606 of the revised judicature act of 1961, Act No. 236 of the Public Acts of 1961, being section 600.606 of the Michigan Compiled Laws, or the recorder's court of the city of Detroit under this section or section 10a(1)(c) of Act No. 369 of the Public Acts of 1919, being section 725.10a of the Michigan Compiled Laws.

(6) If legal counsel has not been retained or appointed to represent the juvenile, the court shall advise the juvenile and his or her parents, guardian, custodian, or guardian ad litem of the juvenile's right to representation and appoint legal counsel. If the court appoints legal counsel, the judge may assess the cost of providing legal counsel as costs against the juvenile or those responsible for his or her support, or both, if the persons to be assessed are financially able to comply.

(7) Legal counsel shall have access to records or reports provided and received by the judge as a basis for decision in proceedings for waiver of jurisdiction. A continuance shall be granted at legal counsel's request if any report, information, or recommendation not previously available is introduced or developed at the hearing and the interests of justice require a continuance.

(8) The court shall enter a written order either granting or denying the motion to waive jurisdiction and the court shall state on the record or in a written opinion the court's findings of fact and conclusions of law forming the basis for entering the order. If a juvenile is waived, a transcript of the court's findings or a copy of the written opinion shall be sent to the court of general criminal jurisdiction.

(9) If the court does not waive jurisdiction, a transcript of the court's findings or, if a written opinion is prepared, a copy of the written opinion shall be sent to the prosecuting attorney, juvenile, or juvenile's attorney upon request.

(10) If the court waives jurisdiction, the juvenile shall be arraigned on an information filed by the prosecutor in the court of general criminal jurisdiction. The probable cause finding under subsection (3) satisfies the requirements of, and is the equivalent of, the preliminary examination required by chapter VI of Act No. 175 of the Public Acts of 1927.

(11) As used in this section, "felony" means an offense punishable by imprisonment for more than 1 year or an offense designated by law as a felony.

History: Add. 1944, 1st Ex. Sess., Act 54, Imd. Eff. Mar. 6, 1944;—Am. 1946, 1st Ex. Sess., Act 22, Imd. Eff. Feb. 26, 1946;—CL 1948, 712A.4;—Am. 1969, Act 140, Eff. Mar. 20, 1970;—Am. 1972, Act 265, Imd. Eff. Oct. 3, 1972;—Am. 1988, Act 182, Eff. Oct. 1, 1988;—Am. 1996, Act 262, Eff. Jan. 1, 1997;—Am. 1996, Act 409, Eff. Jan. 1, 1998.

Former law: See section 26 of Ch. XII of Act 288 of 1939, and CL 1929, § 12839.

Popular name: Probate Code

Popular name: Juvenile Code

712A.13a Definitions; petition; release of juvenile; order removing abusive person from home; placement of child; foster care; conditions; duty of court to inform parties; criminal record check and central registry clearance; family-like setting; parenting time; siblings; joint placement; visitation or other contact; review and modification of orders and plans; release of information; information included with order; "abuse" defined.

Sec. 13a. (1) As used in this section and sections 2, 6b, 13b, 17c, 17d, 18f, 19, 19a, 19b, and 19c of this chapter:

(a) "Agency" means a public or private organization, institution, or facility that is performing the functions under part D of title IV of the social security act, 42 USC 651 to 669b, or that is responsible under court order or contractual arrangement for a juvenile's care and supervision.

(b) "Agency case file" means the current file from the agency providing direct services to the child, that can include the child protective services file if the child has not been removed from the home or the department or contract agency foster care file as provided under 1973 PA 116, MCL 722.111 to 722.128.

(c) "Attorney" means, if appointed to represent a child in a proceeding under section 2(b) or (c) of this chapter, an attorney serving as the child's legal advocate in a traditional attorney-client relationship with the child, as governed by the Michigan rules of professional conduct. An attorney defined under this subdivision owes the same duties of undivided loyalty, confidentiality, and zealous representation of the child's expressed wishes as the attorney would to an adult client. For the purpose of a notice required under these sections, attorney includes a child's lawyer-guardian ad litem.

(d) "Case service plan" means the plan developed by an agency and prepared under section 18f of this chapter that includes services to be provided by and responsibilities and obligations of the agency and activities, responsibilities, and obligations of the parent. The case service plan may be referred to using different names than case service plan including, but not limited to, a parent/agency agreement or a parent/agency treatment plan and service agreement.

(e) "Foster care" means care provided to a juvenile in a foster family home, foster family group home, or child caring institution licensed or approved under 1973 PA 116, MCL 722.111 to 722.128, or care provided to a juvenile in a relative's home under a court order.

(f) "Guardian ad litem" means an individual whom the court appoints to assist the court in determining the child's best interests. A guardian ad litem does not need to be an attorney.

(g) "Lawyer-guardian ad litem" means an attorney appointed under section 17c of this chapter. A lawyer-guardian ad litem represents the child, and has the powers and duties, as set forth in section 17d of this chapter. The provisions of section 17d of this chapter also apply to a lawyer-guardian ad litem appointed under each of the following:

(*i*) Section 5213 or 5219 of the estates and protected individuals code, 1998 PA 386, MCL 700.5213 and 700.5219.

(*ii*) Section 4 of the child custody act of 1970, 1970 PA 91, MCL 722.24.

(*iii*) Section 10 of the child protection law, 1975 PA 238, MCL 722.630.

(h) "Nonparent adult" means a person who is 18 years of age or older and who, regardless of the person's domicile, meets all of the following criteria in relation to a child over whom the court takes jurisdiction under this chapter:

(*i*) Has substantial and regular contact with the child.

(*ii*) Has a close personal relationship with the child's parent or with a person responsible for the child's health or welfare.

(*iii*) Is not the child's parent or a person otherwise related to the child by blood or affinity to the third degree.

(i) "Permanent foster family agreement" means an agreement for a child 14 years old or older to remain with a particular foster family until the child is 18 years old under standards and requirements established by the department, which agreement is among all of the following:

(*i*) The child.

(*ii*) If the child is a temporary ward, the child's family.

(*iii*) The foster family.

(*iv*) The child placing agency responsible for the child's care in foster care.

(j) "Relative" means an individual who is at least 18 years of age and related to the child by blood, marriage, or adoption, as grandparent, great-grandparent, great-great-grandparent, aunt or uncle, great-aunt or great-uncle, great-great-aunt or great-great-uncle, sibling, stepsibling, nephew or niece, first cousin or first cousin once removed, and the spouse of any of the above, even after the marriage has ended by death or divorce. A stepparent, ex-stepparent, or the parent who shares custody of a half-sibling shall be considered a relative for the purpose of placement. Notification to the stepparent, ex-stepparent, or the parent who shares custody of a half-sibling is required as described in section 4a of the foster care and adoption services act, 1994 PA 203, MCL 722.954a. A child may be placed with the parent of a man whom the court has found probable cause to believe is the putative father if there is no man with legally established rights to the child. A placement with the parent of a putative father under this subdivision is not a finding of paternity and does not confer legal standing on the putative father.

(k) "Sex offenders registration act" means the sex offenders registration act, 1994 PA 295, MCL 28.721 to 28.736.

(*l*) "Sibling" means a child who is related through birth or adoption by at least 1 common parent. Sibling includes that term as defined by the American Indian or Alaskan native child's tribal code or custom.

(2) If a juvenile is alleged to be within the provisions of section 2(b) of this chapter, the court may authorize a petition to be filed at the conclusion of the preliminary hearing or inquiry. The court may authorize the petition upon a showing of probable cause that 1 or more of the allegations in the petition are true and fall within the provisions of section 2(b) of this chapter. If a petition is before the court because the department is required to submit the petition under section 17 of the child protection law,

1975 PA 238, MCL 722.637, the court shall hold a hearing on the petition within 24 hours or on the next business day after the petition is submitted, at which hearing the court shall consider at least the matters governed by subsections (4) and (5).

(3) Except as provided in subsections (5) and (6), if a petition under subsection (2) is authorized, the court may release the juvenile in the custody of either of the juvenile's parents or the juvenile's guardian or custodian under reasonable terms and conditions necessary for either the juvenile's physical health or mental well-being.

(4) The court may order a parent, guardian, custodian, nonparent adult, or other person residing in a child's home to leave the home and, except as the court orders, not to subsequently return to the home if all of the following take place:

(a) A petition alleging abuse of the child by the parent, guardian, custodian, nonparent adult, or other person is authorized under subsection (2).

(b) The court after a hearing finds probable cause to believe the parent, guardian, custodian, nonparent adult, or other person committed the abuse.

(c) The court finds on the record that the presence in the home of the person alleged to have committed the abuse presents a substantial risk of harm to the child's life, physical health, or mental well-being.

(5) If a petition alleges abuse by a person described in subsection (4), regardless of whether the court orders the alleged abuser to leave the child's home under subsection (4), the court shall not leave the child in or return the child to the child's home or place the child with a person not licensed under 1973 PA 116, MCL 722.111 to 722.128, unless the court finds that the conditions of custody at the placement and with the individual with whom the child is placed are adequate to safeguard the child from the risk of harm to the child's life, physical health, or mental well-being.

(6) If a court finds a parent is required by court order to register under the sex offenders registration act, the department may, but is not required to, make reasonable efforts to reunify the child with the parent. The court may order reasonable efforts to be made by the department.

(7) In determining whether to enter an order under subsection (4), the court may consider whether the parent who is to remain in the juvenile's home is married to the person to be removed or has a legal right to retain possession of the home.

(8) An order entered under subsection (4) may also contain 1 or more of the following terms or conditions:

(a) The court may require the alleged abusive parent to pay appropriate support to maintain a suitable home environment for the juvenile during the duration of the order.

(b) The court may order the alleged abusive person, according to terms the court may set, to surrender to a local law enforcement agency any firearms or other potentially dangerous weapons the alleged abusive person owns, possesses, or uses.

(c) The court may include any reasonable term or condition necessary for the juvenile's physical or mental well-being or necessary to protect the juvenile.

(9) The court may order placement of the child in foster care if the court finds all of the following conditions:

(a) Custody of the child with the parent presents a substantial risk of harm to the child's life, physical health, or mental well-being.

(b) No provision of service or other arrangement except removal of the child is reasonably available to adequately safeguard the child from risk as described in subdivision (a).

(c) Continuing the child's residence in the home is contrary to the child's welfare.

(d) Consistent with the circumstances, reasonable efforts were made to prevent or eliminate the need for removal of the child.

(e) Conditions of child custody away from the parent are adequate to safeguard the child's health and welfare.

(10) If the court orders placement of the juvenile outside the juvenile's home, the court shall inform the parties of the following:

(a) That the agency has the responsibility to prepare an initial services plan within 30 days of the juvenile's placement.

(b) The general elements of an initial services plan as required by the rules promulgated under 1973 PA 116, MCL 722.111 to 722.128.

(c) That participation in the initial services plan is voluntary without a court order.

(11) Before or within 7 days after a child is placed in a relative's home, the department shall perform a criminal record check and central registry clearance. If the child is placed in the home of a relative, the court shall order a home study to be performed and a copy of the home study to be submitted to the court not more than 30 days after the placement.

(12) In determining placement of a juvenile pending trial, the court shall order the juvenile placed in the most family-like setting available consistent with the juvenile's needs.

(13) If a juvenile is removed from the parent's custody at any time, the court shall permit the juvenile's parent to have regular and frequent parenting time with the juvenile. Parenting time between the juvenile and his or her parent shall not be less than 1 time every 7 days unless the court determines either that exigent circumstances require less frequent parenting time or that parenting time, even if supervised, may be harmful to the juvenile's life, physical health, or mental well-being. If the court determines that parenting time, even if supervised, may be harmful to the juvenile's life, physical health, or mental well-being, the court may suspend parenting time until the risk of harm no longer exists. The court may order the juvenile to have a psychological evaluation or counseling, or both, to determine the appropriateness and the conditions of parenting time.

(14) Reasonable efforts shall be made to do the following:

(a) Place siblings removed from their home in the same foster care, kinship guardianship, or adoptive placement, unless the supervising agency documents that a joint placement would be contrary to the safety or well-being of any of the siblings.

(b) In the case of siblings removed from their home who are not jointly placed, provide for visitation, at least monthly, or other ongoing interaction between the siblings, unless the supervising agency documents that visitation, at least monthly, or other ongoing interaction would be contrary to the safety or well-being of any of the siblings.

(15) If the supervising agency documents that visitation or other contact is contrary to the safety or well-being of any of the siblings and temporarily suspends visitation or contact, the supervising agency shall report its determination to the court for consideration at the next review hearing.

(16) If the supervising agency temporarily suspends visitation or contact, the court shall review the decision and determine whether sibling visitation or contact will be beneficial to the siblings. If so, the court shall order sibling visitation or contact to the extent reasonable.

(17) Upon the motion of any party, the court shall review custody and placement orders and initial services plans pending trial and may modify those orders and plans as the court considers under this section are in the juvenile's best interests.

(18) The court shall include in an order placing a child in foster care an order directing the release of information concerning the child in accordance with this subsection. If a child is placed in foster care, within 10 days after receipt of a written request, the agency shall provide the person who is providing the foster care with copies of all initial, updated, and revised case service plans and court orders relating to the child and all of the child's medical, mental health, and education reports, including reports compiled before the child was placed with that person.

(19) In an order placing a child in foster care, the court shall include both of the following:

(a) An order that the child's parent, guardian, or custodian provide the supervising agency with the name and address of each of the child's medical providers.

(b) An order that each of the child's medical providers release the child's medical records. The order may specify providers by profession or type of institution.

(20) As used in this section, "abuse" means 1 or more of the following:

(a) Harm or threatened harm by a person to a juvenile's health or welfare that occurs through nonaccidental physical or mental injury.

(b) Engaging in sexual contact or sexual penetration as defined in section 520a of the Michigan penal code, 1931 PA 328, MCL 750.520a, with a juvenile.

(c) Sexual exploitation of a juvenile, which includes, but is not limited to, allowing, permitting, or encouraging a juvenile to engage in prostitution or allowing, permitting, encouraging, or engaging in photographing, filming, or depicting a juvenile engaged in a listed sexual act as defined in section 145c of the Michigan penal code, 1931 PA 328, MCL 750.145c.

(d) Maltreatment of a juvenile.

History: Add. 1988, Act 224, Eff. Apr. 1, 1989;—Am. 1993, Act 114, Imd. Eff. July 20, 1993;—Am. 1996, Act 16, Eff. June 1, 1996;—Am. 1996, Act 409, Eff. Jan. 1, 1998;—Am. 1997, Act 163, Eff. Mar. 31, 1998;—Am. 1998, Act 480, Eff. Mar. 1, 1999;—Am. 1998, Act 530, Eff. July 1, 1999;—Am. 2000, Act 55, Eff. Apr. 1, 2000;—Am. 2004, Act 475, Imd. Eff. Dec. 28, 2004;—Am. 2012, Act 115, Imd. Eff. May 1, 2012;—Am. 2012, Act 163, Imd. Eff. June 12, 2012;—Am. 2015, Act 228, Imd. Eff. Dec. 17, 2015;—Am. 2016, Act 191, Eff. Sept. 19, 2016.

Popular name: Probate Code

Popular name: Juvenile Code

712A.18 Orders of disposition; reimbursement; hearing; guidelines; restitution; condition of probation; community service; fingerprints; report to state police; payment of assessment; registration of juvenile provided in MCL 28.721 to 28.736; release from placement in juvenile boot camp; alternative order of disposition; imposition of sentence in county jail facility; violation of personal protection order; costs; remission.

Sec. 18. (1) If the court finds that a juvenile concerning whom a petition is filed is not within this chapter, the court shall enter an order dismissing the petition. Except as otherwise provided in subsection (10), if the court finds that a juvenile is within this chapter, the court may enter any of the following orders of disposition that are appropriate for the welfare of the juvenile and society in view of the facts proven and ascertained:

(a) Warn the juvenile or the juvenile's parents, guardian, or custodian and, except as provided in subsection (7), dismiss the petition.

(b) Place the juvenile on probation, or under supervision in the juvenile's own home or in the home of an adult who is related to the juvenile. As used in this subdivision, "related" means an individual who is not less than 18 years of age and related to the child by blood, marriage, or adoption, as grandparent, great-grandparent, great-great-grandparent, aunt or uncle, great-aunt or great-uncle, great-great-aunt or great-great-uncle, sibling, stepsibling, nephew or niece, first cousin or first cousin once removed, and the spouse of any of the above, even after the marriage has ended by death or divorce. A child may be placed with the parent of a man whom the court has found probable cause to believe is the putative father if there is no man with legally established rights to the child. This placement of the child with the parent of a man whom the court has found probable cause to believe is the putative father is for the purposes of placement only and is not to be construed as a finding of paternity or to confer legal standing. The court shall order the terms and conditions of probation or supervision, including reasonable rules for the conduct of the parents, guardian, or custodian, if any, as the court determines necessary for the physical, mental, or moral well-being and behavior of the juvenile. The court may order that the juvenile participate in a juvenile drug treatment court under chapter 10A of the revised judicature act of 1961, 1961 PA 236, MCL 600.1060 to 600.1084. The court also shall order, as a condition of probation or supervision, that the juvenile shall pay the minimum state cost prescribed by section 18m of this chapter.

(c) If a juvenile is within the court's jurisdiction under section 2(a) of this chapter, or under section 2(h) of this chapter for a supplemental petition, place the juvenile in a suitable foster care home subject to the court's supervision. If a juvenile is within the court's jurisdiction under section 2(b) of this chapter, the court shall not place a juvenile in a foster care home subject to the court's supervision.

(d) Except as otherwise provided in this subdivision, place the juvenile in or commit the juvenile to a private institution or agency approved or licensed by the department's division of child welfare licensing for the care of juveniles of similar age, sex, and characteristics. If the juvenile is not a ward of the court, the court shall commit the juvenile to the department or, if the county is a county juvenile agency, to that county juvenile agency for placement in or commitment to an institution or agency as the department or county juvenile agency determines is most appropriate, subject to any initial level of placement the court designates.

(e) Except as otherwise provided in this subdivision, commit the juvenile to a public institution, county facility, institution operated as an agency of the court or county, or agency authorized by law to receive juveniles of similar age, sex, and characteristics. If the juvenile is not a ward of the court, the court shall commit the juvenile to the department or, if the county is a county juvenile agency, to that county juvenile agency for placement in or commitment to an institution or facility as the department or county juvenile agency determines is most appropriate, subject to any initial level of placement the court designates. If a child is not less than 17 years of age and is in violation of a personal protection order, the court may commit the child to a county jail within the adult prisoner population. In a placement under subdivision (d) or a commitment under this subdivision, except to a state institution or a county juvenile agency institution, the juvenile's religious affiliation shall be protected by placement or commitment to a private child-placing or child-caring agency or institution, if available. Except for commitment to the department or a county juvenile agency, an order of commitment under this subdivision to a state institution or agency described in the youth rehabilitation services act, 1974 PA 150, MCL 803.301 to 803.309, or in 1935 PA 220, MCL 400.201 to 400.214, the court shall name the superintendent of the institution to which the juvenile is committed as a special guardian to receive benefits due the juvenile from the government of the United States. An order of commitment under this subdivision to the department or a county juvenile agency shall name that agency as a special guardian to receive those benefits. The benefits received by the special guardian shall be used to the extent necessary to pay for the portions of the cost of care in the institution or facility that the parent or parents are found unable to pay.

(f) Provide the juvenile with medical, dental, surgical, or other health care, in a local hospital if available, or elsewhere, maintaining as much as possible a local physician-patient relationship, and with clothing and other incidental items the court determines are necessary.

(g) Order the parents, guardian, custodian, or any other person to refrain from continuing conduct that the court determines has caused or tended to cause the juvenile to come within or to remain under this chapter or that obstructs placement or commitment of the juvenile by an order under this section.

(h) Appoint a guardian under section 5204 of the estates and protected individuals code, 1998 PA 386, MCL 700.5204, in response to a petition filed with the court by a person interested in the juvenile's welfare. If the court appoints a guardian as authorized by this subdivision, it may dismiss the petition under this chapter.

(i) Order the juvenile to engage in community service.

(j) If the court finds that a juvenile has violated a municipal ordinance or a state or federal law, order the juvenile to pay a civil fine in the amount of the civil or penal fine provided by the ordinance or law. Money collected from fines levied under this subsection shall be distributed as provided in section 29 of this chapter.

(k) If a juvenile is within the court's jurisdiction under section 2(a)(1) of this chapter, order the juvenile's parent or guardian to personally participate in treatment reasonably available in the parent's or guardian's location.

(*l*) If a juvenile is within the court's jurisdiction under section 2(a)(1) of this chapter, place the juvenile in and order the juvenile to complete satisfactorily a program of training in a juvenile boot camp established by the department under the juvenile boot camp act, 1996 PA 263, MCL 400.1301 to 400.1309, as provided in that act. If the county is a county juvenile agency, the court shall commit the juvenile to that county juvenile agency for placement in the program under that act. Upon receiving a report of satisfactory completion of the program from the department, the court shall authorize the juvenile's release from placement in the juvenile boot camp. Following satisfactory completion of the juvenile boot camp program, the juvenile shall complete an additional period of not less than 120 days or more than 180 days of intensive supervised community reintegration in the juvenile's local community. To place or commit a juvenile under this subdivision, the court shall determine all of the following:

(*i*) Placement in a juvenile boot camp will benefit the juvenile.

(*ii*) The juvenile is physically able to participate in the program.

(*iii*) The juvenile does not appear to have any mental handicap that would prevent participation in the program.

(*iv*) The juvenile will not be a danger to other juveniles in the boot camp.

(*v*) There is an opening in a juvenile boot camp program.

(*vi*) If the court must commit the juvenile to a county juvenile agency, the county juvenile agency is able to place the juvenile in a juvenile boot camp program.

(m) If the court entered a judgment of conviction under section 2d of this chapter, enter any disposition under this section or, if the court determines that the best interests of the public would be served, impose any sentence upon the juvenile that could be imposed upon an adult convicted of the offense for which the juvenile was convicted. If the juvenile is convicted of a violation or conspiracy to commit a violation of section 7403(2)(a)(i) of the public health code, 1978 PA 368, MCL 333.7403, the court may impose the alternative sentence permitted under that section if the court determines that the best interests of the public would be served. The court may delay imposing a sentence of imprisonment under this subdivision for a period not longer than the period during which the court has jurisdiction over the juvenile under this chapter by entering an order of disposition delaying imposition of sentence and placing the juvenile on probation upon the terms and conditions it considers appropriate, including any disposition under this section. If the court delays imposing sentence under this section, section 18i of this chapter applies. If the court imposes sentence, it shall enter a judgment of sentence. If the court imposes a sentence of imprisonment, the juvenile shall receive credit against the sentence for time served before sentencing. In determining whether to enter an order of disposition or impose a sentence under this subdivision, the court shall consider all of the following factors, giving greater weight to the seriousness of the offense and the juvenile's prior record:

(*i*) The seriousness of the offense in terms of community protection, including, but not limited to, the existence of any aggravating factors recognized by the sentencing guidelines, the use of a firearm or other dangerous weapon, and the impact on any victim.

(*ii*) The juvenile's culpability in committing the offense, including, but not limited to, the level of the juvenile's participation in planning and carrying out the offense and the existence of any aggravating or mitigating factors recognized by the sentencing guidelines.

(*iii*) The juvenile's prior record of delinquency including, but not limited to, any record of detention, any police record, any school record, or any other evidence indicating prior delinquent behavior.

(*iv*) The juvenile's programming history, including, but not limited to, the juvenile's past willingness to participate meaningfully in available programming.

(*v*) The adequacy of the punishment or programming available in the juvenile justice system.

(*vi*) The dispositional options available for the juvenile.

(n) In a proceeding under section 2(b) or (c) of this chapter, if a juvenile is removed from the parent's custody at any time, the court shall permit the juvenile's parent to have regular and frequent parenting time with the juvenile. Parenting time between the juvenile and his or her parent shall not be less than 1 time every 7 days unless the court determines either that exigent circumstances require less frequent parenting time or that parenting time, even if supervised, may be harmful to the juvenile's life, physical health, or mental well-being. If the court determines that parenting time, even if supervised, may be harmful to the juvenile's life, physical health, or mental well-being, the court may suspend parenting time until the risk of harm no longer exists. The court may order the juvenile to have a psychological evaluation or counseling, or both, to determine the appropriateness and the conditions of parenting time.

(2) An order of disposition placing a juvenile in or committing a juvenile to care outside of the juvenile's own home and under state, county juvenile agency, or court supervision shall contain a provision for reimbursement by the juvenile, parent, guardian, or custodian to the court for the cost of care or service. The order shall be reasonable, taking into account both the income and resources of the juvenile, parent, guardian, or custodian. The amount may be based upon the guidelines and model schedule created under subsection (6). If the juvenile is receiving an adoption support subsidy under sections 115f to 115m of the social welfare act, 1939 PA 280, MCL 400.115f to 400.115m, the amount shall not exceed the amount of the support subsidy. The reimbursement provision applies during the entire period the juvenile remains in care outside of the juvenile's own home and under state, county juvenile agency, or court supervision, unless the juvenile is in the permanent custody of the court. The court shall provide for the collection of all amounts ordered to be reimbursed and the money collected shall be accounted for and reported to the county board of commissioners. Collections to cover delinquent accounts or to pay the balance due on reimbursement orders may be made after a juvenile is released or discharged from care outside the juvenile's own home and under state, county juvenile agency, or court supervision. Twenty-five percent of all amounts collected under an order entered under this subsection shall be credited to the appropriate fund of the county to offset the administrative cost of collections. The balance of all amounts collected under an order entered under this subsection shall be divided in the same ratio in which the county, state, and federal government participate in the cost of care outside the juvenile's own home and under state, county juvenile agency, or court supervision. The court may also collect from the government of the United States benefits paid for the cost of care of a court ward. Money collected for juveniles placed by the court with or committed to the department or a county juvenile agency shall be accounted for and reported on an individual juvenile basis. In cases of delinquent accounts, the court may also enter an order to intercept state or federal tax refunds of a juvenile, parent, guardian, or custodian and initiate the necessary offset proceedings in order to recover the cost of care or service. The court shall send to the person who is the subject of the intercept order advance written notice of the proposed offset. The notice shall include notice of the opportunity to contest the offset on the grounds that the intercept is not proper because of a mistake of fact concerning the amount of the delinquency or the identity of the person subject to the order. The court shall provide for the prompt reimbursement of an amount withheld in error or an amount found to exceed the delinquent amount.

(3) An order of disposition placing a juvenile in the juvenile's own home under subsection (1)(b) may contain a provision for reimbursement by the juvenile, parent, guardian, or custodian to the court for the cost of service. If an order is entered under this subsection, an amount due shall be determined and treated in the same manner provided for an order entered under subsection (2).

(4) An order directed to a parent or a person other than the juvenile is not effective and binding on the parent or other person unless opportunity for hearing is given by issuance of summons or notice as provided in sections 12 and 13 of this chapter and until a copy of the order, bearing the seal of the court, is served on the parent or other person as provided in section 13 of this chapter.

(5) If the court appoints an attorney to represent a juvenile, parent, guardian, or custodian, the court may require in an order entered under this section that the juvenile, parent, guardian, or custodian reimburse the court for attorney fees.

(6) The office of the state court administrator, under the supervision and direction of the supreme court, shall create guidelines that the court may use in determining the ability of the juvenile, parent, guardian, or custodian to pay for care and any costs of service ordered under subsection (2) or (3). The guidelines shall take into account both the income and resources of the juvenile, parent, guardian, or custodian.

(7) If the court finds that a juvenile comes under section 30 of this chapter, the court shall order the juvenile or the juvenile's parent to pay restitution as provided in sections 30 and 31 of this chapter and in sections 44 and 45 of the crime victim's rights act, 1985 PA 87, MCL 780.794 and 780.795.

(8) If the court imposes restitution as a condition of probation, the court shall require the juvenile to do either of the following as an additional condition of probation:

(a) Engage in community service or, with the victim's consent, perform services for the victim.

(b) Seek and maintain paid employment and pay restitution to the victim from the earnings of that employment.

(9) If the court finds that the juvenile is in intentional default of the payment of restitution, a court may, as provided in section 31 of this chapter, revoke or alter the terms and conditions of probation for nonpayment of restitution. If a juvenile who is ordered to engage in community service intentionally refuses to perform the required community service, the court may revoke or alter the terms and conditions of probation.

(10) The court shall not enter an order of disposition for a juvenile offense as defined in section 1a of 1925 PA 289, MCL 28.241a, or a judgment of sentence for a conviction until the court has examined the court file and has determined that the juvenile's fingerprints have been taken and forwarded as required by section 3 of 1925 PA 289, MCL 28.243, and as required by the sex offenders registration act, 1994 PA 295, MCL 28.721 to 28.736. If a juvenile has not had his or her fingerprints taken, the court shall do either of the following:

(a) Order the juvenile to submit himself or herself to the police agency that arrested or obtained the warrant for the juvenile's arrest so the juvenile's fingerprints can be taken and forwarded.

(b) Order the juvenile committed to the sheriff's custody for taking and forwarding the juvenile's fingerprints.

(11) Upon final disposition, conviction, acquittal, or dismissal of an offense within the court's jurisdiction under section 2(a) (1) of this chapter, using forms approved by the state court administrator, the clerk of the court entering the final disposition, conviction, acquittal, or dismissal shall immediately advise the department of state police of that final disposition, conviction, acquittal, or dismissal as required by section 3 of 1925 PA 289, MCL 28.243. The report to the department of state police shall include information as to the finding of the judge or jury and a summary of the disposition or sentence imposed.

(12) If the court enters an order of disposition based on an act that is a juvenile offense as defined in section 1 of 1989 PA 196, MCL 780.901, the court shall order the juvenile to pay the assessment as provided in that act. If the court enters a judgment of conviction under section 2d of this chapter for an offense that is a felony, misdemeanor, or ordinance violation, the court shall order the juvenile to pay the assessment as provided in that act.

(13) If the court has entered an order of disposition or a judgment of conviction for a listed offense as defined in section 2 of the sex offenders registration act, 1994 PA 295, MCL 28.722, the court, the department, or the county juvenile agency shall register the juvenile or accept the juvenile's registration as provided in the sex offenders registration act, 1994 PA 295, MCL 28.721 to 28.736.

(14) If the court enters an order of disposition placing a juvenile in a juvenile boot camp program, or committing a juvenile to a county juvenile agency for placement in a juvenile boot camp program, and the court receives from the department a report that the juvenile has failed to perform satisfactorily in the program, that the juvenile does not meet the program's requirements or is medically unable to participate in the program for more than 25 days, that there is no opening in a juvenile boot camp program, or that the county juvenile agency is unable to place the juvenile in a juvenile boot camp program, the court shall release the juvenile from placement or commitment and enter an alternative order of disposition. A juvenile shall not be placed in a juvenile boot camp under an order of disposition more than once, except that a juvenile returned to the court for a medical condition, because there was no opening in a juvenile boot camp program, or because the county juvenile agency was unable to place the juvenile in a juvenile boot camp program may be placed again in the juvenile boot camp program after the medical condition is corrected, an opening becomes available, or the county juvenile agency is able to place the juvenile.

(15) If the juvenile is within the court's jurisdiction under section 2(a)(1) of this chapter for an offense other than a listed offense as defined in section 2 of the sex offenders registration act, 1994 PA 295, MCL 28.722, the court shall determine if the offense is a violation of a law of this state or a local ordinance of a municipality of this state that by its nature constitutes a sexual offense against an individual who is less than 18 years of age. If so, the order of disposition is for a listed offense as defined in section 2 of the sex offenders registration act, 1994 PA 295, MCL 28.722, and the court shall include the basis for that determination on the record and include the determination in the order of disposition.

(16) The court shall not impose a sentence of imprisonment in the county jail under subsection (1)(m) unless the present county jail facility for the juvenile's imprisonment would meet all requirements under federal law and regulations for housing

juveniles. The court shall not impose the sentence until it consults with the sheriff to determine when the sentence will begin to ensure that space will be available for the juvenile.

(17) In a proceeding under section 2(h) of this chapter, this section only applies to a disposition for a violation of a personal protection order and subsequent proceedings.

(18) If a juvenile is within the court's jurisdiction under section 2(a)(1) of this chapter, the court shall order the juvenile to pay costs as provided in section 18m of this chapter.

(19) A juvenile who has been ordered to pay the minimum state cost as provided in section 18m of this chapter as a condition of probation or supervision and who is not in willful default of the payment of the minimum state cost may petition the court at any time for a remission of the payment of any unpaid portion of the minimum state cost. If the court determines that payment of the amount due will impose a manifest hardship on the juvenile or his or her immediate family, the court may remit all or part of the amount of the minimum state cost due or modify the method of payment.

History: Add. 1944, 1st Ex. Sess., Act 54, Imd. Eff. Mar. 6, 1944; —CL 1948, 712A.18;—Am. 1953, Act 139, Eff. Oct. 2, 1953;—Am. 1963, Act 65, Imd. Eff. May 8, 1963;—Am. 1972, Act 175, Imd. Eff. June 16, 1972;—Am. 1982, Act 398, Imd. Eff. Dec. 28, 1982;—Am. 1988, Act 71, Eff. June 1, 1988;—Am. 1988, Act 72, Eff. June 1, 1988;—Am. 1988, Act 224, Eff. Apr. 1, 1989;—Am. 1989, Act 112, Imd. Eff. June 23, 1989;—Am. 1990, Act 314, Imd. Eff. Dec. 20, 1990;—Am. 1993, Act 344, Eff. May 1, 1994;—Am. 1994, Act 264, Eff. Jan. 1, 1995;—Am. 1994, Act 355, Eff. Oct. 1, 1995;—Am. 1996, Act 243, Eff. Aug. 1, 1996;—Am. 1996, Act 244, Eff. Aug. 1, 1996;—Am. 1997, Act 163, Eff. Mar. 31, 1998;—Am. 1998, Act 474, Eff. Mar. 1, 1999;—Am. 1998, Act 478, Eff. Jan. 12, 1999;—Am. 1999, Act 86, Eff. Sept. 1, 1999;—Am. 2000, Act 55, Eff. Apr. 1, 2000;—Am. 2003, Act 71, Eff. Oct. 1, 2003;—Am. 2004, Act 102, Imd. Eff. May 13, 2004;—Am. 2004, Act 221, Eff. Jan. 1, 2005;—Am. 2004, Act 475, Imd. Eff. Dec. 28, 2004;—Am. 2011, Act 295, Eff. Apr. 1, 2012;—Am. 2016, Act 191, Eff. Sept. 19, 2016.

Former law: See sections 18, 20, 21, and 22 of Ch. XII of Act 288 of 1939; CL 1929, §§ 12838 and 12840; Act 30 of 1931; and Act 260 of 1937.

Popular name: Probate Code

Popular name: Juvenile Code

712A.18e Application for entry of order setting aside adjudication; filing; contents; submitting copy of application and fingerprints; report; fee; serving copy of application on attorney general and prosecuting attorney; contesting application; notice to victim; definitions; hearing; affidavits; proofs; entry of order; setting aside adjudication as privilege and conditional; effect of entering order; sending copy of order to arresting agency and department of state police; nonpublic record of order and record; availability of nonpublic record; fee; exemption from disclosure; divulging, using, or publishing information as misdemeanor.

Sec. 18e. (1) Except as provided in subsection (2), a person who has been adjudicated of not more than 1 juvenile offense that would be a felony if committed by an adult and not more than 3 juvenile offenses, of which not more than 1 may be a juvenile offense that would be a felony if committed by an adult and who has no felony convictions may file an application with the adjudicating court or adjudicating courts for the entry of an order setting aside the adjudications. A person may have only 1 adjudication for an offense that would be a felony if committed by an adult and not more than 2 adjudications for an offense that would be a misdemeanor if committed by an adult or if there is no adjudication for a felony if committed by an adult, not more than 3 adjudications for an offense that would be a misdemeanor if committed by an adult set aside under this section. Multiple adjudications arising out of a series of acts that were in a continuous time sequence of 12 hours or less and that displayed a single intent and goal constitute 1 offense provided that none of the adjudications constitute any of the following:

(a) An assaultive crime as that term is defined in subsection (7).

(b) An offense involving the use or possession of a weapon.

(c) An offense with a maximum penalty of 10 or more years imprisonment.

(2) A person shall not apply under this section to have set aside, and a judge shall not under this section set aside, any of the following:

(a) An adjudication for an offense that if committed by an adult would be a felony for which the maximum punishment is life imprisonment.

(b) An adjudication for a traffic offense under the Michigan vehicle code, 1949 PA 300, MCL 257.1 to 257.923, or a local ordinance substantially corresponding to that act, that involves the operation of a vehicle and at the time of the violation is a felony or misdemeanor.

(c) A conviction under section 2d of this chapter. This subdivision does not prevent a person convicted under section 2d of this chapter from having that conviction set aside as otherwise provided by law.

(3) An application under this section shall not be filed until the expiration of 1 year following imposition of the disposition for the adjudication that the applicant seeks to set aside, or 1 year following completion of any term of detention for that adjudication, or when the person becomes 18 years of age, whichever occurs later.

(4) An application under this section is invalid unless it contains the following information and is signed under oath by the person whose adjudication is to be set aside:

(a) The full name and current address of the applicant.

(b) A certified record of the adjudication that is to be set aside.

(c) A statement that the applicant has not been adjudicated of a juvenile offense other than the juvenile offenses sought to be set aside as a result of this application.

(d) A statement that the applicant has not been convicted of any felony offense.

(e) A statement as to whether the applicant has previously filed an application to set aside this or any other adjudication and, if so, the disposition of the application.

(f) A statement as to whether the applicant has any other criminal charge pending against him or her in any court in the United States or in any other country.

(g) A consent to the use of the nonpublic record created under subsection (13), to the extent authorized by subsection (13).

(5) The applicant shall submit a copy of the application and 2 complete sets of fingerprints to the department of state police. The department of state police shall compare those fingerprints with the records of the department, including the nonpublic record created under subsection (13), and shall forward a complete set of fingerprints to the Federal Bureau of Investigation for a comparison with the records available to that agency. The department of state police shall report to the court in which the application is filed the information contained in the department's records with respect to any pending charges against the applicant, any record of adjudication or conviction of the applicant, and the setting aside of any adjudication or conviction of the applicant and shall report to the court any similar information obtained from the Federal Bureau of Investigation. The court shall not act upon the application until the department of state police reports the information required by this subsection to the court.

(6) The copy of the application submitted to the department of state police under subsection (5) shall be accompanied by a fee of $25.00 payable to the state of Michigan. The department of state police shall use the fee to defray the expenses incurred in processing the application.

(7) A copy of the application shall be served upon the attorney general and, if applicable, upon the office of the prosecuting attorney who prosecuted the offense. The attorney general and the prosecuting attorney shall have an opportunity to contest the application. If the adjudication was for an offense that if committed by an adult would be an assaultive crime or serious misdemeanor, and if the name of the victim is known to the prosecuting attorney, the prosecuting attorney shall give the victim of that offense written notice of the application and forward a copy of the application to the victim under section 46a of the William Van Regenmorter crime victim's rights act, 1985 PA 87, MCL 780.796a. The notice shall be sent by first-class mail to the victim's last known address. The victim has the right to appear at any proceeding under this section concerning that adjudication and to make a written or oral statement. As used in this subsection:

(a) "Assaultive crime" means that term as defined in section 9a of chapter X of the code of criminal procedure, 1927 PA 175, MCL 770.9a.

(b) "Serious misdemeanor" means that term as defined in section 31 of the William Van Regenmorter crime victim's rights act, 1985 PA 87, MCL 780.781.

(c) "Victim" means that term as defined in section 31 of the William Van Regenmorter crime victim's rights act, 1985 PA 87, MCL 780.781.

(8) Upon the hearing of the application, the court may require the filing of affidavits and the taking of proofs as it considers proper.

(9) Except as provided in subsection (10), if the court determines that the circumstances and behavior of the applicant from the date of the applicant's adjudication to the filing of the application warrant setting aside the 1 adjudication for a juvenile offense that would be a felony if committed by an adult and not more than 2 adjudications for a juvenile offense that would be a misdemeanor if committed by an adult or if there is no adjudication for a felony if committed by an adult, not more than 3 adjudications for an offense that would be a misdemeanor if committed by an adult and that setting aside the adjudication or adjudications is consistent with the public welfare, the court may enter an order setting aside the adjudication. Except as provided in subsection (10), the setting aside of an adjudication under this section is a privilege and conditional, and is not a right.

(10) If the person files an application with the court and he or she otherwise meets all the requirements, notwithstanding subsection (9), the court shall set aside the adjudication of a person as follows:

(a) The person was adjudicated for an offense that if committed by an adult would be a violation or an attempted violation of section 413 of the Michigan penal code, 1931 PA 328, MCL 750.413.

(b) The person was adjudicated for an offense that if committed by an adult would be a violation or an attempted violation of section 448, 449, or 450 of the Michigan penal code, 1931 PA 328, MCL 750.448, 750.449, and 750.450, or a local ordinance substantially corresponding to section 448, 449, or 450 of the Michigan penal code, 1931 PA 328, MCL 750.448, 750.449, and 750.450, and he or she committed the offense as a direct result of his or her being a victim of a human trafficking violation.

(11) Upon the entry of an order under this section, the applicant is considered not to have been previously adjudicated, except as provided in subsection (13) and as follows:

(a) The applicant is not entitled to the remission of any fine, costs, or other money paid as a consequence of an adjudication that is set aside.

(b) This section does not affect the right of the applicant to rely upon the adjudication to bar subsequent proceedings for the same offense.

(c) This section does not affect the right of a victim of an offense to prosecute or defend a civil action for damages.

(d) This section does not create a right to commence an action for damages for detention under the disposition that the applicant served before the adjudication is set aside under this section.

(12) Upon the entry of an order under this section, the court shall send a copy of the order to the arresting agency and the department of state police.

(13) The department of state police shall retain a nonpublic record of the order setting aside an adjudication for a juvenile offense that would be a felony if committed by an adult and not more than 2 juvenile offenses that would be misdemeanors if committed by an adult or if there is no adjudication for a felony if committed by an adult, not more than 3 adjudications for an offense that would be a misdemeanor if committed by an adult and of the record of the arrest, fingerprints, adjudication, and disposition of the applicant in the case to which the order applies. Except as provided in subsection (14), this nonpublic record shall be made available only to a court of competent jurisdiction, an agency of the judicial branch of state government, a law enforcement agency, a prosecuting attorney, the attorney general, or the governor upon request and only for the following purposes:

(a) Consideration in a licensing function conducted by an agency of the judicial branch of state government.

(b) Consideration by a law enforcement agency if a person whose adjudication has been set aside applies for employment with the law enforcement agency.

(c) To show that a person who has filed an application to set aside an adjudication has previously had an adjudication set aside under this section.

(d) The court's consideration in determining the sentence to be imposed upon conviction for a subsequent offense that is punishable as a felony or by imprisonment for more than 1 year.

(e) Consideration by the governor, if a person whose adjudication has been set aside applies for a pardon for another offense.

(14) A copy of the nonpublic record created under subsection (13) shall be provided to the person whose adjudication is set aside under this section upon payment of a fee determined and charged by the department of state police in the same manner as the fee prescribed in section 4 of the freedom of information act, 1976 PA 442, MCL 15.234.

(15) The nonpublic record maintained under subsection (13) is exempt from disclosure under the freedom of information act, 1976 PA 442, MCL 15.231 to 15.246.

(16) Except as provided in subsection (13), a person, other than the applicant, who knows or should have known that an adjudication was set aside under this section, who divulges, uses, or publishes information concerning an adjudication set aside under this section is guilty of a misdemeanor.

History: Add. 1988, Act 72, Eff. June 1, 1988;—Am. 1993, Act 344, Eff. May 1, 1994;—Am. 1996, Act 257, Eff. Jan. 1, 1997;—Am. 2012, Act 527, Imd. Eff. Dec. 28, 2012;—Am. 2016, Act 337, Eff. Mar. 14, 2017.

Popular name: Probate Code

Popular name: Juvenile Code

712A.18g Commitment under MCL 712A.18(1)(e).

Sec. 18g. (1) In addition to any other disposition under this act, a juvenile other than a juvenile sentenced in the same manner as an adult under section 18(1)(n) of this chapter shall be committed under section 18(1)(e) of this chapter to a detention facility for a specified period of time if all of the following circumstances exist:

(a) The juvenile is under the jurisdiction of the juvenile division of the probate court under section 2(a)(1) of this chapter.

(b) The juvenile is adjudicated as or convicted of violating a criminal municipal ordinance or law of this state or the United States.

(c) The juvenile is found to have used a firearm during the criminal violation.

(2) The period of time specified under subsection (1) shall not exceed the length of the sentence that could have been imposed if the juvenile had been sentenced as an adult.

(3) "Firearm" means that term as defined in section 3t of chapter 1 of the Revised Statutes of 1846, being section 8.3t of the Michigan Compiled Laws.

History: Add. 1996, Act 258, Eff. Jan. 1, 1997.

Popular name: Probate Code

Popular name: Juvenile Code

THE MICHIGAN PENAL CODE (EXCERPT)
Act 328 of 1931

AN ACT to revise, consolidate, codify, and add to the statutes relating to crimes; to define crimes and prescribe the penalties and remedies; to provide for restitution under certain circumstances; to provide for the competency of evidence at the trial of persons accused of crime; to provide immunity from prosecution for certain witnesses appearing at criminal trials; to provide for liability for damages; and to repeal certain acts and parts of acts inconsistent with or contravening any of the provisions of this act.

History: 1931, Act 328, Eff. Sept. 18, 1931;—Am. 1991, Act 56, Eff. Jan. 1, 1992;—Am. 2005, Act 105, Eff. Dec. 1, 2005;—Am. 2010, Act 107, Eff. Aug. 1, 2010.

Constitutionality: Michigan's anti-stalking law is not an unconstitutionally vague threat to freedom of speech. Staley v Jones, 239 F3d 769 (CA 6, 2001).

The People of the State of Michigan enact:

CHAPTER XI
ASSAULTS

750.82 Felonious assault; violation of subsection (1) in weapon free school zone; definitions.

Sec. 82. (1) Except as provided in subsection (2), a person who assaults another person with a gun, revolver, pistol, knife, iron bar, club, brass knuckles, or other dangerous weapon without intending to commit murder or to inflict great bodily harm less than murder is guilty of a felony punishable by imprisonment for not more than 4 years or a fine of not more than $2,000.00, or both.

(2) A person who violates subsection (1) in a weapon free school zone is guilty of a felony punishable by 1 or more of the following:

(a) Imprisonment for not more than 4 years.

(b) Community service for not more than 150 hours.

(c) A fine of not more than $6,000.00.

(3) As used in this section:

(a) "School" means a public, private, denominational, or parochial school offering developmental kindergarten, kindergarten, or any grade from 1 through 12.

(b) "School property" means a building, playing field, or property used for school purposes to impart instruction to children or used for functions and events sponsored by a school, except a building used primarily for adult education or college extension courses.

(c) "Weapon free school zone" means school property and a vehicle used by a school to transport students to or from school property.

History: 1931, Act 328, Eff. Sept. 18, 1931;—CL 1948, 750.82;—Am. 1994, Act 158, Eff. Aug. 15, 1994.

Former law: See section 1 of Act 232 of 1913, being CL 1915, § 15228; CL 1929, § 16747; and Act 241 of 1915.

750.89 Assault with intent to rob and steal; armed.

Sec. 89. Assault with intent to rob and steal being armed—Any person, being armed with a dangerous weapon, or any article used or fashioned in a manner to lead a person so assaulted reasonably to believe it to be a dangerous weapon, who shall assault another with intent to rob and steal shall be guilty of a felony, punishable by imprisonment in the state prison for life, or for any term of years.

History: 1931, Act 328, Eff. Sept. 18, 1931;—Am. 1939, Act 94, Eff. Sept. 29, 1939;—CL 1948, 750.89.

Former law: See section 16 of Ch. 153 of R.S. 1846, being CL 1857, § 5726; CL 1871, § 7525; How., § 9090; CL 1897, § 11485; CL 1915, § 15207; CL 1929, § 16723; Act 143 of 1869; and Act 374 of 1927.

CHAPTER XVI
BREAKING AND ENTERING

750.110a Definitions; home invasion; first degree; second degree; third degree; penalties.

Sec. 110a. (1) As used in this section:

(a) "Dwelling" means a structure or shelter that is used permanently or temporarily as a place of abode, including an appurtenant structure attached to that structure or shelter.

(b) "Dangerous weapon" means 1 or more of the following:

(*i*) A loaded or unloaded firearm, whether operable or inoperable.

(*ii*) A knife, stabbing instrument, brass knuckles, blackjack, club, or other object specifically designed or customarily carried or possessed for use as a weapon.

(*iii*) An object that is likely to cause death or bodily injury when used as a weapon and that is used as a weapon or carried or possessed for use as a weapon.

(*iv*) An object or device that is used or fashioned in a manner to lead a person to believe the object or device is an object or device described in subparagraphs (*i*) to (*iii*).

(c) "Without permission" means without having obtained permission to enter from the owner or lessee of the dwelling or from any other person lawfully in possession or control of the dwelling.

(2) A person who breaks and enters a dwelling with intent to commit a felony, larceny, or assault in the dwelling, a person who enters a dwelling without permission with intent to commit a felony, larceny, or assault in the dwelling, or a person who breaks and enters a dwelling or enters a dwelling without permission and, at any time while he or she is entering, present in, or exiting the dwelling, commits a felony, larceny, or assault is guilty of home invasion in the first degree if at any time while the person is entering, present in, or exiting the dwelling either of the following circumstances exists:

(a) The person is armed with a dangerous weapon.

(b) Another person is lawfully present in the dwelling.

(3) A person who breaks and enters a dwelling with intent to commit a felony, larceny, or assault in the dwelling, a person who enters a dwelling without permission with intent to commit a felony, larceny, or assault in the dwelling, or a person who breaks and enters a dwelling or enters a dwelling without permission and, at any time while he or she is entering, present in, or exiting the dwelling, commits a felony, larceny, or assault is guilty of home invasion in the second degree.

(4) A person is guilty of home invasion in the third degree if the person does either of the following:

(a) Breaks and enters a dwelling with intent to commit a misdemeanor in the dwelling, enters a dwelling without permission with intent to commit a misdemeanor in the dwelling, or breaks and enters a dwelling or enters a dwelling without permission and, at any time while he or she is entering, present in, or exiting the dwelling, commits a misdemeanor.

(b) Breaks and enters a dwelling or enters a dwelling without permission and, at any time while the person is entering, present in, or exiting the dwelling, violates any of the following ordered to protect a named person or persons:

(*i*) A probation term or condition.

(*ii*) A parole term or condition.

(*iii*) A personal protection order term or condition.

(*iv*) A bond or bail condition or any condition of pretrial release.

(5) Home invasion in the first degree is a felony punishable by imprisonment for not more than 20 years or a fine of not more than $5,000.00, or both.

(6) Home invasion in the second degree is a felony punishable by imprisonment for not more than 15 years or a fine of not more than $3,000.00, or both.

(7) Home invasion in the third degree is a felony punishable by imprisonment for not more than 5 years or a fine of not more than $2,000.00, or both.

(8) The court may order a term of imprisonment imposed for home invasion in the first degree to be served consecutively to any term of imprisonment imposed for any other criminal offense arising from the same transaction.

(9) Imposition of a penalty under this section does not bar imposition of a penalty under any other applicable law.

History: Add. 1994, Act 270, Eff. Oct. 1, 1994;—Am. 1999, Act 44, Eff. Oct. 1, 1999.

CHAPTER XXVA
CRIMINAL ENTERPRISES

750.159g "Racketeering" defined.

Sec. 159g. As used in this chapter, "racketeering" means committing, attempting to commit, conspiring to commit, or aiding or abetting, soliciting, coercing, or intimidating a person to commit an offense for financial gain, involving any of the following:

(a) A felony violation of section 8 of the tobacco products tax act, 1993 PA 327, MCL 205.428, concerning tobacco product taxes, or section 9 of former 1947 PA 265, concerning cigarette taxes.

(b) A violation of section 11151(3) of the natural resources and environmental protection act, 1994 PA 451, MCL 324.11151, or section 48(3) of former 1979 PA 64, concerning felonious disposal of hazardous waste.

(c) A felony violation of part 74 of the public health code, 1978 PA 368, MCL 333.7401 to 333.7461, concerning controlled substances.

(d) A felony violation of section 7340, 7340c, or 17766c of the public health code, 1978 PA 368, MCL 333.7340, 333.7340c, and 333.17766c, concerning ephedrine or pseudoephedrine.

(e) A felony violation of section 60 of the social welfare act, 1939 PA 280, MCL 400.60, concerning welfare fraud.

(f) A violation of section 4, 5, or 7 of the medicaid false claim act, 1977 PA 72, MCL 400.604, 400.605, and 400.607, concerning medicaid fraud.

(g) A felony violation of section 18 of the Michigan gaming control and revenue act, 1996 IL 1, MCL 432.218, concerning the business of gaming.

(h) A felony violation of section 909(4) of the Michigan liquor control code of 1998, 1998 PA 58, MCL 436.1909, concerning the illegal sale, delivery, or importation of spirits.

(i) A violation of section 508 of the uniform securities act (2002), 2008 PA 551, MCL 451.2508, concerning fraud.
(j) A violation of section 5 or 7 of 1978 PA 33, MCL 722.675 and 722.677, concerning the display or dissemination of obscene matter to minors.
(k) A violation of section 49, concerning animal fighting.
(*l*) A felony violation of section 72, 73, 74, 75, or 77, concerning arson.
(m) A violation of section 93, 94, 95, or 96, concerning bank bonds, bills, notes, and property.
(n) A violation of section 110 or 110a, concerning breaking and entering or home invasion.
(o) A violation of section 117, 118, 119, 120, 121, or 124, concerning bribery.
(p) A violation of section 120a, concerning jury tampering.
(q) A violation of section 145c, concerning child sexually abusive activity or material.
(r) A violation of section 145d, concerning internet or computer crimes.
(s) A felony violation of section 157n, 157p, 157q, 157r, 157s, 157t, or 157u, concerning credit cards or financial transaction devices.
(t) A felony violation of section 174, 175, 176, 180, 181, or 182, concerning embezzlement.
(u) A felony violation of chapter XXXIII, concerning explosives and bombs.
(v) A violation of section 213, concerning extortion.
(w) A felony violation of section 218, concerning false pretenses.
(x) A felony violation of section 223(2), 224(1)(a), (b), or (c), 224b, 224c, 224e(1), 226, 227, 234a, 234b, or 237a, concerning firearms or dangerous weapons.
(y) A felony violation of chapter XLI, concerning forgery and counterfeiting.
(z) A violation of section 271, 272, 273, or 274, concerning securities fraud.
(aa) A violation of section 300a, concerning food stamps or coupons or access devices.
(bb) A violation of section 301, 302, 303, 304, 305, 305a, or 313, concerning gambling.
(cc) A violation of section 316 or 317, concerning murder.
(dd) A violation of section 330, 331, or 332, concerning horse racing.
(ee) A violation of section 349, 349a, or 350, concerning kidnapping.
(ff) A felony violation of chapter LII, concerning larceny.
(gg) A violation of section 411k, concerning money laundering.
(hh) A violation of section 422, 423, 424, or 425, concerning perjury or subornation of perjury.
(ii) A violation of section 452, 455, 457, 458, or 459, concerning prostitution.
(jj) A violation of chapter LXVIIA, concerning human trafficking.
(kk) A violation of section 529, 529a, 530, or 531, concerning robbery.
(*ll*) A felony violation of section 535 or 535a, concerning stolen, embezzled, or converted property.
(mm) A violation of chapter LXXXIII-A, concerning terrorism.
(nn) A violation of section 5 of 1984 PA 343, MCL 752.365, concerning obscenity.
(oo) A felony violation of the identity theft protection act, 2004 PA 452, MCL 445.61 to 445.77.
(pp) An offense committed within this state or another state that constitutes racketeering activity as defined in 18 USC 1961(1).
(qq) An offense committed within this state or another state in violation of a law of the United States that is substantially similar to a violation listed in subdivisions (a) through (pp).
(rr) An offense committed in another state in violation of a statute of that state that is substantially similar to a violation listed in subdivisions (a) through (pp).

History: Add. 1995, Act 187, Eff. Apr. 1, 1996;—Am. 1997, Act 75, Imd. Eff. July 17, 1997;—Am. 2002, Act 124, Eff. Apr. 22, 2002;—Am. 2009, Act 82, Imd. Eff. Aug. 31, 2009;—Am. 2010, Act 176, Imd. Eff. Sept. 30, 2010;—Am. 2010, Act 362, Eff. Apr. 1, 2011;—Am. 2012, Act 172, Imd. Eff. June 19, 2012;—Am. 2012, Act 351, Imd. Eff. Dec. 13, 2012;—Am. 2014, Act 300, Eff. Jan. 1, 2015.

CHAPTER XXVIII
DISORDERLY PERSONS

750.167a Person hunting with firearms while drunk or intoxicated; confiscation and disposition of weapons; application for or possession of hunting license for period of 3 years prohibited.

Sec. 167a. Any person who shall be drunk or intoxicated while hunting with a firearm or other weapon under a valid hunting license shall be deemed to be a disorderly person. Upon conviction of such person, the weapon shall be confiscated and shall be delivered to the department of natural resources for disposition in the same manner as weapons confiscated for other violations of the game laws. Upon conviction under this section, the person so convicted, in addition to any punishment imposed pursuant to section 168, and as a part of any sentence imposed, shall be forbidden to apply for or possess a hunting license for a period of 3 years following the date of conviction. A violation of the conditions of such sentence shall be deemed to be a misdemeanor.

History: Add. 1952, Act 30, Eff. Sept. 18, 1952;—Am. 1987, Act 148, Imd. Eff. Oct. 26, 1987.

Compiler's note: For transfer of powers and duties of department of natural resources to department of natural resources and environment, and abolishment of department of natural resources, see E.R.O. No. 2009-31, compiled at MCL 324.99919.

CHAPTER XXX
DUELLING

750.171 Repealed. 2010, Act 96, Imd. Eff. June 22, 2010.

Compiler's note: The repealed section pertained to engaging in or challenging to fight duel.

750.172 Repealed. 2015, Act 210, Eff. Mar. 14, 2016.

Compiler's note: The repealed section pertained to accepting challenge and abetting duel.

CHAPTER XXXII
ESCAPES, RESCUES, JAIL AND PRISON BREAKING

750.183 Facilitating escape of or assisting prisoners; penalty.

Sec. 183. Any person who conveys into any jail, prison, or other like place of confinement, any disguise or any instrument, tool, weapon, or other thing, adapted or useful to aid any prisoner in making his or her escape, with intent to facilitate the escape of any prisoner there lawfully committed or detained, or shall by any means whatever, aid or assist any prisoner in his or her endeavor to escape therefrom, whether such escape be effected or attempted, or not, and every person who shall forcibly rescue any prisoner, held in custody upon any conviction or charge of an offense, is guilty of a felony punishable by imprisonment in the state prison not more than 7 years; or, if the person whose escape or rescue was effected or intended, was charged with an offense not capital, nor punishable by imprisonment in the state prison, then the offense mentioned in this section shall be a misdemeanor and shall be punishable by imprisonment for not more than 1 year or a fine of not more than $1,000.00.

History: 1931, Act 328, Eff. Sept. 18, 1931;—CL 1948, 750.183;—Am. 2002, Act 672, Eff. Mar. 31, 2003.

Former law: See section 11 of Ch. 156 of R.S. 1846, being CL 1857, § 5830; CL 1871, § 7663; How., § 9245; CL 1897, § 11315; CL 1915, § 14982; and CL 1929, § 16573.

750.197c Breaking or escaping jail, health care facility, or other place of confinement; violation as felony; penalty; definitions.

Sec. 197c. (1) A person lawfully imprisoned in a jail, other place of confinement established by law for any term, or lawfully imprisoned for any purpose at any other place, including, but not limited to, hospitals and other health care facilities or awaiting examination, trial, arraignment, sentence, or after sentence awaiting or during transfer to or from a prison, for a crime or offense, or charged with a crime or offense who, without being discharged from the place of confinement, or other lawful imprisonment by due process of law, through the use of violence, threats of violence or dangerous weapons, assaults an employee of the place of confinement or other custodian knowing the person to be an employee or custodian or breaks the place of confinement and escapes, or breaks the place of confinement although an escape is not actually made, is guilty of a felony punishable by imprisonment for not more than 5 years or a fine of not more than $2,500.00, or both.

(2) As used in this section:

(a) "Place of confinement" includes a correctional facility operated by the department of corrections, a local unit of government, or a private vendor under section 20i of 1953 PA 232, MCL 791.220i.

(b) "Employee" includes persons who are employed by the place of confinement as independent contractors.

History: Add. 1967, Act 59, Eff. Nov. 2, 1967;—Am. 1976, Act 188, Eff. Jan. 1, 1977;—Am. 1998, Act 510, Imd. Eff. Jan. 8, 1999;—Am. 2006, Act 535, Imd. Eff. Dec. 29, 2006.

CHAPTER XXXIII
EXPLOSIVES AND BOMBS, AND HARMFUL DEVICES

750.200 Explosives; common carriers for passengers; transportation.

Sec. 200. (1) A person shall not transport, carry, or convey dynamite, gunpowder, or any other explosive between any places within this state on any vessel, car, or vehicle of any description that is operated by a common carrier and that is carrying passengers for hire. A person who violates this section is guilty of a felony punishable by imprisonment for not more than 5 years or a fine of not more than $3,000.00, or both.

(2) This section does not prohibit the transportation of any of the following:

(a) Small arms ammunition in any quantity.

(b) Fuses, torpedoes, rockets, or other signal devices essential to promote safety in operation.

(c) Properly packed and marked samples for laboratory examination that do not exceed a net weight of 1/2 pound each and that do not exceed 20 samples at 1 time in a single vessel, car, or vehicle if the samples are not carried in that part of a vessel, car, or vehicle that is intended for transporting passengers for hire.

(3) This section does not prohibit the transportation of military or naval forces with their accompanying munitions of war on passenger equipment vessels, cars, or vehicles.

(4) This section does not apply to the transportation of benzine, naphtha, gasoline, or kerosene.

History: 1931, Act 328, Eff. Sept. 18, 1931;—CL 1948, 750.200;—Am. 1998, Act 206, Eff. Oct. 1, 1998.

Former law: See section 1 of Act 182 of 1909, being CL 1915, § 15251; and CL 1929, § 16795.

CHAPTER XXXVII
FIREARMS

750.222 Definitions.

Sec. 222. As used in this chapter:

(a) "Alcoholic liquor" means that term as defined in section 105 of the Michigan liquor control code of 1998, 1998 PA 58, MCL 436.1105.

(b) "Barrel length" means the internal length of a firearm as measured from the face of the closed breech of the firearm when it is unloaded, to the forward face of the end of the barrel.

(c) "Brandish" means to point, wave about, or display in a threatening manner with the intent to induce fear in another person.

(d) "Controlled substance" means a controlled substance or controlled substance analogue as those terms are defined in section 7104 of the public health code, 1978 PA 368, MCL 333.7104.

(e) "Firearm" means any weapon which will, is designed to, or may readily be converted to expel a projectile by action of an explosive.

(f) "Pistol" means a loaded or unloaded firearm that is 26 inches or less in length, or a loaded or unloaded firearm that by its construction and appearance conceals itself as a firearm.

(g) "Pneumatic gun" means that term as defined in section 1 of 1990 PA 319, MCL 123.1101.

(h) "Purchaser" means a person who receives a pistol from another person by purchase, gift, or loan.

(i) "Rifle" means a firearm designed or redesigned, made or remade, and intended to be fired from the shoulder and designed or redesigned and made or remade to use the energy of the explosive in a fixed metallic cartridge to fire only a single projectile through a rifled bore for each single pull of the trigger.

(j) "Seller" means a person who sells, furnishes, loans, or gives a pistol to another person.

(k) "Short-barreled rifle" means a rifle having 1 or more barrels less than 16 inches in length or a weapon made from a rifle, whether by alteration, modification, or otherwise, if the weapon as modified has an overall length of less than 26 inches.

(*l*) "Short-barreled shotgun" means a shotgun having 1 or more barrels less than 18 inches in length or a weapon made from a shotgun, whether by alteration, modification, or otherwise, if the weapon as modified has an overall length of less than 26 inches.

(m) "Shotgun" means a firearm designed or redesigned, made or remade, and intended to be fired from the shoulder and designed or redesigned and made or remade to use the energy of the explosive in a fixed shotgun shell to fire through a smooth bore either a number of ball shot or a single projectile for each single function of the trigger.

History: 1931, Act 328, Eff. Sept. 18, 1931;—CL 1948, 750.222;—Am. 1964, Act 215, Eff. Aug. 28, 1964;—Am. 1978, Act 564, Imd. Eff. Dec. 29, 1978;—Am. 1992, Act 217, Imd. Eff. Oct. 13, 1992;—Am. 2001, Act 135, Eff. Feb. 1, 2002;—Am. 2012, Act 242, Eff. Jan. 1, 2013;—Am. 2015, Act 26, Eff. July 1, 2015;—Am. 2015, Act 28, Eff. Aug. 10, 2015.

750.223 Selling firearms and ammunition; violations; penalties; "licensed dealer" defined.

Sec. 223. (1) A person who knowingly sells a pistol without complying with section 2 of 1927 PA 372, MCL 28.422, is guilty of a misdemeanor, punishable by imprisonment for not more than 90 days, or a fine of not more than $100.00, or both.

(2) A person who knowingly sells a firearm more than 26 inches in length to a person under 18 years of age is guilty of a misdemeanor, punishable by imprisonment for not more than 90 days, or a fine of not more than $500.00, or both. A second or subsequent violation of this subsection is a felony punishable by imprisonment for not more than 4 years, or a fine of not more than $2,000.00, or both. It is an affirmative defense to a prosecution under this subsection that the person who sold the firearm asked to see and was shown a driver's license or identification card issued by a state that identified the purchaser as being 18 years of age or older.

(3) A seller shall not sell a firearm or ammunition to a person if the seller knows that either of the following circumstances exists:

(a) The person is under indictment for a felony. As used in this subdivision, "felony" means a violation of a law of this state, or of another state, or of the United States that is punishable by imprisonment for 4 years or more.

(b) The person is prohibited under section 224f from possessing, using, transporting, selling, purchasing, carrying, shipping, receiving, or distributing a firearm.

(4) A person who violates subsection (3) is guilty of a felony, punishable by imprisonment for not more than 10 years, or by a fine of not more than $5,000.00, or both.

(5) As used in this section, "licensed dealer" means a person licensed under 18 USC 923 who regularly buys and sells firearms as a commercial activity with the principal objective of livelihood and profit.

History: 1931, Act 328, Eff. Sept. 18, 1931;—CL 1948, 750.223;—Am. 1969, Act 210, Eff. Mar. 20, 1970;—Am. 1990, Act 321, Eff. Mar. 28, 1991;—Am. 1992, Act 217, Imd. Eff. Oct. 13, 1992;—Am. 1992, Act 221, Eff. Mar. 31, 1993;—Am. 2012, Act 242, Eff. Jan. 1, 2013.

750.224 Weapons; manufacture, sale, or possession as felony; violation as felony; penalty; exceptions; "muffler" or "silencer" defined.

Sec. 224. (1) A person shall not manufacture, sell, offer for sale, or possess any of the following:

(a) A machine gun or firearm that shoots or is designed to shoot automatically more than 1 shot without manual reloading, by a single function of the trigger.

(b) A muffler or silencer.

(c) A bomb or bombshell.

(d) A blackjack, slungshot, billy, metallic knuckles, sand club, sand bag, or bludgeon.

(e) A device, weapon, cartridge, container, or contrivance designed to render a person temporarily or permanently disabled by the ejection, release, or emission of a gas or other substance.

(2) A person who violates subsection (1) is guilty of a felony, punishable by imprisonment for not more than 5 years, or a fine of not more than $2,500.00, or both.

(3) Subsection (1) does not apply to any of the following:

(a) A self-defense spray or foam device as defined in section 224d.

(b) A person manufacturing firearms, explosives, or munitions of war by virtue of a contract with a department of the government of the United States.

(c) A person licensed by the secretary of the treasury of the United States or the secretary's delegate to manufacture, sell, or possess a machine gun, or a device, weapon, cartridge, container, or contrivance described in subsection (1).

(4) As used in this chapter, "muffler" or "silencer" means 1 or more of the following:

(a) A device for muffling, silencing, or deadening the report of a firearm.

(b) A combination of parts, designed or redesigned, and intended for use in assembling or fabricating a muffler or silencer.

(c) A part, designed or redesigned, and intended only for use in assembling or fabricating a muffler or silencer.

History: 1931, Act 328, Eff. Sept. 18, 1931;—CL 1948, 750.224;—Am. 1959, Act 175, Eff. Mar. 19, 1960;—Am. 1978, Act 564, Imd. Eff. Dec. 29, 1978;—Am. 1980, Act 346, Eff. Mar. 31, 1981;—Am. 1990, Act 321, Eff. Mar. 28, 1991;—Am. 1991, Act 33, Imd. Eff. June 10, 1991;—Am. 2006, Act 401, Eff. Dec. 28, 2006.

Constitutionality: The Michigan supreme court held that the statute was not unconstitutionally vague as applied to the defendant in People v Lynch, 410 Mich 343; 301 NW2d 796 (1981).

Former law: See section 3 of Act 372 of 1927, being CL 1929, § 16751; and Act 206 of 1929.

750.224a Portable device or weapon directing electrical current, impulse, wave, or beam; sale or possession prohibited; exceptions; use of electro-muscular disruption technology; violation; penalty; definitions.

Sec. 224a. (1) Except as otherwise provided in this section, a person shall not sell, offer for sale, or possess in this state a portable device or weapon from which an electrical current, impulse, wave, or beam may be directed, which current, impulse, wave, or beam is designed to incapacitate temporarily, injure, or kill.

(2) This section does not prohibit any of the following:

(a) The possession and reasonable use of a device that uses electro-muscular disruption technology by a peace officer, or by any of the following individuals if the individual has been trained in the use, effects, and risks of the device, and is using the device while performing his or her official duties:

(*i*) An employee of the department of corrections who is authorized in writing by the director of the department of corrections to possess and use the device.

(*ii*) A local corrections officer authorized in writing by the county sheriff to possess and use the device.

(*iii*) An individual employed by a local unit of government that utilizes a jail or lockup facility who has custody of persons detained or incarcerated in the jail or lockup facility and who is authorized in writing by the chief of police, director of public safety, or sheriff to possess and use the device.

(*iv*) A probation officer.

(*v*) A court officer.

(*vi*) A bail agent authorized under section 167b.

(*vii*) A licensed private investigator.

(*viii*) An aircraft pilot or aircraft crew member.

(*ix*) An individual employed as a private security police officer. As used in this subparagraph, "private security police" means that term as defined in section 2 of the private security business and security alarm act, 1968 PA 330, MCL 338.1052.

(b) The possession and reasonable use of a device that uses electro-muscular disruption technology by an individual who holds a valid license to carry a concealed pistol under section 5b of 1927 PA 372, MCL 28.425, and who has been trained under subsection (5) in the use, effects, and risks of the device.

(c) Possession solely for the purpose of delivering a device described in subsection (1) to any governmental agency or to a laboratory for testing, with the prior written approval of the governmental agency or law enforcement agency and under conditions determined to be appropriate by that agency.

(3) A manufacturer, authorized importer, or authorized dealer may demonstrate, offer for sale, hold for sale, sell, give, lend, or deliver a device that uses electro-muscular disruption technology to a person authorized to possess a device that uses electro-muscular disruption technology and may possess a device that uses electro-muscular disruption technology for any of those purposes.

(4) A person who violates subsection (1) is guilty of a felony punishable by imprisonment for not more than 4 years or a fine of not more than $2,000.00, or both.

(5) An authorized dealer or other person who sells a device that uses electro-muscular disruption technology to an individual described in subsection (2)(b) shall verify the individual's identity and verify that the individual holds a valid concealed pistol license issued under section 5b of 1927 PA 372, MCL 28.425b, and shall provide to the individual purchasing the device, at the time of the sale, training on the use, effects, and risks of the device. A person who violates this subsection is guilty of a misdemeanor punishable by imprisonment for not more than 30 days or a fine of not more than $500.00, or both.

(6) An individual described in subsection (2) shall not use a device that uses electro-muscular disruption technology against another person except under circumstances that would justify the individual's lawful use of physical force. An individual who violates this subdivision is guilty of a misdemeanor punishable by imprisonment for not more than 2 years or a fine of not more than $2,000.00, or both.

(7) As used in this section:

(a) "A device that uses electro-muscular disruption technology" means a device to which both of the following apply:

(*i*) The device is capable of creating an electro-muscular disruption and is used or intended to be used as a defensive device capable of temporarily incapacitating or immobilizing a person by the direction or emission of conducted energy.

(*ii*) The device contains an identification and tracking system that, when the device is initially used, dispenses coded material traceable to the purchaser through records kept by the manufacturer, and the manufacturer of the device has a policy of providing that identification and tracking information to a police agency upon written request by that agency. However, this subdivision does not apply to a launchable device that is used only by law enforcement agencies.

(b) "Local corrections officer" means that term as defined in section 2 of the local corrections officers training act, 2003 PA 125, MCL 791.532.

(c) "Peace officer" means any of the following:

(*i*) A police officer or public safety officer of this state or a political subdivision of this state, including motor carrier officers appointed under section 6d of 1935 PA 59, MCL 28.6d, and security personnel employed by the state under section 6c of 1935 PA 59, MCL 28.6c.

(*ii*) A sheriff or a sheriff's deputy.

(*iii*) A police officer or public safety officer of a junior college, college, or university who is authorized by the governing board of that junior college, college, or university to enforce state law and the rules and ordinances of that junior college, college, or university.

(*iv*) A township constable.

(*v*) A marshal of a city, village, or township.

(*vi*) A conservation officer of the department of natural resources or the department of environmental quality.

(*vii*) A reserve peace officer, as that term is defined in section 1 of 1927 PA 372, MCL 28.421.

(*viii*) A law enforcement officer of another state or of a political subdivision of another state or a junior college, college, or university in another state, substantially corresponding to a law enforcement officer described in subparagraphs (*i*) to (*vii*).

(*ix*) A federal law enforcement officer.

History: Add. 1976, Act 106, Eff. July 1, 1976;—Am. 2002, Act 709, Imd. Eff. Dec. 30, 2002;—Am. 2004, Act 338, Imd. Eff. Sept. 23, 2004;—Am. 2006, Act 457, Imd. Eff. Dec. 20, 2006;—Am. 2012, Act 122, Eff. Aug. 6, 2012.

750.224b Short-barreled shotgun or rifle; making, manufacturing, transferring, or possessing as felony; penalty; exceptions; short-barreled shotgun or rifle 26 inches or less; short-barreled shotgun or rifle greater than 26 inches; violation of subsection (5) as civil infraction; seizure and forfeiture; applicability of MCL 776.20 to subsection (3).

Sec. 224b. (1) A person shall not make, manufacture, transfer, or possess a short-barreled shotgun or a short-barreled rifle.

(2) A person who violates subsection (1) is guilty of a felony punishable by imprisonment for not more than 5 years or a fine of not more than $2,500.00, or both.

(3) Subsection (1) does not apply to a short-barreled shotgun or short-barreled rifle that is lawfully made, manufactured, transferred, or possessed under federal law.

(4) A person, excluding a manufacturer, lawfully making, transferring, or possessing a short-barreled shotgun or short-barreled rifle that is 26 inches or less in length under this section shall comply with section 2 or 2a of 1927 PA 372, MCL 28.422 and 28.422a.

(5) A person who possesses a short-barreled shotgun or short-barreled rifle that is greater than 26 inches in length under this section shall possess a copy of the federal registration of that short-barreled shotgun or short-barreled rifle while transporting or using that short-barreled shotgun or short-barreled rifle and shall present that federal registration to a peace officer upon request by that peace officer.

(6) A person who violates subsection (5) is responsible for a state civil infraction and may be fined not more than $100.00. A short-barreled shotgun or short-barreled rifle carried in violation of subsection (5) is subject to immediate seizure by a peace officer. If a peace officer seizes a short-barreled shotgun or short-barreled rifle under this subsection, the person has 45 days in which to display the federal registration to an authorized employee of the law enforcement entity that employs the peace officer. If the person displays the federal registration to an authorized employee of the law enforcement entity that employs the peace

officer within the 45-day period, the authorized employee of that law enforcement entity shall return the short-barreled shotgun or short-barreled rifle to the person unless the person is prohibited by law from possessing a firearm. If the person does not display the federal registration within the 45-day period, the short-barreled shotgun or short-barreled rifle is subject to seizure and forfeiture in the same manner that property is subject to seizure and forfeiture under sections 4701 to 4709 of the revised judicature act of 1961, 1961 PA 236, MCL 600.4701 to 600.4709.

(7) Section 20 of chapter XVI of the code of criminal procedure, 1927 PA 175, MCL 776.20, applies to subsection (3).

History: Add. 1978, Act 564, Imd. Eff. Dec. 29, 1978;—Am. 2008, Act 196, Eff. Jan. 7, 2009;—Am. 2014, Act 63, Imd. Eff. Mar. 27, 2014.

750.224c Armor piercing ammunition; manufacture, distribution, sale, or use prohibited; exceptions; violation as felony; penalty; definitions; exemption of projectile or projectile core; rule.

Sec. 224c. (1) Except as provided in subsection (2), a person shall not manufacture, distribute, sell, or use armor piercing ammunition in this state. A person who willfully violates this section is guilty of a felony, punishable by imprisonment for not more than 4 years, or by a fine of not more than $2,000.00, or both.

(2) This section does not apply to either of the following:

(a) A person who manufactures, distributes, sells, or uses armor piercing ammunition in this state, if that manufacture, distribution, sale, or use is not in violation of chapter 44 of title 18 of the United States Code.

(b) A licensed dealer who sells or distributes armor piercing ammunition in violation of this section if the licensed dealer is subject to license revocation under chapter 44 of title 18 of the United States Code for that sale or distribution.

(3) As used in this section:

(a) "Armor piercing ammunition" means a projectile or projectile core which may be used in a pistol and which is constructed entirely, excluding the presence of traces of other substances, of tungsten alloys, steel, iron, brass, bronze, beryllium copper, or a combination of tungsten alloys, steel, iron, brass, bronze, or beryllium copper. Armor piercing ammunition does not include any of the following:

(*i*) Shotgun shot that is required by federal law or by a law of this state to be used for hunting purposes.

(*ii*) A frangible projectile designed for target shooting.

(*iii*) A projectile that the director of the department of state police finds is primarily intended to be used for sporting purposes.

(*iv*) A projectile or projectile core that the director of the department of state police finds is intended to be used for industrial purposes.

(b) "Licensed dealer" means a person licensed under chapter 44 of title 18 of the United States Code to deal in firearms or ammunition.

(4) The director of the department of state police shall exempt a projectile or projectile core under subsection (3)(a)(*iii*) or (*iv*) if that projectile or projectile core is exempted under chapter 44 of title 18 of the United States Code. The director of state police shall exempt a projectile or projectile core under subsection (3)(a)(*iii*) or (*iv*) only by a rule promulgated in compliance with the administrative procedures act of 1969, Act No. 306 of the Public Acts of 1969, being sections 24.201 to 24.328 of the Michigan Compiled Laws.

History: Add. 1990, Act 318, Eff. Mar. 28, 1991.

750.224d Self-defense spray or foam device.

Sec. 224d. (1) As used in this section and section 224, "self-defense spray or foam device" means a device to which all of the following apply:

(a) The device is capable of carrying, and ejects, releases, or emits 1 of the following:

(*i*) Not more than 35 grams of any combination of orthochlorobenzalmalononitrile and inert ingredients.

(*ii*) A solution containing not more than 10% oleoresin capsicum.

(b) The device does not eject, release, or emit any gas or substance that will temporarily or permanently disable, incapacitate, injure, or harm a person with whom the gas or substance comes in contact, other than the substance described in subdivision (a)(*i*) or (*ii*).

(2) Except as otherwise provided in this section, a person who uses a self-defense spray or foam device to eject, release, or emit orthochlorobenzalmalononitrile or oleoresin capsicum at another person is guilty of a misdemeanor, punishable by imprisonment for not more than 2 years, or a fine of not more than $2,000.00, or both.

(3) If a person uses a self-defense spray or foam device during the commission of a crime to eject, release, or emit orthochlorobenzalmalononitrile or oleoresin capsicum or threatens to use a self-defense spray or foam device during the commission of a crime to temporarily or permanently disable another person, the judge who imposes sentence upon a conviction for that crime shall consider the defendant's use or threatened use of the self-defense spray or foam device as a reason for enhancing the sentence.

(4) A person shall not sell a self-defense spray or foam device to a minor. A person who violates this subsection is guilty of a misdemeanor punishable by imprisonment for not more than 90 days or a fine of not more than $500.00, or both.

(5) Subsection (2) does not prohibit either of the following:

(a) The reasonable use of a self-defense spray or foam device containing not more than 10% oleoresin capsicum by a person who is employed by a county sheriff or a chief of police and who is authorized in writing by the county sheriff or chief of police to carry and use a self-defense spray or foam device and has been trained in the use, effects, and risks of the device, while in performance of his or her official duties.

(b) The reasonable use of a self-defense spray or foam device containing not more than 10% oleoresin capsicum by a person in the protection of a person or property under circumstances that would justify the person's use of physical force.

History: Add. 1980, Act 346, Eff. Mar. 31, 1981;—Am. 1991, Act 33, Imd. Eff. June 10, 1991;—Am. 1992, Act 4, Imd. Eff. Feb. 21, 1992;—Am. 2006, Act 401, Eff. Dec. 28, 2006;—Am. 2010, Act 365, Imd. Eff. Dec. 22, 2010.

750.224e Conversion of semiautomatic firearm to fully automatic firearm; prohibited acts; penalty; applicability; "fully automatic firearm", "licensed collector", and "semiautomatic firearm" defined.

Sec. 224e. (1) A person shall not knowingly do any of the following:

(a) Manufacture, sell, distribute, or possess or attempt to manufacture, sell, distribute, or possess a device that is designed or intended to be used to convert a semiautomatic firearm into a fully automatic firearm.

(b) Demonstrate to another person or attempt to demonstrate to another person how to manufacture or install a device to convert a semiautomatic firearm into a fully automatic firearm.

(2) A person who violates subsection (1) is guilty of a felony punishable by imprisonment for not more than 4 years, or a fine of not more than $2,000.00, or both.

(3) This section does not apply to any of the following:

(a) A police agency of this state, or of a local unit of government of this state, or of the United States.

(b) An employee of an agency described in subdivision (a), if the manufacture, sale, distribution, or possession or attempted manufacture, sale, distribution, or possession or demonstration or attempted demonstration is in the course of his or her official duties as an employee of that agency.

(c) The armed forces.

(d) A member or employee of the armed forces, if the manufacture, sale, distribution, or possession or attempted manufacture, sale, distribution, or possession or demonstration or attempted demonstration is in the course of his or her official duties as a member or employee of the armed forces.

(e) A licensed collector who possesses a device that is designed or intended to be used to convert a semiautomatic firearm into a fully automatic firearm that was lawfully owned by that licensed collector before the effective date of the amendatory act that added this section. This subdivision does not permit a licensed collector who lawfully owned a device that is designed or intended to be used to convert a semiautomatic firearm into a fully automatic firearm before the effective date of the amendatory act that added this section to sell or distribute or attempt to sell or distribute that device to another person after the effective date of the amendatory act that added this section.

(4) As used in this section:

(a) "Fully automatic firearm" means a firearm employing gas pressure or force of recoil to mechanically eject an empty cartridge from the firearm after a shot, and to load the next cartridge from the magazine, without renewed pressure on the trigger for each successive shot.

(b) "Licensed collector" means a person who is licensed under chapter 44 of title 18 of the United States code to acquire, hold, or dispose of firearms as curios or relics.

(c) "Semiautomatic firearm" means a firearm employing gas pressure or force of recoil to mechanically eject an empty cartridge from the firearm after a shot, and to load the next cartridge from the magazine, but requiring renewed pressure on the trigger for each successive shot.

History: Add. 1990, Act 321, Eff. Mar. 28, 1991.

750.224f Possession of firearm or distribution of ammunition by person convicted of felony; circumstances; penalty; applicability of section to expunged or set aside conviction; definitions.

Sec. 224f. (1) Except as provided in subsection (2), a person convicted of a felony shall not possess, use, transport, sell, purchase, carry, ship, receive, or distribute a firearm in this state until the expiration of 3 years after all of the following circumstances exist:

(a) The person has paid all fines imposed for the violation.

(b) The person has served all terms of imprisonment imposed for the violation.

(c) The person has successfully completed all conditions of probation or parole imposed for the violation.

(2) A person convicted of a specified felony shall not possess, use, transport, sell, purchase, carry, ship, receive, or distribute a firearm in this state until all of the following circumstances exist:

(a) The expiration of 5 years after all of the following circumstances exist:

(*i*) The person has paid all fines imposed for the violation.

(*ii*) The person has served all terms of imprisonment imposed for the violation.

(*iii*) The person has successfully completed all conditions of probation or parole imposed for the violation.

(b) The person's right to possess, use, transport, sell, purchase, carry, ship, receive, or distribute a firearm has been restored under section 4 of 1927 PA 372, MCL 28.424.

(3) Except as provided in subsection (4), a person convicted of a felony shall not possess, use, transport, sell, carry, ship, or distribute ammunition in this state until the expiration of 3 years after all of the following circumstances exist:

(a) The person has paid all fines imposed for the violation.

(b) The person has served all terms of imprisonment imposed for the violation.

(c) The person has successfully completed all conditions of probation or parole imposed for the violation.

(4) A person convicted of a specified felony shall not possess, use, transport, sell, carry, ship, or distribute ammunition in this state until all of the following circumstances exist:

(a) The expiration of 5 years after all of the following circumstances exist:

(*i*) The person has paid all fines imposed for the violation.

(*ii*) The person has served all terms of imprisonment imposed for the violation.

(*iii*) The person has successfully completed all conditions of probation or parole imposed for the violation.

(b) The person's right to possess, use, transport, sell, purchase, carry, ship, receive, or distribute ammunition has been restored under section 4 of 1927 PA 372, MCL 28.424.

(5) A person who possesses, uses, transports, sells, purchases, carries, ships, receives, or distributes a firearm in violation of this section is guilty of a felony punishable by imprisonment for not more than 5 years or a fine of not more than $5,000.00, or both.

(6) A person who possesses, uses, transports, sells, carries, ships, or distributes ammunition in violation of this section is guilty of a felony punishable by imprisonment for not more than 5 years or a fine of not more than $5,000.00, or both.

(7) Any single criminal transaction where a person possesses, uses, transports, sells, carries, ships, or distributes ammunition in violation of this section, regardless of the amount of ammunition involved, constitutes 1 offense.

(8) This section does not apply to a conviction that has been expunged or set aside, or for which the person has been pardoned, unless the expunction, order, or pardon expressly provides that the person shall not possess a firearm or ammunition.

(9) As used in this section:

(a) "Ammunition" means any projectile that, in its current state, may be expelled from a firearm by an explosive.

(b) "Felony" means a violation of a law of this state, or of another state, or of the United States that is punishable by imprisonment for 4 years or more, or an attempt to violate such a law.

(10) As used in subsections (2) and (4), "specified felony" means a felony in which 1 or more of the following circumstances exist:

(a) An element of that felony is the use, attempted use, or threatened use of physical force against the person or property of another, or that by its nature, involves a substantial risk that physical force against the person or property of another may be used in the course of committing the offense.

(b) An element of that felony is the unlawful manufacture, possession, importation, exportation, distribution, or dispensing of a controlled substance.

(c) An element of that felony is the unlawful possession or distribution of a firearm.

(d) An element of that felony is the unlawful use of an explosive.

(e) The felony is burglary of an occupied dwelling, or breaking and entering an occupied dwelling, or arson.

History: Add. 1992, Act 217, Imd. Eff. Oct. 13, 1992;—Am. 2014, Act 4, Eff. May 12, 2014.

750.226 Firearm or dangerous or deadly weapon or instrument; carrying with unlawful intent; violation as felony; penalty.

Sec. 226. (1) A person shall not, with intent to use the same unlawfully against the person of another, go armed with a pistol or other firearm, or a pneumatic gun, dagger, dirk, razor, stiletto, or knife having a blade over 3 inches in length, or any other dangerous or deadly weapon or instrument.

(2) A person who violates this section is guilty of a felony punishable by imprisonment for not more than 5 years or a fine of not more than $2,500.00.

History: 1931, Act 328, Eff. Sept. 18, 1931;—CL 1948, 750.226;—Am. 2015, Act 26, Eff. July 1, 2015.

Former law: See section 4 of Act 372 of 1927, being CL 1929, § 16752.

750.227 Concealed weapons; carrying; penalty.

Sec. 227. (1) A person shall not carry a dagger, dirk, stiletto, a double-edged nonfolding stabbing instrument of any length, or any other dangerous weapon, except a hunting knife adapted and carried as such, concealed on or about his or her person, or whether concealed or otherwise in any vehicle operated or occupied by the person, except in his or her dwelling house, place of business or on other land possessed by the person.

(2) A person shall not carry a pistol concealed on or about his or her person, or, whether concealed or otherwise, in a vehicle operated or occupied by the person, except in his or her dwelling house, place of business, or on other land possessed by the person, without a license to carry the pistol as provided by law and if licensed, shall not carry the pistol in a place or manner inconsistent with any restrictions upon such license.

(3) A person who violates this section is guilty of a felony, punishable by imprisonment for not more than 5 years, or by a fine of not more than $2,500.00.

History: 1931, Act 328, Eff. Sept. 18, 1931;—CL 1948, 750.227;—Am. 1973, Act 206, Eff. Mar. 29, 1974;—Am. 1986, Act 8, Eff. July 1, 1986.

Constitutionality: The double jeopardy protection against multiple punishment for the same offense is a restriction on a court's ability to impose punishment in excess of that intended by the Legislature, not a limit on the Legislature's power to define crime and fix punishment. People v Sturgis, 427 Mich 392; 397 NW2d 783 (1986).

Former law: See section 5 of Act 372 of 1927, being CL 1929, § 16753.

750.227a Pistols; unlawful possession by licensee.

Sec. 227a. Any person licensed in accordance with law to carry a pistol because he is engaged in the business of protecting the person or property of another, except peace officers of the United States, the state or any subdivision of the state railroad policemen appointed and commissioned under the provisions of Act No. 114 of the Public Acts of 1941, being sections 470.51 to 470.61 of the Compiled Laws of 1948 or those in the military service of the United States, who shall have a pistol in his possession while not actually engaged in the business of protecting the person or property of another, except in his dwelling house or on other land possessed by him, is guilty of a felony. This section shall not be construed to prohibit such person from carrying an unloaded pistol to or from his place of employment by the most direct route.

History: Add. 1966, Act 100, Eff. Mar. 10, 1967;—Am. 1967, Act 49, Eff. Nov. 2, 1967.

750.227b Carrying or possessing firearm when committing or attempting to commit felony; carrying or possessing pneumatic gun; exception; "law enforcement officer" defined.

Sec. 227b. (1) A person who carries or has in his or her possession a firearm when he or she commits or attempts to commit a felony, except a violation of section 223, 227, 227a, or 230, is guilty of a felony and shall be punished by imprisonment for 2 years. Upon a second conviction under this subsection, the person shall be punished by imprisonment for 5 years. Upon a third or subsequent conviction under this subsection, the person shall be punished by imprisonment for 10 years.

(2) A person who carries or has in his or her possession a pneumatic gun and uses that pneumatic gun in furtherance of committing or attempting to commit a felony, except a violation of section 223, 227, 227a, or 230, is guilty of a felony and shall be punished by imprisonment for 2 years. Upon a second conviction under this subsection, the person shall be punished by imprisonment for 5 years. Upon a third or subsequent conviction under this subsection, the person shall be punished by imprisonment for 10 years.

(3) A term of imprisonment prescribed by this section is in addition to the sentence imposed for the conviction of the felony or the attempt to commit the felony and shall be served consecutively with and preceding any term of imprisonment imposed for the conviction of the felony or attempt to commit the felony.

(4) A term of imprisonment imposed under this section shall not be suspended. The person subject to the sentence mandated by this section is not eligible for parole or probation during the mandatory term imposed under subsection (1) or (2).

(5) This section does not apply to a law enforcement officer who is authorized to carry a firearm while in the official performance of his or her duties and who is in the performance of those duties. As used in this subsection, "law enforcement officer" means a person who is regularly employed as a member of a duly authorized police agency or other organization of the United States, this state, or a city, county, township, or village of this state and who is responsible for the prevention and detection of crime and the enforcement of the general criminal laws of this state.

History: Add. 1976, Act 6, Eff. Jan. 1, 1977;—Am. 1990, Act 321, Eff. Mar. 28, 1991;—Am. 2015, Act 26, Eff. July 1, 2015.

Constitutionality: The double jeopardy protection against multiple punishment for the same offense is a restriction on a court's ability to impose punishment in excess of that intended by the Legislature, not a limit on the Legislature's power to define crime and fix punishment. People v Sturgis, 427 Mich 392; 397 NW2d 783 (1986).

750.227c Transporting or possessing loaded firearm in or upon vehicle propelled by mechanical means; violation as misdemeanor; penalty.

Sec. 227c. (1) Except as otherwise permitted by law, a person shall not transport or possess in or upon a sailboat or a motor vehicle, aircraft, motorboat, or any other vehicle propelled by mechanical means either of the following:

(a) A firearm, other than a pistol, that is loaded.

(b) A pneumatic gun that is loaded and expels a metallic BB or metallic pellet greater than .177 caliber.

(2) A person who violates this section is guilty of a misdemeanor punishable by imprisonment for not more than 2 years or a fine of not more than $2,500.00, or both.

History: Add. 1981, Act 103, Eff. Mar. 31, 1982;—Am. 2015, Act 26, Eff. July 1, 2015.

750.227d Transporting or possessing firearm in or upon motor vehicle or self-propelled vehicle designed for land travel; violation as misdemeanor; penalty.

Sec. 227d. (1) Except as otherwise permitted by law, a person shall not transport or possess in or upon a motor vehicle or any self-propelled vehicle designed for land travel either of the following:

(a) A firearm, other than a pistol, unless the firearm is unloaded and is 1 or more of the following:

(*i*) Taken down.

(*ii*) Enclosed in a case.

(*iii*) Carried in the trunk of the vehicle.

(*iv*) Inaccessible from the interior of the vehicle.

(b) A pneumatic gun that expels a metallic BB or metallic pellet greater than .177 caliber unless the pneumatic gun is unloaded and is 1 or more of the following:

(*i*) Taken down.

(*ii*) Enclosed in a case.

(*iii*) Carried in the trunk of the vehicle.

(*iv*) Inaccessible from the interior of the vehicle.

(2) A person who violates this section is guilty of a misdemeanor punishable by imprisonment for not more than 90 days or a fine of not more than $100.00, or both.

History: Add. 1981, Act 103, Eff. Mar. 31, 1982;—Am. 2015, Act 26, Eff. July 1, 2015.

750.227f Committing or attempting to commit crime involving violent act or threat of violent act against another person while wearing body armor as felony; penalty; consecutive term of imprisonment; exception; definitions.

Sec. 227f. (1) Except as provided in subsection (2), an individual who commits or attempts to commit a crime that involves a violent act or a threat of a violent act against another person while wearing body armor is guilty of a felony, punishable by imprisonment for not more than 4 years, or a fine of not more than $2,000.00, or both. A term of imprisonment imposed for violating this section may be served consecutively to any term of imprisonment imposed for the crime committed or attempted.

(2) Subsection (1) does not apply to either of the following:

(a) A peace officer of this state or another state, or of a local unit of government of this state or another state, or of the United States, performing his or her duties as a peace officer while on or off a scheduled work shift as a peace officer.

(b) A security officer performing his or her duties as a security officer while on a scheduled work shift as a security officer.

(3) As used in this section:

(a) "Body armor" means clothing or a device designed or intended to protect an individual's body or a portion of an individual's body from injury caused by a firearm.

(b) "Security officer" means an individual lawfully employed to physically protect another individual or to physically protect the property of another person.

History: Add. 1990, Act 321, Eff. Mar. 28, 1991;—Am. 1992, Act 218, Imd. Eff. Oct. 13, 1992;—Am. 1996, Act 163, Imd. Eff. Apr. 11, 1996;—Am. 2000, Act 226, Eff. Oct. 1, 2000.

750.227g Body armor; purchase, ownership, possession, or use by convicted felon; prohibition; issuance of written permission; violation as felony; definitions.

Sec. 227g. (1) Except as otherwise provided in this section, a person who has been convicted of a violent felony shall not purchase, own, possess, or use body armor.

(2) A person who has been convicted of a violent felony whose employment, livelihood, or safety is dependent on his or her ability to purchase, own, possess, or use body armor may petition the chief of police of the local unit of government in which he or she resides or, if he or she does not reside in a local unit of government that has a police department, the county sheriff, for written permission to purchase, own, possess, or use body armor under this section.

(3) The chief of police of a local unit of government or the county sheriff may grant a person who properly petitions that chief of police or county sheriff under subsection (2) written permission to purchase, own, possess, or use body armor as provided in this section if the chief of police or county sheriff determines that both of the following circumstances exist:

(a) The petitioner is likely to use body armor in a safe and lawful manner.

(b) The petitioner has reasonable need for the protection provided by body armor.

(4) In making the determination required under subsection (3), the chief of police or county sheriff shall consider all of the following:

(a) The petitioner's continued employment.

(b) The interests of justice.

(c) Other circumstances justifying issuance of written permission to purchase, own, possess, or use body armor.

(5) The chief of police or county sheriff may restrict written permission issued to a petitioner under this section in any manner determined appropriate by that chief of police or county sheriff. If permission is restricted, the chief of police or county sheriff shall state the restrictions in the permission document.

(6) It is the intent of the legislature that chiefs of police and county sheriffs exercise broad discretion in determining whether to issue written permission to purchase, own, possess, or use body armor under this section. However, nothing in this section requires a chief of police or county sheriff to issue written permission to any particular petitioner. The issuance of written permission to purchase, own, possess, or use body armor under this section does not relieve any person or entity from criminal liability that might otherwise be imposed.

(7) A person who receives written permission from a chief of police or county sheriff to purchase, own, possess, or use body armor shall have that written permission in his or her possession when he or she is purchasing, owning, possessing, or using body armor.

(8) A law enforcement agency may issue body armor to a person who is in custody or who is a witness to a crime for his or her own protection without a petition being previously filed under subsection (2). If the law enforcement agency issues body armor to the person under this subsection, the law enforcement agency shall document the reasons for issuing body armor and retain a copy of that document as an official record. The law enforcement agency shall also issue written permission to the person to possess and use body armor under this section.

(9) A person who violates this section is guilty of a crime as follows:

(a) For a violation of subsection (1), the person is guilty of a felony punishable by imprisonment for not more than 4 years or a fine of not more than $2,000.00, or both.

(b) For a violation of subsection (7), the person is guilty of a misdemeanor punishable by imprisonment for not more than 93 days or a fine of not more than $100.00, or both.

(10) As used in this section:

(a) "Body armor" means that term as defined in section 227f.

(b) "Violent felony" means that term as defined in section 36 of 1953 PA 232, MCL 791.236.

History: Add. 2000, Act 224, Eff. Oct. 1, 2000.

750.228 Ownership of pistol greater than 26 inches in length; conditions; election to have firearm not considered as pistol.

Sec. 228. (1) A person may lawfully own, possess, carry, or transport as a pistol a firearm greater than 26 inches in length if all of the following conditions apply:

(a) The person registered the firearm as a pistol under section 2 or 2a of 1927 PA 372, MCL 28.422 and 28.422a, before January 1, 2013.

(b) The person who registered the firearm as described in subdivision (a) has maintained registration of the firearm since January 1, 2013 without lapse.

(c) The person possesses a copy of the license or record issued to him or her under section 2 or 2a of 1927 PA 372, MCL 28.422 and 28.422a.

(2) A person who satisfies all of the conditions listed under subsection (1) nevertheless may elect to have the firearm not be considered to be a pistol. A person who makes the election under this subsection shall notify the department of state police of the election in a manner prescribed by that department.

History: Add. 2012, Act 242, Eff. Jan. 1, 2013.

Compiler's note: Former MCL 750.228, which pertained to penalties to have pistol inspected, was repealed by Act 196 of 2008, Eff. Jan. 7, 2009.

750.229 Pistols accepted in pawn, by second-hand dealer or junk dealer.

Sec. 229. Any pawnbroker who shall accept a pistol in pawn, or any second-hand or junk dealer, as defined in Act No. 350 of the Public Acts of 1917, who shall accept a pistol and offer or display the same for resale, shall be guilty of a misdemeanor.

History: 1931, Act 328, Eff. Sept. 18, 1931;—Am. 1945, Act 236, Eff. Sept. 6, 1945;—CL 1948, 750.229.

Compiler's note: For provisions of Act 350 of 1917, referred to in this section, see MCL 445.401 et seq.

Former law: See section 10 of Act 372 of 1927, being CL 1929, § 16759.

750.230 Firearms; altering, removing, or obliterating marks of identity; presumption.

Sec. 230. A person who shall wilfully alter, remove, or obliterate the name of the maker, model, manufacturer's number, or other mark of identity of a pistol or other firearm, shall be guilty of a felony, punishable by imprisonment for not more than 2 years or fine of not more than $1,000.00. Possession of a firearm upon which the number shall have been altered, removed, or obliterated, other than an antique firearm as defined by section 231a(2)(a) or (b), shall be presumptive evidence that the possessor has altered, removed, or obliterated the same.

History: 1931, Act 328, Eff. Sept. 18, 1931;—CL 1948, 750.230;—Am. 1976, Act 32, Imd. Eff. Mar. 5, 1976.

Constitutionality: The statutory presumption contained in this section is unconstitutional. People v Moore, 402 Mich 538; 266 NW2d 145 (1978).

Former law: See section 11 of Act 372 of 1927, being CL 1929, § 16760.

750.231 MCL 750.224, 750.224a, 750.224b, 750.224d, 750.227, 750.227c, and 750.227d inapplicable to certain persons and organizations.

Sec. 231. (1) Except as provided in subsection (2), sections 224, 224a, 224b, 224d, 227, 227c, and 227d do not apply to any of the following:

(a) A peace officer of an authorized police agency of the United States, of this state, or of a political subdivision of this state, who is regularly employed and paid by the United States, this state, or a political subdivision of this state.

(b) A person who is regularly employed by the state department of corrections and who is authorized in writing by the director of the department of corrections to carry a concealed weapon while in the official performance of his or her duties or while going to or returning from those duties.

(c) A person employed by a private vendor that operates a youth correctional facility authorized under section 20g of the corrections code of 1953, 1953 PA 232, MCL 791.220g, who meets the same criteria established by the director of the state department of corrections for departmental employees described in subdivision (b) and who is authorized in writing by the director of the department of corrections to carry a concealed weapon while in the official performance of his or her duties or while going to or returning from those duties.

(d) A member of the United States Army, Air Force, Navy, or Marine Corps or the United States Coast Guard while carrying weapons in the line of or incidental to duty.

(e) An organization authorized by law to purchase or receive weapons from the United States or from this state.

(f) A member of the National Guard, United States Armed Forces Reserve, the United States Coast Guard Reserve, or any other authorized military organization while on duty or drill, or in going to or returning from a place of assembly or practice, while carrying weapons used for a purpose of the National Guard, United States Armed Forces Reserve, United States Coast Guard Reserve, or other duly authorized military organization.

(g) A security employee employed by the state and granted limited arrest powers under section 6c of 1935 PA 59, MCL 28.6c.

(h) A motor carrier officer appointed under section 6d of 1935 PA 59, MCL 28.6d.

(2) As applied to section 224a(1) only, subsection (1) is not applicable to an individual included under subsection (1)(a), (b), or (c) unless he or she has been trained on the use, effects, and risks of using a portable device or weapon described in section 224a(1).

History: 1931, Act 328, Eff. Sept. 18, 1931;—CL 1948, 750.231;—Am. 1958, Act 107, Eff. Sept. 13, 1958;—Am. 1964, Act 215, Eff. Aug. 28, 1964;—Am. 1981, Act 103, Eff. Mar. 31, 1982;—Am. 1998, Act 510, Imd. Eff. Jan. 8, 1999;—Am. 2002, Act 536, Imd. Eff. July 26, 2002;—Am. 2006, Act 401, Eff. Dec. 28, 2006;—Am. 2017, Act 96, Eff. Oct. 11, 2017.

750.231a Exceptions to MCL 750.227(2); "antique firearm" defined.

Sec. 231a. (1) Subsection (2) of section 227 does not apply to any of the following:

(a) To a person holding a valid license to carry a pistol concealed upon his or her person issued by his or her state of residence except where the pistol is carried in nonconformance with a restriction appearing on the license.

(b) To the regular and ordinary transportation of pistols as merchandise by an authorized agent of a person licensed to manufacture firearms.

(c) To a person carrying an antique firearm, completely unloaded in a closed case or container designed for the storage of firearms in the trunk of a vehicle.

(d) To a person while transporting a pistol for a lawful purpose that is licensed by the owner or occupant of the motor vehicle in compliance with section 2 of 1927 PA 372, MCL 28.422, and the pistol is unloaded in a closed case designed for the storage of firearms in the trunk of the vehicle.

(e) To a person while transporting a pistol for a lawful purpose that is licensed by the owner or occupant of the motor vehicle in compliance with section 2 of 1927 PA 372, MCL 28.422, and the pistol is unloaded in a closed case designed for the storage of firearms in a vehicle that does not have a trunk and is not readily accessible to the occupants of the vehicle.

(2) As used in this section, "antique firearm" means either of the following:

(*i*) A firearm not designed or redesigned for using rimfire or conventional center fire ignition with fixed ammunition and manufactured in or before 1898, including a matchlock, flintlock, percussion cap, or similar type of ignition system or replica of such a firearm, whether actually manufactured before or after 1898.

(*ii*) A firearm using fixed ammunition manufactured in or before 1898, for which ammunition is no longer manufactured in the United States and is not readily available in the ordinary channels of commercial trade.

History: Add. 1964, Act 215, Eff. Aug. 28, 1964;—Am. 1973, Act 191, Eff. Mar. 29, 1974;—Am. 1974, Act 55, Imd. Eff. Apr. 1, 1974;—Am. 1978, Act 280, Imd. Eff. July 6, 1978;—Am. 2002, Act 82, Imd. Eff. Mar. 26, 2002;—Am. 2008, Act 196, Eff. Jan. 7, 2009;—Am. 2012, Act 427, Imd. Eff. Dec. 21, 2012.

750.231b Sale and safety inspection; persons exempt.

Sec. 231b. Sections 223 and 228 do not apply to a duly authorized police or correctional agency of the United States or of the state or any subdivision thereof, nor to the army, air force, navy or marine corps of the United States, nor to organizations authorized by law to purchase or receive weapons from the United States or from this state, nor to the national guard, armed forces reserves or other duly authorized military organizations, nor to a member of such agencies or organizations for weapons used by him for the purposes of such agencies or organizations, nor to a person holding a license to carry a pistol concealed upon his person issued by another state, nor to the regular and ordinary transportation of pistols as merchandise by an authorized agent of a person licensed to manufacture firearms.

History: Add. 1964, Act 215, Eff. Aug. 28, 1964.

750.231c "Aircraft," "approved signaling device," and "vessel" defined; sections inapplicable to approved signaling device; sale, purchase, possession, or use of approved signaling device; violation as misdemeanor; penalties.

Sec. 231c. (1) As used in this section:

(a) "Aircraft" means aircraft as defined in section 43.

(b) "Approved signaling device" means a pistol which is a signaling device approved by the United States coast guard pursuant to regulations issued under former section 4488 of the Revised Statutes of the United States, 46 U.S.C. Appx. 481, or under former section 5 of the federal boat safety act of 1971, Public Law 92-75, 46 U.S.C. 1454.

(c) "Vessel" means every description of watercraft, other than a seaplane on the water, used or capable of being used as a means of transportation on water.

(2) Sections 223, 227, 228, 232, 232a, and 237 shall not apply to an approved signaling device.

(3) A person shall not sell an approved signaling device to a person, nor shall a person purchase an approved signaling device, unless the purchaser is 18 years of age or older and either of the following apply:

(a) The purchaser possesses and displays to the seller any of the following:

(*i*) A valid and current certificate of number issued pursuant to section 80124 of part 801 (marine safety) of the natural resources and environmental protection act, Act No. 451 of the Public Acts of 1994, being section 324.80124 of the Michigan Compiled Laws, for a vessel.

(*ii*) If a vessel is considered in compliance with the numbering requirements of this state pursuant to section 80122 of part 801 of Act No. 451 of the Public Acts of 1994, being section 324.80122 of the Michigan Compiled Laws, proof of ownership or proof of the vessel's being numbered in another state.

(*iii*) If a vessel is not required to be numbered or to display a decal under part 801 of Act No. 451 of the Public Acts of 1994, being sections 324.80101 to 324.80199 of the Michigan Compiled Laws, proof of ownership of the vessel.

(b) The purchaser is the holder of and displays to the seller a valid and effective airman's certificate of competency issued by the United States or a foreign government.

(4) A person may possess an approved signaling device only under the following circumstances:

(a) The possession occurs in the process of manufacturing, marketing, or sale of the device, including the transportation of the device as merchandise, and the device is unloaded.

(b) The device is on a vessel or on an aircraft.

(c) The device is at a person's residence.

(d) The person is en route from the place of purchase to the person's residence or the person's vessel or aircraft or between the person's residence and the person's vessel or aircraft.

(e) The device is in a vehicle other than a vessel or aircraft and all of the following apply:

(*i*) The device is unloaded.

(*ii*) The device is enclosed in a case and either is carried in the trunk of the vehicle which has a trunk or is otherwise not readily accessible to the occupants of the vehicle.

(*iii*) Subdivision (d) applies.

(5) A person shall not use an approved signaling device unless he or she reasonably believes that its use is necessary for the safety of the person or of another person on the waters of this state or in an aircraft emergency situation.

(6) A person who sells, purchases, or possesses an approved signaling device in violation of this section is guilty of a misdemeanor, punishable by imprisonment for not more than 90 days, or a fine of not more than $200.00, or both.

(7) A person who uses an approved signaling device in violation of this section is guilty of a misdemeanor, punishable by a fine of not more than $200.00.

History: Add. 1982, Act 185, Eff. July 1, 1982;—Am. 1996, Act 80, Imd. Eff. Feb. 27, 1996.

750.232 Repealed. 2017, Act 95, Eff. Oct.11, 2017.

Compiler's note: The repealed section pertained to registration of purchasers of firearms.

750.232a Obtaining pistol in violation of MCL 28.422; intentionally making material false statement on application for license to purchase pistol; using or attempting to use false identification or identification of another person to purchase firearm; penalties.

Sec. 232a. (1) Except as provided in subsection (2), a person who obtains a pistol in violation of section 2 of Act No. 372 of the Public Acts of 1927, as amended, being section 28.422 of the Michigan Compiled Laws, is guilty of a misdemeanor, punishable by imprisonment for not more than 90 days or a fine of not more than $100.00, or both.

(2) Subsection (1) does not apply to a person who obtained a pistol in violation of section 2 of Act No. 372 of the Public Acts of 1927 before the effective date of the 1990 amendatory act that added this subsection, who has not been convicted of that violation, and who obtains a license as required under section 2 of Act No. 372 of the Public Acts of 1927 within 90 days after the effective date of the 1990 amendatory act that added this subsection.

(3) A person who intentionally makes a material false statement on an application for a license to purchase a pistol under section 2 of Act No. 372 of the Public Acts of 1927, as amended, is guilty of a felony, punishable by imprisonment for not more than 4 years, or a fine of not more than $2,000.00, or both.

(4) A person who uses or attempts to use false identification or the identification of another person to purchase a firearm is guilty of a misdemeanor, punishable by imprisonment for not more than 90 days or a fine of not more than $100.00, or both.

History: Add. 1943, Act 54, Eff. July 30, 1943;—CL 1948, 750.232a;—Am. 1990, Act 321, Eff. Mar. 28, 1991.

Compiler's note: For provisions of section 2, referred to in this section, see MCL 28.422.

750.233 Pointing or aiming firearm at another person; misdemeanor; penalty; exception; "peace officer defined."

Sec. 233. (1) A person who intentionally but without malice points or aims a firearm at or toward another person is guilty of a misdemeanor punishable by imprisonment for not more than 93 days or a fine of not more than $500.00, or both.

(2) This section does not apply to a peace officer of this state or another state, or of a local unit of government of this state or another state, or of the United States, performing his or her duties as a peace officer. As used in this section, "peace officer" means that term as defined in section 215.

History: 1931, Act 328, Eff. Sept. 18, 1931;—CL 1948, 750.233;—Am. 2005, Act 303, Imd. Eff. Dec. 21, 2005.

Former law: See section 1 of Act 68 of 1869, being CL 1871, § 7548; How., § 9110; CL 1897, § 11509; CL 1915, § 15232; and CL 1929, § 16776.

750.234 Firearm; discharge; intentionally aimed without malice; misdemeanor; penalty; exception; "peace officer" defined.

Sec. 234. (1) A person who discharges a firearm while it is intentionally but without malice aimed at or toward another person, without injuring another person, is guilty of a misdemeanor punishable by imprisonment for not more than 1 year or a fine of not more than $500.00, or both.

(2) This section does not apply to a peace officer of this state or another state, or of a local unit of government of this state or another state, or of the United States, performing his or her duties as a peace officer. As used in this section, "peace officer" means that term as defined in section 215.

History: 1931, Act 328, Eff. Sept. 18, 1931;—CL 1948, 750.234;—Am. 2005, Act 303, Imd. Eff. Dec. 21, 2005.

Former law: See section 2 of Act 68 of 1869, being CL 1871, § 7548; How., § 9111; CL 1897, § 11510; CL 1915, § 15233; and CL 1929, § 16777.

750.234a Intentionally discharging firearm from motor vehicle, snowmobile, or off-road vehicle as crime; penalty; exceptions; other violation; consecutive terms; self-defense; "peace officer" defined.

Sec. 234a. (1) An individual who intentionally discharges a firearm from a motor vehicle, a snowmobile, or an off-road vehicle is guilty of a crime as follows:

(a) If the violation endangers the safety of another individual, the individual is guilty of a felony punishable by imprisonment for not more than 10 years or a fine of not more than $10,000.00, or both.

(b) If the violation causes any physical injury to another individual, the individual is guilty of a felony punishable by imprisonment for not more than 15 years or a fine of not more than $15,000.00, or both.

(c) If the violation causes the serious impairment of a body function of another individual, the individual is guilty of a felony punishable by imprisonment for not more than 20 years or a fine of not more than $25,000.00, or both.

(d) If the violation causes the death of another individual, the individual is guilty of a felony punishable by imprisonment for life or any term of years.

(2) Subsection (1) does not apply to any of the following:

(a) A peace officer of this state or another state, or of a local unit of government of this state or another state, or of the United States, performing his or her duties as a peace officer while on or off a scheduled work shift as a peace officer.

(b) An individual who discharges a firearm in self-defense or the defense of another individual.

(3) This section does not prohibit an individual from being charged with, convicted of, or punished for any other violation of law that is committed by that individual while violating this section.

(4) A term of imprisonment imposed for a violation of this section may run consecutively to any term of imprisonment imposed for another violation arising from the same transaction.

(5) As used in this section:

(a) "Peace officer" means that term as defined in section 215.

(b) "Serious impairment of a body function" means that term as defined in section 58c of the Michigan vehicle code, 1949 PA 300, MCL 257.58c.

History: Add. 1990, Act 321, Eff. Mar. 28, 1991;—Am. 1992, Act 218, Imd. Eff. Oct. 13, 1992;—Am. 1996, Act 163, Imd. Eff. Apr. 11, 1996;—Am. 2005, Act 303, Imd. Eff. Dec. 21, 2005;—Am. 2014, Act 191, Eff. Sept. 22, 2014.

750.234b Intentionally discharging firearm at dwelling or potentially occupied structure as felony; penalty; exceptions; other violation; consecutive terms; definitions.

Sec. 234b. (1) Except as otherwise provided in this section, an individual who intentionally discharges a firearm at a facility that he or she knows or has reason to believe is a dwelling or a potentially occupied structure, whether or not the dwelling or structure is actually occupied at the time the firearm is discharged, is guilty of a felony punishable by imprisonment for not more than 10 years or a fine of not more than $10,000.00, or both.

(2) An individual who intentionally discharges a firearm in a facility that he or she knows or has reason to believe is a dwelling or a potentially occupied structure, in reckless disregard for the safety of any individual and whether or not the dwelling or structure is actually occupied at the time the firearm is discharged, is guilty of a felony punishable by imprisonment for not more than 10 years or a fine of not more than $10,000.00, or both.

(3) If an individual violates subsection (1) or (2) and causes any physical injury to another individual, the individual is guilty of a felony punishable by imprisonment for not more than 15 years or a fine of not more than $15,000.00, or both.

(4) If an individual violates subsection (1) or (2) and causes the serious impairment of a body function of another individual, the individual is guilty of a felony punishable by imprisonment for not more than 20 years or a fine of not more than $25,000.00, or both.

(5) If an individual violates subsection (1) or (2) and causes the death of another individual, the individual is guilty of a felony punishable by imprisonment for life or any term of years.

(6) Subsections (1) and (2) do not apply to a peace officer of this state or another state, or of a local unit of government of this state or another state, or of the United States, performing his or her duties as a peace officer.

(7) Subsections (1) and (2) do not apply to an individual who discharges a firearm in self-defense or the defense of another individual.

(8) This section does not prohibit an individual from being charged with, convicted of, or punished for any other violation of law that is committed by that individual while violating this section.

(9) A term of imprisonment imposed for a violation of this section may run consecutively to any term of imprisonment imposed for another violation arising from the same transaction.

(10) As used in this section:

(a) "Dwelling" means a facility habitually used by 1 or more individuals as a place of abode, whether or not an individual is present in the facility.

(b) "Peace officer" means that term as defined in section 215.

(c) "Potentially occupied structure" means a structure that a reasonable person knows or should know is likely to be occupied by 1 or more individuals due to its nature, function, or location.

(d) "Serious impairment of a body function" means that term as defined in section 58c of the Michigan vehicle code, 1949 PA 300, MCL 257.58c.

History: Add. 1990, Act 321, Eff. Mar. 28, 1991;—Am. 1992, Act 218, Imd. Eff. Oct. 13, 1992;—Am. 2005, Act 303, Imd. Eff. Dec. 21, 2005;—Am. 2014, Act 191, Eff. Sept. 22, 2014.

750.234c Intentionally discharging firearm at emergency or law enforcement vehicle as felony; penalty; "emergency or law enforcement vehicle" defined.

Sec. 234c. (1) An individual who intentionally discharges a firearm at a motor vehicle that he or she knows or has reason to believe is an emergency or law enforcement vehicle is guilty of a felony, punishable by imprisonment for not more than 4 years, or a fine of not more than $2,000.00, or both.

(2) As used in this section, "emergency or law enforcement vehicle" means 1 or more of the following:

(a) A motor vehicle owned or operated by a fire department of a local unit of government of this state.

(b) A motor vehicle owned or operated by a police agency of the United States, of this state, or of a local unit of government of this state.

(c) A motor vehicle owned or operated by the department of natural resources that is used for law enforcement purposes.

(d) A motor vehicle owned or operated by an entity licensed to provide emergency medical services under part 192 of article 17 of the public health code, Act No. 368 of the Public Acts of 1978, being sections 333.20901 to 333.20979 of the Michigan Compiled Laws, and that is used to provide emergency medical assistance to individuals.

(e) A motor vehicle owned or operated by a volunteer employee or paid employee of an entity described in subdivisions (a) to (c) while the motor vehicle is being used to perform emergency or law enforcement duties for that entity.

History: Add. 1990, Act 321, Eff. Mar. 28, 1991.

750.234d Possession of firearm on certain premises prohibited; applicability; violation as misdemeanor; penalty.

Sec. 234d. (1) Except as provided in subsection (2), a person shall not possess a firearm on the premises of any of the following:

(a) A depository financial institution or a subsidiary or affiliate of a depository financial institution.

(b) A church or other house of religious worship.

(c) A court.

(d) A theatre.

(e) A sports arena.

(f) A day care center.

(g) A hospital.

(h) An establishment licensed under the Michigan liquor control act, Act No. 8 of the Public Acts of the Extra Session of 1933, being sections 436.1 to 436.58 of the Michigan Compiled Laws.

(2) This section does not apply to any of the following:

(a) A person who owns, or is employed by or contracted by, an entity described in subsection (1) if the possession of that firearm is to provide security services for that entity.

(b) A peace officer.

(c) A person licensed by this state or another state to carry a concealed weapon.

(d) A person who possesses a firearm on the premises of an entity described in subsection (1) if that possession is with the permission of the owner or an agent of the owner of that entity.

(3) A person who violates this section is guilty of a misdemeanor punishable by imprisonment for not more than 90 days or a fine of not more than $100.00, or both.

History: Add. 1990, Act 321, Eff. Mar. 28, 1991;—Am. 1992, Act 218, Imd. Eff. Oct. 13, 1992;—Am. 1994, Act 158, Eff. Aug. 15, 1994.

750.234e Brandishing firearm in public; applicability; violation as misdemeanor; penalty.

Sec. 234e. (1) Except as provided in subsection (2), a person shall not willfully and knowingly brandish a firearm in public.

(2) Subsection (1) does not apply to either of the following:

(a) A peace officer lawfully performing his or her duties as a peace officer.

(b) A person lawfully acting in self-defense or defense of another under the self-defense act, 2006 PA 309, MCL 780.971 to 780.974.

(3) A person who violates this section is guilty of a misdemeanor punishable by imprisonment for not more than 90 days, or a fine of not more than $100.00, or both.

History: Add. 1990, Act 321, Eff. Mar. 28, 1991;—Am. 2015, Act 27, Eff. Aug. 10, 2015.

750.234f Possession of firearm by person less than 18 years of age; exceptions; violation as misdemeanor; penalty.

Sec. 234f. (1) Except as provided in subsection (2), an individual less than 18 years of age shall not possess a firearm in public except under the direct supervision of an individual 18 years of age or older.

(2) Subsection (1) does not apply to an individual less than 18 years of age who possesses a firearm in accordance with part 401 (wildlife conservation) of the natural resources and environmental protection act, Act No. 451 of the Public Acts of 1994, being sections 324.40101 to 324.40119 of the Michigan Compiled Laws, or part 435 (hunting and fishing licensing) of Act No. 451 of the Public Acts of 1994, being sections 324.43501 to 324.43561 of the Michigan Compiled Laws. However, an individual less than 18 years of age may possess a firearm without a hunting license while at, or going to or from, a recognized target range or trap or skeet shooting ground if, while going to or from the range or ground, the firearm is enclosed and securely fastened in a case or locked in the trunk of a motor vehicle.

(3) An individual who violates this section is guilty of a misdemeanor, punishable by imprisonment for not more than 90 days, or a fine of not more than $100.00, or both.

History: Add. 1990, Act 321, Eff. Mar. 28, 1991;—Am. 1992, Act 218, Imd. Eff. Oct. 13, 1992;—Am. 1996, Act 80, Imd. Eff. Feb. 27, 1996.

750.235 Maiming or injuring person by discharging firearm; intentionally aimed without malice; exception; "peace officer" defined.

Sec. 235. (1) A person who maims or injures another person by discharging a firearm pointed or aimed intentionally but without malice at another person is guilty of a misdemeanor punishable by imprisonment for not more than 1 year or a fine of not more than $500.00, or both.

(2) This section does not apply to a peace officer of this state or another state, or of a local unit of government of this state or another state, or of the United States, performing his or her duties as a peace officer. As used in this section, "peace officer" means that term as defined in section 215.

History: 1931, Act 328, Eff. Sept. 18, 1931;—CL 1948, 750.235;—Am. 2005, Act 303, Imd. Eff. Dec. 21, 2005.

Former law: See section 3 of Act 68 of 1869, being CL 1871, § 7549; How., § 9112; CL 1897, § 11511; CL 1915, § 15234; and CL 1929, § 16778.

750.235a Parent of minor guilty of misdemeanor; conditions; penalty; defense; definitions.

Sec. 235a. (1) The parent of a minor is guilty of a misdemeanor if all of the following apply:

(a) The parent has custody of the minor.

(b) The minor violates this chapter in a weapon free school zone.

(c) The parent knows that the minor would violate this chapter or the parent acts to further the violation.

(2) An individual convicted under subsection (1) may be punished by 1 or more of the following:

(a) A fine of not more than $2,000.00.

(b) Community service for not more than 100 hours.

(c) Probation.

(3) It is a complete defense to a prosecution under this section if the defendant promptly notifies the local law enforcement agency or the school administration that the minor is violating or will violate this chapter in a weapon free school zone.

(4) As used in this section:

(a) "Minor" means an individual less than 18 years of age.

(b) "School" means a public, private, denominational, or parochial school offering developmental kindergarten, kindergarten, or any grade from 1 through 12.

(c) "School property" means a building, playing field, or property used for school purposes to impart instruction to children or used for functions and events sponsored by a school, except a building used primarily for adult education or college extension courses.

(d) "Weapon free school zone" means school property and a vehicle used by a school to transport students to or from school property.

History: Add. 1994, Act 158, Eff. Aug. 15, 1994.

Compiler's note: Former MCL 750.235a, which made the reckless use of firearms a misdemeanor, was repealed by Act 45 of 1952, Eff. Sept. 18, 1952.

750.236 Spring gun, trap or device; setting.

Sec. 236. Setting spring guns, etc.—Any person who shall set any spring or other gun, or any trap or device operating by the firing or explosion of gunpowder or any other explosive, and shall leave or permit the same to be left, except in the immediate presence of some competent person, shall be guilty of a misdemeanor, punishable by imprisonment in the county jail not more than 1 year, or by a fine of not more than 500 dollars, and the killing of any person by the firing of a gun or device so set shall be manslaughter.

History: 1931, Act 328, Eff. Sept. 18, 1931;—CL 1948, 750.236.

Former law: See section 1 of Act 97 of 1875; being How., § 9114; CL 1897, § 11515; CL 1915, § 15250; and CL 1929, § 16782.

750.236a Computer-assisted shooting; prohibited acts; definitions.

Sec. 236a. (1) A person in this state shall not do any of the following:

(a) Engage in computer-assisted shooting.

(b) Provide or operate, with or without remuneration, facilities for computer-assisted shooting.

(c) Provide or offer to provide, with or without remuneration, equipment specially adapted for computer-assisted shooting. This subdivision does not prohibit providing or offering to provide any of the following:

(*i*) General-purpose equipment, including a computer, a camera, fencing, building materials, or a firearm.

(*ii*) General-purpose computer software, including an operating system and communications programs.

(*iii*) General telecommunications hardware or networking services for computers, including adapters, modems, servers, routers, and other facilities associated with internet access.

(d) Provide or offer to provide, with or without remuneration, an animal for computer-assisted shooting.

(2) As used in this section:

(a) "Computer-assisted shooting" means the use of a computer or any other device, equipment, or software to remotely control the aiming and discharge of a firearm to kill an animal, whether or not the animal is located in this state.

(b) "Facilities for computer-assisted remote shooting" includes real property and improvements on the property associated with computer-assisted shooting, such as hunting blinds, offices, and rooms equipped to facilitate computer-assisted shooting.

History: Add. 2005, Act 110, Imd. Eff. Sept. 22, 2005.

750.236b Computer-assisted shooting; prohibited conduct; definitions.

Sec. 236b. (1) A person in this state shall not do any of the following:

(a) Engage in computer-assisted shooting.

(b) Provide or operate, with or without remuneration, facilities for computer-assisted shooting.

(c) Provide or offer to provide, with or without remuneration, equipment specially adapted for computer-assisted shooting. This subdivision does not prohibit providing or offering to provide any of the following:

(*i*) General-purpose equipment, including a computer, a camera, fencing, building materials, or a bow or crossbow.

(*ii*) General-purpose computer software, including an operating system and communications programs.

(*iii*) General telecommunications hardware or networking services for computers, including adapters, modems, servers, routers, and other facilities associated with internet access.

(d) Provide or offer to provide, with or without remuneration, an animal for computer-assisted shooting.

(2) As used in this section:

(a) "Computer-assisted shooting" means the use of a computer or any other device, equipment, or software to remotely control the aiming and discharge of a bow or crossbow to kill an animal, whether or not the animal is located in this state.

(b) "Facilities for computer-assisted remote shooting" includes real property and improvements on the property associated with computer-assisted shooting, such as hunting blinds, offices, and rooms equipped to facilitate computer-assisted shooting.

History: Add. 2005, Act 111, Imd. Eff. Sept. 22, 2005.

750.236c Violation of MCL 750.236a or 750.236b; penalty; forfeiture.

Sec. 236c. (1) A person who violates section 236a or 236b is guilty of a misdemeanor punishable by imprisonment for not more than 93 days or a fine of not more than $500.00, or both.

(2) A person who has been convicted of violating section 236a or 236b and subsequently violates either of those sections is guilty of a misdemeanor punishable by imprisonment for not more than 1 year or a fine of not more than $1,000.00, or both. In addition, the instrumentalities of the crime are subject to forfeiture in the same manner as provided in part 47 of the revised judicature act of 1961, 1961 PA 236, MCL 600.4701 to 600.4709.

History: Add. 2005, Act 112, Eff. Oct. 15, 2005.

750.237 Liquor or controlled substance; possession or use of firearm by person under influence; violation; penalty; chemical analysis.

Sec. 237. (1) An individual shall not carry, have in possession or under control, or use in any manner or discharge a firearm under any of the following circumstances:

(a) The individual is under the influence of alcoholic liquor, a controlled substance, or a combination of alcoholic liquor and a controlled substance.

(b) The individual has an alcohol content of 0.08 or more grams per 100 milliliters of blood, per 210 liters of breath, or per 67 milliliters of urine.

(c) Because of the consumption of alcoholic liquor, a controlled substance, or a combination of alcoholic liquor and a controlled substance, the individual's ability to use a firearm is visibly impaired.

(2) Except as provided in subsections (3) and (4), an individual who violates subsection (1) is guilty of a misdemeanor punishable by imprisonment for not more than 93 days or a fine of not more than $100.00 for carrying or possessing a firearm, or both, and not more than $500.00 for using or discharging a firearm, or both.

(3) An individual who violates subsection (1) and causes a serious impairment of a body function of another individual by the discharge or use in any manner of the firearm is guilty of a felony punishable by imprisonment for not more than 5 years or a fine of not less than $1,000.00 or more than $5,000.00, or both. As used in this subsection, "serious impairment of a body function" includes, but is not limited to, 1 or more of the following:

(a) Loss of a limb or use of a limb.

(b) Loss of a hand, foot, finger, or thumb or use of a hand, foot, finger, or thumb.

(c) Loss of an eye or ear or of use of an eye or ear.

(d) Loss or substantial impairment of a bodily function.

(e) Serious visible disfigurement.

(f) A comatose state that lasts for more than 3 days.

(g) Measurable brain damage or mental impairment.

(h) A skull fracture or other serious bone fracture.

(i) Subdural hemorrhage or subdural hematoma.

(j) Loss of an organ.

(4) An individual who violates subsection (1) and causes the death of another individual by the discharge or use in any manner of a firearm is guilty of a felony punishable by imprisonment for not more than 15 years or a fine of not less than $2,500.00 or more than $10,000.00, or both.

(5) A peace officer who has probable cause to believe an individual violated subsection (1) may require the individual to submit to a chemical analysis of his or her breath, blood, or urine. However, an individual who is afflicted with hemophilia, diabetes, or a condition requiring the use of an anticoagulant under the direction of a physician is not required to submit to a chemical analysis of his or her blood.

(6) Before an individual is required to submit to a chemical analysis under subsection (5), the peace officer shall inform the individual of all of the following:

(a) The individual may refuse to submit to the chemical analysis, but if he or she refuses, the officer may obtain a court order requiring the individual to submit to a chemical analysis.

(b) If the individual submits to the chemical analysis, he or she may obtain a chemical analysis from a person of his or her own choosing.

(7) The failure of a peace officer to comply with the requirements of subsection (6) does not render the results of a chemical analysis inadmissible as evidence in a criminal prosecution for violating this section, in a civil action arising out of a violation of this section, or in any administrative proceeding arising out of a violation of this section.

(8) The collection and testing of breath, blood, or urine specimens under this section shall be conducted in the same manner that breath, blood, or urine specimens are collected and tested for alcohol—and controlled-substance-related driving violations under the Michigan vehicle code, 1949 PA 300, MCL 257.1 to 257.923.

(9) This section does not prohibit the individual from being charged with, convicted of, or sentenced for any other violation of law arising out of the same transaction as the violation of this section in lieu of being charged with, convicted of, or sentenced for the violation of this section.

History: 1931, Act 328, Eff. Sept. 18, 1931;—CL 1948, 750.237;—Am. 2001, Act 135, Eff. Feb. 1, 2002.

Former law: See sections 1 and 2 of Act 25 of 1929, being CL 1929, §§ 16780 and 16781.

750.237a Individual engaging in proscribed conduct in weapon free school zone; violation; penalties; definitions.

Sec. 237a. (1) An individual who engages in conduct proscribed under section 224, 224a, 224b, 224c, 224e, 226, 227, 227a, 227f, 234a, 234b, or 234c, or who engages in conduct proscribed under section 223(2) for a second or subsequent time, in a weapon free school zone is guilty of a felony punishable by 1 or more of the following:

(a) Imprisonment for not more than the maximum term of imprisonment authorized for the section violated.

(b) Community service for not more than 150 hours.

(c) A fine of not more than 3 times the maximum fine authorized for the section violated.

(2) An individual who engages in conduct proscribed under section 223(1), 224d, 227c, 227d, 231c, 232a(1) or (4), 233, 234, 234e, 234f, 235, 236, or 237, or who engages in conduct proscribed under section 223(2) for the first time, in a weapon free school zone is guilty of a misdemeanor punishable by 1 or more of the following:

(a) Imprisonment for not more than the maximum term of imprisonment authorized for the section violated or 93 days, whichever is greater.

(b) Community service for not more than 100 hours.

(c) A fine of not more than $2,000.00 or the maximum fine authorized for the section violated, whichever is greater.

(3) Subsections (1) and (2) do not apply to conduct proscribed under a section enumerated in those subsections to the extent that the proscribed conduct is otherwise exempted or authorized under this chapter.

(4) Except as provided in subsection (5), an individual who possesses a weapon in a weapon free school zone is guilty of a misdemeanor punishable by 1 or more of the following:

(a) Imprisonment for not more than 93 days.

(b) Community service for not more than 100 hours.

(c) A fine of not more than $2,000.00.

(5) Subsection (4) does not apply to any of the following:

(a) An individual employed by or contracted by a school if the possession of that weapon is to provide security services for the school.

(b) A peace officer.

(c) An individual licensed by this state or another state to carry a concealed weapon.

(d) An individual who possesses a weapon provided by a school or a school's instructor on school property for purposes of providing or receiving instruction in the use of that weapon.

(e) An individual who possesses a firearm on school property if that possession is with the permission of the school's principal or an agent of the school designated by the school's principal or the school board.

(f) An individual who is 18 years of age or older who is not a student at the school and who possesses a firearm on school property while transporting a student to or from the school if any of the following apply:

(*i*) The individual is carrying an antique firearm, completely unloaded, in a wrapper or container in the trunk of a vehicle while en route to or from a hunting or target shooting area or function involving the exhibition, demonstration or sale of antique firearms.

(*ii*) The individual is carrying a firearm unloaded in a wrapper or container in the trunk of the person's vehicle, while in possession of a valid Michigan hunting license or proof of valid membership in an organization having shooting range facilities, and while en route to or from a hunting or target shooting area.

(*iii*) The individual is carrying a firearm unloaded in a wrapper or container in the trunk of the individual's vehicle from the place of purchase to his or her home or place of business or to a place of repair or back to his or her home or place of business, or in moving goods from one place of abode or business to another place of abode or business.

(*iv*) The individual is carrying an unloaded firearm in the passenger compartment of a vehicle that does not have a trunk, if the individual is otherwise complying with the requirements of subparagraph (*ii*) or (*iii*) and the wrapper or container is not readily accessible to the occupants of the vehicle.

(6) As used in this section:

(a) "Antique firearm" means either of the following:

(*i*) A firearm not designed or redesigned for using rimfire or conventional center fire ignition with fixed ammunition and manufactured in or before 1898, including a matchlock, flintlock, percussion cap, or similar type of ignition system or a replica of such a firearm, whether actually manufactured before or after the year 1898.

(*ii*) A firearm using fixed ammunition manufactured in or before 1898, for which ammunition is no longer manufactured in the United States and is not readily available in the ordinary channels of commercial trade.

(b) "School" means a public, private, denominational, or parochial school offering developmental kindergarten, kindergarten, or any grade from 1 through 12.

(c) "School property" means a building, playing field, or property used for school purposes to impart instruction to children or used for functions and events sponsored by a school, except a building used primarily for adult education or college extension courses.

(d) "Weapon" includes, but is not limited to, a pneumatic gun.

(e) "Weapon free school zone" means school property and a vehicle used by a school to transport students to or from school property.

History: Add. 1994, Act 158, Eff. Aug. 15, 1994;—Am. 2015, Act 26, Eff. July 1, 2015;—Am. 2017, Act 96, Eff. Oct. 11, 2017.

750.238 Search warrant.

Sec. 238. Search warrant—When complaint shall be made on oath to any magistrate authorized to issue warrants in criminal cases that any pistol or other weapon or device mentioned in this chapter is unlawfully possessed or carried by any person, such magistrate shall, if he be satisfied that there is reasonable cause to believe the matters in said complaint be true, issue his warrant directed to any peace officer, commanding him to search the person or place described in such complaint, and if such pistol, weapon or device be there found, to seize and hold the same as evidence of a violation of this chapter.

History: 1931, Act 328, Eff. Sept. 18, 1931;—CL 1948, 750.238.

750.239 Forfeiture of weapons; disposal; immunity from civil liability.

Sec. 239. (1) Except as provided in subsection (2) and subject to section 239a, all pistols, weapons, or devices carried, possessed, or used contrary to this chapter are forfeited to the state and shall be turned over to the department of state police for disposition as determined appropriate by the director of the department of state police or his or her designated representative.

(2) The director of the department of state police shall dispose of firearms under this section by 1 of the following methods:

(a) By conducting a public auction in which firearms received under this section may be purchased at a sale conducted in compliance with section 4708 of the revised judicature act of 1961, 1961 PA 236, MCL 600.4708, by individuals authorized by law to possess those firearms.

(b) By destroying them.

(c) By any other lawful manner prescribed by the director of the department of state police.

(3) Before disposing of a firearm under this section, the director of the department of state police shall do both of the following:

(a) Determine through the law enforcement information network whether the firearm has been reported lost or stolen. If the firearm has been reported lost or stolen and the name and address of the owner can be determined, the director of the department of state police shall provide 30 days' written notice of his or her intent to dispose of the firearm under this section to the owner, and allow the owner to claim the firearm within that 30-day period if he or she is authorized to possess the firearm.

(b) Provide 30 days' notice to the public on the department of state police website of his or her intent to dispose of the firearm under this section. The notice shall include a description of the firearm and shall state the firearm's serial number, if the serial number can be determined. The department of state police shall allow the owner of the firearm to claim the firearm within that 30-day period if he or she is authorized to possess the firearm. The 30-day period required under this subdivision is in addition to the 30-day period required under subdivision (a).

(4) The department of state police is immune from civil liability for disposing of a firearm in compliance with this section.

History: 1931, Act 328, Eff. Sept. 18, 1931;—CL 1948, 750.239;—Am. 1949, Act 168, Eff. Sept. 23, 1949;—Am. 1964, Act 215, Eff. Aug. 28, 1964;—Am. 2010, Act 294, Imd. Eff. Dec. 16, 2010.

750.239a Disposition of seized weapon; immunity from civil liability; "law enforcement agency" defined.

Sec. 239a. (1) A law enforcement agency that seizes or otherwise comes into possession of a firearm or a part of a firearm subject to disposal under section 239 may, instead of forwarding the firearm or part of a firearm to the director of the department of state police or his or her designated representative for disposal under that section, retain that firearm or part of a firearm for the following purposes:

(a) For legal sale or trade to a federally licensed firearm dealer. The proceeds from any sale or trade under this subdivision shall be used by the law enforcement agency only for law enforcement purposes. The law enforcement agency shall not sell or trade a firearm or part of a firearm under this subdivision to any individual who is a member of that law enforcement agency unless the individual is a federally licensed firearms dealer and the sale is made pursuant to a public auction.

(b) For official use by members of the seizing law enforcement agency who are employed as peace officers. A firearm or part of a firearm shall not be sold under this subdivision.

(2) A law enforcement agency that sells or trades any pistol to a licensed dealer under subsection (1)(a) or retains any pistol under subsection (1)(b) shall complete a record of the transaction under section 2 or section 2a, as applicable.

(3) A law enforcement agency that sells or trades a firearm or part of a firearm under this section shall retain a receipt of the sale or trade for a period of not less than 7 years. The law enforcement agency shall make all receipts retained under this subsection available for inspection by the department of state police upon demand and for auditing purposes by the state and the local unit of government of which the agency is a part.

(4) Before disposing of a firearm under this section, the law enforcement agency shall do both of the following:

(a) Determine through the law enforcement information network whether the firearm has been reported lost or stolen. If the firearm has been reported lost or stolen and the name and address of the owner can be determined, the law enforcement agency shall provide 30 days' written notice of its intent to dispose of the firearm under this section to the owner, and allow the owner to claim the firearm within that 30-day period if he or she is authorized to possess the firearm. If the police agency determines that a serial number has been altered or has been removed or obliterated from the firearm, the police agency shall submit the firearm to the department of state police or a forensic laboratory for serial number verification or restoration to determine legal ownership.

(b) Provide 30 days' notice to the public on a website maintained by the law enforcement agency of its intent to dispose of the firearm under this section. The notice shall include a description of the firearm and shall state the firearm's serial number, if the serial number can be determined. The law enforcement agency shall allow the owner of the firearm to claim the firearm within that 30-day period if he or she is authorized to possess the firearm. The 30-day period required under this subdivision is in addition to the 30-day period required under subdivision (a).

(5) The law enforcement agency is immune from civil liability for disposing of a firearm in compliance with this section.

(6) As used in this section, "law enforcement agency" means any agency that employs peace officers.

History: Add. 1996, Act 496, Eff. Mar. 31, 1997;—Am. 2010, Act 294, Imd. Eff. Dec. 16, 2010.

CHAPTER XXXIX
FIREWORKS

750.243a-750.243e Repealed. 2011, Act 256, Eff. Jan. 1, 2012.

Compiler's note: The repealed sections pertained to prohibited firework sales, permits for use or sale of fireworks, transportation and storage of fireworks, and penalties for violations.

CHAPTER XLV
HOMICIDE

750.329 Discharging firearm pointed or aimed at another person resulting in death; manslaughter; exception; "peace officer" defined.

Sec. 329. (1) A person who wounds, maims, or injures another person by discharging a firearm that is pointed or aimed intentionally but without malice at another person is guilty of manslaughter if the wounds, maiming, or injuries result in death.

(2) This section does not apply to a peace officer of this state or another state, or of a local unit of government of this state or another state, or of the United States, performing his or her duties as a peace officer. As used in this section, "peace officer" means that term as defined in section 215.

History: 1931, Act 328, Eff. Sept. 18, 1931;—CL 1948, 750.329;—Am. 2005, Act 303, Imd. Eff. Dec. 21, 2005.

CHAPTER L
KIDNAPING

750.349b Unlawful imprisonment; circumstances; violation as felony; penalty; definitions; other violation.

Sec. 349b. (1) A person commits the crime of unlawful imprisonment if he or she knowingly restrains another person under any of the following circumstances:

(a) The person is restrained by means of a weapon or dangerous instrument.

(b) The restrained person was secretly confined.

(c) The person was restrained to facilitate the commission of another felony or to facilitate flight after commission of another felony.

(2) A person who commits unlawful imprisonment is guilty of a felony punishable by imprisonment for not more than 15 years or a fine of not more than $20,000.00, or both.

(3) As used in this section:

(a) "Restrain" means to forcibly restrict a person's movements or to forcibly confine the person so as to interfere with that person's liberty without that person's consent or without lawful authority. The restraint does not have to exist for any particular length of time and may be related or incidental to the commission of other criminal acts.

(b) "Secretly confined" means either of the following:

(*i*) To keep the confinement of the restrained person a secret.

(*ii*) To keep the location of the restrained person a secret.

(4) This section does not prohibit the person from being charged with, convicted of, or sentenced for any other violation of law that is committed by that person while violating this section.

History: Add. 2006, Act 160, Eff. Aug. 24, 2006.

CHAPTER LII
LARCENY

750.357b Committing larceny by stealing firearm of another person as felony; penalty.

Sec. 357b. A person who commits larceny by stealing the firearm of another person is guilty of a felony, punishable by imprisonment for not more than 5 years or by a fine of not more than $2,500.00, or both.

History: Add. 1990, Act 321, Eff. Mar. 28, 1991.

CHAPTER LIX
MILITARY

750.406 Military stores, larceny, embezzlement or destruction.

Sec. 406. Larceny, embezzlement or destruction of military stores—Any person who, during any war, rebellion or insurrection against the United States, or against this state, shall wilfully and maliciously embezzle, steal, injure, destroy or secrete any arms or ammunition, or military stores or equipments of the United States, or of this state, or of any officer, soldier or soldiers in the service of the United States, or of this state, or shall wilfully and maliciously destroy, remove or injure any buildings, machinery or material used or intended to be used in the making, repairing or storing of any arms, ammunition, military stores or equipments for the service of the United States, or of this state, whether such buildings, machinery or materials be public or private property, shall be guilty of a felony, punishable by imprisonment in the state prison for not more than 5 years or by a fine of not more than 2,500 dollars.

History: 1931, Act 328, Eff. Sept. 18, 1931;—CL 1948, 750.406.

Former law: See section 3 of Act 128 of 1863, being CL 1871, § 7763; How., § 9360; CL 1897, § 11389; CL 1915, § 15107; and CL 1929, § 16640.

CHAPTER LXI
MOTOR VEHICLES

750.421 Motor vehicles; trailer designed for defense or attack.

Sec. 421. Motor vehicle or trailer designed for purpose of defense or attack—Any person who shall construct, reconstruct, devise, manufacture, purchase, sell, possess or operate any motor vehicle or other vehicle capable of being drawn by a motor vehicle, designed for the use or purpose of defense or attack, from or by explosives, projectiles, ammunition, gases, fumes or other missiles, weapons and firearms, without first obtaining a license therefor from the commissioner of the department of public safety, or his duly authorized deputy, shall be guilty of a felony, punishable by imprisonment in the state prison not more than 5 years or by a fine not more than 2,500 dollars: Provided, That the provisions of this section shall not apply to any person constructing, reconstructing, devising, manufacturing, purchasing, selling, possessing or operating such vehicles by virtue of any contract with any department of the government of the United States, or with any foreign government, state, municipality or any subdivision thereof.

Applications for said license shall be upon forms provided by said commissioner of public safety. The applicant shall possess the same qualifications and said license shall be issued and revoked in the same manner and subject to the same conditions as are prescribed by law for the issuing and revoking of licenses for carrying concealed weapons, insofar as the same are applicable. The said commissioner may prescribe such other rules and regulations as are necessary to carry out the purpose of this section.

History: 1931, Act 328, Eff. Sept. 18, 1931;—CL 1948, 750.421.

CHAPTER LXX
PUBLIC OFFICES AND OFFICERS

750.479b Taking of firearm or other weapon from peace officer or corrections officer; penalty; commission of other violation; consecutive terms of imprisonment; definitions.

Sec. 479b. (1) An individual who takes a weapon other than a firearm from the lawful possession of a peace officer or a corrections officer is guilty of a felony punishable by imprisonment for not more than 4 years or a fine of not more than $2,500.00, or both, if all of the following circumstances exist at the time the weapon is taken:

(a) The individual knows or has reason to believe the person from whom the weapon is taken is a peace officer or a corrections officer.

(b) The peace officer or corrections officer is performing his or her duties as a peace officer or a corrections officer.

(c) The individual takes the weapon without consent of the peace officer or corrections officer.

(d) The peace officer or corrections officer is authorized by his or her employer to carry the weapon in the line of duty.

(2) An individual who takes a firearm from the lawful possession of a peace officer or a corrections officer is guilty of a felony punishable by imprisonment for not more than 10 years or a fine of not more than
$5,000.00, or both, if all of the following circumstances exist at the time the firearm is taken:

(a) The individual knows or has reason to believe the person from whom the firearm is taken is a peace officer or a corrections officer.

(b) The peace officer or corrections officer is performing his or her duties as a peace officer or a corrections officer.

(c) The individual takes the firearm without the consent of the peace officer or corrections officer.

(d) The peace officer or corrections officer is authorized by his or her employer to carry the firearm in the line of duty.

(3) This section does not prohibit an individual from being charged with, convicted of, or punished for any other violation of law that is committed by that individual while violating this section.

(4) A term of imprisonment imposed for a violation of this section may run consecutively to any term of imprisonment imposed for another violation arising from the same transaction.

(5) As used in this section:

(a) "Corrections officer" means a prison or jail guard or other employee of a jail or a state or federal correctional facility, who performs duties involving the transportation, care, custody, or supervision of prisoners.

(b) "Peace officer" means 1 or more of the following:

(*i*) A police officer of this state or a political subdivision of this state.

(*ii*) A police officer of any entity of the United States.

(*iii*) The sheriff of a county of this state or the sheriff's deputy.

(*iv*) A public safety officer of a college or university who is authorized by the governing board of that college or university to enforce state law and the rules and ordinances of that college or university.

(*v*) A conservation officer of the department of natural resources.

(*vi*) A conservation officer of the United States department of interior.

History: Add. 1994, Act 33, Eff. June 1, 1994.

CHAPTER LXXVI
RAPE

750.520b Criminal sexual conduct in the first degree; circumstances; felony; consecutive terms.

Sec. 520b. (1) A person is guilty of criminal sexual conduct in the first degree if he or she engages in sexual penetration with another person and if any of the following circumstances exists:

(a) That other person is under 13 years of age.

(b) That other person is at least 13 but less than 16 years of age and any of the following:

(*i*) The actor is a member of the same household as the victim.

(*ii*) The actor is related to the victim by blood or affinity to the fourth degree.

(*iii*) The actor is in a position of authority over the victim and used this authority to coerce the victim to submit.

(*iv*) The actor is a teacher, substitute teacher, or administrator of the public school, nonpublic school, school district, or intermediate school district in which that other person is enrolled.

(*v*) The actor is an employee or a contractual service provider of the public school, nonpublic school, school district, or intermediate school district in which that other person is enrolled, or is a volunteer who is not a student in any public school or nonpublic school, or is an employee of this state or of a local unit of government of this state or of the United States assigned to provide any service to that public school, nonpublic school, school district, or intermediate school district, and the actor uses his or her employee, contractual, or volunteer status to gain access to, or to establish a relationship with, that other person.

(*vi*) The actor is an employee, contractual service provider, or volunteer of a child care organization, or a person licensed to operate a foster family home or a foster family group home in which that other person is a resident, and the sexual penetration occurs during the period of that other person's residency. As used in this subparagraph, "child care organization", "foster family home", and "foster family group home" mean those terms as defined in section 1 of 1973 PA 116, MCL 722.111.

(c) Sexual penetration occurs under circumstances involving the commission of any other felony.

(d) The actor is aided or abetted by 1 or more other persons and either of the following circumstances exists:

(*i*) The actor knows or has reason to know that the victim is mentally incapable, mentally incapacitated, or physically helpless.

(*ii*) The actor uses force or coercion to accomplish the sexual penetration. Force or coercion includes, but is not limited to, any of the circumstances listed in subdivision (f).

(e) The actor is armed with a weapon or any article used or fashioned in a manner to lead the victim to reasonably believe it to be a weapon.

(f) The actor causes personal injury to the victim and force or coercion is used to accomplish sexual penetration. Force or coercion includes, but is not limited to, any of the following circumstances:

(*i*) When the actor overcomes the victim through the actual application of physical force or physical violence.

(*ii*) When the actor coerces the victim to submit by threatening to use force or violence on the victim, and the victim believes that the actor has the present ability to execute these threats.

(*iii*) When the actor coerces the victim to submit by threatening to retaliate in the future against the victim, or any other person, and the victim believes that the actor has the ability to execute this threat. As used in this subdivision, "to retaliate" includes threats of physical punishment, kidnapping, or extortion.

(*iv*) When the actor engages in the medical treatment or examination of the victim in a manner or for purposes that are medically recognized as unethical or unacceptable.

(*v*) When the actor, through concealment or by the element of surprise, is able to overcome the victim.

(g) The actor causes personal injury to the victim, and the actor knows or has reason to know that the victim is mentally incapable, mentally incapacitated, or physically helpless.

(h) That other person is mentally incapable, mentally disabled, mentally incapacitated, or physically helpless, and any of the following:

(*i*) The actor is related to the victim by blood or affinity to the fourth degree.

(*ii*) The actor is in a position of authority over the victim and used this authority to coerce the victim to submit.

(2) Criminal sexual conduct in the first degree is a felony punishable as follows:

(a) Except as provided in subdivisions (b) and (c), by imprisonment for life or for any term of years.

(b) For a violation that is committed by an individual 17 years of age or older against an individual less than 13 years of age by imprisonment for life or any term of years, but not less than 25 years.

(c) For a violation that is committed by an individual 18 years of age or older against an individual less than 13 years of age, by imprisonment for life without the possibility of parole if the person was previously convicted of a violation of this section or section 520c, 520d, 520e, or 520g committed against an individual less than 13 years of age or a violation of law of the United States, another state or political subdivision substantially corresponding to a violation of this section or section 520c, 520d, 520e, or 520g committed against an individual less than 13 years of age.

(d) In addition to any other penalty imposed under subdivision (a) or (b), the court shall sentence the defendant to lifetime electronic monitoring under section 520n.

(3) The court may order a term of imprisonment imposed under this section to be served consecutively to any term of imprisonment imposed for any other criminal offense arising from the same transaction.

History: Add. 1974, Act 266, Eff. Apr. 1, 1975;—Am. 1983, Act 158, Eff. Mar. 29, 1984;—Am. 2002, Act 714, Eff. Apr. 1, 2003;—Am. 2006, Act 165, Eff. Aug. 28, 2006;—Am. 2006, Act 169, Eff. Aug. 28, 2006;—Am. 2007, Act 163, Eff. July 1, 2008;—Am. 2012, Act 372, Eff. Apr. 1, 2013;—Am. 2014, Act 23, Imd. Eff. Mar. 4, 2014.

Constitutionality: The provision in the criminal sexual conduct statute which permits elevation of a criminal sexual conduct offense from a lesser to a higher degree on the basis of proof of personal injury to the victim in the form of mental anguish is not unconstitutionally vague. People v Petrella, 424 Mich 221; 380 NW2d 11 (1985).

Compiler's note: Section 2 of Act 266 of 1974 provides:

"Saving clause.

"All proceedings pending and all rights and liabilities existing, acquired, or incurred at the time this amendatory act takes effect are saved and may be consummated according to the law in force when they are commenced. This amendatory act shall not be construed to affect any prosecution pending or begun before the effective date of this amendatory act."

750.520c Criminal sexual conduct in the second degree; felony.

Sec. 520c. (1) A person is guilty of criminal sexual conduct in the second degree if the person engages in sexual contact with another person and if any of the following circumstances exists:

(a) That other person is under 13 years of age.

(b) That other person is at least 13 but less than 16 years of age and any of the following:

(*i*) The actor is a member of the same household as the victim.

(*ii*) The actor is related by blood or affinity to the fourth degree to the victim.

(*iii*) The actor is in a position of authority over the victim and the actor used this authority to coerce the victim to submit.

(*iv*) The actor is a teacher, substitute teacher, or administrator of the public school, nonpublic school, school district, or intermediate school district in which that other person is enrolled.

(*v*) The actor is an employee or a contractual service provider of the public school, nonpublic school, school district, or intermediate school district in which that other person is enrolled, or is a volunteer who is not a student in any public school or nonpublic school, or is an employee of this state or of a local unit of government of this state or of the United States assigned to provide any service to that public school, nonpublic school, school district, or intermediate school district, and the actor uses his or her employee, contractual, or volunteer status to gain access to, or to establish a relationship with, that other person.

(*vi*) The actor is an employee, contractual service provider, or volunteer of a child care organization, or a person licensed to operate a foster family home or a foster family group home in which that other person is a resident and the sexual contact occurs during the period of that other person's residency. As used in this subdivision, "child care organization", "foster family home", and "foster family group home" mean those terms as defined in section 1 of 1973 PA 116, MCL 722.111.

(c) Sexual contact occurs under circumstances involving the commission of any other felony.

(d) The actor is aided or abetted by 1 or more other persons and either of the following circumstances exists:

(*i*) The actor knows or has reason to know that the victim is mentally incapable, mentally incapacitated, or physically helpless.

(*ii*) The actor uses force or coercion to accomplish the sexual contact. Force or coercion includes, but is not limited to, any of the circumstances listed in section 520b(1)(f).

(e) The actor is armed with a weapon, or any article used or fashioned in a manner to lead a person to reasonably believe it to be a weapon.

(f) The actor causes personal injury to the victim and force or coercion is used to accomplish the sexual contact. Force or coercion includes, but is not limited to, any of the circumstances listed in section 520b(1)(f).

(g) The actor causes personal injury to the victim and the actor knows or has reason to know that the victim is mentally incapable, mentally incapacitated, or physically helpless.

(h) That other person is mentally incapable, mentally disabled, mentally incapacitated, or physically helpless, and any of the following:

(*i*) The actor is related to the victim by blood or affinity to the fourth degree.

(*ii*) The actor is in a position of authority over the victim and used this authority to coerce the victim to submit.

(i) That other person is under the jurisdiction of the department of corrections and the actor is an employee or a contractual employee of, or a volunteer with, the department of corrections who knows that the other person is under the jurisdiction of the department of corrections.

(j) That other person is under the jurisdiction of the department of corrections and the actor is an employee or a contractual employee of, or a volunteer with, a private vendor that operates a youth correctional facility under section 20g of the corrections code of 1953, 1953 PA 232, MCL 791.220g, who knows that the other person is under the jurisdiction of the department of corrections.

(k) That other person is a prisoner or probationer under the jurisdiction of a county for purposes of imprisonment or a work program or other probationary program and the actor is an employee or a contractual employee of or a volunteer with the county or the department of corrections who knows that the other person is under the county's jurisdiction.

(*l*) The actor knows or has reason to know that a court has detained the victim in a facility while the victim is awaiting a trial or hearing, or committed the victim to a facility as a result of the victim having been found responsible for committing an act that would be a crime if committed by an adult, and the actor is an employee or contractual employee of, or a volunteer with, the facility in which the victim is detained or to which the victim was committed.

(2) Criminal sexual conduct in the second degree is a felony punishable as follows:

(a) By imprisonment for not more than 15 years.

(b) In addition to the penalty specified in subdivision (a), the court shall sentence the defendant to lifetime electronic monitoring under section 520n if the violation involved sexual contact committed by an individual 17 years of age or older against an individual less than 13 years of age.

History: Add. 1974, Act 266, Eff. Apr. 1, 1975;—Am. 1983, Act 158, Eff. Mar. 29, 1984;—Am. 2000, Act 227, Eff. Oct. 1, 2000;—Am. 2002, Act 714, Eff. Apr. 1, 2003;—Am. 2006, Act 171, Eff. Aug. 28, 2006;—Am. 2007, Act 163, Eff. July 1, 2008;—Am. 2012, Act 372, Eff. Apr. 1, 2013.

Compiler's note: Section 2 of Act 266 of 1974 provides:

"Saving clause.

"All proceedings pending and all rights and liabilities existing, acquired, or incurred at the time this amendatory act takes effect are saved and may be consummated according to the law in force when they are commenced. This amendatory act shall not be construed to affect any prosecution pending or begun before the effective date of this amendatory act."

CHAPTER LXXVII
RIOTS AND UNLAWFUL ASSEMBLIES

750.528a Definitions; firearm or explosive or incendiary device; teaching or demonstrating use, application, or construction in furtherance of civil disorder; unlawful assembly; exception; violation as felony.

Sec. 528a. (1) As used in this section:

(a) "Civil disorder" means any public disturbance involving the use of any firearm, explosive, or incendiary device by 3 or more assembled persons that causes an immediate danger to, or that results in damage or injury to, any property or person.

(b) "Explosive or incendiary device" means:

(*i*) Dynamite, gunpowder, or other similarly explosive substance.

(*ii*) Any bomb, grenade, missile, or similar device designed to expand suddenly and release internal energy resulting in an explosion.

(*iii*) Any incendiary bomb or grenade, fire bomb, or similar device designed to ignite, including any device that consists of or includes a breakable container containing a flammable liquid or compound and a wick composed of any material that, if ignited, is capable of igniting the flammable liquid or compound; and that may be carried or thrown by a person.

(c) "Firearm" means any weapon that will, is designed to, or may readily be converted to expel a projectile by action of an explosive.

(d) "Law enforcement officer" means any of the following:

(*i*) A sheriff or sheriff's deputy, a village marshal or township constable, an officer of the police department of any city, village, or township, an officer of the Michigan state police, or a peace officer who is trained and licensed or certified under the Michigan commission on law enforcement standards act, 1965 PA 203, MCL 28.601 to 28.615.

(*ii*) Any officer or employee of the United States, its possessions, or territories who is authorized to enforce the laws of the United States, its possessions, or its territories.

(*iii*) Any member of the National Guard, coast guard, military reserve, or the armed forces of the United States when acting in his or her official capacity.

(2) A person shall not teach or demonstrate to another person the use, application, or construction of any firearm, or any explosive or incendiary device, if that person knows, has reason to know, or intends that what is taught or demonstrated will be used in, or in furtherance of, a civil disorder.

(3) A person shall not assemble with 1 or more persons for the purpose of training with, practicing with, or being instructed in the use of any firearm, or any explosive or incendiary device, if that person intends to use that firearm or device in, or in furtherance of, a civil disorder.

(4) This section does not apply to any act of a law enforcement officer that is performed in the lawful performance of his or her official duties as a law enforcement officer, or any activity of any hunting club, rifle club, rifle range, pistol range, shooting range, or other program or individual instruction intended to teach the safe handling or use of firearms, archery equipment, or other weapons or techniques employed in connection with lawful sports, self-defense, or other lawful activities.

(5) A person who violates this section is guilty of a felony.

History: Add. 1986, Act 113, Eff. Mar. 31, 1987;—Am. 2015, Act 26, Eff. July 1, 2015;—Am. 2016, Act 297, Eff. Jan. 2, 2017.

CHAPTER LXXVIII
ROBBERY

750.529 Use or possession of dangerous weapon; aggravated assault; penalty.

Sec. 529. A person who engages in conduct proscribed under section 530 and who in the course of engaging in that conduct, possesses a dangerous weapon or an article used or fashioned in a manner to lead any person present to reasonably believe the article is a dangerous weapon, or who represents orally or otherwise that he or she is in possession of a dangerous weapon, is guilty of a felony punishable by imprisonment for life or for any term of years. If an aggravated assault or serious injury is inflicted by any person while violating this section, the person shall be sentenced to a minimum term of imprisonment of not less than 2 years.

History: 1931, Act 328, Eff. Sept. 18, 1931;—CL 1948, 750.529;—Am. 1959, Act 71, Eff. Mar. 19, 1960;—Am. 2004, Act 128, Eff. July 1, 2004.

Constitutionality: A defendant's convictions of both armed robbery and the lesser included offenses of larceny of property with a value over $100 and of larceny in a building cannot be allowed to stand as a violation of the defendant's protection against double jeopardy. People v Jankowski, 408 Mich 79; 289 NW2d 674 (1980).

In People v Wilder, 411 Mich 328; 308 NW2d 112 (1981), the Michigan supreme court held that conviction and sentence for both first-degree felony murder and the underlying felony of armed robbery violates the state constitutional prohibition against double jeopardy.

Former law: See section 15 of Ch. 153 of R.S. 1846, being CL 1857, § 5725; CL 1871, § 7524; How., § 9089; CL 1897, § 11484; CL 1915, § 15206; CL 1929, § 16722; and Act 374 of 1927.

CHAPTER LXXXI
STOLEN, EMBEZZLED OR CONVERTED PROPERTY

750.535b Transporting or shipping stolen firearm or stolen ammunition as felony; receiving, concealing, storing, bartering, selling, disposing of, pledging, or accepting as security for a loan a stolen firearm as felony; penalties.

Sec. 535b. (1) A person who transports or ships a stolen firearm or stolen ammunition, knowing that the firearm or ammunition was stolen, is guilty of a felony, punishable by imprisonment for not more than 10 years or by a fine of not more than $5,000.00, or both.

(2) A person who receives, conceals, stores, barters, sells, disposes of, pledges, or accepts as security for a loan a stolen firearm or stolen ammunition, knowing that the firearm or ammunition was stolen, is guilty of a felony, punishable by imprisonment for not more than 10 years or by a fine of not more than $5,000.00, or both.

History: Add. 1990, Act 321, Eff. Mar. 28, 1991.

750.536a Rendering goods or property unidentifiable; possession or sale of goods or property with identifying number obscured, defaced, altered, obliterated, removed, destroyed, or otherwise concealed or disguised.

Sec. 536a. (1) A person who obscures, defaces, alters, obliterates, removes, destroys, or otherwise conceals or disguises any registration, serial, or other identifying number embossed, engraved, carved, stamped, welded, or otherwise placed or situated in or upon goods or property held for sale in the ordinary course of business with the intent to render the goods or property unidentifiable shall be guilty of a misdemeanor.

(2) A person who is a dealer in or collector of any merchandise or personal property or the agent, employee, or representative of a dealer or collector and who possesses goods or property with the intent to sell the goods or property in the ordinary course of business knowing the registration, serial, or other identifying number has been obscured, defaced, altered, obliterated, removed, destroyed, or otherwise concealed or disguised shall be guilty of a misdemeanor.

(3) A person who is a dealer or collector of any merchandise or personal property or the agent, employee, or representative of a dealer or collector and who sells goods or property in the ordinary course of business knowing that the registration, serial, or other identifying number has been obscured, defaced, altered, obliterated, removed, destroyed, or otherwise concealed or disguised shall be guilty of a misdemeanor.

History: Add. 1980, Act 44, Eff. July 1, 1980;—Am. 1984, Act 407, Eff. Apr. 1, 1985.

DEATH OR INJURIES FROM FIREARMS
Act 10 of 1952

AN ACT to define the duties of any person who discharges a firearm and thereby injures any person; and to prescribe penalties for violations of the provisions of this act.

History: 1952, Act 10, Eff. Sept. 18, 1952.

The People of the State of Michigan enact:

752.841 "Firearm" defined.

Sec. 1. As used in this act, "firearm" means any weapon which will, is designed to, or may readily be converted to expel a projectile by action of an explosive.

History: 1952, Act 10, Eff. Sept. 18, 1952;—Am. 2015, Act 23, Eff. July 1, 2015.

752.842 Firearms; discharging; injuries.

Sec. 2. Any person who discharges a firearm and thereby injures or fatally wounds another person, or has reason to believe he has injured or fatally wounded another person, shall immediately stop at the scene and shall give his name and address to the injured person, or any member of his party, and shall render to the person so injured immediate assistance and reasonable assistance in securing medical and hospital care and transportation for such injured person.

History: 1952, Act 10, Eff. Sept. 18, 1952.

752.843 Firearms; report of injury or death.

Sec. 3. Every person who shall have caused or been involved in an accident in which a human being was killed or injured by means of a firearm, shall, in addition to complying with the provisions of section 2 of this act, immediately thereafter report such injury or death to the nearest office of the state police, or to the sheriff of the county wherein the death or injury occurred, unless such person be physically incapable of making the required report, in which event it shall be the duty of such person or persons to designate an agent to file the report. It shall be the duty of the sheriff, upon receipt of the report herein required, to transmit the same forthwith to the nearest office of the state police.

History: 1952, Act 10, Eff. Sept. 18, 1952.

752.844 Reports; availability for use.

Sec. 4. Reports required to be filed under the provisions of this act shall not be available for use in any way in any court action, civil or criminal, and shall not be open to general public inspection, but shall be for the purpose of furnishing statistical information as to the number and cause of such accidents. This act shall be construed to supplement the law of this state with respect to evidence and its admissibility.

History: 1952, Act 10, Eff. Sept. 18, 1952.

752.845 Firearms; injury to person, penalty, suspension of hunting privileges.

Sec. 5. Any person violating any of the provisions of this act shall, upon conviction thereof, be fined not more than $100.00 and costs of prosecution, or imprisonment in the county jail for not to exceed 90 days, or both such fine and imprisonment in the discretion of the court. In addition to any fine or imprisonment, the court may suspend the hunting privileges of such person for a period of not to exceed 3 years from the date of conviction.

History: 1952, Act 10, Eff. Sept. 18, 1952;—Am. 1958, Act 12, Eff. Sept. 13, 1958.

CARELESS, RECKLESS, OR NEGLIGENT USE OF FIREARMS
Act 45 of 1952

AN ACT to prohibit the careless, reckless or negligent use of firearms and to provide penalties for the violation of this act; and to repeal certain acts and parts of acts.

History: 1952, Act 45, Eff. Sept. 18, 1952.

The People of the State of Michigan enact:

752.861 Careless, reckless or negligent use of firearms; penalty.

Sec. 1. Any person who, because of carelessness, recklessness or negligence, but not wilfully or wantonly, shall cause or allow any firearm under his immediate control, to be discharged so as to kill or injure another person, shall be guilty of a misdemeanor, punishable by imprisonment in the state prison for not more than 2 years, or by a fine of not more than $2,000.00, or by imprisonment in the county jail for not more than 1 year, in the discretion of the court.

History: 1952, Act 45, Eff. Sept. 18, 1952.

752.862 Careless, reckless or negligent use of firearms; injury of property; penalty.

Sec. 2. Any person who, because of carelessness, recklessness or negligence, but not wilfully or wantonly, shall cause or allow any firearm under his control to be discharged so as to destroy or injure the property of another, real or personal, shall be guilty of a misdemeanor, punishable by imprisonment in the county jail for not more than 90 days or by a fine of not more than $100.00, if the injury to such property shall not exceed the sum of $50.00, but in the event that such injury shall exceed the sum of $50.00, then said offense shall be punishable by imprisonment in the county jail for not more than 1 year or by a fine not exceeding $500.00.

History: 1952, Act 45, Eff. Sept. 18, 1952.

752.863 Section repealed.

Sec. 3. Section 235a of Act No. 328 of the Public Acts of 1931, being section 750.235a of the Compiled Laws of 1948, is hereby repealed.

History: 1952, Act 45, Eff. Sept. 18, 1952.

752.863a Reckless, wanton use or negligent discharge of firearm; penalty.

Sec. 3. Any person who shall recklessly or heedlessly or wilfully or wantonly use, carry, handle or discharge any firearm without due caution and circumspection for the rights, safety or property of others shall be guilty of a misdemeanor.

History: Add. 1955, Act 14, Eff. Oct. 14, 1955.

Compiler's note: Section 3, as added by Act 14 of 1955, was compiled as MCL 752.863[a] to distinguish it from another section 3, deriving from Act 45 of 1952 and pertaining to the repeal of MCL 750.235a. The compilation number formerly assigned to this section was MCL 752.a863.

752.864 Firearms; injury to person or property, suspension of hunting privileges.

Sec. 4. In addition to the penalties provided in other sections of this act, the court may suspend the hunting privileges of any person convicted of violating any provision of this act for a period of not to exceed 3 years from the date of conviction.

History: Add. 1958, Act 15, Eff. Sept. 13, 1958.

SPRING, GAS, OR AIR OPERATED HANDGUNS
Act 186 of 1959

752.891 to 752.892 Repealed. 2015, Act 21, Eff. July 1, 2015.

THE CODE OF CRIMINAL PROCEDURE (EXCERPT)
Act 175 of 1927

AN ACT to revise, consolidate, and codify the laws relating to criminal procedure and to define the jurisdiction, powers, and duties of courts, judges, and other officers of the court under the provisions of this act; to provide laws relative to the rights of persons accused of criminal offenses and ordinance violations; to provide for the arrest of persons charged with or suspected of criminal offenses and ordinance violations; to provide for bail of persons arrested for or accused of criminal offenses and ordinance violations; to provide for the examination of persons accused of criminal offenses; to regulate the procedure relative to grand juries, indictments, informations, and proceedings before trial; to provide for trials of persons complained of or indicted for criminal offenses and ordinance violations and to provide for the procedure in those trials; to provide for judgments and sentences of persons convicted of criminal offenses and ordinance violations; to establish a sentencing commission and to prescribe its powers and duties; to provide for procedure relating to new trials and appeals in criminal and ordinance violation cases; to provide a uniform system of probation throughout this state and the appointment of probation officers; to prescribe the powers, duties, and compensation of probation officers; to provide penalties for the violation of the duties of probation officers; to provide for procedure governing proceedings to prevent crime and proceedings for the discovery of crime; to provide for fees of officers, witnesses, and others in criminal and ordinance violation cases; to set forth miscellaneous provisions as to criminal procedure in certain cases; to provide penalties for the violation of certain provisions of this act; and to repeal all acts and parts of acts inconsistent with or contravening any of the provisions of this act.

History: 1927, Act 175, Eff. Sept. 5, 1927;—Am. 1980, Act 506, Imd. Eff. Jan. 22, 1981;—Am. 1994, Act 445, Imd. Eff. Jan. 10, 1995.

The People of the State of Michigan enact:

CHAPTER IV
ARREST

764.1f Juvenile; filing complaint and warrant with magistrate; "specified juvenile violation" defined.

Sec. 1f. (1) If the prosecuting attorney has reason to believe that a juvenile 14 years of age or older but less than 17 years of age has committed a specified juvenile violation, the prosecuting attorney may authorize the filing of a complaint and warrant on the charge with a magistrate concerning the juvenile.

(2) As used in this section, "specified juvenile violation" means any of the following:

(a) A violation of section 72, 83, 86, 89, 91, 316, 317, 349, 520b, 529, 529a, or 531 of the Michigan penal code, 1931 PA 328, MCL 750.72, 750.83, 750.86, 750.89, 750.91, 750.316, 750.317, 750.349, 750.520b, 750.529, 750.529a, and 750.531.

(b) A violation of section 84 or 110a(2) of the Michigan penal code, 1931 PA 328, MCL 750.84 and 750.110a, if the juvenile is armed with a dangerous weapon. As used in this subdivision, "dangerous weapon" means 1 or more of the following:

(*i*) A loaded or unloaded firearm, whether operable or inoperable.

(*ii*) A knife, stabbing instrument, brass knuckles, blackjack, club, or other object specifically designed or customarily carried or possessed for use as a weapon.

(*iii*) An object that is likely to cause death or bodily injury when used as a weapon and that is used as a weapon or carried or possessed for use as a weapon.

(*iv*) An object or device that is used or fashioned in a manner to lead a person to believe the object or device is an object or device described in subparagraphs (*i*) to (*iii*).

(c) A violation of section 186a of the Michigan penal code, 1931 PA 328, MCL 750.186a, regarding escape or attempted escape from a juvenile facility, but only if the juvenile facility from which the individual escaped or attempted to escape was 1 of the following:

(*i*) A high-security or medium-security facility operated by the family independence agency or a county juvenile agency.

(*ii*) A high-security facility operated by a private agency under contract with the family independence agency or a county juvenile agency.

(d) A violation of section 7401(2)(a)(*i*) or 7403(2)(a)(*i*) of the public health code, 1978 PA 368, MCL 333.7401 and 333.7403.

(e) An attempt to commit a violation described in subdivisions (a) to (d).

(f) Conspiracy to commit a violation described in subdivisions (a) to (d).

(g) Solicitation to commit a violation described in subdivisions (a) to (d).

(h) Any lesser included offense of a violation described in subdivisions (a) to (g) if the individual is charged with a violation described in subdivisions (a) to (g).

(i) Any other violation arising out of the same transaction as a violation described in subdivisions (a) to (g) if the individual is charged with a violation described in subdivisions (a) to (g).

History: Add. 1988, Act 67, Eff. Oct. 1, 1988;—Am. 1994, Act 195, Eff. Oct. 1, 1994;—Am. 1996, Act 255, Eff. Jan. 1, 1997;—Am. 1998, Act 520, Imd. Eff. Jan. 12, 1999.

Compiler's note: Section 3 of Act 67 of 1988 provides: "This amendatory act shall take effect June 1, 1988." This section was amended by Act 173 of 1988 to read as follows: "This amendatory act shall take effect October 1, 1988."

764.15b Arrest without warrant for violation of personal protection order; answering to charge of contempt; hearing; bond; show cause order; jurisdiction to conduct contempt proceedings; prosecution of criminal contempt; prohibited actions by court; definitions.

Sec. 15b. (1) A peace officer, without a warrant, may arrest and take into custody an individual when the peace officer has or receives positive information that another peace officer has reasonable cause to believe all of the following apply:

(a) A personal protection order has been issued under section 2950 or 2950a of the revised judicature act of 1961, 1961 PA 236, MCL 600.2950 and 600.2950a, or is a valid foreign protection order.

(b) The individual named in the personal protection order is violating or has violated the order. An individual is violating or has violated the order if that individual commits 1 or more of the following acts the order specifically restrains or enjoins the individual from committing:

(*i*) Assaulting, attacking, beating, molesting, or wounding a named individual.

(*ii*) Removing minor children from an individual having legal custody of the children, except as otherwise authorized by a custody or parenting time order issued by a court of competent jurisdiction.

(*iii*) Entering onto premises.

(*iv*) Engaging in conduct prohibited under section 411h or 411i of the Michigan penal code, 1931 PA 328, MCL 750.411h and 750.411i.

(*v*) Threatening to kill or physically injure a named individual.

(*vi*) Purchasing or possessing a firearm.

(*vii*) Interfering with petitioner's efforts to remove petitioner's children or personal property from premises that are solely owned or leased by the individual to be restrained or enjoined.

(*viii*) Interfering with petitioner at petitioner's place of employment or education or engaging in conduct that impairs petitioner's employment or educational relationship or environment.

(*ix*) Any other act or conduct specified by the court in the personal protection order.

(c) If the personal protection order was issued under section 2950 or 2950a, the personal protection order states on its face that a violation of its terms subjects the individual to immediate arrest and either of the following:

(*i*) If the individual restrained or enjoined is 17 years of age or older, to criminal contempt of court and, if found guilty of criminal contempt, to imprisonment for not more than 93 days and to a fine of not more than
$500.00.

(*ii*) If the individual restrained or enjoined is less than 17 years of age, to the dispositional alternatives listed in section 18 of chapter XIIA of the probate code of 1939, 1939 PA 288, MCL 712A.18.

(2) An individual arrested under this section shall be brought before the family division of the circuit court having jurisdiction in the cause within 24 hours after arrest to answer to a charge of contempt for violating the personal protection order, at which time the court shall do each of the following:

(a) Set a time certain for a hearing on the alleged violation of the personal protection order. The hearing shall be held within 72 hours after arrest, unless extended by the court on the motion of the arrested individual or the prosecuting attorney.

(b) Set a reasonable bond pending a hearing of the alleged violation of the personal protection order.

(c) Notify the prosecuting attorney of the criminal contempt proceeding.

(d) Notify the party who procured the personal protection order and his or her attorney of record, if any, and direct the party to appear at the hearing and give evidence on the charge of contempt.

(3) In circuits in which the circuit court judge may not be present or available within 24 hours after arrest, an individual arrested under this section shall be taken before the district court within 24 hours after arrest, at which time the district court shall set bond and order the defendant to appear before the family division of circuit court in the county for a hearing on the charge. If the district court will not be open within 24 hours after arrest, a judge or district court magistrate shall set bond and order the defendant to appear before the circuit court in the county for a hearing on the charge.

(4) If a criminal contempt proceeding for violation of a personal protection order is not initiated by an arrest under this section but is initiated as a result of a show cause order or other process or proceedings, the court shall do all of the following:

(a) Notify the party who procured the personal protection order and his or her attorney of record, if any, and direct the party to appear at the hearing and give evidence on the contempt charge.

(b) Notify the prosecuting attorney of the criminal contempt proceeding.

(5) The family division of circuit court in each county of this state has jurisdiction to conduct contempt proceedings based upon a violation of a personal protection order described in this section issued by the circuit court in any county of this state or upon a violation of a valid foreign protection order. The court of arraignment shall notify the court that issued the personal protection order or foreign protection order that the issuing court may request that the defendant be returned to that court for violating the personal protection order or foreign protection order. If the court that issued the personal protection order or foreign protection order requests that the defendant be returned to that court to stand trial, the county of the requesting court shall bear the cost of transporting the defendant to that county.

(6) The family division of circuit court has jurisdiction to conduct contempt proceedings based upon a violation of a personal protection order issued pursuant to section 2(h) of chapter XIIA of the probate code of 1939, 1939 PA 288, MCL 712A.2, by the family division of circuit court in any county of this state or a valid foreign protection order issued against a respondent who is less than 18 years of age at the time of the alleged violation of the foreign protection order in this state. The family

division of circuit court that conducts the preliminary inquiry shall notify the court that issued the personal protection order or foreign protection order that the issuing court may request that the respondent be returned to that county for violating the personal protection order or foreign protection order. If the court that issued the personal protection order or foreign protection order requests that the respondent be returned to that court to stand trial, the county of the requesting court shall bear the cost of transporting the respondent to that county.

(7) The prosecuting attorney shall prosecute a criminal contempt proceeding initiated by the court under subsection (2) or initiated by a show cause order under subsection (4), unless the party who procured the personal protection order retains his or her own attorney for the criminal contempt proceeding or the prosecuting attorney determines that the personal protection order was not violated or that it would not be in the interest of justice to prosecute the criminal contempt violation. If the prosecuting attorney prosecutes the criminal contempt proceeding, the court shall grant an adjournment for not less than 14 days or a lesser period requested if the prosecuting attorney moves for adjournment. If the prosecuting attorney prosecutes the criminal contempt proceeding, the court may dismiss the proceeding upon motion of the prosecuting attorney for good cause shown.

(8) A court shall not rescind a personal protection order, dismiss a contempt proceeding based on a personal protection order, or impose any other sanction for a failure to comply with a time limit prescribed in this section.

(9) As used in this section:

(a) "Foreign protection order" means that term as defined in section 2950h of the revised judicature act of 1961, 1961 PA 236, MCL 600.2950h.

(b) "Personal protection order" means a personal protection order issued under section 2950 or 2950a of the revised judicature act of 1961, 1961 PA 236, MCL 600.2950 and 600.2950a, and, unless the context indicates otherwise, includes a valid foreign protection order.

(c) "Valid foreign protection order" means a foreign protection order that satisfies the conditions for validity provided in section 2950i of the revised judicature act of 1961, 1961 PA 236, MCL 600.2950i.

History: Add. 1980, Act 471, Eff. Mar. 31, 1981;—Am. 1983, Act 230, Imd. Eff. Nov. 28, 1983;—Am. 1992, Act 251, Eff. Jan. 1, 1993;—Am. 1994, Act 59, Eff. July 1, 1994;—Am. 1994, Act 62, Eff. July 1, 1994;—Am. 1994, Act 418, Eff. Apr. 1, 1995;—Am. 1996, Act 15, Eff. June 1, 1996;—Am. 1998, Act 475, Eff. Mar. 1, 1999;—Am. 1999, Act 269, Eff. July 1, 2000;—Am. 2001, Act 209, Eff. Apr. 1, 2002.

764.15c Investigation or intervention in domestic violence dispute; providing victim with notice of rights; report; retention and filing of report; development of standard domestic violence incident report form; definitions.

Sec. 15c. (1) After investigating or intervening in a domestic violence incident, a peace officer shall provide the victim with a copy of the notice in this section. The notice shall be written and shall include all of the following:

(a) The name and telephone number of the responding police agency.

(b) The name and badge number of the responding peace officer.

(c) Substantially the following statement:

"You may obtain a copy of the police incident report for your case by contacting this law enforcement agency at the telephone number provided.

The domestic violence shelter program and other resources in your area are (include local information).

Information about emergency shelter, counseling services, and the legal rights of domestic violence victims is available from these resources.

Your legal rights include the right to go to court and file a petition requesting a personal protection order to protect you or other members of your household from domestic abuse which could include restraining or enjoining the abuser from doing the following:

(a) Entering onto premises.

(b) Assaulting, attacking, beating, molesting, or wounding you.

(c) Threatening to kill or physically injure you or another person.

(d) Removing minor children from you, except as otherwise authorized by a custody or parenting time order issued by a court of competent jurisdiction.

(e) Engaging in stalking behavior.

(f) Purchasing or possessing a firearm.

(g) Interfering with your efforts to remove your children or personal property from premises that are solely owned or leased by the abuser.

(h) Interfering with you at your place of employment or education or engaging in conduct that impairs your employment relationship or your employment or educational environment.

(i) Engaging in any other specific act or conduct that imposes upon or interferes with your personal liberty or that causes a reasonable apprehension of violence.

(j) Having access to information in records concerning any minor child you have with the abuser that would inform the abuser about your address or telephone number, the child's address or telephone number, or your employment address.

Your legal rights also include the right to go to court and file a motion for an order to show cause and a hearing if the abuser is violating or has violated a personal protection order and has not been arrested.".

(2) The peace officer shall prepare a domestic violence report after investigating or intervening in a domestic violence incident. Effective October 1, 2002, a peace officer shall use the standard domestic violence incident report form developed under subsection (4) or a form substantially similar to that standard form to report a domestic violence incident. The report shall contain, but is not limited to containing, all of the following:

(a) The address, date, and time of the incident being investigated.

(b) The victim's name, address, home and work telephone numbers, race, sex, and date of birth.

(c) The suspect's name, address, home and work telephone numbers, race, sex, date of birth, and information describing the suspect and whether an injunction or restraining order covering the suspect exists.

(d) The name, address, home and work telephone numbers, race, sex, and date of birth of any witness, including a child of the victim or suspect, and the relationship of the witness to the suspect or victim.

(e) The following information about the incident being investigated:

(*i*) The name of the person who called the law enforcement agency.

(*ii*) The relationship of the victim and suspect.

(*iii*) Whether alcohol or controlled substance use was involved in the incident, and by whom it was used.

(*iv*) A brief narrative describing the incident and the circumstances that led to it.

(*v*) Whether and how many times the suspect physically assaulted the victim and a description of any weapon or object used.

(*vi*) A description of all injuries sustained by the victim and an explanation of how the injuries were sustained.

(*vii*) If the victim sought medical attention, information concerning where and how the victim was transported, whether the victim was admitted to a hospital or clinic for treatment, and the name and telephone number of the attending physician.

(*viii*) A description of any property damage reported by the victim or evident at the scene.

(f) A description of any previous domestic violence incidents between the victim and the suspect.

(g) The date and time of the report and the name, badge number, and signature of the peace officer completing the report.

(3) The law enforcement agency shall retain the completed domestic violence report in its files. The law enforcement agency shall also file a copy of the completed domestic violence report with the prosecuting attorney within 48 hours after the domestic violence incident is reported to the law enforcement agency.

(4) By June 1, 2002, the department of state police shall develop a standard domestic violence incident report form.

(5) As used in this section:

(a) "Dating relationship" means that term as defined in section 2950 of the revised judicature act of 1961, 1961 PA 236, MCL 600.2950.

(b) "Domestic violence incident" means an incident reported to a law enforcement agency involving allegations of 1 or both of the following:

(*i*) A violation of a personal protection order issued under section 2950 of the revised judicature act of 1961, 1961 PA 236, MCL 600.2950, or a violation of a valid foreign protection order.

(*ii*) A crime committed by an individual against his or her spouse or former spouse, an individual with whom he or she has had a child in common, an individual with whom he or she has or has had a dating relationship, or an individual who resides or has resided in the same household.

(c) "Foreign protection order" means that term as defined in section 2950h of the revised judicature act of 1961, 1961 PA 236, MCL 600.2950h.

(d) "Valid foreign protection order" means a foreign protection order that satisfies the conditions for validity provided in section 2950i of the revised judicature act of 1961, 1961 PA 236, MCL 600.2950i.

History: Add. 1985, Act 222, Eff. Mar. 31, 1986;—Am. 1994, Act 60, Eff. July 1, 1994;—Am. 1994, Act 63, Eff. July 1, 1994;—Am. 1994, Act 418, Eff. Apr. 1, 1995;—Am. 1996, Act 15, Eff. June 1, 1996;—Am. 1998, Act 475, Eff. Mar. 1, 1999;—Am. 1999, Act 269, Eff. July 1, 2000;—Am. 2001, Act 207, Eff. Apr. 1, 2002;—Am. 2001, Act 210, Eff. Apr. 1, 2002.

764.15d Federal law enforcement officer; powers.

Sec. 15d. (1) A federal law enforcement officer may enforce state law to the same extent as a state or local officer only if all of the following conditions are met:

(a) The officer is authorized under federal law to arrest a person, with or without a warrant, for a violation of a federal statute.

(b) The officer is authorized by federal law to carry a firearm in the performance of his or her duties.

(c) One or more of the following apply:

(*i*) The officer possesses a state warrant for the arrest of the person for the commission of a felony.

(*ii*) The officer has received positive information from an authoritative source, in writing or by telegraph, telephone, teletype, radio, computer, or other means, that another federal law enforcement officer or a peace officer possesses a state warrant for the arrest of the person for the commission of a felony.

(*iii*) The officer is participating in a joint investigation conducted by a federal agency and a state or local law enforcement agency.

(*iv*) The officer is acting pursuant to the request of a state or local law enforcement officer or agency.

(*v*) The officer is responding to an emergency.

(2) Except as otherwise provided in subsection (3), a federal law enforcement officer who meets the requirements of subsection (1) has the privileges and immunities of a peace officer of this state.
(3) This section does not impose liability upon or require indemnification by the state or a local unit of government for an act performed by a federal law enforcement officer under this section.
(4) As used in this section:
(a) "Emergency" means a sudden or unexpected circumstance that requires immediate action to protect the health, safety, welfare, or property of an individual from actual or threatened harm or from an unlawful act.
(b) "Local unit of government" means a county, city, village, or township.

History: Add. 1987, Act 256, Imd. Eff. Dec. 28, 1987;—Am. 1999, Act 64, Eff. Oct. 1, 1999.

764.25 Arrest; weapons and articles on prisoner; seizure, disposal.

Sec. 25. Any person making an arrest shall take from the person arrested, all offensive weapons or incriminating articles which he may have about his person and must deliver them to the sheriff of the county, chief of police of the city or to the magistrate before whom he is taken.

History: 1927, Act 175, Eff. Sept. 5, 1927;—CL 1929, 17159;—CL 1948, 764.25.

764.25a Strip search.

Sec. 25a. (1) As used in this section, "strip search" means a search which requires a person to remove his or her clothing to expose underclothing, breasts, buttocks, or genitalia.
(2) A person arrested or detained for a misdemeanor offense, or an offense which is punishable only by a civil fine shall not be strip searched unless both of the following occur:
(a) The person arrested is being lodged into a detention facility by order of a court or there is reasonable cause to believe that the person is concealing a weapon, a controlled substance, or evidence of a crime.
(b) The strip search is conducted by a person who has obtained prior written authorization from the chief law enforcement officer of the law enforcement agency conducting the strip search, or from that officer's designee; or if the strip search is conducted upon a minor in a juvenile detention facility which is not operated by a law enforcement agency, the strip search is conducted by a person who has obtained prior written authorization from the chief administrative officer of that facility, or from that officer's designee.
(3) A strip search conducted under this section shall be performed by a person of the same sex as the person being searched and shall be performed in a place that prevents the search from being observed by a person not conducting or necessary to assist with the search. A law enforcement officer who assists in the strip search shall be of the same sex as the person being searched.
(4) If a strip search is conducted under this section, the arresting officer shall prepare a report of the strip search. The report shall include the following information:
(a) The name and sex of the person subjected to the strip search.
(b) The name and sex of the person conducting the strip search.
(c) The name and sex of a person who assists in conducting the strip search.
(d) The time, date, and place of the strip search.
(e) The justification for conducting a strip search.
(f) A list of all items recovered from the person who was strip searched.
(g) A copy of the written authorization required under subsection (2)(b).
(5) A copy of the report required by subsection (4) shall be given without cost to the person who has been searched, subject to deletions permitted by section 13 of the freedom of information act, 1976 PA 442, MCL 15.243.
(6) A law enforcement officer, any employee of the law enforcement agency, or a chief administrative officer or employee of a juvenile detention facility who conducts or authorizes a strip search in violation of this section is guilty of a misdemeanor.
(7) This section shall not apply to the strip search of a person lodged in a detention facility by an order of a court or in a state correctional facility housing prisoners under the jurisdiction of the department of corrections, including a youth correctional facility operated by the department of corrections or a private vendor under section 20g of 1953 PA 232, MCL 791.220g.

History: Add. 1979, Act 185, Eff. Mar. 27, 1980;—Am. 1983, Act 92, Eff. Mar. 29, 1984;—Am. 1999, Act 65, Imd. Eff. June 24, 1999.

CHAPTER V
BAIL

765.6b Release of defendant subject to protective conditions; contents of order; purchase or possession of firearm; entering or removing order from LEIN; order to wear electronic monitoring device; other orders; definitions; authority to impose other conditions not limited; "LEIN" defined.

Sec. 6b. (1) A judge or district court magistrate may release a defendant under this subsection subject to conditions reasonably necessary for the protection of 1 or more named persons. If a judge or district court magistrate releases a defendant under this subsection subject to protective conditions, the judge or district court magistrate shall make a finding of the need for protective conditions and inform the defendant on the record, either orally or by a writing that is personally delivered to the defendant, of the specific conditions imposed and that if the defendant violates a condition of release, he or she will be subject to arrest without a warrant and may have his or her bail forfeited or revoked and new conditions of release imposed, in addition to the penalty provided under section 3f of chapter XI and any other penalties that may be imposed if the defendant is found in contempt of court.

(2) An order or amended order issued under subsection (1) shall contain all of the following:

(a) A statement of the defendant's full name.

(b) A statement of the defendant's height, weight, race, sex, date of birth, hair color, eye color, and any other identifying information the judge or district court magistrate considers appropriate.

(c) A statement of the date the conditions become effective.

(d) A statement of the date on which the order will expire.

(e) A statement of the conditions imposed.

(3) An order or amended order issued under this subsection and subsection (1) may impose a condition that the defendant not purchase or possess a firearm. However, if the court orders the defendant to carry or wear an electronic monitoring device as a condition of release as described in subsection (6), the court shall also impose a condition that the defendant not purchase or possess a firearm.

(4) The judge or district court magistrate shall immediately direct the issuing court or a law enforcement agency within the jurisdiction of the court, in writing, to enter an order or amended order issued under subsection (1) or subsections (1) and (3) into LEIN. If the order or amended order is rescinded, the judge or district court magistrate shall immediately order the issuing court or law enforcement agency to remove the order or amended order from LEIN.

(5) The issuing court or a law enforcement agency within the jurisdiction of the court shall immediately enter an order or amended order into LEIN or shall remove the order or amended order from the law enforcement information network upon expiration of the order or as directed by the court under subsection (4).

(6) If a defendant who is charged with a crime involving domestic violence, or any other assaultive crime, is released under this subsection and subsection (1), the judge or district court magistrate may order the defendant to wear an electronic monitoring device as a condition of release. With the informed consent of the victim, the court may also order the defendant to provide the victim of the charged crime with an electronic receptor device capable of receiving the global positioning system information from the electronic monitoring device worn by the defendant that notifies the victim if the defendant is located within a proximity to the victim as determined by the judge or district court magistrate in consultation with the victim. The victim shall also be furnished with a telephone contact with the local law enforcement agency to request immediate assistance if the defendant is located within that proximity to the victim. In addition, the victim may provide the court with a list of areas from which he or she would like the defendant excluded. The court shall consider the victim's request and shall determine which areas the defendant shall be prohibited from accessing. The court shall instruct the entity monitoring the defendant's position to notify the proper authorities if the defendant violates the order. In determining whether to order a defendant to wear an electronic monitoring device, the court shall consider the likelihood that the defendant's participation in electronic monitoring will deter the defendant from seeking to kill, physically injure, stalk, or otherwise threaten the victim prior to trial. The victim may request the court to terminate the victim's participation in the monitoring of the defendant at any time. The court shall not impose sanctions on the victim for refusing to participate in monitoring under this subsection. A defendant described in this subsection shall only be released if he or she agrees to pay the cost of the device and any monitoring as a condition of release or to perform community service work in lieu of paying that cost. An electronic monitoring device ordered to be worn under this subsection shall provide reliable notification of removal or tampering. As used in this subsection:

(a) "Assaultive crime" means that term as defined in section 9a of chapter X.

(b) "Domestic violence" means that term as defined in section 1 of 1978 PA 389, MCL 400.1501.

(c) "Electronic monitoring device" includes any electronic device or instrument that is used to track the location of an individual or to monitor an individual's blood alcohol content, but does not include any technology that is implanted or violates the corporeal body of the individual.

(d) "Informed consent" means that the victim was given information concerning all of the following before consenting to participate in electronic monitoring:

(*i*) The victim's right to refuse to participate in that monitoring and the process for requesting the court to terminate the victim's participation after it has been ordered.

(*ii*) The manner in which the monitoring technology functions and the risks and limitations of that technology, and the extent to which the system will track and record the victim's location and movements.

(*iii*) The boundaries imposed on the defendant during the monitoring program.

(*iv*) Sanctions that the court may impose on the defendant for violating an order issued under this subsection.

(*v*) The procedure that the victim is to follow if the defendant violates an order issued under this subsection or if monitoring equipment fails to operate properly.

(*vi*) Identification of support services available to assist the victim to develop a safety plan to use if the court's order issued under this subsection is violated or if the monitoring equipment fails to operate properly.

(*vii*) Identification of community services available to assist the victim in obtaining shelter, counseling, education, child care, legal representation, and other help in addressing the consequences and effects of domestic violence.

(*viii*) The nonconfidential nature of the victim's communications with the court concerning electronic monitoring and the restrictions to be imposed upon the defendant's movements.

(7) A judge or district court magistrate may release under this subsection a defendant subject to conditions reasonably necessary for the protection of the public if the defendant has submitted to a preliminary roadside analysis that detects the presence of alcoholic liquor, a controlled substance, or other intoxicating substance, or any combination of them, and that a subsequent chemical test is pending. The judge or district court magistrate shall inform the defendant on the record, either orally or by a writing that is personally delivered to the defendant, of all of the following:

(a) That if the defendant is released under this subsection, he or she shall not operate a motor vehicle under the influence of alcoholic liquor, a controlled substance, or another intoxicating substance, or any combination of them, as a condition of release.

(b) That if the defendant violates the condition of release under subdivision (a), he or she will be subject to arrest without a warrant, shall have his or her bail forfeited or revoked, and shall not be released from custody prior to arraignment.

(8) The judge or district court magistrate shall immediately direct the issuing court or a law enforcement agency within the jurisdiction of the court, in writing, to enter an order or amended order issued under subsection (7) into LEIN. If the order or amended order is rescinded, the judge or district court magistrate shall immediately order the issuing court or law enforcement agency to remove the order or amended order from LEIN.

(9) The issuing court or a law enforcement agency within the jurisdiction of the court shall immediately enter an order or amended order into LEIN. If the order or amended order is rescinded, the court or law enforcement agency shall immediately remove the order or amended order from LEIN upon expiration of the order under subsection (8).

(10) This section does not limit the authority of judges or district court magistrates to impose protective or other release conditions under other applicable statutes or court rules, including ordering a defendant to wear an electronic monitoring device.

(11) As used in this section, "LEIN" means the law enforcement information network regulated under the C.J.I.S. policy council act, 1974 PA 163, MCL 28.211 to 28.215, or by the department of state police.

History: Add. 1993, Act 53, Eff. July 1, 1993;—Am. 1994, Act 335, Eff. Apr. 1, 1996;—Am. 2008, Act 192, Imd. Eff. July 10, 2008;—Am. 2013, Act 54, Imd. Eff. June 11, 2013;—Am. 2014, Act 316, Eff. Jan. 12, 2015.

Compiler's note: Enacting section 1 of Act 192 of 2008 provides:
"Enacting section 1. This amendatory act shall be known and cited as 'Mary's Law'".

CHAPTER VI
EXAMINATION OF OFFENDERS

766.14 Proceedings where offense charged not felony; transfer of case to family division of circuit court; waiver of jurisdiction; "specified juvenile violation" defined.

Sec. 14. (1) If the court determines at the conclusion of the preliminary examination of a person charged with a felony that the offense charged is not a felony or that an included offense that is not a felony has been committed, the accused shall not be dismissed but the magistrate shall proceed in the same manner as if the accused had initially been charged with an offense that is not a felony.

(2) If at the conclusion of the preliminary examination of a juvenile the magistrate finds that a specified juvenile violation did not occur or that there is not probable cause to believe that the juvenile committed the violation, but that there is probable cause to believe that some other offense occurred and that the juvenile committed that other offense, the magistrate shall transfer the case to the family division of circuit court of the county where the offense is alleged to have been committed.

(3) A transfer under subsection (2) does not prevent the family division of circuit court from waiving jurisdiction over the juvenile under section 4 of chapter XIIA of 1939 PA 288, MCL 712A.4.

(4) As used in this section, "specified juvenile violation" means any of the following:

(a) A violation of section 72, 83, 86, 89, 91, 316, 317, 349, 520b, 529, 529a, or 531 of the Michigan penal code, 1931 PA 328, MCL 750.72, 750.83, 750.89, 750.91, 750.316, 750.317, 750.349, 750.520b, 750.529, 750.529a, and 750.531.

(b) A violation of section 84 or 110a(2) of the Michigan penal code, 1931 PA 328, MCL 750.84 and 750.110a, if the juvenile is armed with a dangerous weapon. As used in this subdivision, "dangerous weapon" means 1 or more of the following:

(*i*) A loaded or unloaded firearm, whether operable or inoperable.

(*ii*) A knife, stabbing instrument, brass knuckles, blackjack, club, or other object specifically designed or customarily carried or possessed for use as a weapon.

(*iii*) An object that is likely to cause death or bodily injury when used as a weapon and that is used as a weapon or carried or possessed for use as a weapon.

(*iv*) An object or device that is used or fashioned in a manner to lead a person to believe the object or device is an object or device described in subparagraphs (*i*) to (*iii*).

(c) A violation of section 186a of the Michigan penal code, 1931 PA 328, MCL 750.186a, regarding escape or attempted escape from a juvenile facility, but only if the juvenile facility from which the individual escaped or attempted to escape was 1 of the following:

(*i*) A high-security or medium-security facility operated by the family independence agency or a county juvenile agency.

(*ii*) A high-security facility operated by a private agency under contract with the family independence agency or a county juvenile agency.

(d) A violation of section 7401(2)(a)(*i*) or 7403(2)(a)(*i*) of the public health code, 1978 PA 368, MCL 333.7401 and 333.7403.
(e) An attempt to commit a violation described in subdivisions (a) to (d).
(f) Conspiracy to commit a violation described in subdivisions (a) to (d).
(g) Solicitation to commit a violation described in subdivisions (a) to (d).
(h) Any lesser included offense of a violation described in subdivisions (a) to (g) if the individual is charged with a violation described in subdivisions (a) to (g).
(i) Any other violation arising out of the same transaction as a violation described in subdivisions (a) to (g) if the individual is charged with a violation described in subdivisions (a) to (g).

History: 1927, Act 175, Eff. Sept. 5, 1927;—CL 1929, 17206;—CL 1948, 766.14;—Am. 1974, Act 63, Eff. May 1, 1974;—Am. 1988, Act 67, Eff. Oct. 1, 1988;—Am. 1994, Act 195, Eff. Oct. 1, 1994;—Am. 1996, Act 255, Eff. Jan. 1, 1997;—Am. 1996, Act 418, Eff. Jan. 1, 1998;—Am. 1998, Act 520, Imd. Eff. Jan. 12, 1999.

Compiler's note: Section 2 of Act 63 of 1974 provides:
"Section 2. To give judges, prosecutors, and defense counsel a reasonable opportunity to become aware of and familiar with the time periods and sequence prescribed in this amendatory act and the effects of noncompliance, sections 20 and 21 of chapter 8 of Act No. 175 of the Public Acts of 1927, being sections 768.20 and 768.21 of the Michigan Compiled Laws, as amended by this amendatory act shall take effect May 1, 1974, and apply to cases in which the arraignment on an information occurs on or after that date. The other provisions of this amendatory act shall take effect May 1, 1974 and apply to offenses committed on or after that date."
Section 3 of Act 67 of 1988 provides: "This amendatory act shall take effect June 1, 1988." This section was amended by Act 173 of 1988 to read as follows: "This amendatory act shall take effect October 1, 1988."

CHAPTER VIII
TRIALS

768.21c Use of deadly force by individual in own dwelling; "dwelling" defined.

Sec. 21c. (1) In cases in which section 2 of the self-defense act does not apply, the common law of this state applies except that the duty to retreat before using deadly force is not required if an individual is in his or her own dwelling or within the curtilage of that dwelling.
(2) As used in this section, "dwelling" means a structure or shelter that is used permanently or temporarily as a place of abode, including an appurtenant structure attached to that structure or shelter.

History: Add. 2006, Act 313, Eff. Oct. 1, 2006.

CHAPTER IX
JUDGMENT AND SENTENCE

769.1 Authority and power of court; crimes for which juvenile to be sentenced as adult; fingerprints as condition to sentencing; hearing at juvenile's sentencing; determination; criteria; waiver; violation of MCL 333.7403; statement on record; transcript; reimbursement provision in order of commitment; disposition of collections; order to intercept tax refunds and initiate offset proceedings; notice; order directed to person responsible for juvenile's support; hearing; copy of order; retention of jurisdiction over juvenile; annual review; examination of juvenile's annual report; forwarding report.

Sec. 1. (1) A judge of a court having jurisdiction may pronounce judgment against and pass sentence upon a person convicted of an offense in that court. The sentence shall not exceed the sentence prescribed by law. The court shall sentence a juvenile convicted of any of the following crimes in the same manner as an adult:
(a) Arson of a dwelling in violation of section 72 of the Michigan penal code, 1931 PA 328, MCL 750.72.
(b) Assault with intent to commit murder in violation of section 83 of the Michigan penal code, 1931 PA 328, MCL 750.83.
(c) Assault with intent to maim in violation of section 86 of the Michigan penal code, 1931 PA 328, MCL 750.86.
(d) Attempted murder in violation of section 91 of the Michigan penal code, 1931 PA 328, MCL 750.91.
(e) Conspiracy to commit murder in violation of section 157a of the Michigan penal code, 1931 PA 328, MCL 750.157a.
(f) Solicitation to commit murder in violation of section 157b of the Michigan penal code, 1931 PA 328, MCL 750.157b.
(g) First degree murder in violation of section 316 of the Michigan penal code, 1931 PA 328, MCL 750.316.
(h) Second degree murder in violation of section 317 of the Michigan penal code, 1931 PA 328, MCL 750.317.
(i) Kidnapping in violation of section 349 of the Michigan penal code, 1931 PA 328, MCL 750.349.
(j) First degree criminal sexual conduct in violation of section 520b of the Michigan penal code, 1931 PA 328, MCL 750.520b.
(k) Armed robbery in violation of section 529 of the Michigan penal code, 1931 PA 328, MCL 750.529.
(*l*) Carjacking in violation of section 529a of the Michigan penal code, 1931 PA 328, MCL 750.529a.
(2) A person convicted of a felony or of a misdemeanor punishable by imprisonment for more than 92 days shall not be sentenced until the court has examined the court file and has determined that the person's fingerprints have been taken.
(3) Unless a juvenile is required to be sentenced in the same manner as an adult under subsection (1), a judge of a court having jurisdiction over a juvenile shall conduct a hearing at the juvenile's sentencing to determine if the best interests of the

public would be served by placing the juvenile on probation and committing the juvenile to an institution or agency described in the youth rehabilitation services act, 1974 PA 150, MCL 803.301 to 803.309, or by imposing any other sentence provided by law for an adult offender. Except as provided in subsection (5), the court shall sentence the juvenile in the same manner as an adult unless the court determines by a preponderance of the evidence that the interests of the public would be best served by placing the juvenile on probation and committing the juvenile to an institution or agency described in the youth rehabilitation services act, 1974 PA 150, MCL 803.301 to 803.309. The rules of evidence do not apply to a hearing under this subsection. In making the determination required under this subsection, the judge shall consider all of the following, giving greater weight to the seriousness of the alleged offense and the juvenile's prior record of delinquency:

(a) The seriousness of the alleged offense in terms of community protection, including, but not limited to, the existence of any aggravating factors recognized by the sentencing guidelines, the use of a firearm or other dangerous weapon, and the impact on any victim.

(b) The juvenile's culpability in committing the alleged offense, including, but not limited to, the level of the juvenile's participation in planning and carrying out the offense and the existence of any aggravating or mitigating factors recognized by the sentencing guidelines.

(c) The juvenile's prior record of delinquency including, but not limited to, any record of detention, any police record, any school record, or any other evidence indicating prior delinquent behavior.

(d) The juvenile's programming history, including, but not limited to, the juvenile's past willingness to participate meaningfully in available programming.

(e) The adequacy of the punishment or programming available in the juvenile justice system.

(f) The dispositional options available for the juvenile.

(4) With the consent of the prosecutor and the defendant, the court may waive the hearing required under subsection (3). If the court waives the hearing required under subsection (3), the court may place the juvenile on probation and commit the juvenile to an institution or agency described in the youth rehabilitation services act, 1974 PA 150, MCL 803.301 to 803.309, but shall not impose any other sentence provided by law for an adult offender.

(5) If a juvenile is convicted of a violation or conspiracy to commit a violation of section 7403(2)(a)(*i*) of the public health code, 1978 PA 368, MCL 333.7403, the court shall determine whether the best interests of the public would be served by imposing the sentence provided by law for an adult offender, by placing the individual on probation and committing the individual to an institution or agency under subsection (3), or by imposing a sentence of imprisonment for any term of years but not less than 25 years. If the court determines by clear and convincing evidence that the best interests of the public would be served by imposing a sentence of imprisonment for any term of years but not less than 25 years, the court may impose that sentence. In making its determination, the court shall use the criteria specified in subsection (3).

(6) The court shall state on the record the court's findings of fact and conclusions of law for the probation and commitment decision or sentencing decision made under subsection (3). If a juvenile is committed under subsection (3) to an institution or agency described in the youth rehabilitation services act, 1974 PA 150, MCL 803.301 to 803.309, a transcript of the court's findings shall be sent to the family independence agency or county juvenile agency, as applicable.

(7) If a juvenile is committed under subsection (3) or (4) to an institution or agency described in the youth rehabilitation services act, 1974 PA 150, MCL 803.301 to 803.309, the written order of commitment shall contain a provision for the reimbursement to the court by the juvenile or those responsible for the juvenile's support, or both, for the cost of care or service. The amount of reimbursement ordered shall be reasonable, taking into account both the income and resources of the juvenile and those responsible for the juvenile's support. The amount may be based upon the guidelines and model schedule prepared under section 18(6) of chapter XIIA of the probate code of 1939, 1939 PA 288, MCL 712A.18. The reimbursement provision applies during the entire period the juvenile remains in care outside the juvenile's own home and under court supervision. The court shall provide for the collection of all amounts ordered to be reimbursed, and the money collected shall be accounted for and reported to the county board of commissioners. Collections to cover delinquent accounts or to pay the balance due on reimbursement orders may be made after a juvenile is released or discharged from care outside the juvenile's own home and under court supervision. Twenty-five percent of all amounts collected pursuant to an order entered under this subsection shall be credited to the appropriate fund of the county to offset the administrative cost of collections. The balance of all amounts collected pursuant to an order entered under this subsection shall be divided in the same ratio in which the county, state, and federal government participate in the cost of care outside the juvenile's own home and under county, state, or court supervision. The court may also collect benefits paid by the government of the United States for the cost of care of the juvenile. Money collected for juveniles placed with or committed to the family independence agency or a county juvenile agency shall be accounted for and reported on an individual basis. In cases of delinquent accounts, the court may also enter an order to intercept state tax refunds or the federal income tax refund of a child, parent, guardian, or custodian and initiate the necessary offset proceedings in order to recover the cost of care or service. The court shall send to the person who is the subject of the intercept order advance written notice of the proposed offset. The notice shall include notice of the opportunity to contest the offset on the grounds that the intercept is not proper because of a mistake of fact concerning the amount of the delinquency or the identity of the person subject to the order. The court shall provide for the prompt reimbursement of an amount withheld in error or an amount found to exceed the delinquent amount.

(8) If the court appoints an attorney to represent a juvenile, an order entered under this section may require the juvenile or person responsible for the juvenile's support, or both, to reimburse the court for attorney fees.

(9) An order directed to a person responsible for the juvenile's support under this section is not binding on the person unless an opportunity for a hearing has been given and until a copy of the order is served on the person, personally or by first-class mail to the person's last known address.

(10) If a juvenile is placed on probation and committed under subsection (3) or (4) to an institution or agency described in the youth rehabilitation services act, 1974 PA 150, MCL 803.301 to 803.309, the court shall retain jurisdiction over the juvenile while the juvenile is on probation and committed to that institution or agency.

(11) If the court has retained jurisdiction over a juvenile under subsection (10), the court shall conduct an annual review of the services being provided to the juvenile, the juvenile's placement, and the juvenile's progress in that placement. In conducting this review, the court shall examine the juvenile's annual report prepared under section 3 of the juvenile facilities act, 1988 PA 73, MCL 803.223. The court may order changes in the juvenile's placement or treatment plan including, but not limited to, committing the juvenile to the jurisdiction of the department of corrections, based on the review.

(12) If an individual who is under the court's jurisdiction under section 4 of chapter XIIA of the probate code of 1939, 1939 PA 288, MCL 712A.4, is convicted of a violation or conspiracy to commit a violation of section 7403(2)(a)(*i*) of the public health code, 1978 PA 368, MCL 333.7403, the court shall determine whether the best interests of the public would be served by imposing the sentence provided by law for an adult offender or by imposing a sentence of imprisonment for any term of years but not less than 25 years. If the court determines by clear and convincing evidence that the best interests of the public would be served by imposing a sentence of imprisonment for any term of years but not less than 25 years, the court may impose that sentence. In making its determination, the court shall use the criteria specified in subsection (3) to the extent they apply.

(13) If the defendant is sentenced for an offense other than a listed offense as defined in section 2(d)(*i*) to (*ix*) and (*xi*) to (*xiii*) of the sex offenders registration act, 1994 PA 295, MCL 28.722, the court shall determine if the offense is a violation of a law of this state or a local ordinance of a municipality of this state that by its nature constitutes a sexual offense against an individual who is less than 18 years of age. If so, the conviction is for a listed offense as defined in section 2(d)(*x*) of the sex offenders registration act, 1994 PA 295, MCL 28.722, and the court shall include the basis for that determination on the record and include the determination in the judgment of sentence.

(14) When sentencing a person convicted of a misdemeanor involving the illegal delivery, possession, or use of alcohol or a controlled substance or a felony, the court shall examine the presentence investigation report and determine if the person being sentenced is licensed or registered under article 15 of the public health code, 1978 PA 368, MCL 333.16101 to 333.18838. The court shall also examine the court file and determine if a report of the conviction upon which the person is being sentenced has been forwarded to the department of consumer and industry services as provided in section 16a. If the report has not been forwarded to the department of consumer and industry services, the court shall order the clerk of the court to immediately prepare and forward the report as provided in section 16a.

History: 1927, Act 175, Eff. Sept. 5, 1927;—CL 1929, 17329;—CL 1948, 769.1;—Am. 1980, Act 506, Imd. Eff. Jan. 22, 1981;—Am. 1986, Act 232, Eff. June 1, 1987;—Am. 1988, Act 78, Eff. Oct. 1, 1988;—Am. 1989, Act 113, Imd. Eff. June 23, 1989;—Am. 1993, Act 85, Eff. Apr. 1, 1994;—Am. 1996, Act 247, Eff. Jan. 1, 1997;—Am. 1996, Act 248, Eff. Jan. 1, 1997;—Am. 1998, Act 520, Imd. Eff. Jan. 12, 1999;—Am. 1999, Act 87, Eff. Sept. 1, 1999.

Compiler's note: Section 3 of Act 78 of 1988 provides: "This amendatory act shall take effect June 1, 1988." This section was amended by Act 181 of 1988 to read as follows: "This amendatory act shall take effect October 1, 1988."

Former law: See section 3 of Act 162 of 1850, being CL 1857, § 6113; CL 1871, § 7997; How., § 9613; CL 1897, § 11983; CL 1915, § 15856; and Act 166 of 1851.

CHAPTER XVI
MISCELLANEOUS PROVISIONS

776.20 Firearms violations; burden of establishing exception.

Sec. 20. In any prosecution for the violation of any acts of the state relative to use, licensing and possession of pistols or firearms, the burden of establishing any exception, excuse, proviso or exemption contained in any such act shall be upon the defendant but this does not shift the burden of proof for the violation.

History: Add. 1968, Act 299, Eff. Nov. 15, 1968.

CHAPTER XVII
SENTENCING GUIDELINES

PART 2
INCLUDED FELONIES

777.11b Applicability of chapter to certain felonies; MCL 28.214(6)(b) to 28.754(1).

Sec. 11b. This chapter applies to the following felonies enumerated in chapter 28 of the Michigan Compiled Laws:

M.C.L.	Category	Class	Description	Stat Max
28.214(6)(b)	Pub trst	F	Unauthorized disclosure of information from LEIN — subsequent offense	4
28.293(1)	Pub ord	E	False information when applying for state ID	5

28.293(2)	Pub ord	D	False information when applying for state ID — second offense	7
28.293(3)	Pub ord	C	False information when applying for state ID — third or subsequent offense	15
28.295(1)(a)	Pub ord	D	Counterfeiting or forging state ID card or using counterfeited or forged state ID card to commit felony punishable by imprisonment for 10 years or more	10
28.295(1)(b)	Pub ord	E	Counterfeiting or forging state ID card or using counterfeited or forged state ID card to commit felony punishable by imprisonment for less than 10 years or a misdemeanor punishable by more than 6 months	5
28.295(2)	Pub ord	E	Selling counterfeited or forged state ID card or possessing counterfeited or forged state ID card with intent to deliver to another person or possessing 2 or more counterfeited or forged state ID cards	5
28.295(5)	Property	H	Using stolen state ID card to commit felony	Variable
28.295a(1)	Pub ord	H	False representation to obtain or misuse personal information	4
28.295a(2)	Pub ord	G	False representation to obtain or misuse personal information — second offense	7
28.295a(3)	Pub ord	C	False representation to obtain or misuse personal information — third or subsequent offense	15
28.308	Pub saf	E	False certification or statement in application for enhanced driver license or enhanced official state personal identification card	5
28.422(14)	Pub saf	F	Forgery on pistol license application	4
28.422a(5)	Pub saf	F	False statement on pistol sales record	4
28.425b(3)	Pub saf	F	False statement on concealed pistol permit application	4
28.425j(3)	Pub saf	F	Unlawful granting or presenting of pistol training certificate	4
28.425o(6)(c)	Pub saf	F	Carrying concealed pistol or electro-muscular disruption device in prohibited place — third or subsequent offense	4
28.435(14)(c)	Pub saf	G	Firearm sale without trigger lock, gun case, or storage container — third or subsequent offense	2
28.454(1)	Pub saf	G	Consumer fireworks certificate violation	2
28.468(1)(c)	Pub saf	E	Michigan fireworks safety act violation causing serious impairment	5
28.468(1)(d)	Pub saf	C	Michigan fireworks safety act violation causing death	15
28.516(2)	Pub saf	F	False statement on concealed firearm certificate application	4
28.674	Pub saf	F	False report of a public threat	4
28.729(1)(a)	Pub ord	F	Failure to register as a sex offender, first offense	4
28.729(1)(b)	Pub ord	D	Failure to register as a sex offender, second offense	7
28.729(1)(c)	Pub ord	D	Failure to register as a sex offender, third or subsequent offense	10
28.729(2)	Pub ord	F	Failure to update sex offender registration information	2
28.734(2)(b)	Pub trst	G	Student safety zone violation involving work or loitering — subsequent offense	2
28.735(2)(b)	Pub trst	G	Student safety zone violation involving residency — subsequent offense	2
28.754(1)	Pub ord	F	False report of a child abduction	4

History: Add. 2002, Act 31, Eff. Apr. 1, 2002;—Am. 2004, Act 150, Eff. Sept. 1, 2004;—Am. 2005, Act 122, Eff. Jan. 1, 2006;—Am. 2005, Act 139, Eff. Jan. 1, 2006;—Am. 2005, Act 207, Eff. Feb. 1, 2006;—Am. 2008, Act 24, Imd. Eff. Mar. 13, 2008;—Am. 2008, Act 538, Eff. Mar. 31, 2009;—Am. 2011, Act 19, Eff. July 1, 2011;—Am. 2011, Act 257, Imd. Eff. Dec. 14, 2011;—Am. 2012, Act 124, Eff. Aug. 6, 2012;—Am. 2015, Act 4, Eff. Oct. 1, 2015;—Am. 2015, Act 201, Eff. Feb. 22, 2016;—Am. 2016, Act 234, Eff. Sept. 22, 2016.

777.12k Chapters 258 to 260; felonies.

Sec. 12k. This chapter applies to the following felonies enumerated in chapters 258 to 260 of the Michigan Compiled Laws:

M.C.L.	Category	Class	Description	Stat Max
259.80f(3)	Pub saf	D	Possessing weapon in sterile area of commercial airport	10
259.83(2)(b)	Pub saf	G	Aircraft — failure to comply with certification requirements — second violation	2
259.83(2)(c)	Pub saf	F	Aircraft — failure to comply with certification requirements — third or subsequent violation	4
259.83b(2)(a)	Pub saf	F	Conducting flight operations without certificate	4
259.83b(2)(b)	Pub saf	E	Conducting flight operations without certificate — second violation	5
259.83b(2)(c)	Pub saf	D	Conducting flight operations without certificate — third or subsequent violation	10
259.183	Property	E	Aircraft — unlawful taking or tampering	5
259.185(4)	Person	C	Operating or serving as crew of aircraft while under the influence causing death	15
259.185(5)	Person	E	Operating or serving as crew of aircraft while under the influence causing serious impairment	5
259.185(8)	Pub saf	E	Operating or serving as crew of aircraft while under the influence — third or subsequent offense	5

History: Add. 2002, Act 34, Eff. Apr. 1, 2002.

777.13m Applicability of chapter to certain felonies; MCL 333.7340 to 333.7417.

Sec. 13m. This chapter applies to the following felonies enumerated in chapter 333 of the Michigan Compiled Laws:

M.C.L.	Category	Class	Description	Stat Max
333.7340	CS	F	Sale, distribution, or delivery of product containing ephedrine or pseudoephedrine by mail, internet, or telephone	4
333.7340c(2)	CS	D	Soliciting another person to purchase or obtain ephedrine or pseudoephedrine to manufacture methamphetamine	10
333.7341(8)	CS	G	Delivery or manufacture of imitation controlled substance	2
333.7401(2)(a)(*i*)	CS	A	Delivery or manufacture of 1,000 or more grams of certain schedule 1 or 2 controlled substances	Life
333.7401(2)(a)(*ii*)	CS	A	Delivery or manufacture of 450 or more but less than 1,000 grams of certain schedule 1 or 2 controlled substances	30
333.7401(2)(a)(*iii*)	CS	B	Delivery or manufacture of 50 or more but less than 450 grams of certain schedule 1 or 2 controlled substances	20
333.7401(2)(a)(*iv*)	CS	D	Delivery or manufacture of less than 50 grams of certain schedule 1 or 2 controlled substances	20
333.7401(2)(b)(*i*)	CS	B	Delivery or manufacture of methamphetamine or 3, 4-methylenedioxymethamphetamine	20
333.7401(2)(b)(*ii*)	CS	E	Delivery or manufacture of certain schedule 1, 2, or 3 controlled substances	7

333.7401(2)(c)	CS	F	Delivery or manufacture of schedule 4 controlled substance	4
333.7401(2)(d)(*i*)	CS	C	Delivery or manufacture of 45 or more kilograms of marihuana or synthetic equivalents of marihuana	15
333.7401(2)(d)(*ii*)	CS	D	Delivery or manufacture of 5 or more but less than 45 kilograms of marihuana or synthetic equivalents of marihuana	7
333.7401(2)(d)(*iii*)	CS	F	Delivery or manufacture of less than 5 kilograms or 20 plants of marihuana or synthetic equivalents of marihuana	4
333.7401(2)(e)	CS	G	Delivery or manufacture of schedule 5 controlled substance	2
333.7401(2)(f)	CS	D	Delivery or manufacture of a prescription form or counterfeit prescription form	7
333.7401a	Person	B	Delivering a controlled substance or GBL with intent to commit criminal sexual conduct	20
333.7401b(3)(a)	CS	E	Delivery or manufacture of GBL	7
333.7401b(3)(b)	CS	G	Possession of GBL	2
333.7401c(2)(a)	CS	D	Operating or maintaining controlled substance laboratory	10
333.7401c(2)(b)	CS	B	Operating or maintaining controlled substance laboratory in presence of minor	20
333.7401c(2)(c)	CS	B	Operating or maintaining controlled substance laboratory involving hazardous waste	20
333.7401c(2)(d)	CS	B	Operating or maintaining controlled substance laboratory near certain places	20
333.7401c(2)(e)	CS	A	Operating or maintaining controlled substance laboratory involving firearm or other harmful device	25
333.7401c(2)(f)	CS	B	Operating or maintaining controlled substance laboratory involving methamphetamine	20
333.7402(2)(a)	CS	D	Delivery or manufacture of certain counterfeit controlled substances	10
333.7402(2)(b)	CS	E	Delivery or manufacture of schedule 1, 2, or 3 counterfeit controlled substance	5
333.7402(2)(c)	CS	F	Delivery or manufacture of counterfeit schedule 4 controlled substance	4
333.7402(2)(d)	CS	G	Delivery or manufacture of counterfeit schedule 5 controlled substance	2
333.7402(2)(e)	CS	C	Delivery or manufacture of controlled substance analogue	15
333.7403(2)(a)(*i*)	CS	A	Possession of 1,000 or more grams of certain schedule 1 or 2 controlled substances	Life
333.7403(2)(a)(*ii*)	CS	A	Possession of 450 or more but less than 1,000 grams of certain schedule 1 or 2 controlled substances	30
333.7403(2)(a)(*iii*)	CS	B	Possession of 50 or more but less than 450 grams of certain schedule 1 or 2 controlled substances	20
333.7403(2)(a)(*iv*)	CS	G	Possession of 25 or more but less than 50 grams of certain schedule 1 or 2 controlled substances	4
333.7403(2)(a)(*v*)	CS	G	Possession of less than 25 grams of certain schedule 1 or 2 controlled substances	4
333.7403(2)(b)(*i*)	CS	D	Possession of methamphetamine or 3, 4-methylenedioxymethamphetamine	10
333.7403(2)(b)(*ii*)	CS	G	Possession of certain schedule 1, 2, 3, or 4 controlled substances or controlled substances analogue	2

333.7403a	CS	F	Fraudulently obtaining controlled substance or prescription for controlled substance	4
333.7405(1)(a)	CS	G	Controlled substance violations by licensee	2
333.7405(1)(b)	CS	G	Manufacturing or distribution violations by licensee	2
333.7405(1)(c)	CS	G	Refusing lawful inspection	2
333.7405(1)(d)	CS	G	Maintaining drug house	2
333.7405(1)(e)	CS	G	Unlawfully dispensing out-of-state prescription	2
333.7407(1)(a)	CS	G	Controlled substance violations by licensee	4
333.7407(1)(b)	CS	G	Use of fictitious, revoked, or suspended license number	4
333.7407(1)(c)	CS	G	Obtaining controlled substance by fraud	4
333.7407(1)(d)	CS	G	False reports under controlled substance article	4
333.7407(1)(e)	CS	G	Possession of counterfeiting implements	4
333.7407(1)(f)	CS	F	Disclosing or obtaining prescription information	4
333.7407(1)(g)	CS	F	Possession of counterfeit prescription form	4
333.7407(2)	CS	G	Refusing to furnish records under controlled substance article	4
333.7410a	CS	G	Controlled substance offense or offense involving GBL in or near a park	2
333.7417	CS	F	Sell or offer to sell named product producing same or similar effect as scheduled ingredient	4

History: Add. 2002, Act 30, Eff. Apr. 1, 2002;—Am. 2002, Act 666, Eff. Mar. 1, 2003;—Am. 2002, Act 711, Eff. Apr. 1, 2003;—Am. 2003, Act 311, Eff. Apr. 1, 2004;—Am. 2006, Act 259, Eff. Oct. 1, 2006;—Am. 2010, Act 170, Eff. Oct. 1, 2010;—Am. 2010, Act 355, Imd. Eff. Dec. 22, 2010;—Am. 2013, Act 124, Imd. Eff. Oct. 1, 2013;—Am. 2014, Act 218, Eff. Jan. 1, 2015;—Am. 2016, Act 126, Eff. Aug. 23, 2016;—Am. 2016, Act 549, Eff. Apr. 10, 2017.

777.16d MCL 750.81(5) to 750.91; felonies to which chapter applicable.

Sec. 16d. This chapter applies to the following felonies enumerated in chapter 750 of the Michigan Compiled Laws:

M.C.L.	Category	Class	Description	Stat Max
750.81(5)	Person	E	Domestic assault or assault of a pregnant individual with prior convictions	5
750.81a(3)	Person	E	Aggravated domestic assault with prior convictions	5
750.81d(1)	Person	G	Assaulting, resisting, or obstructing certain persons	2
750.81d(2)	Person	F	Assaulting, resisting, or obstructing certain persons causing injury	4
750.81d(3)	Person	C	Assaulting, resisting, or obstructing certain persons causing serious impairment	15
750.81d(4)	Person	B	Assaulting, resisting, or obstructing certain persons causing death	20
750.81e(2)	Person	G	Assault on utility worker causing bodily injury requiring medical attention	2
750.81e(3)	Person	E	Assault on utility worker causing serious impairment of a body function	5
750.82(1)	Person	F	Felonious assault	4
750.82(2)	Person	F	Felonious assault — weapon-free school zone	4
750.83	Person	A	Assault with intent to murder	Life
750.84(1)(a)	Person	D	Assault with intent to do great bodily harm less than murder	10
750.84(1)(b)	Person	D	Assault by strangulation or suffocation	10
750.85	Person	A	Torture	Life
750.86	Person	D	Assault with intent to maim	10
750.87	Person	D	Assault with intent to commit a felony	10
750.88	Person	C	Assault with intent to commit unarmed robbery	15
750.89	Person	A	Assault with intent to commit armed robbery	Life

750.90	Person	D	Sexual intercourse under pretext of medical treatment	10
750.90a	Person	A	Assault against a pregnant individual causing miscarriage, stillbirth, or death to embryo or fetus with intent or recklessness	Life
750.90b(a)	Person	C	Assault against a pregnant individual resulting in miscarriage, stillbirth, or death to embryo or fetus	15
750.90b(b)	Person	D	Assault against a pregnant individual resulting in great bodily harm to embryo or fetus	10
750.90c(a)	Person	C	Gross negligence against a pregnant individual resulting in miscarriage, stillbirth, or death to embryo or fetus	15
750.90c(b)	Person	E	Gross negligence against a pregnant individual resulting in great bodily harm to embryo or fetus	5
750.90d(a)	Person	C	Operating a vehicle under the influence or while impaired causing miscarriage, stillbirth, or death to embryo or fetus	15
750.90d(b)	Person	E	Operating a vehicle under the influence or while impaired causing serious or aggravated injury to embryo or fetus	5
750.90e	Person	G	Careless or reckless driving causing miscarriage, stillbirth, or death to embryo or fetus	2
750.90g(3)	Person	A	Performance of procedure on live infant with intent to cause death	Life
750.90h	Person	G	Performing or assisting in performance of partial-birth abortion	2
750.91	Person	A	Attempted murder	Life

History: Add. 1998, Act 317, Eff. Dec. 15, 1998;—Am. 1999, Act 192, Eff. Mar. 10, 2000;—Am. 2000, Act 279, Eff. Oct. 1, 2000;—Am. 2001, Act 2, Eff. June 1, 2001;—Am. 2001, Act 20, Eff. Sept. 1, 2001;—Am. 2002, Act 269, Eff. July 15, 2002;—Am. 2005, Act 336, Eff. Mar. 1, 2006;—Am. 2010, Act 132, Imd. Eff. July 21, 2010;—Am. 2011, Act 169, Eff. Jan. 1, 2012;—Am. 2012, Act 365, Eff. Apr. 1, 2013;—Am. 2016, Act 88, Eff. July 25, 2016.

777.16m MCL 750.223(2) to 750.237(4); felonies to which chapter applicable.

Sec. 16m. This chapter applies to the following felonies enumerated in chapter 750 of the Michigan Compiled Laws:

M.C.L.	Category	Class	Description	Stat Max
750.223(2)	Pub saf	F	Sale of firearm to minor — subsequent offense	4
750.223(3)	Pub ord	D	Sale of firearm to person prohibited from possessing	10
750.224	Pub saf	E	Manufacture or sale of silencer, bomb, blackjack, automatic weapon, gas spray, etc.	5
750.224a(4)	Pub saf	F	Possession or sale of electrical current weapons	4
750.224a(6)	Pub saf	G	Improper use of electro-muscular disruption device	2
750.224b	Pub saf	E	Possession of short barreled shotgun or rifle	5
750.224c	Pub saf	F	Armor piercing ammunition	4
750.224d(2)	Person	G	Using self-defense spray device	2
750.224e	Pub saf	F	Manufacture/sale/possession of devices to convert semiautomatic weapons	4
750.224f(5)	Pub saf	E	Possession or sale of firearm by felon	5
750.224f(6)	Pub saf	E	Possession or sale of ammunition by felon	5
750.226	Pub saf	E	Carrying firearm or dangerous weapon with unlawful intent	5
750.227	Pub saf	E	Carrying a concealed weapon	5
750.227a	Pub saf	F	Unlawful possession of pistol	4
750.227c	Pub saf	G	Possessing a loaded firearm in or upon a vehicle	2
750.227f	Pub saf	F	Wearing body armor during commission of certain crimes	4

750.227g(1)	Pub saf	F	Felon purchasing, owning, possessing, or using body armor	4
750.230	Pub saf	G	Altering ID mark on firearm	2
750.232a(3)	Pub saf	G	False statement in a pistol application	4
750.234a(1)(a)	Pub saf	D	Discharging firearm from vehicle	10
750.234a(1)(b)	Person	C	Discharging firearm from vehicle causing physical injury	15
750.234a(1)(c)	Person	B	Discharging firearm from vehicle causing serious impairment	20
750.234a(1)(d)	Person	A	Discharging firearm from vehicle causing death	Life
750.234b(1)	Pub saf	D	Discharging firearm at a dwelling or potentially occupied structure	10
750.234b(2)	Pub saf	D	Discharging firearm in a dwelling or potentially occupied structure	10
750.234b(3)	Pub saf	C	Discharging firearm in or at a dwelling or potentially occupied structure causing physical injury	15
750.234b(4)	Person	B	Discharging firearm in or at a dwelling or potentially occupied structure causing serious impairment	20
750.234b(5)	Person	A	Discharging firearm in or at a dwelling or potentially occupied structure causing death	Life
750.234c	Pub saf	F	Discharging firearm at emergency/police vehicle	4
750.236	Person	C	Setting spring gun — death resulting	15
750.237(3)	Person	E	Using firearm while under the influence or impaired causing serious impairment	5
750.237(4)	Person	C	Using firearm while under the influence or impaired causing death	15

History: Add. 1998, Act 317, Eff. Dec. 15, 1998;—Am. 2000, Act 225, Eff. Oct. 1, 2000;—Am. 2000, Act 279, Eff. Oct. 1, 2000;—Am. 2001, Act 166, Eff. Feb. 1, 2002;—Am. 2005, Act 106, Imd. Eff. Sept. 14, 2005;—Am. 2012, Act 124, Eff. Aug. 6, 2012;—Am. 2014, Act 5, Eff. May 12, 2014;—Am. 2014, Act 192, Eff. Sept. 22, 2014.

777.16p MCL 750.317 to 750.329a; felonies to which chapter applicable.

Sec. 16p. This chapter applies to the following felonies enumerated in chapter 750 of the Michigan Compiled Laws:

M.C.L.	Category	Class	Description	Stat Max
750.317	Person	M2	Second degree murder	Life
750.317a	Person	A	Delivery of controlled substance causing death	Life
750.321	Person	C	Manslaughter	15
750.322	Person	C	Willful killing of unborn quick child	15
750.323	Person	C	Abortion resulting in death	15
750.327	Person	A	Death by explosives on vehicle or vessel	Life
750.328	Person	A	Death by explosives in or near building	Life
750.329	Person	C	Homicide — weapon aimed with intent but not malice	15
750.329a	Person	E	Assisting a suicide	5

History: Add. 1998, Act 317, Eff. Dec. 15, 1998;—Am. 2000, Act 279, Eff. Oct. 1, 2000;—Am. 2005, Act 168, Eff. Jan. 1, 2006;—Am. 2008, Act 467, Eff. Oct. 31, 2010.

777.16r MCL 750.356(2) to 750.374; felonies to which chapter applicable.

Sec. 16r. This chapter applies to the following felonies enumerated in chapter 750 of the Michigan Compiled Laws:

M.C.L.	Category	Class	Description	Stat Max
750.356(2)	Property	D	Larceny involving $20,000 or more or with prior convictions	10

750.356(3)	Property	E	Larceny involving $1,000 to $20,000 or with prior convictions	5
750.356a(1)	Property	G	Larceny from a motor vehicle	5
750.356a(2)(c)	Property	E	Breaking and entering a vehicle to steal $1,000 to $20,000 or with prior convictions	5
750.356a(2)(d)	Property	D	Breaking and entering a vehicle to steal $20,000 or more or with prior convictions	10
750.356a(3)	Property	G	Breaking and entering a vehicle to steal causing damage	5
750.356b	Property	G	Breaking and entering a coin telephone	4
750.356c	Property	E	Retail fraud — first degree	5
750.357	Person	D	Larceny from the person	10
750.357a	Property	G	Larceny of livestock	4
750.357b	Property	E	Larceny — stealing firearms of another	5
750.358	Property	G	Larceny from burning building	5
750.36	Property	G	Larceny in a building	4
750.360a(2)(b)	Property	F	Theft detection device offense with prior conviction	4
750.361	Property	H	Trains — stealing/maliciously removing parts	2
750.362	Property	E	Larceny by conversion involving $1,000 to $20,000 or with prior convictions	5
	Property	D	Larceny by conversion involving $20,000 or more or with prior convictions	10
750.362a(2)	Property	D	Larceny of rental property involving $20,000 or more or with prior convictions	10
750.362a(3)	Property	E	Larceny of rental property involving $1,000 to $20,000 or with prior convictions	5
750.363	Property	E	Larceny by false personation involving $1,000 to $20,000 or with prior convictions	5
	Property	D	Larceny by false personation involving $20,000 or more	10
750.365	Person	D	Larceny from car or persons detained or injured by accident	20
750.367	Property	E	Larceny of trees or shrubs involving $1,000 to $20,000 or with prior convictions	5
	Property	D	Larceny of a tree or shrub involving $20,000 or more or with prior convictions	10
750.367b	Property	E	Airplanes — taking possession	5
750.368(5)	Pub ord	G	Preparing, serving, or executing unauthorized process — third or subsequent offense	4
750.372	Pub ord	H	Running or allowing lottery	2
750.373	Pub ord	H	Selling or possessing lottery tickets	2
750.374	Pub ord	H	Lottery violations — subsequent offense	4

History: Add. 1998, Act 317, Eff. Dec. 15, 1998;—Am. 2000, Act 279, Eff. Oct. 1, 2000;—Am. 2002, Act 102, Eff. July 1, 2002;—Am. 2002, Act 279, Imd. Eff. May 9, 2002.

777.16x MCL 750.478a(2) to 750.512; felonies to which chapter applicable.

Sec. 16x. This chapter applies to the following felonies enumerated in chapter 750 of the Michigan Compiled Laws:

M.C.L.	Category	Class	Description	Stat Max
750.478a(2)	Pub ord	H	Unauthorized process to obstruct a public officer or employee	2
750.478a(3)	Pub ord	G	Unauthorized process to obstruct a public officer or employee — subsequent offense	4
750.479(2)	Person	G	Assaulting or obstructing certain officials	2

750.479(3)	Person	G	Assaulting or obstructing certain officials causing injury	4
750.479(4)	Person	D	Assaulting or obstructing certain officials causing serious impairment	10
750.479(5)	Person	B	Assaulting or obstructing certain officials causing death	20
750.479a(2)	Pub saf	G	Fleeing and eluding — fourth degree	2
750.479a(3)	Pub saf	E	Fleeing and eluding — third degree	5
750.479a(4)	Person	C	Fleeing and eluding — second degree	10
750.479a(5)	Person	B	Fleeing and eluding — first degree	15
750.479b(1)	Person	F	Disarming peace officer — nonfirearm	4
750.479b(2)	Person	D	Disarming peace officer — firearm	10
750.479c(2)(c)	Pub ord	G	Providing false information to peace officer conducting criminal investigation	2
750.479c(2)(d)	Pub ord	F	Providing false or misleading information to peace officer conducting criminal investigation regarding certain felonies	4
750.48	Pub trst	F	Public officers — refusing to turn over books/money to successor	4
750.483a(2)(b)	Person	D	Withholding evidence, preventing report of crime, or retaliating for reporting crime punishable by more than 10 years	10
750.483a(4)(b)	Person	D	Interfering with police investigation by committing crime or threatening to kill or injure	10
750.483a(6)(a)	Pub ord	F	Tampering with evidence or offering false evidence	4
750.483a(6)(b)	Pub ord	D	Tampering with evidence or offering false evidence in case punishable by more than 10 years	10
750.488	Pub trst	H	Public officers — state official — retaining fees	2
750.49	Pub trst	H	Public money — safekeeping	2
750.491	Pub trst	H	Public records — removal/mutilation/destruction	2
750.492a(1)(a)	Pub trst	G	Medical record — intentional place false information — health care provider	4
750.492a(2)	Pub trst	G	Medical record — health care provider — altering to conceal injury/death	4
750.495a(2)	Person	F	Concealing objects in trees or wood products — causing injury	4
750.495a(3)	Person	C	Concealing objects in trees or wood products — causing death	15
750.498b(2)(a)	Person	E	Tampering with, taking, or removing marine safety device without authority causing serious impairment	5
750.498b(2)(b)	Person	C	Tampering with, taking, or removing marine safety device without authority causing death	15
750.502d	Pub saf	F	Unlawfully possessing or transporting anhydrous ammonia or tampering with containers	4
750.505	Pub ord	E	Common law offenses	5
750.508(2)(b)	Pub ord	G	Carrying or possessing a scanner in the commission of a crime	2
750.511	Person	A	Blocking or wrecking railroad track	Life
750.512	Property	E	Uncoupling railroad cars	10

History: Add. 1998, Act 317, Eff. Dec. 15, 1998;—Am. 2000, Act 279, Eff. Oct. 1, 2000;—Am. 2000, Act 473, Eff. Mar. 28, 2001;—Am. 2002, Act 271, Eff. July 15, 2002;—Am. 2002, Act 320, Eff. July 15, 2002;—Am. 2003, Act 313, Eff. Apr. 1, 2004;—Am. 2006, Act 40, Imd. Eff. Mar. 2, 2006;—Am. 2006, Act 234, Eff. July 1, 2006; —Am. 2012, Act 105, Eff. July 20, 2012; —Am. 2012, Act 323, Eff. Jan. 1, 2013.

777.16y MCL 750.520b(2) to 750.532; felonies to which chapter applicable.

Sec. 16y. This chapter applies to the following felonies enumerated in chapter 750 of the Michigan Compiled Laws:

M.C.L.	Category	Class	Description	Stat Max
750.520b(2)	Person	A	First degree criminal sexual conduct	Life
750.520c	Person	C	Second degree criminal sexual conduct	15
750.520d	Person	B	Third degree criminal sexual conduct	15
750.520e	Person	G	Fourth degree criminal sexual conduct	2
750.520g(1)	Person	D	Assault with intent to commit sexual penetration	10
750.520g(2)	Person	E	Assault with intent to commit sexual contact	5
750.520n	Pub saf	G	Electronic monitoring device violation	2
750.528	Pub saf	F	Destroying dwelling house or other property during riot or unlawful assembly	4
750.528a	Pub saf	F	Civil disorders — firearms/explosives	4
750.529	Person	A	Armed robbery	Life
750.529a	Person	A	Carjacking	Life
750.530	Person	C	Unarmed robbery	15
750.531	Person	C	Bank robbery/safebreaking	Life
750.532	Person	H	Seduction	5

History: Add. 1998, Act 317, Eff. Dec. 15, 1998;—Am. 2000, Act 279, Eff. Oct. 1, 2000;—Am. 2005, Act 304, Eff. Apr. 15, 2006;—Am. 2006, Act 166, Eff. Aug. 28, 2006;—Am. 2006, Act 655, Imd. Eff. Jan. 9, 2007.

777.16z MCL 750.535(2) to 750.535b; felonies to which chapter applicable.

Sec. 16z. This chapter applies to the following felonies enumerated in chapter 750 of the Michigan Compiled Laws:

M.C.L.	Category	Class	Description	Stat Max
750.535(2)	Property	D	Receiving or concealing stolen property having a value of $20,000 or more or with prior convictions	10
750.535(3)	Property	E	Receiving or concealing stolen property having a value of $1,000 to $20,000 or with prior convictions	5
750.535(7)	Property	E	Receiving or concealing stolen motor vehicle	5
750.535(8)	Property	D	Receiving or concealing stolen motor vehicle — second or subsequent offense	10
750.535a(2)	Pub ord	D	Operating a chop shop	10
750.535a(3)	Pub ord	D	Operating a chop shop, subsequent violation	10
750.535b	Pub saf	E	Stolen firearms or ammunition	10

History: Add. 1998, Act 317, Eff. Dec. 15, 1998;—Am. 1999, Act 186, Eff. Apr. 1, 2000;—Am. 2000, Act 279, Eff. Oct. 1, 2000;—Am. 2002, Act 122, Eff. Apr. 22, 2002;—Am. 2002, Act 271, Imd. Eff. May 9, 2002;—Am. 2004, Act 2, Imd. Eff. Feb. 12, 2004;—Am. 2004, Act 157, Imd. Eff. June 16, 2004;—Am. 2006, Act 62, Eff. June 1, 2006;—Am. 2006, Act 655, Imd. Eff. Jan. 9, 2007;—Am. 2007, Act 20, Imd. Eff. June 19, 2007;—Am. 2014, Act 222, Eff. Mar. 31, 2015.

Compiler's note: Enacting section 1 of Act 20 of 2007 provides:

"Enacting section 1. The citation correction in section 16z of chapter XVII of the code of criminal procedure, 1927 PA 175, MCL 777.16z, changing the reference of 750.520b(2) to 750.535(2), applies retroactively to January 9, 2007."

777.17 Applicability of chapter to certain felonies; chapters 751 to 830.

Sec. 17. This chapter applies to the following felonies enumerated in chapters 751 to 830 of the Michigan Compiled Laws as set forth in sections 17a to 17g of this chapter.

History: Add. 1998, Act 317, Eff. Dec. 15, 1998;—Am. 1999, Act 67, Eff. Aug. 1, 1999;—Am. 2000, Act 178, Eff. Sept. 18, 2000;—Am. 2000, Act 279, Eff. Oct. 1, 2000;—Am. 2000, Act 300, Eff. Jan. 1, 2001;—Am. 2001, Act 136, Eff. Feb. 1, 2002;—Am. 2002, Act 28, Eff. Apr. 1, 2002.

777.17d Applicability of chapter to certain felonies; MCL 752.802 to 752.1084.

Sec. 17d. This chapter applies to the following felonies enumerated in chapter 752 of the Michigan Compiled Laws:

M.C.L.	Category	Class	Description	Stat Max
752.802	Property	H	Manufacture or sale of slugs for use in vending machines	5

752.811	Property	H	Breaking and entering a coin operated device	3
752.861	Person	G	Careless discharge of firearm causing injury or death	2
752.881	Person	G	Reckless use of bow and arrow resulting in injury or death	2
752.1003	Property	F	False claim, statement, or representation to obtain health care benefits	4
752.1004	Property	F	Soliciting, paying, or receiving kickback or receiving referral fee for health care payment	4
752.1005	Property	H	Conspiring to commit health care fraud	10
752.1006	Property	D	Health care fraud — subsequent offense	20
752.1054(2)	Property	G	Copying audio or video recordings for gain	5
752.1084	Property	E	Organized retail crime act violation	5

History: Add. 2002, Act 28, Eff. Apr. 1, 2002;—Am. 2012, Act 456, Eff. Mar. 31, 2013;—Am. 2013, Act 124, Imd. Eff. Oct. 1, 2013.

777.17g Applicability of chapter to certain felonies; MCL 800.281(1) to 801.263(2).

Sec. 17g. This chapter applies to the following felonies enumerated in chapters 800 to 830 of the Michigan Compiled Laws:

M.C.L.	Category	Class	Description	Stat Max
800.281(1)	Pub saf	H	Furnishing prisoner with contraband	5
800.281(2)	Pub saf	H	Furnishing prisoner with contraband outside	5
800.281(3)	Pub saf	H	Bringing contraband into prisons	5
800.281(4)	Pub saf	E	Prisoner possessing contraband	5
800.283(1)	Pub saf	E	Furnishing weapon to prisoner in prison	5
800.283(2)	Pub saf	E	Prisons — knowledge of a weapon in a correctional facility	5
800.283(3)	Pub saf	E	Bringing weapon into prison	5
800.283(4)	Pub saf	E	Prisoner possessing weapon	5
800.283a	Pub saf	E	Furnishing cell phone to prisoner	5
801.262(1)(a)	Pub saf	E	Bringing weapon into jail	5
801.262(1)(b)	Pub saf	E	Furnishing weapon to prisoner in jail	5
801.262(2)	Pub saf	E	Prisoner in jail possessing weapon	5
801.262a	Pub saf	E	Furnishing cell phone or other wireless device to prisoner in jail	5
801.263(1)	Pub saf	H	Furnishing contraband to prisoner in jail	5
801.263(2)	Pub saf	H	Prisoner in jail possessing contraband	5

History: Add. 2002, Act 28, Eff. Apr. 1, 2002;—Am. 2006, Act 541, Imd. Eff. Dec. 29, 2006;—Am. 2013, Act 124, Imd. Eff. Oct. 1, 2013.

777.18 MCL 333.7410 to 750.367a; felonies to which chapter applicable.

Sec. 18. This chapter applies to the following felonies:

M.C.L.	Category	Description	Stat Max
333.7410	CS	Controlled substance offense or offense involving GBL on or near school property or library	Variable
333.7413(2) or (3)	Pub trst	Subsequent controlled substance violations	Variable
333.7416(1)(a)	CS	Recruiting or inducing a minor to commit a controlled substance felony	Variable
750.157a(a)	Pub saf	Conspiracy	Variable
750.157c	Person	Inducing minor to commit a felony	Variable
750.188	Pub ord	Voluntarily suffering prisoner to	
750.237a	Pub saf	Felony committed in a weapon-free school zone	Variable
750.367a	Property	Larceny of rationed goods	Variable

History: Add. 1998, Act 317, Eff. Dec. 15, 1998;—Am. 2000, Act 279, Eff. Oct. 1, 2000;—Am. 2000, Act 304, Eff. Jan. 1, 2001;—Am. 2006, Act 553, Eff. Mar. 30, 2007.

PART 4
OFFENSE VARIABLES

777.31 Aggravated use of weapon; definitions.

Sec. 31. (1) Offense variable 1 is aggravated use of a weapon. Score offense variable 1 by determining which of the following apply and by assigning the number of points attributable to the one that has the highest number of points:

(a) A firearm was discharged at or toward a human being or a victim was cut or stabbed with a knife or other cutting or stabbing weapon .... 25 points

(b) The victim was subjected or exposed to a harmful biological substance, harmful biological device, harmful chemical substance, harmful chemical device, harmful radioactive material, harmful radioactive device, incendiary device, or explosive device .... 20 points

(c) A firearm was pointed at or toward a victim or the victim had a reasonable apprehension of an immediate battery when threatened with a knife or other cutting or stabbing weapon. .... 15 points

(d) The victim was touched by any other type of weapon .... 10 points

(e) A weapon was displayed or implied .... 5 points

(f) No aggravated use of a weapon occurred .... 0 points

(2) All of the following apply to scoring offense variable 1:

(a) Count each person who was placed in danger of injury or loss of life as a victim.

(b) In multiple offender cases, if 1 offender is assessed points for the presence or use of a weapon, all offenders shall be assessed the same number of points.

(c) Score 5 points if an offender used an object to suggest the presence of a weapon.

(d) Score 5 points if an offender used a chemical irritant, chemical irritant device, smoke device, or imitation harmful substance or device.

(e) Do not score 5 points if the conviction offense is a violation of section 82 or 529 of the Michigan penal code, 1931 PA 328, MCL 750.82 and 750.529.

(3) As used in this section:

(a) "Chemical irritant", "chemical irritant device", "harmful biological substance", "harmful biological device", "harmful chemical substance", "harmful chemical device", "harmful radioactive material", "harmful radioactive device", and "imitation harmful substance or device" mean those terms as defined in section 200h of the Michigan penal code, 1931 PA 328, MCL 750.200h.

(b) "Incendiary device" includes gasoline or any other flammable substance, a blowtorch, fire bomb, Molotov cocktail, or other similar device.

History: Add. 1998, Act 317, Eff. Dec. 15, 1998;—Am. 1999, Act 227, Imd. Eff. Dec. 28, 1999;—Am. 2001, Act 136, Imd. Eff. Oct. 23, 2001;—Am. 2002, Act 137, Eff. Apr. 22, 2002.

777.32 Lethal potential of weapon possessed or used.

Sec. 32. (1) Offense variable 2 is lethal potential of the weapon possessed or used. Score offense variable 2 by determining which of the following apply and by assigning the number of points attributable to the one that has the highest number of points:

(a) The offender possessed or used a harmful biological substance, harmful biological device, harmful chemical substance, harmful chemical device, harmful radioactive material, or harmful radioactive device........ 15 points

(b) The offender possessed or used an incendiary device, an explosive device, or a fully automatic weapon... 15 points

(c) The offender possessed or used a short-barreled rifle or a short-barreled shotgun .... 10 points

(d) The offender possessed or used a pistol, rifle, shotgun, or knife or other cutting or stabbing weapon .... 5 points

(e) The offender possessed or used any other potentially lethal weapon .... 1 point

(f) The offender possessed or used no weapon .... 0 points

(2) In multiple offender cases, if 1 offender is assessed points for possessing a weapon, all offenders shall be assessed the same number of points.

(3) As used in this section:

(a) "Harmful biological substance", "harmful biological device", "harmful chemical substance", "harmful chemical device", "harmful radioactive material", and "harmful radioactive device" mean those terms as defined in section 200h of the Michigan penal code, 1931 PA 328, MCL 750.200h.

(b) "Fully automatic weapon" means a firearm employing gas pressure or force of recoil or other means to eject an empty cartridge from the firearm after a shot, and to load and fire the next cartridge from the magazine, without renewed pressure on the trigger for each successive shot.

(c) "Pistol", "rifle", or "shotgun" includes a revolver, semi-automatic pistol, rifle, shotgun, combination rifle and shotgun, or other firearm manufactured in or after 1898 that fires fixed ammunition, but does not include a fully automatic weapon or short-barreled shotgun or short-barreled rifle.

(d) "Incendiary device" includes gasoline or any other flammable substance, a blowtorch, fire bomb, Molotov cocktail, or other similar device.

History: Add. 1998, Act 317, Eff. Dec. 15, 1998;—Am. 2001, Act 136, Imd. Eff. Oct. 23, 2001.

PART 5
PRIOR RECORD VARIABLES

777.55 Prior misdemeanor convictions or prior misdemeanor juvenile adjudications.

Sec. 55. (1) Prior record variable 5 is prior misdemeanor convictions or prior misdemeanor juvenile adjudications. Score prior record variable 5 by determining which of the following apply and by assigning the number of points attributable to the one that has the highest number of points:

(a) The offender has 7 or more prior misdemeanor convictions or prior misdemeanor juvenile adjudications.. 20 points

(b) The offender has 5 or 6 prior misdemeanor convictions or prior misdemeanor juvenile adjudications........ 15 points

(c) The offender has 3 or 4 prior misdemeanor convictions or prior misdemeanor juvenile adjudications........ 10 points

(d) The offender has 2 prior misdemeanor convictions or prior misdemeanor juvenile adjudications .... 5 points

(e) The offender has 1 prior misdemeanor conviction or prior misdemeanor juvenile adjudication.................. 2 points

(f) The offender has no prior misdemeanor convictions or prior misdemeanor juvenile adjudications............. 0 points

(2) All of the following apply to scoring record variable 5:

(a) Except as provided in subdivision (b), count a prior misdemeanor conviction or prior misdemeanor juvenile adjudication only if it is an offense against a person or property, a controlled substance offense, or a weapon offense. Do not count a prior conviction used to enhance the sentencing offense to a felony.

(b) Count all prior misdemeanor convictions and prior misdemeanor juvenile adjudications for operating or attempting to operate a vehicle, vessel, ORV, snowmobile, aircraft, or locomotive while under the influence of or impaired by alcohol, a controlled substance, or a combination of alcohol and a controlled substance. Do not count a prior conviction used to enhance the sentencing offense to a felony.

(3) As used in this section:

(a) "Prior misdemeanor conviction" means a conviction for a misdemeanor under a law of this state, a political subdivision of this state, another state, a political subdivision of another state, or the United States if the conviction was entered before the sentencing offense was committed.

(b) "Prior misdemeanor juvenile adjudication" means a juvenile adjudication for conduct that if committed by an adult would be a misdemeanor under a law of this state, a political subdivision of this state, another state, a political subdivision of another state, or the United States if the order of disposition was entered before the sentencing offense was committed.

History: Add. 1998, Act 317, Eff. Dec. 15, 1998;—Am. 2000, Act 279, Eff. Oct. 1, 2000.

777.57 Subsequent or concurrent felony convictions.

Sec. 57. (1) Prior record variable 7 is subsequent or concurrent felony convictions. Score prior record variable 7 by determining which of the following apply and by assigning the number of points attributable to the one that has the highest number of points:

(a) The offender has 2 or more subsequent or concurrent convictions.. 20 points

(b) The offender has 1 subsequent or concurrent conviction .... 10 points

(c) The offender has no subsequent or concurrent convictions... 0 points

(2) All of the following apply to scoring record variable 7:

(a) Score the appropriate point value if the offender was convicted of multiple felony counts or was convicted of a felony after the sentencing offense was committed.

(b) Do not score a felony firearm conviction in this variable.

(c) Do not score a concurrent felony conviction if a mandatory consecutive sentence or a consecutive sentence imposed under section 7401(3) of the public health code, 1978 PA 368, MCL 333.7401, will result from that conviction.

History: Add. 1998, Act 317, Eff. Dec. 15, 1998;—Am. 1999, Act 227, Imd. Eff. Dec. 28, 1999;—Am. 2002, Act 666, Eff. Mar. 1, 2003.

WILLIAM VAN REGENMORTER CRIME VICTIM'S RIGHTS ACT (EXCERPT)
Act 87 of 1985

AN ACT to establish the rights of victims of crime and juvenile offenses; to provide for certain procedures; to establish certain immunities and duties; to limit convicted criminals from deriving profit under certain circumstances; to prohibit certain conduct of employers or employers' agents toward victims; and to provide for penalties and remedies.

History: 1985, Act 87, Eff. Oct. 9, 1985;—Am. 1988, Act 22, Eff. June 1, 1988.

The People of the State of Michigan enact:

ARTICLE 1

780.754 Return of property to victim; retention of evidence.

Sec. 4. (1) The law enforcement agency having responsibility for investigating a reported crime shall promptly return to the victim property belonging to that victim which is taken in the course of the investigation, except as provided in subsections (2) to (4).

(2) The agency shall not return property which is contraband.

(3) The agency shall not return property if the ownership of the property is disputed until the dispute is resolved.

(4) The agency shall retain as evidence any weapon used in the commission of the crime and any other evidence if the prosecuting attorney certifies that there is a need to retain that evidence in lieu of a photograph or other means of memorializing its possession by the agency.

History: 1985, Act 87, Eff. Oct. 9, 1985.

ARTICLE 2

780.781 Definitions; designation of person to act in place of victim; individual charged with offense arising out of same transaction; eligibility to exercise privileges and rights established for victims.

Sec. 31. (1) Except as otherwise defined in this article, as used in this article:

(a) "County juvenile agency" means that term as defined in section 2 of the county juvenile agency act, 1998 PA 518, MCL 45.622.

(b) "Court" means the family division of circuit court.

(c) "Crime victim services commission" means that term as described in section 2 of 1976 PA 223, MCL 18.352.

(d) "Designated case" means a case designated as a case in which the juvenile is to be tried in the same manner as an adult under section 2d of chapter XIIA of the probate code of 1939, 1939 PA 288, MCL 712A.2d.

(e) "Juvenile" means an individual alleged or found to be within the court's jurisdiction under section 2(a)(1) of chapter XIIA of the probate code of 1939, 1939 PA 288, MCL 712A.2, for an offense, including, but not limited to, an individual in a designated case.

(f) "Juvenile facility" means a county facility, an institution operated as an agency of the county or the court, or an institution or agency described in the youth rehabilitation services act, 1974 PA 150, MCL 803.301 to 803.309, to which a juvenile has been committed or in which a juvenile is detained.

(g) "Offense" means 1 or more of the following:

(*i*) A violation of a penal law of this state for which a juvenile offender, if convicted as an adult, may be punished by imprisonment for more than 1 year or an offense expressly designated by law as a felony.

(*ii*) A violation of section 81 (assault and battery, including domestic violence), 81a (assault; infliction of serious injury, including aggravated domestic violence), 115 (breaking and entering or illegal entry), 136b(7) (child abuse in the fourth degree), 145 (contributing to the neglect or delinquency of a minor), 145d (using the internet or a computer to make a prohibited communication), 233 (intentionally aiming a firearm without malice), 234 (discharge of a firearm intentionally aimed at a person), 235 (discharge of an intentionally aimed firearm resulting in injury), 335a (indecent exposure), or 411h (stalking) of the Michigan penal code, 1931 PA 328, MCL 750.81, 750.81a, 750.115, 750.136b, 750.145, 750.145d, 750.233, 750.234, 750.235, 750.335a, and 750.411h.

(*iii*) A violation of section 601b(2) (injuring a worker in a work zone) or 617a (leaving the scene of a personal injury accident) of the Michigan vehicle code, 1949 PA 300, MCL 257.601b and 257.617a, or a violation of section 625 (operating a vehicle while under the influence of or impaired by intoxicating liquor or a controlled substance, or with unlawful blood alcohol content) of that act, MCL 257.625, if the violation involves an accident resulting in damage to another individual's property or physical injury or death to another individual.

(*iv*) Selling or furnishing alcoholic liquor to an individual less than 21 years of age in violation of section 33 of the former 1933 (Ex Sess) PA 8, or section 701 of the Michigan liquor control code of 1998, 1998 PA 58, MCL 436.1701, if the violation results in physical injury or death to any individual.

(*v*) A violation of section 80176(1) or (3) (operating a vessel while under the influence of or impaired by intoxicating liquor or a controlled substance, or with unlawful blood alcohol content) of the natural resources and environmental protection act, 1994 PA 451, MCL 324.80176, if the violation involves an accident resulting in damage to another individual's property or physical injury or death to any individual.

(*vi*) A violation of a local ordinance substantially corresponding to a law enumerated in subparagraphs (*i*) to (*v*).

(*vii*) A violation described in subparagraphs (*i*) to (*vi*) that is subsequently reduced to a violation not included in subparagraphs (*i*) to (*vi*).

(h) "Person" means an individual, organization, partnership, corporation, or governmental entity.

(i) "Prosecuting attorney" means the prosecuting attorney for a county, an assistant prosecuting attorney for a county, the attorney general, the deputy attorney general, an assistant attorney general, a special prosecuting attorney, or, in connection with the prosecution of an ordinance violation, an attorney for the political subdivision that enacted the ordinance upon which the violation is based.

(j) "Victim" means any of the following:

(*i*) A person who suffers direct or threatened physical, financial, or emotional harm as a result of the commission of an offense, except as provided in subparagraph (*ii*), (*iii*), or (*iv*).

(*ii*) The following individuals other than the juvenile if the victim is deceased:

(A) The spouse of the deceased victim.

(B) A child of the deceased victim if the child is 18 years of age or older and sub-subparagraph (A) does not apply.

(C) A parent of a deceased victim if sub-subparagraphs (A) and (B) do not apply.

(D) The guardian or custodian of a child of a deceased victim if the child is less than 18 years of age and sub-subparagraphs (A) to (C) do not apply.

(E) A sibling of the deceased victim if sub-subparagraphs (A) to (D) do not apply.

(F) A grandparent of the deceased victim if sub-subparagraphs (A) to (E) do not apply.

(*iii*) A parent, guardian, or custodian of a victim who is less than 18 years of age and who is neither the defendant nor incarcerated, if the parent, guardian, or custodian so chooses. For the purpose of making an impact statement only, a parent, guardian, or custodian of a victim who is less than 18 years of age at the time of the commission of the crime and who is neither the defendant nor incarcerated, if the parent, guardian, or custodian so chooses.

(*iv*) A parent, guardian, or custodian of a victim who is mentally or emotionally unable to participate in the legal process if he or she is neither the defendant nor incarcerated.

(2) If a victim as defined in subsection (1)(j)(*i*) is physically or emotionally unable to exercise the privileges and rights under this article, the victim may designate his or her spouse, child 18 years of age or older, parent, sibling, grandparent, or any other person 18 years of age or older who is neither the defendant nor incarcerated to act in his or her place while the physical or emotional disability continues. The victim shall provide the prosecuting attorney with the name of the person who is to act in his or her place. During the physical or emotional disability, notices to be provided under this article to the victim shall continue to be sent only to the victim.

(3) An individual who is charged with an offense arising out of the same transaction from which the charge against the defendant arose is not eligible to exercise the privileges and rights established for victims under this article.

History: Add. 1988, Act 22, Eff. June 1, 1988;—Am. 1993, Act 341, Eff. May 1, 1994;—Am. 1996, Act 82, Imd. Eff. Feb. 27, 1996;—Am. 1998, Act 523, Imd. Eff. Jan. 12, 1999;—Am. 2000, Act 503, Eff. June 1, 2001;—Am. 2005, Act 184, Eff. Jan. 1, 2006;—Am. 2006, Act 461, Eff. Jan. 1, 2007;—Am. 2009, Act 28, Eff. July 1, 2009;—Am. 2014, Act 134, Eff. July 1, 2014.

Compiler's note: Enacting section 1 of Act 28 of 2009 provides:

"Enacting section 1. This amendatory act takes effect July 1, 2009, and applies only to crimes committed on and after that date."

ARTICLE 3

780.811 Definitions; physical or emotional inability of victim to exercise privileges and rights; ineligibility to exercise privileges and rights.

Sec. 61. (1) Except as otherwise defined in this article, as used in this article:

(a) "Serious misdemeanor" means 1 or more of the following:

(*i*) A violation of section 81 of the Michigan penal code, 1931 PA 328, MCL 750.81, assault and battery, including domestic violence.

(*ii*) A violation of section 81a of the Michigan penal code, 1931 PA 328, MCL 750.81a, assault; infliction of serious injury, including aggravated domestic violence.

(*iii*) A violation of section 115 of the Michigan penal code, 1931 PA 328, MCL 750.115, breaking and entering or illegal entry.

(*iv*) A violation of section 136b(7) of the Michigan penal code, 1931 PA 328, MCL 750.136b, child abuse in the fourth degree.

(*v*) A violation of section 145 of the Michigan penal code, 1931 PA 328, MCL 750.145, contributing to the neglect or delinquency of a minor.

(*vi*) A misdemeanor violation of section 145d of the Michigan penal code, 1931 PA 328, MCL 750.145d, using the internet or a computer to make a prohibited communication.

(*vii*) A violation of section 233 of the Michigan penal code, 1931 PA 328, MCL 750.233, intentionally aiming a firearm without malice.

(*viii*) A violation of section 234 of the Michigan penal code, 1931 PA 328, MCL 750.234, discharge of a firearm intentionally aimed at a person.

(*ix*) A violation of section 235 of the Michigan penal code, 1931 PA 328, MCL 750.235, discharge of an intentionally aimed firearm resulting in injury.

(*x*) A violation of section 335a of the Michigan penal code, 1931 PA 328, MCL 750.335a, indecent exposure.

(*xi*) A violation of section 411h of the Michigan penal code, 1931 PA 328, MCL 750.411h, stalking.

(*xii*) A violation of section 601b(2) of the Michigan vehicle code, 1949 PA 300, MCL 257.601b, injuring a worker in a work zone.

(*xiii*) A violation of section 617a of the Michigan vehicle code, 1949 PA 300, MCL 257.617a, leaving the scene of a personal injury accident.

(*xiv*) A violation of section 625 of the Michigan vehicle code, 1949 PA 300, MCL 257.625, operating a vehicle while under the influence of or impaired by intoxicating liquor or a controlled substance, or with an unlawful blood alcohol content, if the violation involves an accident resulting in damage to another individual's property or physical injury or death to another individual.

(*xv*) Selling or furnishing alcoholic liquor to an individual less than 21 years of age in violation of section 701 of the Michigan liquor control code of 1998, 1998 PA 58, MCL 436.1701, if the violation results in physical injury or death to any individual.

(*xvi*) A violation of section 80176(1) or (3) of the natural resources and environmental protection act, 1994 PA 451, MCL 324.80176, operating a vessel while under the influence of or impaired by intoxicating liquor or a controlled substance, or with an unlawful blood alcohol content, if the violation involves an accident resulting in damage to another individual's property or physical injury or death to any individual.

(*xvii*) A violation of a local ordinance substantially corresponding to a violation enumerated in subparagraphs (*i*) to (*xvi*).

(*xviii*) A violation charged as a crime or serious misdemeanor enumerated in subparagraphs (*i*) to (*xvii*) but subsequently reduced to or pleaded to as a misdemeanor. As used in this subparagraph, "crime" means that term as defined in section 2.

(b) "Crime victim services commission" means that term as described in section 2 of 1976 PA 223, MCL 18.352.

(c) "Defendant" means a person charged with or convicted of having committed a serious misdemeanor against a victim.

(d) "Final disposition" means the ultimate termination of the criminal prosecution of a defendant including, but not limited to, dismissal, acquittal, or imposition of a sentence by the court.

(e) "Person" means an individual, organization, partnership, corporation, or governmental entity.

(f) "Prisoner" means a person who has been convicted and sentenced to imprisonment for having committed a serious misdemeanor against a victim.

(g) "Prosecuting attorney" means the prosecuting attorney for a county, an assistant prosecuting attorney for a county, the attorney general, the deputy attorney general, an assistant attorney general, a special prosecuting attorney, or, in connection with the prosecution of an ordinance violation, an attorney for the political subdivision that enacted the ordinance upon which the violation is based.

(h) "Victim" means any of the following:

(*i*) An individual who suffers direct or threatened physical, financial, or emotional harm as a result of the commission of a serious misdemeanor, except as provided in subparagraph (*ii*), (*iii*), or (*iv*).

(*ii*) The following individuals other than the defendant if the victim is deceased:

(A) The spouse of the deceased victim.

(B) A child of the deceased victim if the child is 18 years of age or older and sub-subparagraph (A) does not apply.

(C) A parent of a deceased victim if sub-subparagraphs (A) and (B) do not apply.

(D) The guardian or custodian of a child of a deceased victim if the child is less than 18 years of age and sub-subparagraphs (A) to (C) do not apply.

(E) A sibling of the deceased victim if sub-subparagraphs (A) to (D) do not apply.

(F) A grandparent of the deceased victim if sub-subparagraphs (A) to (E) do not apply.

(*iii*) A parent, guardian, or custodian of a victim who is less than 18 years of age and who is neither the defendant nor incarcerated, if the parent, guardian, or custodian so chooses. For the purpose of making an impact statement only, a parent, guardian, or custodian of a victim who is less than 18 years of age at the time of the commission of the crime and who is neither the defendant nor incarcerated, if the parent, guardian, or custodian so chooses.

(*iv*) A parent, guardian, or custodian of a victim who is so mentally incapacitated that he or she cannot meaningfully understand or participate in the legal process if he or she is not the defendant and is not incarcerated.

(2) If a victim as defined in subsection (1)(h)(*i*) is physically or emotionally unable to exercise the privileges and rights under this article, the victim may designate his or her spouse, child 18 years of age or older, parent, sibling, or grandparent or any other person 18 years of age or older who is neither the defendant nor incarcerated to act in his or her place while the physical or emotional disability continues. The victim shall provide the prosecuting attorney with the name of the person who is to act

in place of the victim. During the physical or emotional disability, notices to be provided under this article to the victim shall continue to be sent only to the victim.

(3) An individual who is charged with a serious misdemeanor, a crime as defined in section 2, or an offense as defined in section 31 arising out of the same transaction from which the charge against the defendant arose is not eligible to exercise the privileges and rights established for victims under this article.

(4) An individual who is incarcerated is not eligible to exercise the privileges and rights established for victims under this article except that he or she may submit a written statement to the court for consideration at sentencing.

History: Add. 1988, Act 21, Eff. June 1, 1988;—Am. 1993, Act 341, Eff. May 1, 1994;—Am. 1996, Act 82, Imd. Eff. Feb. 27, 1996;—Am. 2000, Act 503, Eff. June 1, 2001;—Am. 2005, Act 184, Eff. Jan. 1, 2006;—Am. 2006, Act 461, Eff. Jan. 1, 2007;—Am. 2009, Act 28, Eff. July 1, 2009;—Am. 2014, Act 130, Eff. July 1, 2014.

Compiler's note: Enacting section 1 of Act 28 of 2009 provides:

"Enacting section 1. This amendatory act takes effect July 1, 2009, and applies only to crimes committed on and after that date."

780.814 Return of property to victim; exceptions.

Sec. 64. (1) The law enforcement agency having responsibility for investigating a reported serious misdemeanor shall promptly return to the victim property belonging to that victim which is taken in the course of the investigation, except as provided in subsections (2) to (4).

(2) The agency shall not return property which is contraband.

(3) The agency shall not return property if the ownership of the property is disputed until the dispute is resolved.

(4) The agency shall retain as evidence any weapon used in the commission of the serious misdemeanor and any other evidence if the prosecuting attorney certifies that there is a need to retain that evidence in lieu of a photograph or other means of memorializing its possession by the agency.

History: Add. 1988, Act 21, Eff. June 1, 1988.

PRESUMPTION REGARDING SELF-DEFENSE
Act 311 of 2006

AN ACT to create a rebuttable presumption regarding the use of self-defense or the defense of others.
History: 2006, Act 311, Eff. Oct. 1, 2006.

The People of the State of Michigan enact:

780.951 Individual using deadly force or force other than deadly force; presumption; definitions.

Sec. 1. (1) Except as provided in subsection (2), it is a rebuttable presumption in a civil or criminal case that an individual who uses deadly force or force other than deadly force under section 2 of the self-defense act has an honest and reasonable belief that imminent death of, sexual assault of, or great bodily harm to himself or herself or another individual will occur if both of the following apply:

(a) The individual against whom deadly force or force other than deadly force is used is in the process of breaking and entering a dwelling or business premises or committing home invasion or has broken and entered a dwelling or business premises or committed home invasion and is still present in the dwelling or business premises, or is unlawfully attempting to remove another individual from a dwelling, business premises, or occupied vehicle against his or her will.

(b) The individual using deadly force or force other than deadly force honestly and reasonably believes that the individual is engaging in conduct described in subdivision (a).

(2) The presumption set forth in subsection (1) does not apply if any of the following circumstances exist:

(a) The individual against whom deadly force or force other than deadly force is used, including an owner, lessee, or titleholder, has the legal right to be in the dwelling, business premises, or vehicle and there is not an injunction for protection from domestic violence or a written pretrial supervision order, a probation order, or a parole order of no contact against that person.

(b) The individual removed or being removed from the dwelling, business premises, or occupied vehicle is a child or grandchild of, or is otherwise in the lawful custody of or under the lawful guardianship of, the individual against whom deadly force or force other than deadly force is used.

(c) The individual who uses deadly force or force other than deadly force is engaged in the commission of a crime or is using the dwelling, business premises, or occupied vehicle to further the commission of a crime.

(d) The individual against whom deadly force or force other than deadly force is used is a peace officer who has entered or is attempting to enter a dwelling, business premises, or vehicle in the performance of his or her official duties in accordance with applicable law.

(e) The individual against whom deadly force or force other than deadly force is used is the spouse or former spouse of the individual using deadly force or force other than deadly force, an individual with whom the individual using deadly force or other than deadly force has or had a dating relationship, an individual with whom the individual using deadly force or other than deadly force has had a child in common, or a resident or former resident of his or her household, and the individual using deadly force or other than deadly force has a prior history of domestic violence as the aggressor.

(3) As used in this section:

(a) "Domestic violence" means that term as defined in section 1 of 1978 PA 389, MCL 400.1501.

(b) "Business premises" means a building or other structure used for the transaction of business, including an appurtenant structure attached to that building or other structure.

(c) "Dwelling" means a structure or shelter that is used permanently or temporarily as a place of abode, including an appurtenant structure attached to that structure or shelter.

(d) "Law enforcement officer of a Michigan Indian tribal police force" means a regularly employed member of a police force of a Michigan Indian tribe who is appointed pursuant to former 25 CFR 12.100 to 12.103.

(e) "Michigan Indian tribe" means a federally recognized Indian tribe that has trust lands located within this state.

(f) "Peace officer" means any of the following:

(*i*) A regularly employed member of a law enforcement agency authorized and established pursuant to law, including common law, who is responsible for the prevention and detection of crime and the enforcement of the general criminal laws of this state. Peace officer does not include a person serving solely because he or she occupies any other office or position.

(*ii*) A law enforcement officer of a Michigan Indian tribal police force.

(*iii*) The sergeant at arms or any assistant sergeant at arms of either house of the legislature who is commissioned as a police officer by that respective house of the legislature as provided by the legislative sergeant at arms police powers act, 2001 PA 185, MCL 4.381 to 4.382.

(*iv*) A law enforcement officer of a multicounty metropolitan district.

(*v*) A county prosecuting attorney's investigator sworn and fully empowered by the sheriff of that county.

(*vi*) Until December 31, 2007, a law enforcement officer of a school district in this state that has a membership of at least 20,000 pupils and that includes in its territory a city with a population of at least 180,000 as of the most recent federal decennial census.

(*vii*) A fire arson investigator from a fire department within a city with a population of not less than 750,000 who is sworn and fully empowered by the city chief of police.

(*viii*) A security employee employed by the state pursuant to section 6c of 1935 PA 59, MCL 28.6c.

(*ix*) A motor carrier officer appointed pursuant to section 6d of 1935 PA 59, MCL 28.6d.

(*x*) A police officer or public safety officer of a community college, college, or university who is authorized by the governing board of that community college, college, or university to enforce state law and the rules and ordinances of that community college, college, or university.

(g) "Vehicle" means a conveyance of any kind, whether or not motorized, that is designed to transport people or property.

History: 2006, Act 311, Eff. Oct. 1, 2006.

SELF-DEFENSE ACT
Act 309 of 2006

AN ACT to clarify the rights and duties of self-defense and the defense of others.

History: 2006, Act 309, Eff. Oct. 1, 2006.

The People of the State of Michigan enact:

780.971 Short title.

Sec. 1. This act shall be known and may be cited as the "self-defense act".

History: 2006, Act 309, Eff. Oct. 1, 2006.

780.972 Use of deadly force by individual not engaged in commission of crime; conditions.

Sec. 2. (1) An individual who has not or is not engaged in the commission of a crime at the time he or she uses deadly force may use deadly force against another individual anywhere he or she has the legal right to be with no duty to retreat if either of the following applies:

(a) The individual honestly and reasonably believes that the use of deadly force is necessary to prevent the imminent death of or imminent great bodily harm to himself or herself or to another individual.

(b) The individual honestly and reasonably believes that the use of deadly force is necessary to prevent the imminent sexual assault of himself or herself or of another individual.

(2) An individual who has not or is not engaged in the commission of a crime at the time he or she uses force other than deadly force may use force other than deadly force against another individual anywhere he or she has the legal right to be with no duty to retreat if he or she honestly and reasonably believes that the use of that force is necessary to defend himself or herself or another individual from the imminent unlawful use of force by another individual.

History: 2006, Act 309, Eff. Oct. 1, 2006.

780.973 Duty to retreat; effect of act on common law.

Sec. 3. Except as provided in section 2, this act does not modify the common law of this state in existence on October 1, 2006 regarding the duty to retreat before using deadly force or force other than deadly force.

History: 2006, Act 309, Eff. Oct. 1, 2006.

780.974 Right to use deadly force; effect of act on common law.

Sec. 4. This act does not diminish an individual's right to use deadly force or force other than deadly force in self-defense or defense of another individual as provided by the common law of this state in existence on October 1, 2006.

History: 2006, Act 309, Eff. Oct. 1, 2006.

CORRECTIONS CODE OF 1953 (EXCERPT)
Act 232 of 1953

AN ACT to revise, consolidate, and codify the laws relating to probationers and probation officers, to pardons, reprieves, commutations, and paroles, to the administration of correctional institutions, correctional farms, and probation recovery camps, to prisoner labor and correctional industries, and to the supervision and inspection of local jails and houses of correction; to provide for the siting of correctional facilities; to create a state department of corrections, and to prescribe its powers and duties; to provide for the transfer to and vesting in said department of powers and duties vested by law in certain other state boards, commissions, and officers, and to abolish certain boards, commissions, and offices the powers and duties of which are transferred by this act; to allow for the operation of certain facilities by private entities; to prescribe the powers and duties of certain other state departments and agencies; to provide for the creation of a local lockup advisory board; to provide for a lifetime electronic monitoring program; to prescribe penalties for the violation of the provisions of this act; to make certain appropriations; to repeal certain parts of this act on specific dates; and to repeal all acts and parts of acts inconsistent with the provisions of this act.

History: 1953, Act 232, Eff. Oct. 2, 1953;—Am. 1980, Act 303, Imd. Eff. Nov. 26, 1980;—Am. 1984, Act 102, Imd. Eff. May 8, 1984;—Am. 1988, Act 510, Eff. Mar. 30, 1989;—Am. 1992, Act 22, Imd. Eff. Mar. 19, 1992;—Am. 1993, Act 184, Imd. Eff. Sept. 30, 1993;—Am. 1996, Act 164, Eff. Mar. 31, 1997;—Am. 2006, Act 172, Eff. Aug. 28, 2006.

Compiler's note: For transfer of the Department of Corrections to a new Department of Corrections, see E.R.O. No. 1991-12, compiled at MCL 791.302 of the Michigan Compiled Laws.

For abolition of the Michigan Corrections Commission and transferring its powers, duties, and functions to the Director of the new Department of Corrections with the exception that the power to appoint the Director shall be vested with the Governor, see E.R.O. No. 1991-12, compiled at MCL 791.302 of the Michigan Compiled Laws.

Popular name: Department of Corrections Act

The People of the State of Michigan enact:

CHAPTER I
DEPARTMENT OF CORRECTIONS.

791.206 Rules.

Sec. 6. (1) The director may promulgate rules pursuant to the administrative procedures act of 1969, 1969 PA 306, MCL 24.201 to 24.328, to provide for all of the following:

(a) The control, management, and operation of the general affairs of the department.

(b) Supervision and control of probationers and probation officers throughout this state.

(c) The manner in which applications for pardon, reprieve, medical commutation, or commutation shall be made to the governor; the procedures for handling applications and recommendations by the parole board; the manner in which paroles shall be considered, the criteria to be used to reach release decisions, the procedures for medical and special paroles, and the duties of the parole board in those matters; interviews on paroles and for the notice of intent to conduct an interview; the entering of appropriate orders granting or denying paroles; the supervision and control of paroled prisoners; and the revocation of parole.

(d) The management and control of state penal institutions, correctional farms, probation recovery camps, and programs for the care and supervision of youthful trainees separate and apart from persons convicted of crimes within the jurisdiction of the department. Except as provided for in section 62(3), this subdivision does not apply to detention facilities operated by local units of government used to detain persons less than 72 hours. The rules may permit the use of portions of penal institutions in which persons convicted of crimes are detained. The rules shall provide that decisions as to the removal of a youth from the youthful trainee facility or the release of a youth from the supervision of the department shall be made by the department and shall assign responsibility for those decisions to a committee.

(e) The management and control of prison labor and industry.

(f) The director may promulgate rules providing for the creation and operation of a lifetime electronic monitoring program to conduct electronic monitoring of individuals, who have served sentences imposed for certain crimes, following their release from parole, prison, or both parole and prison.

(2) The director may promulgate rules providing for a parole board structure consisting of 3-member panels.

(3) The director may promulgate further rules with respect to the affairs of the department as the director considers necessary or expedient for the proper administration of this act. The director may modify, amend, supplement, or rescind a rule.

(4) The director and the corrections commission shall not promulgate a rule or adopt a guideline that does either of the following:

(a) Prohibits a probation officer or parole officer from carrying a firearm while on duty.

(b) Allows a prisoner to have his or her name changed. If the Michigan supreme court rules that this subdivision is violative of constitutional provisions under the first and fourteenth amendments to the United States constitution and article I, sections 2 and 4 of the state constitution of 1963, the remaining provisions of the code shall remain in effect.

History: 1953, Act 232, Eff. Oct. 2, 1953;—Am. 1966, Act 210, Imd. Eff. July 11, 1966;—Am. 1982, Act 314, Imd. Eff. Oct. 15, 1982;—Am. 1984, Act 102, Imd. Eff. May 8, 1984;—Am. 1986, Act 271, Imd. Eff. Dec. 19, 1986;—Am. 1996, Act 104, Eff. Apr. 1, 1996;—Am. 2006, Act 172, Eff. Aug. 28, 2006.

Compiler's note: In separate opinions, the Michigan Supreme Court held that Section 45(8), (9), (10), and (12) and the second sentence of Section 46(1) ("An agency shall not file a rule ... until at least 10 days after the date of the certificate of approval by the committee or after the legislature adopts a concurrent resolution approving the rule.") of the Administrative Procedures Act of 1969, in providing for the Legislature's reservation of authority to approve or disapprove rules proposed by executive branch agencies, did not comply with the enactment and presentment requirements of Const 1963, Art 4, and violated the separation of powers provision of Const 1963, Art 3, and, therefore, were unconstitutional. These specified portions were declared to be severable with the remaining portions remaining effective. Blank v Department of Corrections, 462 Mich 103 (2000).

Popular name: Department of Corrections Act

Administrative rules: R 791.1101 et seq. of the Michigan Administrative Code.

LIQUOR, NARCOTICS, AND WEAPONS PROHIBITED IN PRISONS (EXCERPT)
Act 17 of 1909

AN ACT to prohibit or limit the access by prisoners and by employees of correctional facilities to certain weapons and wireless communication devices and to alcoholic liquor, drugs, medicines, poisons, and controlled substances in, on, or outside of correctional facilities; to prohibit or limit the bringing into or onto certain facilities and real property, and the disposition of, certain weapons, substances, and wireless communication devices; to prohibit or limit the selling, giving, or furnishing of certain weapons, substances, and wireless communication devices to prisoners; to prohibit the control or possession of certain weapons, substances, and wireless communication devices by prisoners; and to prescribe penalties.

History: 1909, Act 17, Eff. Sept. 1, 1909;—Am. 1977, Act 164, Imd. Eff. Nov. 10, 1977;—Am. 1982, Act 343, Imd. Eff. Dec. 21, 1982;—Am. 2006, Act 540, Imd. Eff. Dec. 29, 2006.

The People of the State of Michigan enact:

800.283 Weapons; prohibitions.

Sec. 3. (1) Unless authorized by the chief administrator of the correctional facility, a weapon or other implement which may be used to injure a prisoner or other person, or in assisting a prisoner to escape from imprisonment, shall not be sold, given, or furnished, either directly or indirectly, to a prisoner who is in or on the correctional facility, or be disposed of in a manner or in a place that it may be secured by a prisoner who is in or on the correctional facility.

(2) Unless authorized by the chief administrator of the correctional facility, a person, who knows or has reason to know that another person is a prisoner, shall not sell, give, or furnish, either directly or indirectly, to that prisoner anywhere outside of a correctional facility a weapon or other implement which may be used to injure a prisoner or other person or in assisting a prisoner to escape from imprisonment.

(3) Unless authorized by the chief administrator of the correctional facility, a weapon or other implement which may be used to injure a prisoner or other person, or in assisting a prisoner to escape from imprisonment, shall not be brought into or onto any correctional facility.

(4) Unless authorized by the chief administrator of the correctional facility, a prisoner shall not have in his or her possession or under his or her control a weapon or other implement which may be used to injure a prisoner or other person, or to assist a prisoner to escape from imprisonment.

History: 1909, Act 17, Eff. Sept. 1, 1909;—CL 1915, 1829;—CL 1929, 17655;—CL 1948, 800.283;—Am. 1972, Act 105, Imd. Eff. Mar. 29, 1972;—Am. 1982, Act 343, Imd. Eff. Dec. 21, 1982.

Constitutionality: In People v Stanton, 400 Mich. 192; 253 NW2d 650 (1977), the Michigan supreme court declared 1972 PA 105, which amended this section, unconstitutional due to a defect in the title to 1909 PA 17. The law as embodied in the 1972 amendment was voided, not the act title. The amendment of the title by 1977 PA 164 following the declaration of unconstitutionality of a portion of the act itself did not suffice to resurrect the voided portion. If the voided portion is to be once again considered a part of the law, it must be "revised, altered, or amended" and "re-enacted and published at length" pursuant to Const 1963, art IV, § 25. People v Clabin, 411 Mich 472; 307 NW2d 682 (1981). This section and the title to 909 PA 17 were subsequently amended by 1982 PA 343.

800.284 Search of persons coming to correctional facility.

Sec. 4. The chief administrator of a correctional facility may search, or have searched, any person coming to the correctional facility as a visitor, or in any other capacity, who is suspected of having any weapon or other implement which may be used to injure a prisoner or other person or in assisting a prisoner to escape from imprisonment, or any alcoholic liquor, prescription drug, poison, or controlled substance upon his or her person.

History: 1909, Act 17, Eff. Sept. 1, 1909;—CL 1915, 1830;—CL 1929, 17656;—CL 1948, 800.284;—Am. 1982, Act 343, Imd. Eff. Dec. 21, 1982.

ALCOHOLIC LIQUOR, CONTROLLED SUBSTANCES, AND WEAPONS (EXCERPT)
Act 7 of 1981

AN ACT to prohibit without authorization the bringing into jails and other specified areas any alcoholic liquor, controlled substances, weapons, and certain other items; the selling or furnishing to prisoners, and the improper disposal of any alcoholic liquor, controlled substances, weapons, and certain other items; the possession or control by prisoners of any alcoholic liquor, controlled substances, weapons, and certain other items; to prescribe a penalty; and to repeal certain acts and parts of acts.

History: 1981, Act 7, Eff. June 1, 1981.

The People of the State of Michigan enact:

801.262 Prohibited acts; weapons.

Sec. 2. (1) Unless authorized by the chief administrator of the jail, a person shall not do either of the following:

(a) Bring into a jail or a building appurtenant to a jail, or onto the grounds used for jail purposes, for the use or benefit of a prisoner, any weapon or other item that may be used to injure a prisoner or other person, or used to assist a prisoner in escaping from jail.

(b) Sell or furnish to a prisoner, or dispose of in a manner that allows a prisoner access to the weapon or other item, any weapon or other item which may be used to injure a prisoner or other person, or used to assist a prisoner in escaping from jail.

(2) Unless authorized by the chief administrator of the jail, a prisoner shall not possess or have under his or her control any weapon or other item that may be used to injure a prisoner or other person, or used to assist a prisoner in escaping from jail.

History: 1981, Act 7, Eff. June 1, 1981.

OPINIONS OF THE ATTORNEY GENERAL

Opinion No. 3158
February, 1945

CONCEALED WEAPONS:
General discussion relative to concealed weapons.

MR. CLYDE H. EDGAR,
Sheriff,
Jackson County,
Jackson, Michigan.

DEAR SIR:

Your letter addressed to the Michigan State Police and dated January 31, 1945 has been referred to me for reply. In your letter you ask substantially the following questions on weapons or firearms:

1. Is a weapon considered concealed when carried in a holster outside of all the clothing of a person?
2. Is it necessary to have a license to carry a concealed pistol when such pistol is being transported from a city home to a place in the country, each of which places is owned by the party transporting the pistol, when the purpose of such transportation is target practice? Would the answer be the same if the place to which the pistol was being transported was owned by a near relative?
3. If a pistol is carried concealed or openly, with clip or cylinder removed, must a license be obtained?
4. A number of our local factories hire men for guard work only and furnish them with guns while on duty only. Is it necessary for them to have licenses to carry such guns?

The late Wm. W. Potter rendered an opinion in April of 1927 on the subject of your first question and I quote the following from that opinion:

> "The statute does not mean or import that no part of the weapons should be concealed, but the offense is only committed when the weapon is so concealed that it is impossible for one approaching in view of the person carrying the weapon to see any part of it. All that the Legislature meant when it prohibited the carrying of concealed weapons was to compel persons to so wear them that others who might come in contact with them might see that they were armed and dangerous persons, who were to be avoided in consequence, for, if it should be required that no part of the weapon should be concealed, the statute would amount to an infringement of the constitutional right of citizens to have and bear arms, since it would be impossible for one to have and bear about his person a pistol or weapon of any kind without having some part of it concealed.
>
> "*Stockdale v. State*, 32 Ga. 225, 227.
>
> "I am, therefore, of the opinion that if a pistol is carried in a holster or belt, on the outside of the clothing so as to be in plain view, it does not constitute carrying a concealed weapon. If it is worn under a coat, it would be, in my judgment, a violation of the statute, as the same would then not be in plain view."

I agree with the conclusions reached in that opinion.

Relative to your second question, it is my opinion that Section 231 of Chapter 27 of the Penal Code of the State of Michigan (Sec. 28.428, Mich. Stat. Ann.) fairly defines the exceptions to the licensing act and therefore it is quoted:

> "The provisions of the second (2nd), third (3rd), sixth (6th) and seventh (7th) sections of this chapter shall not apply to any peace officer of the state or any subdivision thereof who is regularly employed and paid by the state or such subdivision, or to any member of the army, navy or marine corps of the United States or of organizations authorized by law to purchase or receive weapons from the United States or from this state, nor to the national guard or other duly authorized military organizations when on duty or drill, nor to the members thereof in going to or returning from their customary places of assembly or practice, nor to a person licensed to carry a pistol concealed upon his person issued by another state, nor to the regular and ordinary transportation of pistols as merchandise, or to any person while carrying a pistol unloaded in a wrapper from the place of purchase to his home or place of business or to a place of repair or back to his home or place of business, or in moving goods from one place of abode or business to another."

This section does not except the case of a person transporting a pistol from his city to his country home for target practice and it is therefore my opinion that it would be illegal to do so without the license to carry concealed weapons. The same would certainly be true in case the pistol was being transported to a place owned by a near relative.

Answering your third question, it is my opinion that, if carried openly, no license would be required since the weapon would not be concealed. However, if carried concealed, a license would be required regardless of whether the clip or cylinder were removed.

People v. Williamson, 200 Mich. 342.

Replying to your fourth question, Opinion No. O-926, dated July 6, 1942, copy of which is enclosed, relative to plant protection men who are members of the auxiliary military police, seems to cover that situation adequately. However, as to plant protection men who are not members of military police auxiliary, it is my opinion that a license to carry concealed weapons is required. No license would be required if the weapons are carried openly.

Very truly yours,
JOHN R. DETHMERS,
Attorney General.

WHT:mp

Opinion No. 5215
August 26, 1977

FIREARMS:
Return of stolen firearm to owner.
The State Police may return a pistol whose serial number has been altered or removed by another person to its owner after the State Police has restamped the weapon with either its original serial number or a new number issued by the Department and the owner may not be prosecuted for possession of a firearm whose number has been altered, removed or obliterated by another person.

Colonel Gerald L. Hough
Director
Department of State Police
714 South Harrison Road
East Lansing, Michigan 48823

You have requested my opinion on the following questions:

> '1. Can the Department of State Police return to its rightful owner, a pistol whose serial number has been either altered or removed if, prior to being returned, the department restamps the weapon with either its original serial number or a new number issued by the department?
>
> '2. In following the procedure suggested in question number 1, would the owner then be secure from prosecution under MCL Sec. 750.230; MSA Sec. 28.427? (The assumption is made that the weapon would be properly registered once returned.)'

Section 230 of the Michigan Penal Code, 1931 PA 328, Sec. 230, provides in pertinent part:

> 'A person who shall wilfully alter, remove or obliterate the name of the maker, model, manufacturer's number or other mark of identify of a pistol, shall be guilty of a felony, punishable by imprisonment for not more than 2 years or a fine of not more than $1,000.00. Possession of a firearm upon which the number shall have been altered, removed or obliterated, . . . shall be presumptive evidence that the possessor has altered, removed or obliterated the same.'

Thus, although the statute prohibits the alteration, removal, or obliteration of the name of the maker, model, manufacturer's number or other mark of identity of any pistol, it does not prohibit possession of a pistol on which the mark of identity has been altered. It merely creates a rebuttal presumption that the person in possession of such a weapon is the one who altered the identification. *People v Petro*, 342 Mich 299, 306; 70 NW2d 69, 70 (1955). It must also be noted that the role of a statutory presumption is to establish a prima facie case; however, if the presumption is challenged by rebuttal evidence, the presumption cannot be weighed against the evidence. *Gillette v Michigan United Tractor Co*, 205 Mich 410; 171 NW 576 (1919).

In response to question number 1, it is therefore my opinion that the Department of the State Police may return the weapon in question to its owner, in the event the department restamps the weapon with either its original or a new serial number issued by the department and, in answer to your second question, since the owner can show that he did not alter the identification of the pistol, he may not be prosecuted for violation of 1931 PA 328, Sec. 230, *supra*.

Frank J. Kelley
Attorney General

Opinion No. 5960
August 18, 1981

FIREARMS:
Limitation on target practice within a township
The Game Law of 1929, 1929 PA 286, Sec. 10b does not prohibit target practice within a township.
A hunting area control committee is empowered to adopt regulations prohibiting the discharge of firearms in a township or portions thereof in accordance with 1967 PA 159.

Mr. Doyle A. Rowland
Prosecuting Attorney
County of Midland
Courthouse
Midland, Michigan 48640

You have requested my opinion on the following question:

Does MCLA 312.10b(2) prohibit a land-owner from target practicing on his own property located in a township where other residences are within 150 yards, even though such target practicing is carried on in a safe and prudent manner?

The Game Law of 1929, 1929 PA 286, Sec. 10b, as added by 1968 PA 61, MCLA 312.10b; MSA 13.1339(2),(1) provides as follows:

> '(1) For the purpose of this section, 'safety zone' means any area within 150 yards of any occupied dwelling house, residence, or any other building, cabin, camp or cottage when occupied by human beings or any barn or other building used in connection therewith.
>
> '(2) No person, other than the owner, tenant or occupant, shall shoot or discharge any firearm or other dangerous weapon, or hunt for or shoot any wild bird or wild animal while it is within such safety zone, without the specific permission of the owner, tenant or occupant thereof.
>
> '(3) The provisions of this section shall not apply to any landowner, tenant or occupant thereof or their invited guest while hunting on their own property, or to any riparian owner or their tenant or guest while shooting waterfowl lakeward over water from their upland or lakeward from a boat or blind over their submerged soil.'

At the time the Legislature enacted amendatory 1968 PA 61, the title to 1929 PA 286, *supra*, stated:

> 'AN ACT to provide for the protection of wild animals and wild birds; to regulate the taking, possession, use and transportation of same; to prohibit the sale of game animals and birds; to regulate the manner of hunting, pursuing and killing game animals, birds and fur-bearing animals; to provide for the issuing of licenses and permits for the taking, hunting or killing of all wild animals and birds and the disposition of the moneys derived therefrom; to provide penalties for the violation of any of the provisions of this act, and to repeal certain acts relating thereto.'

1968 PA 61 did not amend the title to 1929 PA 286, *supra*.

It is a cardinal rule of statutory construction that the Legislature is presumed to have intended the plain meaning of words used by it. *Florentine Ristorante, Inc v City of Grandville*, 88 Mich App 614, 619; 278 NW2d 694, *lv den* 406 Mich 963 (1979).

The Legislature in the enactment of 1929 PA 286, *supra*, indicated in the title thereof its intention to provide for the protection of wild animals and wild birds; to regulate the taking, possession, use and transportation of same; and, to regulate the manner of hunting, pursuing and killing game animals, birds and fur-bearing animals.

1929 PA 286, Sec. 10b, *supra*, as set forth above in (2) thereof, further regulates the hunting and taking of wild birds or wild animals within the safety zone as defined in (1). The focus of this section is the hunting and taking of wild birds and wild animals.

Thus, the intention of the Legislature, 1929 PA 286, Sec. 10b, *supra*, was the control and limitation of the discharge of weapons in the hunting and taking of wild birds and wild game and not the discharge of weapons in target practice activities.

It is my opinion, therefore, that 1929 PA 286, Sec. 10b(2), *supra*, does not prohibit a landowner from target practicing on his own property where other residences are within 150 yards, even though target practice is carried on in a safe and prudent manner.

---

(1) The Legislature has enacted the Hunting and Fishing License Act, 1980 PA 86, MCLA 316.10 *et seq*; MSA 13.1350(101) *et seq*, repealing many sections of 1929 PA 286, *supra*, but leaving Sec. 10b intact.

While 1929 PA 286, Sec. 10b, *supra*, does not regulate or prohibit target practice within a township not involving hunting, the Legislature has provided for the regulation and prohibition of the discharge of firearms in townships by 1967 PA 159, MCLA 317.331 *et seq*; MSA 13.1397(101) *et seq.* In 1967 PA 159, *supra*, Sec. 1, the Legislature has authorized the creation of a hunting area control committee and empowered it, in the interest of public safety and general welfare, to regulate and prohibit the discharge of firearms upon resolution of the township board that the safety and well being of persons or property are in danger because of the discharge of firearms. 1967 PA 159, *supra*, Sec. 2. After a public hearing, the committee submits its findings and recommendations in the form of proposed regulations to the township board for its approval. 1967 PA 159, *supra*, Sec. 3. If the township board approves the proposed regulations, the committee reports them in accordance with 1969 PA 306, MCLA 24.201 *et seq*; MSA 3.560(101) *et seq.* For examples of regulations promulgated by such committees, see 1979 MAC R 317.120.3 *et seq.*

It is further my opinion that a hunting area control committee is empowered to prohibit the discharge of firearms in the township or portions thereof.

Frank J. Kelley
Attorney General

Opinion No. 6015
November 30, 1981

WEAPONS:

Peace officers possessing automatic weapons

A peace officer may acquire and possess, without a license, an automatic weapon provided that the employer of the peace officer does not adopt a rule or policy prohibiting the acquisition or possession of such automatic weapons.

Honorable Dan L. DeGrow
State Representative
State Capitol Building
Lansing, Michigan

You have requested my opinion on whether peace officers may possess automatic weapons.

The Michigan Penal Code, 1931 PA 328, Ch XXXVII, Sec. 224(1), as last amended by 1980 PA 346; MCLA 750.224; MSA 28.421, provides:

> 'A person shall not manufacture, sell, offer for sale, or possess a machine gun or firearm which shoots or is designed to shoot automatically more than 1 shot without manual reloading, by a single function of the trigger; a muffler, silencer, or device for deadening or muffling the sound of a discharged firearm; a bomb or bombshell; a blackjack, slungshot, billy, metallic knuckles, sand club, sand bag, or bludgeon; or any type of device, weapon, cartridge, container, or contrivance designed for the purpose of rendering a person either temporarily or permanently disabled by the ejection, release, or emission of a gas or other substance. A person who violates this section is guilty of a felony, punishable by imprisonment for not more than 5 years, or a fine of not more than $2,500.00, or both.' *(Emphasis added.)*

OAG, 1977-1978, No 5210, p 189 (August 10, 1977), concluded that it is unlawful for a private citizen to acquire or possess, without a license, a machine gun or a weapon with a silencer.

In 1931 PA 328, Ch XXXVII, Sec. 231; MCLA 750.231; MSA 28.428, the Legislature has provided an exception to the restrictions of 1931 PA 328, Ch XXXVII, Sec. 224, *supra*, as follows:

> 'Sections 224 and 227 do not apply to any peace officer of a duly authorized police agency of the United States or of the state or any subdivision thereof who is regularly employed and paid by the United States or the state or such subdivision, nor to any person regularly employed by the state department of corrections, and authorized in writing by the director of corrections to carry a concealed weapon while in the official performance of his duties or while going to or returning from such duties, nor to any member of the army, air force, navy or marine corps of the United States when carrying weapons in line of or incidental to duty, nor to organizations authorized by law to purchase or receive weapons from the United States or from this state, nor to members of the national guard, armed forces reserves or other duly authorized military organizations when on duty or drill, or in going to or returning from their places of assembly or practice by a direct route or otherwise, while carrying weapons used for purposes of the national guard, armed forces reserves or other duly authorized military organizations.' *(Emphasis added.)*

A plain reading of 1931 PA 328, Ch XXXVII, Sec. 231, *supra*, indicates that the proscriptions contained in 1931 PA 328, Ch XXXVII, Sec. 224, *supra*, have no application to peace officers who are regularly employed and paid by the State of Michigan or any subdivision thereof. The Legislature has imposed no conditions upon the peace officer exemption other than the requirements that the peace officer be regularly employed and paid by the state or any subdivision thereof. On the other hand, persons employed by the Department of Corrections are exempted from 1931 PA 328, Ch XXXVII, Sec. 224, *supra*, only if that person has authorization in writing to carry a concealed weapon and only 'while in the official performance of his duties or while going to or returning from such duties.' Similarly, members of the Army, Air Force, Navy or Marine Corps are exempt only 'when carrying weapons in the line of or incidental to duty.' Likewise, members of the National Guard, Armed Forces Reserves or other duly authorized military organizations are exempt 'when on duty or drill,' in transportation of these weapons by direct route or otherwise, or while carrying such weapons for purposes arising out of their military duties.

> If a statute is clear and unambiguous, judicial construction or interpretation is unwarranted. *Nordman v Calhoun*, 332 Mich 460; 51 NW2d 906 (1952). Moreover, because 1931 PA 328, Ch XXXVII, Secs. 224 and 231, *supra*, are penal in nature, they must be strictly construed. *People v Lockwood*, 308 Mich 618, 622; 14 NW2d 517, 518 (1944); *People v Reynolds*, 71 Mich 343, 348; 38 NW 923, 925 (1888). 1931 PA 328, Ch XXXVII, Sec. 231, *supra*, is clear and unambiguous. Unlike employees of the Department of Corrections or military personnel, no conditions are attached to the exemption as it relates to peace officers regularly employed and paid by the state or any subdivision thereof.

While the wisdom of a public policy permitting peace officers to acquire automatic weapons is open to doubt, I am constrained to conclude that the Legislature has permitted regularly employed and paid peace officers to acquire and possess automatic weapons without a license.

However, there is nothing in 1931 PA 328, Ch XXXVII, Sec. 231, *supra*, which would prevent or limit the director of the Department of State Police, county sheriffs, local chiefs of police, or other police supervisory councils from placing restrictions upon the acquisition and possession of such weapons. In *Eaton County Deputy Sheriffs Associations v Eaton County Sheriff*, 37 Mich App 427; 195 NW2d 12 (1971), the court held that a sheriff has the authority to prohibit his deputies from carrying their own service revolvers while off duty notwithstanding the statutory exemption for peace officers contained in 1931 PA 328, Ch XXXVII, Sec. 231, *supra*. In its opinion, the court noted:

> 'We find that the exemption of peace officers from obtaining licenses to carry concealed weapons in no way limits the power inherent in the office of sheriff to promulgate rules and regulations pertaining to the employment of deputies. MCLA Sec. 750.231 (Stat Ann 1971 Cum Supp Sec. 28.428) merely provides that Secs. 224 and 227 do not apply to peace officers. Therefore, the officers may carry concealed weapons without being guilty of a felony.
>
> 'However, in our opinion, MCLA Sec. 750.231 in no way limits the power of the sheriff to make rules and regulations which, in his opinion, improve the quality of law enforcement and increase the safety of the citizens in the community. We therefore hold that the trial court was correct in dismissing the plaintiff's complaint.'

It also should be observed that 1935 PA 59, Sec. 9; MCLA 28.9; MSA 4.439, vests the director of the Department of State Police with authority to adopt rules and regulations for the control, discipline and conduct of members of the department; 1895 PA 3, Ch VII, Sec. 45; MCLA 67.45; MSA 5.1329, authorizes the village council to make all necessary rules for the government of the village police department; and 1951 PA 181, Sec. 5; MCLA 41.855; MSA 5.2640(35), empowers the township board of any township to establish rules and regulations for the operation of the township police department and its officers, detectives and employees. As to cities, the Michigan Supreme Court has held that members of a city police department subject themselves to reasonable rules and regulations adopted by the board of control of the department. *Aller v Detroit Police Department Trial Board*, 309 Mich 382; 15 NW2d 676 (1944).

It is my opinion, therefore, that peace officers in Michigan may possess, without a license, machine guns or other automatic weapons, subject to restrictions placed upon such acquisition or possession by their supervisory board or official, as the case may be.

Frank J. Kelley
Attorney General

Opinion No. 6798
May 16, 1994

CONCEALED WEAPON LICENSE:
Michigan resident with a concealed weapon license acquired from another state
A Michigan resident may not carry a concealed pistol in Michigan if the resident has only acquired a license to carry a concealed pistol from another state.

Honorable David Jaye
State Representative
The Capitol
Lansing, MI

You have asked whether a Michigan resident may carry a concealed pistol in Michigan if the resident has only acquired a license to carry a concealed pistol from another state.

MCL 28.432a; MSA 28.98(1), provides:

Section 6 [requiring a concealed weapon license to carry a concealed pistol] does not apply to:

> (f) A person licensed to carry a pistol concealed upon his or her person issued by another state.

Similarly, MCL 750.231a; MSA 28.428(1), states:

> (1) Section 227 [prohibiting carrying a concealed pistol without a license] does not apply to any of the following:
>
> (a) To a person holding a valid license to carry a pistol concealed upon his or her person issued by another state except where the pistol is carried in non-conformance with a restriction appearing on the license.

The above-quoted statutory provisions clearly apply to a resident of another state that obtains a license to carry a concealed pistol in that state and then comes into the State of Michigan. The question is whether the exemption is also applicable to a Michigan resident that obtains a license to carry a concealed pistol from another state and, on that basis, claims an exemption from the requirements of Michigan's concealed weapon laws.

In section 6 of 1927 PA 372, MCL 28.426; MSA 28.93, the Legislature has established a comprehensive procedure for determining whether a Michigan resident should be issued a license to carry a pistol concealed on the person or in a vehicle operated or occupied by the applicant. Subsection (1) of section 6 provides:

> The prosecuting attorney, the sheriff, and the director of the department of state police, or their respective authorized deputies, shall constitute boards exclusively authorized to issue a license to an applicant residing within their respective counties, to carry a pistol concealed on the person and to carry a pistol, whether concealed or otherwise, in a vehicle operated or occupied by the applicant. The county clerk of each county shall be clerk of the licensing board, which board shall be known as the concealed weapon licensing board. A license to carry a pistol concealed on the person or to carry a pistol, whether concealed or otherwise, in a vehicle operated or occupied by the person applying for the license, shall not be granted to a person unless the person is 18 years of age or older, is a citizen of the United States, and has resided in this state 6 months or more. A license shall not be issued unless it appears that the applicant has good reason to fear injury to his or her person or property, or has other proper reasons, and is a suitable person to be licensed. A license shall not be issued to a person who was convicted of a felony or confined for a felony conviction in this state or elsewhere during the 8-year period immediately preceding the date of the application or was adjudged insane unless the person was restored to sanity and so declared by court order. *[Emphasis added.]*

Subsection (4) requires fingerprinting the applicant and sending the fingerprints to the Michigan Department of State Police and the Federal Bureau of Investigation to ascertain whether there has been a felony conviction or confinement for a felony conviction within the 8-year period. Subsection (5) provides that the concealed pistol license may be restricted, on the face of the license, consistent with the reasons the license was issued. Under subsection (6), a concealed pistol license may not be issued for more than three years and a renewal may not be granted unless a new application is filed.

Michigan's appellate courts have consistently recognized that the Legislature has imposed comprehensive requirements an applicant must meet to obtain a concealed pistol license from a county gun board. In *People v McFadden*, 31 Mich App 512, 516; 188 NW2d 141 (1971), the court stated:

> Pursuant to constitutional requirements, the statute enumerates explicit criteria to guide the concealed weapon licensing board in processing applications. Thus, any suggestion that absence of standards creates a potential for arbitrary action lacks merit.

Subsequently, in *Hanselman v Wayne County Weapon Bd*, 419 Mich 168, 189; 351 NW2d 544 (1984), the Supreme Court declared:

> Each concealed weapon licensing board must determine "proper reason" and "suitability" based upon consideration of local needs and an exercise of its discretion. As the Court of Appeals recognized in *Bay County Concealed Weapons Licensing Board v Gasta*, 96 Mich App 784, 789-791; 293 NW2d 707 (1980), the Legislature intends the concealed weapon licensing boards to apply local and discretionary standards in deciding whether to grant an applicant a concealed weapon license:
>
> "The licensing board is comprised of one representative each from the County Prosecutor's Office, the State Police, and the County Sheriff's Department. By creating a board composed of law enforcement officials and giving it the exclusive authority to issue, deny and revoke permits for concealed weapons, the Legislature has insured that an individual's perceived need to carry a concealed weapon will be evaluated in light of the experience and knowledge of community needs possessed by these local officials. The potential danger which a concealed weapon poses to the unsuspecting public justifies that licensing procedures be entrusted to a board comprised of law enforcement officials.
>
> "In view of the inherent potential danger which accompanies the issuance of a permit to carry a concealed weapon, the licensing board as composed reflects the Legislature's intent that power to issue and revoke such [concealed weapon] licenses is properly placed with those professionals most able to assess community needs and problems in this area." *[Emphasis added.]*

There are many rules for interpreting statutes. The ultimate goal of all such rules is to ascertain and implement the legislative intent, even if the intent might appear in conflict with the literal language of the statute. *People v Stoudemire*, 429 Mich 262, 266; 414 NW2d 693 (1987). Also, statutes must be interpreted to avoid absurd consequences. *Webster v Rotary Electric Steel Co*, 321 Mich 526, 531; 33 NW2d 69 (1948).

Here, the Legislature has created local gun boards with the exclusive authority to issue concealed pistol licenses. The Legislature has imposed specific statutory requirements applicants must meet to obtain these licenses. In addition, whether applicants have good reasons and are suitable persons to be licensed is within the sound discretion of a board of local professionals who apply their knowledge of community needs and problems in evaluating applications. It is inconceivable that the Legislature, after crafting these statutory requirements for obtaining a concealed pistol license, intended to permit Michigan residents to avoid them by obtaining a concealed pistol license in another state that may not impose many of the Michigan requirements. That construction of the statute would result in the absurd consequence that a Michigan resident could avoid the legislatively imposed requirements for obtaining a concealed pistol license in Michigan by obtaining that type of license in another state without having to meet the Michigan requirements. Thus, it must be concluded that a Michigan resident with a concealed pistol license obtained in another state may not carry a concealed pistol in Michigan unless the resident first obtains a concealed pistol license in Michigan by meeting the requirements for obtaining the license imposed by Michigan law.

It is my opinion, therefore, that a Michigan resident may not carry a concealed pistol in Michigan if the resident has only acquired a license to carry a concealed pistol from another state.

Frank J. Kelley
Attorney General

Opinion No. 7020
May 25, 1999

EXPLOSIVES:

FIREARMS:

HUNTING:

Small arms ammunition primers and caps as explosives

Small arms ammunition primers and black powder ignition caps do not fall within the definition of "explosive" regulated by the Explosives Act of 1970.

Honorable Christopher D. Dingell
State Senator
The Capitol
Lansing, MI 48909-7536

You have asked if small arms ammunition primers and black powder ignition caps fall within the definition of "explosive" regulated by the Explosives Act of 1970.

Information supplied with your request indicates that small arms ammunition primers are devices used to detonate the explosive in firearm cartridges. Black powder ignition caps are devices used to detonate the explosive in black powder weapons. Both of these devices are commonly understood to contain a small quantity of explosive material to serve as a detonator or detonating device for a larger quantity of explosive material which, when detonated, propels the bullet or other projectile.

The Explosives Act of 1970, 1970 PA 202, MCL 29.41 *et seq*; MSA 4.559(41) *et seq* (Act), regulates and requires a permit for the possession, storage, sale, use, and other disposition of explosives. Violations of the Act are punishable by a monetary fine and/or imprisonment. Section 15. Because the Act is a penal statute, its provisions must be strictly construed. *People v Gilbert*, 414 Mich 191, 211; 324 NW2d 834 (1982).

For the purposes of the Act, the Legislature has defined the term "explosive" in section 2(a), which provides in pertinent part that:

> "Explosive" means blasting powder, nitroglycerine, dynamite, TNT and any other form of high explosive, blasting material, fuse other than an electric circuit breaker, detonator and other detonating agent, a chemical compound or mechanical mixture containing oxidizing or combustible units, or other ingredients, in such proportions, quantities or packing that ignition by fire, friction, concussion or other means of detonation of the compound or mixture or any part thereof may result in the sudden generation and release of highly heated gases or gaseous pressures capable of producing effects damaging or detrimental to or destructive of life, limb or property.

(Emphasis added.)

The first step in ascertaining legislative intent is to look to the text of the statute. *Piper v Pettibone Corp*, 450 Mich 565, 571; 542 NW2d 269 (1995). A clear and unambiguous statement must be enforced by the court as written according to its plain meaning. *Dean v Dep't of Corrections*, 453 Mich 448, 454; 556 NW2d 458 (1996). The first sentence of section 2(a) of the Act lists specific exclusions from the Act's definition of "explosive," the operative words being *other than an electric circuit breaker, detonator or other detonating agent*. Thus, if small arms ammunition primers and ignition caps constitute detonators or detonating agents, they are not an "explosive" under the Act.

The Act does not define *detonator or other detonating agent*. Where statutory terms are not defined, it is customary to consult dictionary definitions. *People v Lee*, 447 Mich 552, 558; 526 NW2d 882 (1994). The word "detonator" is defined as "[a]n explosive (as mercury fulminate) that is more sensitive to heat or shock than the common high explosives and is used in small quantity to detonate another explosive." *Websters Third New International Dictionary*, Unabridged Edition (1986), p 617. "Primer" is defined as "[a] cap or tube containing a small amount of explosive used to detonate the main explosive charge of a firearm or mine." *American Heritage College Dictionary* (1997), p 1087. "Percussion cap" is defined as "[a] thin metal cap containing gunpowder or another detonator that explodes on being struck." *Id*, p 1014. Based on these definitions, I am constrained to conclude that ammunition primers and ignition caps constitute "detonators" and, as such, are excluded from the Act's definition of "explosive."

This result is consistent with the conclusion reached in Letter Opinion of the Attorney General to Colonel John R. Plants, dated March 30, 1972, which concluded that smokeless and black gun powder do not constitute an "explosive" as defined by the Act. The opinion reasoned that, because smokeless and black gun powder were originally included in the bill's definition of "explosive," but were subsequently deleted before enactment, the Legislature must have intended to exclude these items from the definition of an "explosive" under the Act. The Legislature has not since amended the Act to include smokeless and black gun powder. It is, therefore, reasonable to conclude that, since the Legislature has chosen not to regulate smokeless and black gun powder, it likewise did not intend to include small arms ammunition primers and black powder ignition caps which contain smaller explosive charges used to detonate these materials.

It is my opinion, therefore, that small arms ammunition primers and black powder ignition caps do not fall within the definition of "explosive" regulated by the Explosives Act of 1970.

The Legislature is, of course, free to amend the Act if it determines that these devices should be regulated under its provisions.

JENNIFER M. GRANHOLM
Attorney General

Opinion No. 7098
January 11, 2002

CONCEALED WEAPONS: Application of Concealed Pistol Licensing Act's licensing requirement to police officer and reserve police officer

FIREARMS:

LAW ENFORCEMENT: Application of Concealed Pistol Licensing Act's gun-free zone restrictions to police officer and reserve police officer

PEACE OFFICERS:

POLICE:

A police officer, including a reserve police officer, is exempt from the licensing requirements of the Concealed Pistol Licensing Act if the officer possesses the full authority of a peace officer and is regularly employed and paid by a police agency of the United States, this state, or a political subdivision of the state.

A police officer who is exempt from the licensing requirements of the Concealed Pistol Licensing Act, but who voluntarily obtains a concealed pistol license under that act, is not subject to the act's gun-free zone restrictions unless the officer is off-duty and is relying solely on the authority of that license.

Honorable Christopher D. Dingell
State Senator
The Capitol
Lansing, MI 48913

Honorable Ruth Johnson
State Representative
The Capitol
Lansing, MI 48913

You have asked two questions regarding the treatment of police officers under the Concealed Pistol Licensing Act as most recently amended by 2000 PA 381.

Your first question asks whether a police officer, including a reserve police officer, is required to obtain a concealed pistol license under section 6 of the Concealed Pistol Licensing Act in order to lawfully carry a concealed pistol.

The Concealed Pistol Licensing Act (Act), 1927 PA 372, MCL 28.421 *et seq*, regulates the possession and carrying of certain firearms. As originally enacted, section 6 of the Act created a county concealed weapon licensing board and granted to that board considerable discretion in determining whether to issue a license to carry a concealed pistol to individual residents of the county. 2000 PA 381 made substantial amendments to the Act and added numerous new provisions. Among these new provisions is a new section 5b(7) that now sets forth the specific qualifications a person must possess in order to receive a concealed pistol license and further provides that the county concealed weapon licensing board "shall issue" licenses to persons meeting all of those qualifications.

Section 12a of the Act, as added by 1964 PA 216, has long provided that the licensure provisions of section 6 do not apply to various classes of persons, including peace officers who are regularly employed and paid by a police agency of the United States, this state, or a political subdivision. That exemption is continued in the current version of the Act. As most recently amended by 2000 PA 381, section 12a of the Act provides, in pertinent part, that:

> The requirements of this act for obtaining a license to carry a concealed pistol do not apply to any of the following:
>
> (a) *A peace officer* of a duly authorized police agency of the United States or of this state or *a political subdivision of this state*, who is *regularly employed and paid* by the United States or this state or of *a subdivision of this state*, except a township constable. *[Emphasis added.]*

Thus, in order to come within the scope of this exemption, a person must be a "peace officer" and must be "regularly employed and paid" by a qualifying unit of government.

The term "peace officer" as used in the Concealed Pistol Licensing Act refers to members of police forces of governmental units who have been given broad, general authority by law to enforce and preserve the public peace. *People v Bissonette*, 327 Mich 349, 356; 42 NW2d 113 (1950). Police officers of a police department of a political subdivision of this state possess such authority and are, therefore, "peace officers." 1 OAG, 1955, No 1891, p 72 (February 24, 1955); 2 OAG, 1958, No 3212, p 60 (February 21, 1958). Conversely, police officers who possess only restricted or special enforcement authority do not meet this standard and therefore do not qualify as "peace officers." *People v Bissonette, supra*; OAG, 1987-1988, No 6530, p 362 (August 5, 1988).

The phrase "regularly employed" as used in section 12a of the Act has not been defined by the Legislature. The meaning of this phrase, however, was addressed in OAG, 1973-1974, No 4792, p 78 (August 27, 1973), which concluded that in order to be considered "regularly employed," a peace officer's work should be "substantial rather than merely occasional" and should form "at least a large part of his daily activity." *Id*, at 79. See also OAG, 1979-1980, No 5806, p 1055 (October 28, 1980). Under this standard, a regular police officer who is employed on a full-time basis clearly is "regularly employed" for purposes of section 12a of the Act.

A more difficult problem is presented in the case of reserve police officers who are typically employed on less than a full-time basis. In such cases, it is necessary to address the factual issue of whether the individual officer in question is "regularly employed and paid" within the meaning of section 12a of the Act. OAG No 5806, *supra*, at 1054, considered the status of such reserve officers and concluded that, in order to be exempt from the Act's licensing requirement, a reserve police officer must first apply to the county concealed weapon licensing board to obtain a determination by the board whether the individual officer qualifies for the section 12a exemption. The board must determine, *inter alia*, whether the individual officer is "regularly employed," i.e., whether the officer performs substantial work that constitutes a large part of the officer's daily activity. OAG No 4792, *supra*. If the board finds that a particular reserve police officer is "regularly employed and paid" by a police agency of the United States, this state, or a political subdivision of this state, the officer is exempt from the Act's licensing requirements for carrying a concealed pistol. If, however, the licensing board finds that the reserve officer is not regularly employed and paid by one of such police agencies, licensure is required under the Act before the officer may carry a concealed pistol. OAG No 4792, *supra*, reached the same conclusion with respect to constables.

It is my opinion, therefore, in answer to your first question, that a police officer, including a reserve police officer, is exempt from the licensing requirements of the Concealed Pistol Licensing Act if the officer possesses the full authority of a peace officer and is regularly employed and paid by a police agency of the United States, this state, or a political subdivision of the state.

Your second question asks if a police officer who is exempt from the licensure requirements of the Concealed Pistol Licensing Act, by voluntarily obtaining a license under that Act, becomes subject to the Act's gun-free zone restrictions, either while on or off duty.

As noted in the answer to your first question, the Act clearly and unambiguously exempts regularly employed peace officers from its licensing requirements. Accordingly, such officers need not obtain a license under the Act in order to lawfully carry a concealed pistol. Nothing in the Act, however, prohibits a police officer from voluntarily applying for and obtaining a concealed pistol license if that officer chooses to do so. Moreover, assuming that the officer meets all of the statutory requirements specified in section 5b(7) of the Act, the county licensing board "shall issue" a license to that individual. In these circumstances, the officer would then possess two separate and independent sources of authority for carrying such a concealed pistol: (1) the officer's authority as a regularly employed peace officer; and (2) the authority conferred by the license issued under the Act. Your questions asks, in effect, whether the statutory restrictions attached to the latter source of authority might somehow modify or restrict the officer's separate authority as a peace officer. Specifically, you inquire about the effect of section 5o of the Act, as added by 2000 PA 381, which creates certain gun-free zones as follows:

> (1) An individual licensed under this act to carry a concealed pistol . . . shall not carry a concealed pistol on the premises of any of the following:
>
> (a) A school or school property except that a parent or legal guardian of a student of the school is not precluded from carrying a concealed pistol while in a vehicle on school property, if he or she is dropping the student off at the school or picking up the child from the school. As used in this section, "school" and "school property" mean those terms as defined in section 237a of the Michigan penal code, 1931 PA 328, MCL 750.237a.
>
> (b) A public or private day care center, public or private child caring agency, or public or private child placing agency.
>
> (c) A sports arena or stadium.
>
> (d) A dining room, lounge, or bar area of a premises licensed under the Michigan liquor control code of 1998, 1998 PA 58, MCL 436.1101 to 436.2303. This subdivision shall not apply to an owner or employee of the premises.
>
> (e) Any property or facility owned or operated by a church, synagogue, mosque, temple, or other place of worship, unless the presiding official or officials of the church, synagogue, mosque, temple, or other place of worship permit the carrying of concealed pistol on that property or facility.
>
> (f) An entertainment facility that the individual knows or should know has a seating capacity of 2,500 or more individuals or that has a sign above each public entrance stating in letters not less than 1-inch high a seating capacity of 2,500 or more individuals.
>
> (g) A hospital.

(h) A dormitory or classroom of a community college, college, or university.

The first step in ascertaining legislative intent is to look to the text of the statute. *Piper v Pettibone Corp*, 450 Mich 565, 571; 542 NW2d 269 (1995). Where the language of the statute is clear and unambiguous, the Legislature's intent must be carried out according to its plain meaning. *Dean v Dep't of Corrections*, 453 Mich 448, 454; 556 NW2d 458 (1996). In such instances, statutory construction is neither required nor permitted; rather, the court must apply the statutory language as written. Piper, *supra*, at 572.

The gun-free zone restrictions described in section 5o of the Act, by their express terms, apply only to a person who is carrying a concealed pistol under the authority of a license issued under the Act. Nothing in the Act in any way indicates or suggests that the gun-free zone restrictions are to be extended to a police officer acting under his or her authority as a regularly employed peace officer, even if that officer has elected to apply for and obtain a concealed pistol license under the Act. Thus, as a practical matter, the application of these gun-free zone restrictions to a police officer would depend upon the facts and circumstances of the incident. If the officer is off-duty and chooses to rely solely on his or her concealed pistol license under the Act, the Act's gun-free zone restrictions applicable to that license would apply. But those restrictions plainly do not apply if the police officer, whether on or off duty, can and does rely on his or her independent authority to carry a concealed pistol as a peace officer regularly employed and paid by a police agency of the United States, this state, or a political subdivision.

It is my opinion, therefore, in answer to your second question, that a police officer who is exempt from the licensing requirements of the Concealed Pistol Licensing Act, but who voluntarily obtains a concealed pistol license under that Act, is not subject to the act's gun-free zone restrictions unless the officer is off-duty and is relying solely on the authority of that license.

JENNIFER M. GRANHOLM
Attorney General

Opinion No. 7101
February 6, 2002

CRIMINAL LAW: Reserve police officer carrying exposed but holstered handgun is not brandishing firearm in violation of Michigan Penal Code

FIREARMS:

LAW ENFORCEMENT:

PEACE OFFICERS:

POLICE:

A reserve police officer, by carrying a handgun in a holster that is in plain view, does not violate section 234e of the Michigan Penal Code, which prohibits brandishing a firearm in public.

Honorable Bill Bullard, Jr.
State Senator
The Capitol
Lansing, MI

You have asked if a reserve police officer, by carrying a handgun in a holster that is in plain view, violates section 234e of the Michigan Penal Code, which prohibits brandishing a firearm in public.

The Michigan Penal Code, MCL 750.1 *et seq*, revises, consolidates, and codifies the state's criminal statutes. Section 234e(1) of the Code criminalizes[1] the brandishing of a firearm in public as follows:

> (1) Except as provided in subsection (2), a person shall not knowingly brandish a firearm in public.

Subsection (2) of the same section states that "[s]ubsection (1) does not apply to . . . [a] peace officer lawfully performing his or her duties as a peace officer."

The term "peace officer" refers to members of governmental police forces who have been given broad, general authority by law to enforce and preserve the public peace. *People v Bissonette*, 327 Mich 349, 356; 42 NW2d 113 (1950). Most governmental police officers, i.e., officers who are employed by the state or its political subdivisions, possess such authority and are, therefore, "peace officers." 1 OAG, 1955, No 1891, p 72 (February 24, 1955); 2 OAG, 1958, No 3212, p 60 (February 21, 1958). Conversely, police officers such as motor carrier enforcement officers who possess only restricted or special enforcement authority do not meet this standard and therefore do not qualify as "peace officers." *People v Bissonette, supra*; OAG, 1987-1988, No 6530, p 362 (August 5, 1988). Thus, a reserve police officer with limited law enforcement authority would not qualify as a "peace officer" under subsection 2 of section 234e of the Michigan Penal Code. A reserve police officer with general law enforcement authority who is regularly employed would qualify as a "peace officer" under subsection (2) of section 234e. See OAG, 1973-1974, No 4792, p 78 (August 27, 1973), and OAG, 1979-1980, No 5806, p 1055 (October 28, 1980).

Section 234e of the Michigan Penal Code does not define the crime of brandishing a firearm in public. The Michigan Criminal Jury Instructions, published by the Committee on Standard Criminal Jury Instructions, does not include a recommended jury instruction on brandishing a firearm. Research discloses that while the term "brandishing" appears in reported Michigan cases,[2] none of the cases define the term.

In the absence of any reported Michigan appellate court decisions defining "brandishing," it is appropriate to rely upon dictionary definitions. *People v Denio*, 454 Mich 691, 699; 564 NW2d 13 (1997). According to *The American Heritage Dictionary, Second College Edition (1982)*, at p 204, the term brandishing is defined as: "1. To wave or flourish menacingly, as a weapon. 2. To display ostentatiously. –n. A menacing or defiant wave or flourish." This definition comports with the meaning ascribed to this term by courts of other jurisdictions. For example, in *United States v Moerman*, 233 F3d 379, 380 (CA 6, 2000), the court recognized that in federal sentencing guidelines, "brandishing" a weapon is defined to mean "that the weapon was pointed or waved about, or displayed in a threatening manner."

---

[1] Violation of this section is a misdemeanor punishable by imprisonment for up to 90 days, or a fine of not more than $100, or both.

[2] See, for example: *People v Jones*, 443 Mich 88, 90; 504 NW2d 158 (1993), *People v Kreger*, 214 Mich App 549, 552; 543 NW2d 55 (1995), and *People v Stubbs*, 15 Mich App 453, 455; 166 NW2d 477 (1968).

Applying these definitions to your question, it is clear that a reserve police officer, regardless whether he or she qualifies as a "peace officer," when carrying a handgun in a holster in plain view, is not waving or displaying the firearm in a threatening manner. Thus, such conduct does not constitute brandishing a firearm in violation of section 234e of the Michigan Penal Code.

It is my opinion, therefore, that a reserve police officer, by carrying a handgun in a holster that is in plain view, does not violate section 234e of the Michigan Penal Code, which prohibits brandishing a firearm in public.

JENNIFER M. GRANHOLM
Attorney General

Opinion No. 7113
June 28, 2002

CONCEALED WEAPONS: Reserve police officer carrying exposed pistol in gun-free zones established by Concealed Pistol Licensing Act

FIREARMS: Reserve police officer carrying exposed pistol in gun-free zones established by Michigan Penal Code.

LAW ENFORCEMENT:

PEACE OFFICERS:
A uniformed reserve police officer acting as an unpaid volunteer for a local police agency may carry an exposed, holstered pistol within the gun-free zones established by the Concealed Pistol Licensing Act; and if the officer is either a fully authorized "peace officer" or, alternatively, possesses a valid concealed pistol license issued under the Concealed Pistol Licensing Act, he or she may also carry an exposed, holstered pistol within the gun-free zones established by the Michigan Penal Code.

Honorable Gary C. Peters
State Senator
The Capitol
Lansing, MI

Honorable Mary Ann Middaugh
State Representative
The Capitol
Lansing, MI

Honorable Larry Julian
State Representative
The Capitol
Lansing, MI

You have asked whether a uniformed reserve police officer acting as an unpaid volunteer for a local police agency may carry an exposed, holstered pistol within a "gun-free zone" established by the Concealed Pistol Licensing Act.

Your inquiry is governed by the interplay between two separate but related statutes, both of which regulate the possession of firearms.

The Concealed Pistol Licensing Act, 1927 PA 372, MCL 28.421 *et seq*, regulates the possession and carrying of concealed pistols. The Act prohibits persons from carrying a concealed pistol unless they have been licensed in accordance with the provisions of that Act. Amendatory 2000 PA 381 made significant changes to the Act. Section 5b(7) sets forth specific qualifications a person must possess in order to receive a license to carry a concealed pistol and further provides that a county concealed weapon licensing board "shall issue a license" to an applicant who meets those requirements. The Act also provides that a person who is issued a license under the Act may carry a concealed pistol "anywhere in this state" except in certain designated classes of locations listed in section 5o of the Act. Those exceptions, commonly referred to as "gun free zones," include the following:

> a) A school or school property…
>
> b) A public or private day care center, public or private child caring agency, or public or private child placing agency.
>
> c) A sports arena or stadium.
>
> d) A dining room, lounge, or bar area of a premises licensed under the Michigan liquor control code of 1998… This subdivision shall not apply to an owner or employee of the premises.
>
> e) Any property or facility owned or operated by a church, synagogue, mosque, temple, or other place of worship, unless the presiding official or officials of the church, synagogue, mosque, temple, or other place of worship permit the carrying of concealed pistol on that property or facility.
>
> f) An entertainment facility [that has a seating capacity of 2,500 or more]…
>
> g) A hospital.
>
> h) A dormitory or classroom of a community college, college, or university. [Section 5o(1).]

Section 12a of the Act expressly exempts certain persons from the requirements of the Act, including:

> (a) A *peace officer* of a duly authorized police agency of the United States or of this state or a political subdivision of this state, *who is regularly employed* and paid by the United States or this state or a subdivision of this state, except a township constable. *[Emphasis added.]*

Under the express terms of this section, a police officer or reserve police officer is exempt from the requirements of the Concealed Pistol Licensing Act, including the prohibition against carrying a concealed weapon in a "gun free zone," but only if the officer (1) possesses the full authority of a peace officer, and not merely special or limited law enforcement authority; and (2) is regularly employed and paid for those services. See OAG, 2001-2002, No 7098, p 74 (January 11, 2002). Your inquiry does not specify whether the uniformed reserve officer in question possesses the full authority of a peace officer. You do, however, specify that the officer in question serves as an unpaid volunteer. Because the exemption contained in section 12a(a) is limited to officers who are "regularly employed," an unpaid volunteer officer is not exempt from the provisions of the Concealed Pistol Licensing Act and is, therefore, prohibited from carrying a *concealed* pistol in a designated "gun free zone." OAG No 7098, *supra*.

A plain reading of section 5o(1) of the Concealed Pistol Licensing Act discloses, however, that its prohibition applies only to the carrying of pistols that are "concealed." A holstered pistol carried openly and in plain view is not "concealed" and therefore does not violate the prohibition contained in that section. See, e.g., OAG, 1951-1952, No 1388, p 228 (April 18, 1951) ("Should they be so directed by their superior officers, auxiliary police while on duty may carry weapons openly, the prohibition in the Penal Code applying only to 'concealed' weapons."), Cf., *People v Johnnie W. Jones*, 12 Mich App 293, 296; 162 NW2d 847 (1968); and *People v Kincade*, 61 Mich App 498, 502; 233 NW2d 54 (1975).

This, however, does not end the analysis of your question. The carrying of firearms in public is also restricted by the Michigan Penal Code, 1931 PA 328, MCL 750.1 *et seq*. Section 234d of the Penal Code identifies certain "gun free zones" similar to those enumerated in section 5o of the Concealed Pistol Licensing Act; within those specified zones, the possession of firearms is strictly prohibited, subject to limited exceptions. Specifically, section 234d(1) of the Penal Code provides that:

> (1) Except as provided in subsection (2), a person shall not possess a firearm on the premises of any of the following:
>
> (a) A depository financial institution or a subsidiary or affiliate of a depository financial institution.
>
> (b) A church or other house of religious worship.
>
> (c) A court.
>
> (d) A theatre.
>
> (e) A sports arena.
>
> (f) A day care center.
>
> (g) A hospital.
>
> (h) An establishment licensed under the Michigan liquor control act, Act No. 8 of the Public Acts of the Extra Session of 1933, being sections 436.1 to 436.58 of the Michigan Compiled Laws.

This language is significantly broader than that employed by section 5o of the Concealed Pistol Licensing Act. By its express terms, section 234d(1) of the Penal Code applies to firearms generally, not merely to pistols, and applies to firearms whether concealed or not. Subsection (2) of this provision creates several specific exceptions to this prohibition, two of which are germane to your inquiry. It provides, in pertinent part that:

> (2) This section does not apply to any of the following:
>
> * * *
>
> (b) A peace officer.
>
> (c) A person licensed by this state or another state to carry a concealed weapon.

Similarly, section 237a(4) of the Penal Code prohibits possession of a firearm in a weapon free school zone, a term defined in section 237a(6)(d) as "school property and a vehicle used by a school to transport students to or from school property." Like section 234d(2), the prohibition against possessing firearms in a school zone does not apply to a peace officer or to a person licensed to carry a concealed weapon. Section 237a(5).

If a reserve officer qualifies as a peace officer, then the officer is exempt from the prohibition contained in sections 234d(1) and 237a(4) of the Penal Code concerning the possession of firearms on specified premises. If not, sections 234d(2)(c) and

237a(5)(c) of the Penal Code also exempt "[a] person licensed by this state or another state to carry a concealed weapon." A license issued by a county concealed weapon licensing board under section 5b(7) of the Concealed Pistol Licensing Act clearly satisfies the latter exemption. Thus, possession of such a license would enable a reserve police officer to carry an exposed, holstered pistol in the "gun free zones" described in sections 234d and 237a of the Penal Code.

It is my opinion, therefore, that a uniformed reserve police officer acting as an unpaid volunteer for a local police agency may carry an exposed, holstered pistol within the gun-free zones established by the Concealed Pistol Licensing Act; and if the officer is either a fully authorized "peace officer" or, alternatively, possesses a valid concealed pistol license issued under the Concealed Pistol Licensing Act, he or she may also carry an exposed, holstered pistol within the gun-free zones established by the Michigan Penal Code.

JENNIFER M. GRANHOLM
Attorney General

Opinion No. 7120
December 4, 2002

CONCEALED WEAPONS: Outdoor park as "entertainment facility" constituting gun-free zone established by Concealed Pistol Licensing Act

FIREARMS:

LAW ENFORCEMENT:

MUNICIPALITIES:

POLICE:

A municipal outdoor recreation park does not, by itself, constitute an "entertainment facility" within the meaning of section 5o(1)(f) of the Concealed Pistol Licensing Act, and thus is not a gun-free zone as established by that statute.

Honorable Mike Kowall
State Representative
The Capitol
Lansing, Michigan 48913

You have asked whether a municipal outdoor recreation park, by itself, constitutes an "entertainment facility" within the meaning of section 5o(1)(f) of the Concealed Pistol Licensing Act that creates gun-free zones.

We understand that by the use of the term "outdoor recreation park" you mean a natural area of land and water, consisting of lawns, trees, gardens, picnic tables, baseball diamonds, tennis courts, ponds, lakes, or rivers.

The Concealed Pistol Licensing Act, 1927 PA 372, MCL 28.421 *et şeq*, regulates the possession and carrying of concealed pistols. The Act prohibits persons from carrying a concealed pistol unless they have been licensed in accordance with the provisions of that Act. Amendatory 2000 PA 381 made significant changes to the Act. Section 5b(7) sets forth specific qualifications a person must possess in order to receive a license to carry a concealed pistol and further provides that a county concealed weapon licensing board "shall issue a license" to an applicant who meets those requirements. The Act also provides that a person who is issued a license under the Act may carry a concealed pistol "anywhere in this state" except in certain designated classes of locations listed in section 5o of the Act. Section 5c(2). Those excepted locations, commonly referred to as "gun free zones," include the following:

> (f) An entertainment facility that the individual knows or should know has a seating capacity of 2,500 or more individuals or that has a sign above each public entrance stating in letters not less than 1-inch high a seating capacity of 2,500 or more individuals.

The statutory term "entertainment facility" is not defined by the Legislature. The question therefore arises whether a municipal outdoor park, as described in your request, constitutes an entertainment facility for purposes of the gun-free zones created by section 5o(1)(f) of the Act. Words not defined by the Legislature are to be given their generally understood meaning consistent with the intent of the Legislature. *Royal Globe Ins Co v Frankenmuth Mutual Ins Co*, 419 Mich 565, 573; 357 NW2d 652 (1984). Courts will consult dictionaries to ascertain the meaning of undefined statutory terms unless the legislative intent may be discerned from the statute itself. *People v Stone*, 463 Mich 558, 563; 621 NW2d 702 (2001). The term "entertainment" is defined as an act to divert, amuse or to cause someone's time to pass agreeably, such as a concert. *Webster's Third New International Dictionary, Unabridged* (1964). The term "facility" is defined as something built or constructed to perform some particular function. *Id.*

A reading of all the words contained in section 5o(1)(f) of the Act supports the conclusion that the Legislature intended that the term "entertainment facility" constitute a structure or building that has a known seating capacity of 2,500 or more persons, or that has signs above each public entrance stating that the facility has a seating capacity of 2,500 or more persons. Since the Legislature has not required that an entertainment facility be totally self-enclosed, such a facility could consist of a bandshell, amphitheater, or similar structure, provided it has the required, known seating capacity noted above or has appropriate signage above each public entrance indicating a seating capacity of 2,500 or more. This reading of section 5o(1)(f) is supported by the legislative history of 2000 HB 4530, enacted as 2000 PA 231. Both House Legislative Analyses, HB 4530, June 8, 1999, and January 4, 2001, state that HB 4530 would "[p]rohibit a licensee from carrying a concealed weapon in certain public places, such as a school, theater, sports arena, library, or hospital." There is no mention in either bill analysis that an outdoor recreation park, by itself, would constitute a gun-free zone. It is appropriate to rely on the legislative history because of the ambiguity in the statutory language. *Luttrell v Dep't of Corr*, 421 Mich 93, 103; 365 NW2d 74 (1985).

While the Legislature could certainly have included municipal and other outdoor recreation parks within the Act's list of gun-free zones, it chose not to do so. An entertainment facility having a seating capacity of 2,500 or more persons clearly refers to a building or other structure. Accordingly, if an outdoor recreation park includes a band shell, amphitheater, or similar structure that has the required seating capacity, that portion of the park would constitute a gun-free zone under section 5o(f) of the Act.

Finally, section 5o of the Act is a penal statute that must be strictly construed unless the Legislature indicates otherwise. MCL 750.2; *People v Gilbert*, 414 Mich 191, 211; 324 NW2d 834 (1982). There is nothing in the Concealed Pistol Licensing Act or in its legislative history to suggest that this statute be construed in a manner different from the plain language adopted by the Legislature.

It is my opinion, therefore, that a municipal outdoor recreation park does not, by itself, constitute an "entertainment facility" within the meaning of section 5o(1)(f) of the Concealed Pistol Licensing Act, and thus is not a gun-free zone as established by that statute.

JENNIFER M. GRANHOLM
Attorney General

Opinion No. 7133
May 2, 2003

CONCEALED WEAPONS: Eligibility for concealed pistol license of persons whose felony convictions have been set aside

FIREARMS:

CRIMINAL LAW:
A person convicted of a felony whose conviction has been set aside by order of a Michigan court in accordance with 1965 PA 213, as amended, if otherwise qualified, may not be denied a concealed pistol license under section 5b(7)(f) of the Concealed Pistol Licensing Act. A person convicted of one of the offenses described under section 5b(8) of the Concealed Pistol Licensing Act, whose conviction has been set aside, may nevertheless be denied a concealed pistol license on the basis of information concerning that conviction if the concealed weapon licensing board determines that denial is warranted under section 5b(7)(o) of the Act.

Col. Tadarial J. Sturdivant, Director
Department of State Police
714 South Harrison Road
East Lansing, MI 48823

Your predecessor has asked whether a person convicted of a felony whose conviction has been set aside by order of a Michigan court in accordance with 1965 PA 213, as amended, if otherwise qualified, may apply for and obtain a concealed pistol license under the Concealed Pistol Licensing Act.

The Concealed Pistol Licensing Act (CPLA), 1927 PA 372, as amended, MCL 28.421 *et seq*, authorizes a county concealed weapon licensing board to issue a license to carry a concealed pistol to an eligible applicant. MCL 28.425b. An applicant is required to provide a statement whether the applicant "has ever been convicted" of a felony or a misdemeanor. MCL 28.425b(1)(e). A concealed weapon licensing board "shall issue" a license to qualified persons who have "never been convicted of a felony." MCL 28.425b(7)(f). Thus, it must be determined whether a person who has had his or her felony conviction set aside by order of a Michigan court is properly considered "never" to have been convicted of a felony for purposes of the CPLA.

The Legislature has addressed this question in the Set Aside Law, 1965 PA 213, as amended, MCL 780.621 *et seq*. Under section 1 of this law, courts are empowered to set aside the conviction of a person for certain criminal offenses, provided that the person has been convicted only once, five years have expired since the date sentencing was imposed or the term of imprisonment was completed, whichever is later, and the applicant satisfies the other requirements of the act. MCL 780.621. The court may not enter its order setting aside the conviction unless it determines that the circumstances and behavior of the applicant since his or her conviction warrant setting it aside and that such an order "is consistent with the public welfare." MCL 780.621. Once entered, the effect of a court order setting aside a conviction is plainly stated in section 2(1) of the Set Aside Law:

> Upon the entry of an order pursuant to section 1, the applicant, for purposes of the law, *shall be considered not to have been previously convicted*, except as provided in this section [2] and section 3. [MCL 780.622(1); *emphasis added.*]

Thus, unless one of the exceptions stated in section 2 or 3 of the Set Aside Law applies for licensing purposes under the CPLA, the effect of section 2 is clear and unmistakable and must be given effect. *Storey v Meijer Inc*, 431 Mich 368, 376; 429 NW2d 169 (1988).

None of the exceptions set out in section 2 implicate the CPLA. Thus, the answer to the question turns on an analysis of section 3.

Subsection 1 of section 3 requires the court to send a copy of an order setting aside a conviction to the arresting agency and the Department of State Police. Subsection 2 then describes certain obligations of the State Police regarding that order and strictly limits the persons or entities who may have access to that order and the purposes for which such an order may be used:

> (2) The department of state police shall retain a nonpublic record of the order setting aside a conviction and of the record of the arrest, fingerprints, conviction, and sentence of the applicant in the case to which the order applies. Except as provided in subsection (3),[1] this nonpublic record shall be made available only to a court of competent

[1] Subsection (3), which permits a person whose conviction was set aside to obtain a copy of the nonpublic record upon payment of a fee, is not impacted here and need not be discussed.

> jurisdiction, an agency of the judicial branch of state government, a law enforcement agency, a prosecuting attorney, the attorney general, or the governor upon request and *only* for the following purposes:
>
> (a) Consideration in a licensing function conducted by an agency of the judicial branch of state government.
>
> (b) To show that a person who has filed an application to set aside a conviction has previously had a conviction set aside pursuant to this act.
>
> (c) The court's consideration in determining the sentence to be imposed upon conviction for a subsequent offense that is punishable as a felony or by imprisonment for more than 1 year.
>
> (d) Consideration by the governor if a person whose conviction has been set aside applies for a pardon for another offense.
>
> (e) Consideration by a law enforcement agency if a person whose conviction has been set aside applies for employment with the law enforcement agency.
>
> (f) Consideration by a court, law enforcement agency, prosecuting attorney, or the attorney general in determining whether an individual required to be registered under the sex offenders registration act has violated that act, or for use in a prosecution for violating that act. [MCL 780.623(2); *emphasis added.*]

Significantly, the Legislature has also prescribed criminal penalties for a violation of these provisions:

> (5) Except as provided in subsection (2), a person, other than the applicant, who knows or should have known that a conviction was set aside under this section and who divulges, uses, or publishes information concerning a conviction set aside under this section is guilty of a misdemeanor punishable by imprisonment for not more than 90 days or a fine of not more than $500.00, or both. [MCL 780.623(5).]

A concealed weapon licensing board is not among the agencies or persons to whom the state police may provide access to its nonpublic record of the set aside order and related documents. Moreover, consideration in determining eligibility for licensure under the CPLA is not among the limited purposes for which a set aside conviction may be used. Indeed, the only licensing function for which the Legislature has carved out an exception is one "conducted by an agency of the judicial branch of state government." Words in a statute must be construed according to the common and approved usage of the language. MCL 8.3a. Affording the words of section 3(2) their commonly understood meaning, this exception must be read as written and may not be extended to a concealed weapon licensing board in the executive branch of government. See *Taylor v Michigan Public Utilities Comm*, 217 Mich 400, 402-403; 186 NW 485 (1922). Moreover, the express mention of one thing in a statute implies the exclusion of all other similar things. *Jennings v Southwood*, 446 Mich 125, 142; 521 NW2d 230 (1994).

The legislative history of the Set Aside Law is also instructive. When first enacted in 1965, the Set Aside Law consisted of only two sections. Section 2 of the act then provided, like its modern counterpart, that a successful applicant for an order setting aside a conviction "shall be deemed not to have been previously convicted." 1965 PA 213, section 2. Unlike current section 2, however, the original version included no exceptions to this general rule.[2] Most of the exceptions contained in current section 3 were added in 1982 by 1982 PA 495. The exception stated in subsection 3(2)(e) was added in 1988 by 1988 PA 11 and subsection 3(2)(f) was added in 1994 by 1994 PA 294. Thus, when the Legislature has seen fit to add to the limited purposes for which a set aside conviction may be used, it has done so, but it has not done so with regard to licensing purposes under the CPLA.

The Attorney General has considered the meaning and effect of sections 2 and 3 of the Set Aside Law and has construed that law as requiring that a person whose conviction has been set aside by a court is deemed not to have been previously convicted of the crime, except for those express limited purposes identified in the statute. See, e.g., OAG, 1973-1974, No 4774, pp 53, 55 (June 15, 1973); OAG, 1977-1978, No 5349, p 568 (August 9, 1978); OAG, 1993-1994, No 6780, p 89 (January 4, 1994). These opinions also construed the phrase "purposes of the law" contained in section 2(1) of the Act to apply to statutes of this state. OAG, 1973-1974, No 4774, and OAG, 1977-1978, No 5349, *supra*. See also *McBride v Callahan*, 173 Wash 609; 24 P 2d 105, 112 (1933). Thus, as the Set Aside Law contains no exceptions relevant to licensing under the CPLA, a person whose felony conviction has been set aside may be considered as "never having been convicted" for purposes of applying for a concealed weapon license and may not be denied a license to carry a concealed pistol under section 5b(7)(f) of the CPLA. MCL 28.425b(7)(f).

Under the Set Aside Law, the Department of State Police is required to retain a nonpublic record of the order setting aside a conviction and shall make it available to the courts and court agencies, law enforcement agencies, a prosecuting attorney, the Attorney General, or the Governor for the specific purposes enumerated in that statute. MCL 780.623(2). Section 5b(8) of the CPLA similarly requires the Department of State Police to maintain certain conviction information:

---

[2] Also, only a person whose crime was committed before he or she reached 21 years of age could apply for a set aside under the original act. The 1982 amendment extended the law's reach beyond persons who made "one youthful mistake" to everyone, regardless of age. House Legislative Analysis, HB 5229, H-3, September 21, 1982.

> Upon entry of a court order[3] or conviction of 1 of the enumerated prohibitions for using, transporting, selling, purchasing, carrying, shipping, receiving or distributing a firearm in this section [section 5b] the department of state police shall immediately enter the order or conviction into the law enforcement network. *For purposes of this act, information of the court order or conviction shall not be removed from the law enforcement information network, but may be moved to a separate file intended for the use of the county concealed weapon licensing boards, the courts, and other government entities as necessary and exclusively to determine eligibility to be licensed under this act.* [MCL 28.425b(8). *Emphasis added.*]

The "prohibitions" referred to in section 5b(8) above are enumerated in section 5b(7) of the Act.[4] Section 5b(7)(d) refers to certain court orders that would prohibit a person subject to the order from obtaining a permit to carry a concealed pistol. In addition, section 5b(7)(e) refers to section 224f of the Penal Code, MCL 750.224f, as a provision that prohibits a person from "possessing, using, transporting, selling, purchasing, carrying, shipping, receiving, or distributing a firearm." MCL 750.224f removes these gun rights from a convicted felon for a period of at least three years, depending on the crime committed. Even though persons described in these sections may later have their gun rights restored or convictions or other orders set aside, section 5b(8) nonetheless prohibits the State Police from removing the information from the Law Enforcement Information Network, but allows the Department to move the information "to a separate file intended for the use of the county concealed weapon licensing boards, the courts, and other government entities as necessary and exclusively to determine eligibility to be licensed under this act." Thus, the court orders and convictions referred to in section 5b(8) of the CPLA are those that the Legislature has determined bear on the ability of persons to exercise their firearm rights.

Reading the Set Aside Law and the CPLA together, the question arises whether the State Police may divulge information concerning a set aside conviction to a concealed weapon licensing board, and whether the board may use such information, without violating sections 3(3) and 3(5) of the Set Aside Law. In that regard, statutes should be harmonized and meaning and effect given to each of them wherever possible. *Nelson v Transamerica Ins Services*, 441 Mich 508, 513; 495 NW2d 370 (1992).

The Legislature has provided guidance in addressing this issue in section 5b(7)(o) of the CPLA. This section provides the following among the several circumstances that must exist for a concealed weapon licensing board to issue a license:

> Issuing a license to the applicant to carry a concealed pistol in this state is not detrimental to the safety of the applicant or to any other individual. A determination under this subdivision shall be based on clear and convincing evidence of civil infractions, crimes, personal protection orders or injunctions, or police reports or other clear and convincing evidence of the actions of, or statements of, the applicant that bear directly on the applicant's ability to carry a concealed pistol. [MCL 28.425b(7)(o).]

Under this section, evidence of a crime that bears directly on the applicant's ability to carry a concealed pistol is appropriately considered by the boards.

The reading of sections 5b(7)(f), 5b(7)(o), and 5b(8) of the CPLA and the Set Aside Law that best harmonizes them all and gives effect to each is one that allows the State Police to share with concealed weapon licensing boards only that information pertaining to set aside "conviction[s] of 1 of the enumerated prohibitions for using, transporting, selling, purchasing, carrying, shipping, receiving or distributing a firearm in [section 5b]." This conviction information, in turn, may be used by concealed weapon licensing boards in making the determinations required under section 5b(7)(o) of the CPLA, but may not be used under section 5b(f).

This interpretation gives effect to the Legislature's unmistakable intent to make information "that bear[s] directly on the applicant's ability to carry a concealed pistol" available "for the use" of the gun boards "as necessary and exclusively to determine eligibility to be licensed" under the CPLA. MCL 28.425b(8) and MCL 28.425b(7)(o). It is also consistent with the provision of the CPLA that requires an applicant to authorize the licensing board to access any records, including otherwise privileged information, that may pertain to the applicant's qualifications to carry a concealed pistol license. MCL 28.425b(c).

It is my opinion, therefore, that a person convicted of a felony whose conviction has been set aside by order of a Michigan court in accordance with 1965 PA 213, as amended, if otherwise qualified, may not be denied a concealed pistol license under section 5b(7)(f) of the Concealed Pistol Licensing Act. A person convicted of one of the offenses described under section 5b(8) of the Concealed Pistol Licensing Act, whose conviction has been set aside, may nevertheless be denied a concealed pistol license on the basis of information concerning that conviction if the concealed weapon licensing board determines that denial is warranted under section 5b(7)(o) of the Act.

MIKE COX
Attorney General

---

[3] The court order referred to here is one that has the effect of removing or limiting certain of a person's firearm rights as enumerated in section 5b(7)(d) of the CPLA, MCL 28.425b(7)(d). This section does not refer to orders setting aside felony convictions.

[4] No other provisions of section 5b can reasonably be construed as enumerating the "prohibitions" described in section 5b(8).

Opinion No. 7136
July 30, 2003

CONCEALED WEAPONS: Carrying of a pistol in a motor vehicle

FIREARMS:

CRIMINAL LAW:

A person licensed to carry a concealed pistol may lawfully occupy a motor vehicle in which a pistol has been left that belongs to another person who has exited the vehicle.

A person who is not licensed to carry a concealed pistol may lawfully occupy a vehicle in which a pistol has been left that is lawfully contained and that belongs to another person who has exited the vehicle, only if the occupant is not carrying the weapon, a determination that depends on the facts of each case.

Honorable Scott Shackleton
State Representative
The Capitol
Lansing, Michigan

You have asked two questions concerning the carrying of a pistol in a motor vehicle. You first ask if a person licensed to carry a concealed pistol may lawfully occupy a motor vehicle in which a pistol has been left that belongs to another person who has exited the vehicle.

Section 227(2) of the Michigan Penal Code, MCL 750.227(2), makes it a crime to carry a pistol, whether concealed or otherwise, in a vehicle. Section 227(2) states, in pertinent part, as follows:

> A person shall not carry a pistol concealed on or about his or her person, or, whether concealed or otherwise, in a vehicle operated or occupied by the person, except in his or her dwelling house, place of business, or on other land possessed by the person, *without a license to carry the pistol as provided by law* and if licensed, shall not carry the pistol in a place or manner inconsistent with any restrictions upon such license. *[Emphasis added.]*

By its express terms, the criminal prohibition in section 227(2) does not apply to a person licensed to carry a pistol, provided that the pistol is carried in a manner or place consistent with any restriction upon that license. This conclusion is further supported by section 425c(2) of the Concealed Pistol Licensing Act, MCL 28.425c(2), which expressly authorizes a concealed pistol licensee to "[c]arry a pistol in a vehicle, whether concealed or not concealed, anywhere in this state." Moreover, section 231a(1)(a) of the Penal Code, MCL 750.231a(1)(a), provides that the prohibition against carrying a concealed pistol in a motor vehicle does not apply to a person holding a valid license to carry a concealed pistol, provided that the pistol is carried in conformity with any restrictions appearing on the license.[1]

The primary rule of statutory construction is to effectuate the intent of the Legislature. *Wickens v Oakwood Healthcare System*, 465 Mich 53, 60; 631 NW2d 686 (2001). If the language of a statute is clear and unambiguous, it is assumed the Legislature intended its plain meaning to be enforced as written. *People v Stone*, 463 Mich 558, 562; 621 NW2d 702 (2001). Here, the statutes clearly provide that a person licensed to carry a concealed pistol is not subject to the prohibition against carrying a pistol in a motor vehicle, regardless of whether the pistol belongs to the licensee or another person.

It is my opinion, therefore, in answer to your first question, that a person licensed to carry a concealed pistol may lawfully occupy a motor vehicle in which a pistol has been left that belongs to another person who has exited the vehicle.

Your second question asks if a person who is not licensed to carry a concealed pistol may lawfully occupy a vehicle in which a pistol has been left that is lawfully contained,[2] and that belongs to another person who has exited the vehicle.

As previously noted, MCL 750.227(2) generally prohibits a person from carrying a concealed pistol in a motor vehicle unless that person is licensed to carry a concealed pistol. MCL 750.231a(1) contains several exceptions to the prohibition. Subsection (d) exempts a person "while transporting a pistol for a lawful purpose that is licensed by the owner or occupant of the motor vehicle in compliance with section 2 of 1927 PA 372, MCL 28.422, and the pistol is unloaded in a closed case designed

[1] This analysis is limited to consideration of a violation of MCL 750.227 only and assumes that the pistol is lawfully owned, inspected, and has not been used in the commission of a crime.

[2] By using the term "lawfully contained," it is understood that the pistol left in the vehicle is either (1) unloaded in a closed case designed for the storage of firearms in the trunk of the vehicle; or (2) unloaded in a closed case designed for the storage of firearms in a vehicle that does not have a trunk and is not readily accessible to the occupants of the vehicle. See MCL 750.231a(1)(d) and (e).

for the storage of firearms in the trunk of the vehicle."[3] MCL 750.231a(1)(d). Subsection (e) applies to vehicles without trunks by requiring that the firearm not be readily accessible to the occupants of the vehicle. MCL 750.231a(1)(e).

Under the facts provided in your request, the passenger has remained in the vehicle with a properly stored pistol belonging to the driver. Under these facts, the exceptions contained in MCL 750.231a(d) and (e) are inapplicable since the passenger is not "transporting" the firearm. "To transport is to convey from one place or station to another..." *People v Al-Saiegh*, 244 Mich App 391, 399; 625 NW2d 419 (2001).

Nonetheless, a violation of MCL 750.227(2) must be proven by evidence of the following: (1) that a weapon is present in a vehicle operated or occupied by the defendant; (2) that the defendant knew or was aware of its presence; and (3) that the defendant was "carrying" the weapon. *People v Courier*, 122 Mich App 88; 322 NW2d 421 (1982), citing *People v Butler*, 414 Mich 377; 319 NW2d 540 (1982). "Carrying" is an essential element that must be proven to establish a violation of the prohibition in section 227(2) and may not automatically be inferred from evidence that the defendant had knowledge that the weapon was present in the vehicle. *People v Emery*, 150 Mich App 657; 667; 389 NW2d 472 (1986).

The element of "carrying" depends on the particular facts of each case. It cannot be stated, as a definitive matter of law, what conduct constitutes carrying for the purposes of section 227(2). Nevertheless, Michigan courts have articulated several factors to be considered in resolving whether the essential element of "carrying" a weapon in a vehicle has been established. Factors that have been considered include: (1) the defendant's awareness of the weapon; (2) the accessibility or proximity of the weapon to the defendant; (3) the defendant's possession of items which connect him to the weapon, such as ammunition; (4) the defendant's ownership or operation of the vehicle; and (5) the length of time during which the defendant drove or occupied the vehicle. *People v Emery*, 150 Mich App at 667.

The fact that a pistol is lawfully contained does not necessarily exempt a person from possible prosecution under section 227(2). See, for example, *People v Wilson*, 2001 Mich App LEXIS 1144 (unpublished), in which the Court of Appeals held that the defendant was subject to prosecution under section 227(2), notwithstanding that the pistol was locked in the truck of a vehicle.

It is my opinion, therefore, in answer to your second question, that a person who is not licensed to carry a concealed pistol may lawfully occupy a vehicle in which a pistol has been left that is lawfully contained and that belongs to another person who has exited the vehicle, only if the occupant is not carrying the weapon, a determination that depends on the facts of each case.

MIKE COX
Attorney General

[3] Section 2 of 1927 PA 372, MCL 28.422, provides the qualifications for the purchase of a pistol.

Opinion No. 7152
March 29, 2004

FIREARMS: License to purchase pistols

LICENSES:
A local unit of government may not require an applicant for a license to purchase a pistol to provide his or her fingerprints before issuing the license. Where an applicant's identity is reasonably called into question, a local law enforcement official who is unable for that reason to determine that the applicant has demonstrated the existence of all the circumstances necessary to deem that applicant "qualified" may deny the application. If the applicant chooses to provide his or her fingerprints, the local law enforcement official may accept them to attempt to resolve the matter.

Honorable John Garfield
State Representative
The Capitol
Lansing, Michigan

You have asked whether a local unit of government may require an applicant for a license to purchase a pistol to provide his or her fingerprints before issuing the license.

The Legislature has established the circumstances under which a person may obtain a license to purchase a pistol, commonly referred to as a "pistol purchase permit." Section 2(3) of the Firearms Law, 1927 PA 372, MCL 28.422(3), provides that "[t]he commissioner or chief of police of a city, township, or village police department that issues licenses to purchase, carry, or transport pistols, or his or her duly authorized deputy, or the sheriff or his or her duly authorized deputy, in the parts of a county not included within a city, township, or village having an organized police department...shall with due speed and diligence issue licenses to purchase, carry, or transport pistols to qualified applicants" unless the local official has probable cause to believe that the applicant would be a threat to himself or herself or to other individuals, or would commit an offense with the pistol that would violate a law of this or another state or of the United States. The statute provides that an applicant is qualified if all of the following circumstances exist:

> (a) The person is not subject to an order or disposition for which he or she has received notice and an opportunity for a hearing, and which was entered into the law enforcement information network pursuant to [seven specified statutes].
>
> (b) The person is 18 years of age or older or, if the seller is licensed pursuant to section 923 of title 18 of the United States Code, 18 U.S.C. 923, is 21 years of age or older.
>
> (c) The person is a citizen of the United States and is a legal resident of this state.
>
> (d) A felony charge against the person is not pending at the time of application.
>
> (e) The person is not prohibited from possessing, using, transporting, selling, purchasing, carrying, shipping, receiving, or distributing a firearm under section 224f of the Michigan penal code, Act No. 328 of the Public Acts of 1931, being section 750.224f of the Michigan Compiled Laws.
>
> (f) The person has not been adjudged insane in this state or elsewhere unless he or she has been adjudged restored to sanity by court order.
>
> (g) The person is not under an order of involuntary commitment in an inpatient or outpatient setting due to mental illness.
>
> (h) The person has not been adjudged legally incapacitated in this state or elsewhere. This subdivision does not apply to a person who has had his or her legal capacity restored by order of the court.
>
> (i) The person correctly answers 70% or more of the questions on a basic pistol safety review questionnaire approved by the basic pistol safety review board and provided to the individual free of charge by the licensing authority... [MCL 28.422(3)(a)-(i).]

Applications for licenses must be signed by the applicant under oath on forms provided by the Department of State Police. MCL 28.422(4). Under MCL 28.422(11), a person who forges any matter on an application for a license under this section is guilty of a felony. As you observe in your letter, however, no provision of MCL 28.422 requires that an applicant provide his or her fingerprints in order to receive a license to purchase a pistol or authorizes a local law enforcement officer to impose such a requirement.[1]

MCL 28.422 differs in this respect from section 5b of the Firearms Law, MCL 28.425b, which describes the process for obtaining a license to carry a concealed pistol. Section 5b(9), MCL 28.425b(9), states in pertinent part: "An individual, after submitting an application and paying the fee prescribed under subsection (5), shall request and have classifiable fingerprints taken by the county sheriff or a local police agency if that local police agency maintains fingerprinting capability... The county sheriff or local police agency shall take the fingerprints within 5 business days after the request." The fingerprints must be taken on forms and in a manner prescribed by the Department of State Police. MCL 28.425b(10). They are then forwarded to the Department of State Police for comparison with fingerprints already on file with the department, which then forwards the fingerprints to the Federal Bureau of Investigation. MCL 28.425b(10). Under this section, the concealed weapon licensing board may deny a license if an individual's fingerprints are not "classifiable" by the Federal Bureau of Investigation. MCL 28.425b(10).[2]

In construing a statute, the primary task is to discern and give effect to the intent of the Legislature. *Dan De Farms Inc v Sterling Farm Supply Inc*, 465 Mich 872; 633 NW2d 824 (2001). Provisions that the Legislature did not include may not be added into a statute. *In re Wayne County Prosecutor*, 232 Mich App 482, 486; 591 NW2d 359 (1998). In the absence of a statutory provision authorizing a local law enforcement agency to impose such a requirement, as here, one cannot be read into the statute.

Further support for this conclusion is found in MCL 123.1102, which provides:

> A local unit of government shall not impose special taxation on, enact or enforce any ordinance or regulation pertaining to, *or regulate in any other manner the* ownership, registration, *purchase*, sale, transfer, transportation, or possession *of pistols* or other firearms, ammunition for pistols or other firearms, or components of pistols or other firearms, *except as otherwise provided by federal law or a law of this state. [Emphasis added.]*

While this section refers to a "local unit of government" and not individual local officers, its meaning is plain. The Legislature has occupied the field of firearm regulation and has authorized local regulation in this area only to the extent expressly provided by law. *Michigan Coalition for Responsible Gun Owners v City of Ferndale*, 256 Mich App 401, 418; 662 NW2d 864 (2003).

It is important to emphasize, however, that section 2(3) of the Firearms Law, MCL 28.422(3), confers discretion on the law enforcement officials specified in that section to deny an application for a license to purchase a pistol where he or she has probable cause to believe the applicant would be a threat to himself or herself or to other individuals, or would commit an offense with the pistol that would violate the law. Moreover, if the official processing an individual's application reasonably believes the applicant has falsified his or her identity such that the official cannot adequately determine that the applicant has demonstrated the existence of all the necessary circumstances establishing that the applicant is "qualified," such a belief would also justify denying the application. Under these circumstances, if the applicant chooses to provide his or her fingerprints, the local law enforcement official may accept them to attempt to resolve the matter.

It is my opinion, therefore, that a local unit of government may not require an applicant for a license to purchase a pistol to provide his or her fingerprints before issuing the license. Where an applicant's identity is reasonably called into question, a local law enforcement official who is unable for that reason to determine that the applicant has demonstrated the existence of all the circumstances necessary to deem that applicant "qualified" may deny the application. If the applicant chooses to provide his or her fingerprints, the local law enforcement official may accept them to attempt to resolve the matter.

MIKE COX
Attorney General

---

[1] A review of the current form the Department of State Police provides law enforcement officers for their use in processing applications for a license to purchase a pistol reveals no provision requiring an applicant to provide fingerprints or authorizing a law enforcement officer to impose such a requirement. This opinion should not be read to foreclose the state police from making a change in the form to add such a requirement. This opinion only addresses the authority of a local unit of government or its officers to impose such a requirement in the absence of such a form.

In addition, administrative rules promulgated by the Department of State Police, 1979 AC, R 28.91 and R 28.92, do not apply here. Each of these rules was adopted pursuant to authority in MCL 28.422 and MCL 28.426. The latter of these statutes was repealed by 2000 PA 381. The rules, while they remain in effect, appear to address circumstances that do not apply to your question.

[2] For other statutes in which the Legislature has expressly authorized or required the taking of fingerprints under certain circumstances, see, e.g., MCL 207.1056 (application for license under Motor Fuel Tax Act); MCL 256.604(1) (application for license to engage in driver training school business); MCL 257.248f(2) (applications for vehicle dealer or salvage vehicle agent license under Michigan Vehicle Code); MCL 257.307 (application for operator's or chauffeur's license under Michigan Vehicle Code); MCL 338.1710 (application for license under Forensic Polygraph Examiners Act); MCL 451.602 (application for registration under Uniform Securities Act); MCL 600.949 (application for admission to state bar); and MCL 711.1 (petition for name change under Probate Code).

Opinion No. 7182
October 19, 2005

FIREARMS: Meaning of retired police or law enforcement officer in the Concealed Pistol Licensing Act

LAW ENFORCEMENT OFFICERS:
The terms "retired police officer" or "retired law enforcement officer," as used in the Concealed Pistol Licensing Act, MCL 28.421 *et seq*, mean a certified police or law enforcement officer who retired in good standing from his or her employment as a police or law enforcement officer and who is receiving a retirement benefit.

Honorable Herb Kehrl
State Representative
The Capitol
Lansing, MI 48909

You have asked several questions concerning the meaning of the terms "retired police officer" or "retired law enforcement officer" as used in the Michigan Concealed Pistol Licensing Act (CPLA), 2000 PA 381, MCL 28.421 *et seq.*

Section 5b(7)(c) of the CPLA, MCL 28.425b(7)(c), provides that, in order to become licensed to carry a concealed pistol, the applicant must have successfully completed a firearms course that satisfies the basic requirements of section 5j, MCL 28.425j, which includes such subjects as the safe handling of a pistol, fundamentals of pistol shooting, legal issues relating to firearms, avoiding confrontation, as well as training and practice on a firing range. Section 5l(2), MCL 28.425l(2), exempts from the educational requirements of section 5b(7)(c) an applicant "who is a retired police officer or retired law enforcement officer." The CPLA also prohibits licensees from carrying a concealed pistol in certain locations, such as schools, hospitals, and day care centers. MCL 28.425o. However, that prohibition does not apply to a licensee who is a "retired police officer or retired law enforcement officer." MCL 28.425o(4)(a).

You ask whether the term "retired police officer" or "retired law enforcement officer" includes an officer who worked part time and is not eligible for retirement benefits. Your other questions present additional factual variations on the first, including whether an officer would be deemed "retired" under the CPLA if the officer was receiving less that full benefits, lacks a retirement card, or retired for medical reasons and was collecting workers compensation benefits. By way of background, you advise that a prosecutor who serves as the chairperson of a county concealed weapon licensing board has taken the position that a retired police or law enforcement officer must be receiving retirement benefits in order to be eligible for the exemptions found in the CPLA.

The terms "retired police officer" and "retired law enforcement officer" are defined in section 1(h) of the CPLA, MCL 28.421(h):

> "Retired police officer" or "retired law enforcement officer" means an individual who was a certified police officer or certified law enforcement officer as those terms are defined under section 2(k) of the commission on law enforcement standards act, 1965 PA 203, MCL 28.602,[1] and retired in good standing from his or her employment as a police officer or law enforcement officer.

The Michigan Commission on Law Enforcement Standards Act (MCOLES Act), MCL 28.601 *et seq*, does not expressly define the terms "certified police officer" or "certified law enforcement officer." Section 2(*l*) of that act, however, does define "police officer" or "law enforcement officer":

> "Police officer" or "law enforcement officer" means, unless the context requires otherwise, any of the following:
>
> (i) A regularly employed member of a law enforcement agency authorized and established pursuant to law, including common law, who is responsible for the prevention and detection of crime and the enforcement of the general criminal laws of this state. Police officer or law enforcement officer does not include a person serving solely because he or she occupies any other office or position.
>
> (ii) A law enforcement officer of a Michigan Indian tribal police force, subject to the limitations set forth in section 9(3).
>
> (iii) The sergeant at arms or any assistant sergeant at arms of either house of the legislature who is commissioned

---

[1] Former section 2(k) of the Commission on Law Enforcement Standards Act is now section 2(*l*) by virtue of an amendment to that act by 2004 PA 379.

as a police officer by that respective house of the legislature as provided by the legislative sergeant at arms police powers act, 2001 PA 185, MCL 4.381 to 4.382.

(iv) A law enforcement officer of a multicounty metropolitan district, subject to the limitations of section 9(7).

(v) A county prosecuting attorney's investigator sworn and fully empowered by the sheriff of that county.

(vi) Until December 31, 2007, a law enforcement officer of a school district in this state that has a membership of at least 20,000 pupils and that includes in its territory a city with a population of at least 180,000 as of the most recent federal decennial census. [MCL 28.602(l).]

The MCOLES Act further defines "certification" in section 2(b), MCL 28.602(b):

"Certification" means either of the following:

(*i*) A determination by the commission that a person meets the law enforcement officer minimum standards to be employed as a commission certified law enforcement officer and that the person is authorized under this act to be employed as a law enforcement officer.

(*ii*) A determination by the commission that a person was employed as a law enforcement officer before January 1, 1977 and that the person is authorized under this act to be employed as a law enforcement officer.

The primary rule of statutory construction is to discern and effectuate the intent of the Legislature. *Sun Valley Foods Co v Ward*, 460 Mich 230; 236; 596 NW2d 119 (1999). Reading the relevant definitions together, it is reasonable to conclude that, for the purposes of the CPLA, the Legislature intended "certified police or law enforcement officer" to mean a person who meets the definition of a police or law enforcement officer in the MCOLES Act and who has met the qualifications for certification under that act.[2]

The question then turns to whether an officer who meets these requirements is "retired." Again, the primary goal of statutory construction is to ascertain and give effect to legislative intent. *People v Stanaway*, 446 Mich 643, 658; 521 NW2d 557 (1994). The word "retired" is not defined in either the CPLA or the MCOLES Act. The rules of statutory construction also require that every word or phrase of a statute be given its commonly accepted meaning. *Western Michigan Univ Bd of Control v Michigan*, 455 Mich 531, 539; 565 NW2d 828 (1997); MCL 8.3a. In the absence of a statutory definition, it is proper to resort to dictionary definitions. *State ex rel Wayne County Prosecuting Attorney v Levenburg*, 406 Mich 455, 465; 280 NW2d 810 (1979). *Webster's Third New International Dictionary, Unabridged Edition* (1964), defines "retired" as having "withdrawn from active duty or business" while "retire" is defined as "to withdraw from office, public station, business, occupation, or active duty." A person who is retired is a "retiree," which is synonymous with "retirant." *Id. Black's Law Dictionary* (7th ed) defines "retirement" as the "voluntary termination of one's own employment or career, [especially] upon reaching a certain age."

Applying these definitions alone, however, does not answer the question of whether an officer must be receiving retirement benefits in order to be deemed "retired" for the purposes of the CPLA. A literal application of the dictionary definition could lead to the conclusion that any certified officer who is separated from his or her position as a police or law enforcement officer, regardless of whether the officer meets the age and longevity requirement needed to qualify for retirement benefits, would qualify as "retired." By requiring that the officer be "retired," however, rather than merely a "former" officer, it is apparent that the Legislature contemplated more than that the officer has received basic training, been employed for the minimum period of time to become certified, and then left that position.

It is helpful in determining legislative intent to examine other statutes that relate to the same subject or share a common purpose. Such statutes are *in pari materia*, and may be read together as one law, even if they contain no reference to one another and were enacted on different dates. *Palmer v State Land Office Bd*, 304 Mich 628, 636; 8 NW2d 664 (1943). The purpose of the in pari materia rule is to give effect to the legislative purpose as found in harmonious statutes. *Jennings v Southwood*, 446 Mich 125, 136-137; 521 NW2d 230 (1994). In addition, the Legislature is deemed to be aware of the meaning given to the words it uses, *Anzaldua v Band*, 457 Mich 530, 543; 578 NW2d 306 (1998), and of the existence of the law in effect at the time of its enactments. *Malcolm v East Detroit*, 437 Mich 132, 139; 468 NW2d 479 (1991).

The term "retired" person or "retirant" has a particular meaning under various pension and employment statutes that are, therefore, relevant in determining the meaning of the terms "retired police officer" and "retired law enforcement officer" under the CPLA. For retirement purposes, a "retirant" is defined in section 2(c) of the Public Employee Retirement Benefits Forfeiture Act, 1994 PA 350, MCL 38.2702(c), as a "person who has retired with a retirement benefit payable from a retirement system." A "member" is defined as a person who is "a member, vested former member, or deferred member of a retirement system." MCL

[2] Michigan Administrative Code, 1988 AACS, R 28.4151(c) defines the term "certified as a police officer" as a "person who has met all the selection, employment, training, or waiver of training standards and who is approved by the training council or pursuant to the act to exercise the authority of a police officer."

38.2702(b). Thus, different terminology is employed for a person who is receiving a pension benefit (a "retirant") and a person who may qualify for a pension benefit but is not yet receiving it (a "member").[3]

The Fire Fighters and Police Officers Retirement Act, 1937 PA 345, MCL 38.551 *et seq*, provides that a "member" who is at least 55 years of age and has 25 years of service may "retire." MCL 38.556(1)(a). A member who becomes incapacitated due to a duty-related injury or disease "shall be retired" and receive a disability retirement pension. MCL 38.556(2)(d). A member who has at least five years of service and suffers a non-duty related injury or disease "may be retired by the retirement board" and receive a formula-based disability retirement pension. MCL 38.556(2)(e). In either case, "a retired member restored to active service shall again become a member of the retirement system" and any workers disability compensation benefits are to be offset against any retirement benefits. MCL 38.556(2)(f). The State Police Retirement Act of 1986, 1986 PA 182, MCL 38.1601 *et seq*, defines a "retirant" as "a member who separates from service and retires with a retirement allowance payable from the appropriate reserve of the retirement system." MCL 38.1604(3). These statutes governing retirement benefits, including those applicable to police officers, support the conclusion that a "retired" police or law enforcement officer is one who separates from service with a retirement benefit. This conclusion would apply regardless of the amount of retirement benefit the officer receives, whether the benefit is based on the officer being injured in the line of duty, or whether the officer receives a retirement card.[4] Given the changes that are being made in retirement benefits in various communities – such as "401(k)" defined contribution plans replacing defined benefit plans, and the possibility of delayed receipt of vested retirement benefits – the Legislature may wish to consider amending MCL 28.421(h) to assure that the language of the statute continues to reflect the underlying intent of the Legislature.

It is my opinion, therefore, that the terms "retired police officer" or "retired law enforcement officer," as used in the Concealed Pistol Licensing Act, MCL 28.421 *et seq*, mean a certified police or law enforcement officer who retired in good standing from his or her employment as a police or law enforcement officer and who is receiving a retirement benefit.

MIKE COX
Attorney General

[3] A similar distinction in terminology is also found in section 2 of the Public Employee Retirement Benefit Protection Act, 2002 PA 100, under which "retirant" means a person "who has retired with a retirement benefit payable from a retirement system," MCL 38.1682(e), and "member" means "a member, vested former member, deferred member . . . . " MCL 38.1682(c).

[4] This conclusion is also supported by the decision in *Clexton v Detroit*, 179 Mich App 209, 214; 445 NW2d 201 (1989). That case involved the interpretation of a city charter provision that defined a "retirant" as a member of the City's retirement system "who retires with a retirement allowance or pension paid by the retirement system." The plaintiff had left his employment before becoming eligible to receive his pension, retaining the right to a retirement allowance upon reaching retirement age. The plaintiff sought to receive payment of unused sick leave payable by the City to a "retirant." Since the plaintiff was not receiving a retirement benefit, the court found he was not a "retirant."

Opinion No. 7183
December 27, 2005

FIREARMS: Possession and transfer of a machine gun

MICHIGAN PENAL CODE:
A person in Michigan may only possess a machine gun if it was lawfully possessed before May 19, 1986, and is properly registered under federal law. A person in Michigan may only transfer possession of a machine gun if authorized to do so by the federal Director of the Bureau of Alcohol, Tobacco, Firearms and Explosives.

Honorable Leon Drolet
State Representative
The Capitol
Lansing, Michigan 48909

You have asked whether a person[1] in Michigan may transfer possession of a federally registered machine gun.

Possession of a machine gun by a person in Michigan is controlled by section 224 of the Michigan Penal Code, MCL 750.224:

> (1) A person shall not manufacture, sell, offer for sale, or possess any of the following:
>
> (a) A machine gun or firearm that shoots or is designed to shoot automatically more than 1 shot without manual reloading, by a single function of the trigger.
>
> * * *
>
> (3) Subsection (1) does not apply to any of the following:
>
> (a) A self-defense spray device as defined in section 224d.
>
> (b) A person manufacturing firearms, explosives, or munitions of war by virtue of a contract with a department of the government of the United States.
>
> (c) *A person licensed by the secretary of the treasury of the United States or the secretary's delegate*[2] *to* manufacture, sell, or *possess a machine gun*, or a device, weapon, cartridge, container, or contrivance described in subsection (1). *[Emphasis added.]*

Of greatest relevance to your question is the exception stated in subsection 3(c) above. Michigan law, therefore, prohibits the possession of a machine gun by a person unless that person has been "licensed" by the United States Government to manufacture, sell, or possess the weapon.

To determine how one becomes "licensed" by the federal government, the governing provision is subsection (o) of section 922 of the federal Firearms Owners' Protection Act of 1986 (FOPA), 18 USC 922(o). That subsection states in relevant part:

> (1) Except as provided in paragraph (2), it shall be unlawful for any person to transfer or possess a machinegun.
>
> (2) This subsection does not apply with respect to—
>
> * * *
>
> (B) any lawful transfer or lawful possession of a machinegun that was lawfully possessed before the date this subsection takes effect [effective May 19, 1986]. [18 USC 922(o)(1) and (2)(B).]

After enactment of the FOPA, the Bureau of Alcohol, Tobacco, Firearms and Explosives promulgated implementing regulations permitting private ownership of a machine gun under specified circumstances. One of those regulations, 27 CFR 479.105, provides:

> (a) General. As provided by 26 U.S.C. 5812 and 26 U.S.C. 5822, an application to make or transfer a firearm shall be denied if the making, transfer, receipt, or possession of the firearm would place the maker or transferee in

---

[1] Because your request only concerns private individuals, this opinion does not address any other classes of persons, such as law enforcement officers and military personnel.

[2] The historical responsibility of the Secretary of Treasury of the United States to regulate firearms through the Bureau of Alcohol, Tobacco, Firearms and Explosives was transferred by Congress to the United States Attorney General by Public Law No 107-296, Title XI, Subtitle B, § 1112(f)(4), (6), 116 Stat 2276 (2002).

violation of law...

(b) Machine guns lawfully possessed prior to May 19, 1986. A machine gun possessed in compliance with the provisions of this part prior to May 19, 1986, may continue to be lawfully possessed by the person to whom the machine gun is registered and may, upon compliance with the provisions of this part, be lawfully transferred to and possessed by the transferee.

Thus, under federal law, a person may possess a machine gun if that person lawfully possessed it before May 19, 1986, or if the person is one to whom a person in lawful possession lawfully transferred possession after that date. Another regulation, 27 CFR 479.84, generally prohibits the transfer of a firearm "unless an application, Form 4 (Firearms), Application for Transfer and Registration of Firearm, in duplicate, executed under the penalties of perjury to transfer the firearm and register it to the transferee has been filed with and approved by the Director [of the Bureau of Alcohol, Tobacco, Firearms and Explosives]." The regulation further requires that the application provide a complete description of the firearm and detailed identification of both parties to the transfer. Under the current Form 4 (copy attached), the transferee is required to certify whether the transferee has been convicted of or is facing criminal felony charges, whether the transferee is a fugitive, illegal alien, addicted to controlled substances, subject to a domestic relations restraining order, has received a military dishonorable discharge, has been adjudicated mentally defective, or has been convicted of domestic violence. An affirmative answer to any of these questions results in a denial of the application. Another regulation, 27 CFR 479.85, requires that the application include the transferee's photograph and set of fingerprints. The application must also be certified by the appropriate state or local law enforcement official as to whether the official has any information indicating that the machine gun will be used for other than a lawful purpose or that possession of the gun by the transferee would be in violation of state or federal law. 27 CFR 479.85. The Form 4 application is then reviewed by the Director and, if approved, is returned to the transferor who may then transfer the weapon. The transferee is required to retain the approved Form 4 application as proof that the firearm is properly registered. 27 CFR 479.86.

In light of this federal regulatory background, it must next be determined whether this federal approval process culminates in the issuance of a "license" for purposes of the exception to the prohibition on the possession of a machine gun found in MCL 750.224.

The foremost rule in construing a statute is to discern and give effect to the intent of the Legislature. *Nastal v Henderson & Associates Investigations, Inc*, 471 Mich 712, 720; 691 NW2d 1 (2005). The first step in ascertaining that intent is to review the language of the statute. The plain meaning of the critical word itself as well as its placement and purpose in the statutory scheme must be considered. *Sun Valley Foods Co v Ward*, 460 Mich 230, 236-237; 596 NW2d 119 (1999).

The concept of licensure was discussed in *Bostrom v Jennings*, 326 Mich 146, 167; 40 NW2d 97 (1949) (Boyles, J. concurring):

[A] license means "to confer on a person the right to do something which otherwise he would not have the right to do." 33 Am Jur, "Licenses," § 2, p 325.

"The object of a license is to confer a right that does not exist without a license." Chilvers v. People, 11 Mich 43, 49.

"The popular understanding of the word license undoubtedly is, a permission to do something which without the license would not be allowable..." *Youngblood v. Sexton*, 32 Mich 406, 419 (20 Am Rep 654).

The general understanding of a license is stated in Webster's New International Dictionary (2d ed), p 1425, as follows:

"License, license, n * * * Authority or liberty given to do or forebear any act; permission to do something."

Although the application and registration scheme provided for under the federal laws and regulations discussed above do not result in the issuance of a document labeled "license,"[3] the Form 4 application and resulting approval process bears all the hallmarks of licensure. The permission granted by the Director of the Bureau of Alcohol, Tobacco, Firearms and Explosives to transfer and possess a machine gun is the official authority required in order to avoid the federal proscription. Absent such approval, a person possessing a machine gun would be subject to serious sanctions, including prosecution and incarceration under both federal and state law. See 18 USC 924 and MCL 750.224(2).

Moreover, there is no indication in the plain text of MCL 750.224 that the Legislature intended the word "license" to have a meaning other than its ordinary meaning as described by the Court in *Bostrom*. Its purpose in the statutory scheme appears to be to assure that only those persons receiving the proper authorization from the appropriate federal officials are allowed to manufacture, sell, or possess a machine gun. The statute does not focus on the particular title or name given to that authorizing instrument. Accordingly, the authorization provided under the federal regulatory scheme embodied in 18 USC 922(o) and

[3] Compare 18 USC 923 (providing for the licensure of manufacturers, importers, dealers, and collectors).

related regulations constitutes a "license" within the meaning of MCL 750.224.[4]

It is my opinion, therefore, that a person in Michigan may only possess a machine gun if it was lawfully possessed before May 19, 1986, and is properly registered under federal law. A person in Michigan may only transfer possession of a machine gun if authorized to do so by the federal Director of the Bureau of Alcohol, Tobacco, Firearms and Explosives.

MIKE COX
Attorney General

---

[4] OAG, 1977-1978, No 5210, p 189 (August 10, 1977), reached the opposite conclusion on this question. However, at the time that opinion was issued, MCL 750.224 allowed a person to possess a machine gun if the person was"duly licensed to manufacture, sell, or possess any machine gun." As that opinion noted, when MCL 750.224 was amended in 1959, the Legislature considered a companion bill to license the possession of machine guns. The opinion concluded that the failure to enact the bill was evidence that no law existed to allow for the possession of a machine gun. The opinion further noted that then existing federal law only provided for the registration and not the licensing of machine guns. As discussed above, Congress subsequently enacted legislation authorizing the Director of Alcohol, Tobacco, Firearms and Explosives to formally approve the possession of certain machine guns. Moreover, soon after the issuance of OAG No 5210, the Legislature amended MCL 750.224 by 1978 PA 564 to specifically recognize an exception for a license issued by the United States Government. The Attorney General was also quick to recognize that with the amendment, the machine gun prohibition in MCL 750.224 did not apply to a person duly licensed by the Secretary of Treasury of the United States or the Secretary's delegate to possess a machine gun. Letter opinion of the Attorney General to Phillip Price, Chief, National Firearms Act Branch, United States Department of Treasury, dated April 25, 1979. Accordingly, OAG No 5210 is superseded by this opinion.

Opinion No. 7253
October 26, 2010

FIREARMS: Possession of a firearm that shoots shotgun shells, has not been modified from a shotgun, and has a barrel length of less than 18 inches, and an overall length of less than 26 inches

FIREARMS ACT:

MICHIGAN PENAL CODE:

SHORT-BARRELED SHOTGUN:
A person in Michigan may lawfully possess a weapon that fires shotgun shells; has not been constructed from a modified shotgun; has an overall length of less than 26 inches and a barrel length of less than 18 inches; and is not designed or intended to be fired from the shoulder, if the person complies with the purchase and registration requirements for owning a pistol set forth in the Firearms Act, 1929 PA 372, MCL 28.421 *et seq.*

Honorable Phillip Pavlov
State Representative
The Capitol
Lansing, MI 48909

You ask whether a person may legally own a weapon that fires shotgun shells; was not constructed from a modified shotgun; has an overall length of less than 26 inches and a barrel length of less than 18 inches; and is registered as a pistol.

Answering your question requires addressing two initial issues. The first is whether the weapon you have described is an unlawful short-barreled shotgun. MCL 750.224b(1) provides that "[a] person shall not manufacture, sell, offer for sale, or possess a short-barreled shotgun or short-barreled rifle." Violation of this prohibition is a felony punishable by up to five years imprisonment or a fine of up to $42,500. MCL 750.224b(2). [1] Short-barreled shotgun is defined in MCL 750.222(i) as:

> [A] ***shotgun*** having 1 or more barrels less than 18 inches in length or a weapon made from a ***shotgun***, whether by alteration, modification, or otherwise, if the weapon as modified has an overall length of less than 26 inches. [Emphasis added.]

The term "shotgun" is defined as "a firearm designed or redesigned, made or remade, and *intended to be fired from the shoulder* and designed or redesigned and made or remade to use the energy of the explosive in a fixed *shotgun shell* to fire through a smooth bore either a number of ball shot or a single projectile for each single function of the trigger." MCL 750.222(h) (emphasis added).

The primary goal of statutory interpretation is to give effect to the intent of the Legislature as expressed in the plain language of the statute. *Brown v Detroit Mayor*, 478 Mich 589, 593; 734 NW2d 514 (2007); *Houdek v Centerville Twp*, 276 Mich App 568, 581; 741 NW2d 587 (2007). "[I]f the language of the statute is clear and unambiguous, no interpretation is necessary and the court must follow the clear wording of the statute." *American Alternative Ins Co v Farmers Ins Exchange*, 470 Mich 28, 30; 679 NW2d 306 (2004).

Based on the plain language of the definitions quoted above, an illegal short-barreled shotgun is either a firearm: (1) designed or intended to be fired from the shoulder and having a barrel length of less than 18 inches; or (2) modified from a shotgun to be less than 26 inches in overall length. MCL 750.222(i) and 750.222(h); *People v Walker*, 166 Mich App 299, 301; 420 NW2d 194 (1988). A number of unmodified weapons fire shotgun shells, have barrel lengths of less than 18 inches, but are not designed or intended to be fired from the shoulder, and therefore do not fall within the statutory definition of "short-barreled shotgun."[2] It is, however, illegal to possess a weapon with a barrel length of less than 18 inches or an overall length of less than 26 inches created by modifying a shotgun originally designed or intended to be fired from the shoulder.

The second issue is whether a weapon that fires shotgun shells but does not meet the definition of a shotgun, and which has a barrel length of less than 18 inches and an overall length of less than 26 inches, may be possessed in Michigan. In other words, if such a weapon is not a shotgun, how should it be classified for purposes of ownership in Michigan.

---

[1] MCL 750.224b(3) exempts from the prohibition short-barreled shotguns that have been deemed by the United States Secretary of Treasury to be a "curio, relic, antique, museum piece, or collector's item" and not likely to be used as a weapon, and the owner has registered the weapon as a pistol in accordance with MCL 28.422 and 28.422a.

[2] An example of such a weapon is the "Super-Shorty" manufactured by Serbu Firearms, Inc. The company describes the weapon as a short 12-gauge pump shotgun available with pistol grips (its overall length is 16.5 inches), and markets the firearm as being concealable. Its overall design reveals that it is not designed or intended to be fired from the shoulder. See (accessed October 20, 2010).

MCL 750.222(e) defines a "pistol" as "a loaded or unloaded *firearm* that is 30 inches or less in length, or a loaded or unloaded firearm that by its construction and appearance conceals itself as a firearm." (Emphasis added.) "Firearm" is defined as "a weapon from which a dangerous projectile may be propelled by an explosive, or by gas or air." MCL 750.222(d).

Based on the plain language of these definitions, the weapon described in your request is plainly a "firearm" since it is a weapon that projects or fires shotgun shells. It also falls within the definition of "pistol" because it is a firearm with an overall length of less than 30 inches. The weapon is not designed or intended to be fired from the shoulder and is concealable. This further supports a conclusion that the weapon is a pistol under Michigan law.

As a pistol, the weapon you describe may not be owned or lawfully possessed unless the requirements of the Firearms Act, 1929 PA 372, MCL 28.421 *et seq*, are met. Under that Act, "a person shall not purchase, carry, possess, or transport a pistol in this state without first having obtained a license for the pistol as prescribed in this section." MCL 28.422(1).[3]

It is my opinion, therefore, that a person in Michigan may lawfully possess a weapon that fires shotgun shells; has not been constructed from a modified shotgun; has an overall length of less than 26 inches and a barrel length of less than 18 inches; and is not designed or intended to be fired from the shoulder, if the person complies with the purchase and registration requirements for owning a pistol set forth in the Firearms Act, 1929 PA 372, MCL 28.421 *et seq*.

MIKE COX
Attorney General

[3] The federal government treats pistols with a smooth barrel as an "any other weapon" (AOW), rather than a pistol. 26 USC 5845(e). However, Michigan law makes no such distinction over barrel rifling. Thus, for federal purposes the weapon is taxed as an AOW, while for state purposes it is a pistol.

Opinion No. 7254
October 26, 2010

CONST 1963, ART 1, § 6: Restrictions on right to bear arms under Const 1963, art 1, § 6

FIREARMS:

NATURAL RESOURCES COMMISSION:
Const 1963, art 1, § 6 provides a constitutional right in Michigan to bear firearms for self defense, subject to reasonable regulation by the State.

The firearm and ammunition restrictions set forth in Wildlife Conservation Order section 2.1(3) dealing with the possession of a rifle or shotgun in areas frequented by deer during the five-day period immediately preceding the beginning of firearm deer season are a reasonable exercise of the State's police power, and do not violate the right to bear arms established by Const 1963, art 1, § 6.

The Legislature may, by statute, amend or repeal the firearm and ammunition restrictions set forth in Wildlife Conservation Order section 2.1(3).

Honorable Michael Prusi
State Senator
The Capitol
Lansing, MI 48909

You have asked two questions regarding a provision within the Wildlife Conservation Order (WCO)[1] that restricts possession of certain firearms and types of ammunition during the five days preceding opening day of Michigan's firearm deer season on November 15.

The WCO is issued under Part 401, Wildlife Conservation, of the Natural Resources and Environmental Protection Act (NREPA), 1994 PA 451, MCL 324.40101 *et seq.* Part 401 vests the authority for managing wild birds and mammals in the Department of Natural Resources and Environment (Department),[2] and the Natural Resources Commission (Commission). Section 40113a of the NREPA, MCL 324.40113a, shifted primary responsibility for one aspect of wildlife management, regulating the taking of game, to the Commission from the Department:

> The commission of natural resources shall have the exclusive authority to regulate the taking of game as defined in section 40103 in this state. The commission of natural resources shall, to the greatest extent practicable, utilize principles of sound scientific management in making decisions regarding the taking of game. Issuance of orders by the commission of natural resources regarding the taking of game shall be made following a public meeting and an opportunity for public input. [MCL 324.40113a(2).][3]

The particular provision of the WCO identified in your request is found in Chapter II, section 2.1, which states:

> (1) Unless otherwise specified in this order, a person shall not do any of the following:
>
> * * *
>
> (3) During the five days immediately preceding November 15, transport or possess in an area frequented by deer a rifle or shotgun with buckshot, slug load, ball load, or cut shell. A person may transport a rifle or shotgun to or from a hunting camp if the rifle or shotgun is unloaded and securely encased or carried in the trunk of a vehicle. This section shall not prohibit a resident who holds a fur harvester's license from carrying a rimfire firearm .22 caliber or smaller while hunting or checking a trap line during the open season for hunting or trapping fur-bearing animals.

The origins of this provision can be found in an amendment to the Game Law, 1929 PA 286, by 1947 PA 326, which stated, in part, in Chapter IV, section 6, 1948 CL 314.6:

---

[1] The Wildlife Conservation Order is actually made up of numerous orders that have been issued and amended over the course of many decades. It may be viewed by accessing the Michigan Department of Natural Resources and Environment website at: <http://michigan.gov/documents/Wcao_134367_7.html> (accessed August 19, 2010).

[2] All statutory functions and authorities of the former Department of Natural Resources were transferred to the new Michigan Department of Natural Resources and Environment by Executive Order 2009-45, effective January 17, 2010.

[3] Section 40113a was added to Part 401 by 1996 PA 377. In the past, the Department's and the Commission's authority were indistinguishable because the Commission was the head of the Department. But through a series of Executive Orders, beginning in 1991, the Commission's role has changed, and it now only retains certain authority including authority over the taking of game.

> Provided further, That during the 5 days immediately preceding the opening of the season for the taking of deer with firearms it shall be unlawful to transport or possess in any area frequented by deer a rifle larger than .22 caliber rim fire, or shotgun with buckshot, or slug load or ball load or cut shell. [Emphasis in original.]

This statutory provision and other sections of the Game Law were repealed by 1980 PA 86, the Hunting and Fishing License Act. That Act, however, included a prohibition similar to 1948 CL 314.6 at Article 8, section 805, MCL 316.805:

> During the 5 days immediately preceding the opening of the earliest season for the taking of deer with firearms, a person shall not transport or possess in any area frequented by deer a rifle or shotgun with buckshot, slug load, ball load, or cut shell. A person may transport a rifle or shotgun to or from a hunting camp if the rifle or shotgun is unloaded and locked in the trunk of a motor vehicle or otherwise inaccessible to an occupant of the motor vehicle from the interior of the vehicle.

The authority of the Commission was later expanded by 1988 PA 256, the Wildlife Conservation Act, which stated that the Commission "shall manage animals in this state," and authorized the Commission to "issue orders" to do so, including orders establishing the lawful time, place, and method of hunting. The Act also required the Commission to issue orders that would take the place of the remaining sections of the Game Law, effectively repealing those sections. These changes consolidated the various game regulations under the Commission, and were intended to provide for the more consistent and efficient management of the State's wildlife resources. Senate Fiscal Analysis, SB 374, July 12, 1988, p 1.

Subsequently, many of the regulations in the Hunting and Fishing License Act, 1980 PA 86, were repealed by 1993 PA 144. This included MCL 316.805, which was described as having been superseded by the earlier Wildlife Conservation Act, 1988 PA 256. Senate Fiscal Analysis, SB 147, August 8, 1994, pp 2-3. 1993 PA 144 was signed by the Governor on August 13, 1993, and took immediate effect. On September 9, 1993, the Department issued amendment 19 to the WCO, adding section 2.1(3).

This history reveals that the ammunition and firearm restrictions set forth in section 2.1(3), or at least similar provisions, have been in force since 1947. As your letter acknowledges, the Department's position is that section 2.1(3) was intended to, and does, help prevent the poaching of deer during the five days preceding opening day. This intent is demonstrated by the fact that the types of ammunition and firearms subject to the five-day period are those typically used when hunting deer. Furthermore, embedded within the protection against poaching immediately before the season opens are the concepts of fair play and a level playing field for hunters. The restriction helps ensure that all hunters enter the season with an equal opportunity for the taking of game.

You first ask whether this provision of the WCO violates an individual's right to bear arms as established by Const 1963, art 1, § 6.

Section 6 states: "Every person has a right to keep and bear arms for the defense of himself and the state." Const 1963, art 1, § 6. It was preceded by Const 1908, art 2, § 5, which provided: "Every person has a right to bear arms for the defense of himself and the state." Because of the similarity of the provisions and since the Convention Comment to Const 1963, art 1, § 6 indicates no intent to reduce the protection of the right to bear arms granted by the 1908 Constitution, the rights guaranteed under both provisions have been viewed as identical. *People v Swint*, 225 Mich App 353, 359, n 2; 572 NW 2d 666 (1997).

Const 1963, art 1, § 6 is similar to the Second Amendment of the United States Constitution, which provides that "the right of the people to keep and bear Arms, shall not be infringed." *In McDonald v Chicago*, 561 US ___; 130 S Ct 3020, 3042; 177 L Ed 2d 894, 921 (2010), the United States Supreme Court confirmed that this provision provides a "fundamental" and "basic" right of self defense, and that it is applicable to the States by virtue of the Fourteenth Amendment of the United States Constitution:

> In sum, it is clear that the Framers and ratifiers of the Fourteenth Amendment counted the right to keep and bear arms among those fundamental rights necessary to our system of ordered liberty.

In reaching that conclusion, however, the Supreme Court recognized that the right was not without limits. Quoting from its decision in *District of Columbia v Heller*, 554 US ___; 128 S Ct 2783; 171 L Ed 2d 637 (2008), the *McDonald Court* stated:

> It is important to keep in mind that *Heller*, while striking down a law that prohibited the possession of handguns in the home, recognized that the right to keep and bear arms is not "a right to keep and carry any weapon whatsoever in any manner whatsoever and for whatever purpose." 554 US, at ___; 128 S Ct 2783; 171 L Ed 2d at 678. We made it clear in *Heller* that our holding did not cast doubt on such longstanding regulatory measures as "prohibitions on the possession of firearms by felons and the mentally ill," "laws forbidding the carrying of firearms in sensitive places such as schools and government buildings, or laws imposing conditions and qualifications on the commercial sale of arms." *Id.*, at ___; 128 S Ct 2783; 171 L Ed 2d at 678. We repeat those assurances here.

Consistent with *McDonald*, the Michigan Supreme Court construed former Const 1908, art 2, § 5, which created a right to bear arms for specific purposes, as being subject to the reasonable exercise of the State's police power. In *People v Brown*, 253 Mich 537, 539-541; 235 NW 245 (1931) (citations omitted), the Court observed:

> It is generally recognized that the constitutional declaration, in both Federal and State constitutions, of the right to bear arms had its origin in the fear of the American colonists of a standing army and its use to oppress the people, and in their attachment to a militia composed of all able-bodied men. Probably the necessity of self-protection in a frontier society also was a factor.
>
> * * *
>
> *The protection of the Constitution is not limited to militiamen nor military purposes, in terms, but extends to "every person" to bear arms for the "defense of himself" as well as of the State*. This includes the right of a foreigner to possess a revolver for the legitimate defense of his person and property, *subject, however, to the valid exercise of the police power of the State to regulate the carrying of firearms*. [Emphasis added.]

More recently, the Court of Appeals in *People v Swint*, recognizing the State's police power, upheld as constitutional under Const 1963, art 1, § 6, a statute that restricted the right of felons to possess firearms.

Applying the *Brown* and *Swint* Courts' reasoning to the WCO's prohibition on possessing certain types of firearms and ammunition in the field before the opening day of deer season, the restriction does not violate Const 1963, art 1, § 6. The WCO imposes a restriction of short duration that only applies to a limited number of specifically described firearms and ammunition, which are typically used to hunt deer. A person subject to section 2.1(3) may otherwise possess a handgun for self defense. Consequently, the WCO would not violate the Second Amendment as interpreted by the United States Supreme Court in *Heller* and *McDonald*. As there is a legitimate police power justification for the WCO – the prevention of poaching and the assurance of a level playing field for all hunters awaiting opening day – and it only places reasonable limits on the right to carry firearms, it is not unconstitutional.

It is my opinion, therefore, that Const 1963, art 1, § 6 provides a constitutional right in Michigan to bear firearms for self defense, subject to reasonable regulation by the State. The firearm and ammunition restrictions set forth in Wildlife Conservation Order section 2.1(3) dealing with the possession of a rifle or shotgun in areas frequented by deer during the five-day period immediately preceding the beginning of firearm deer season are a reasonable exercise of the State's police power, and do not violate the right to bear arms established by Const 1963, art 1 § 6.

You next ask whether the Legislature may "rescind" section 2.1(3) of the WCO by legislation. It is a general rule of law that: "An agency has no inherent power. Any authority it may have is vested by the Legislature, in statutes, or by the Constitution." *Deleeuw v Bd of State Canvassers*, 263 Mich App 497, 500; 688 NW2d 847 (2004), quoting *Belanger & Sons, Inc v Dep't of State*, 176 Mich App 59, 62-63; 438 NW2d 885 (1989).

The Commission's authority to adopt section 2.1(3) is not derived from the Michigan Constitution. The Commission was vested with exclusive authority to regulate the taking of game by the enactment of 1996 PA 377, which was submitted by the Legislature to the electors for vote under the referendum process provided for in Const 1963, art 4, § 34. It was approved by a majority of the electors on November 5, 1996. While a citizen initiated law under art 2, § 9 of the Constitution expressly requires the votes of three-fourths of the members of each house of the legislature to amend or repeal it, art 4, § 34 lacks that requirement and thus laws adopted through referendum may be amended at any time by a simple majority vote of the Legislature:

> No law initiated or adopted by the people shall be subject to the veto power of the governor, and no law adopted by the people at the polls under the initiative provisions of this section shall be amended or repealed, except by a vote of the electors unless otherwise provided in the initiative measure or by three-fourths of the members elected to and serving in each house of the legislature. Laws approved by the people under the referendum provision of this section may be amended by the legislature at any subsequent session thereof. [Const 1963, art 2, § 9.]

OAG, 1997-1998, No 6990, p 161 (August 10, 1998), addressed the Legislature's power to make, amend or repeal a law:

> Const 1963, art 4, § 1, provides that: "The legislative power of the State of Michigan is vested in a senate and a house of representatives." This legislative power has been described as plenary and equivalent to the legislative powers asserted by the Parliament of the United Kingdom, except so far as the people of this state have limited it. *Harsha v Detroit*, 261 Mich 586, 590; 246 NW 849 (1933); *Advisory Opinion on Constitutionality of 1976 PA 240*, 400 Mich 311; 254 NW2d 544 (1977); and *Sessa v State Treasurer*, 117 Mich App 46, 54; 323 NW2d 586 (1982).

The Legislature has plenary authority, except where specifically limited by the Constitution. The WCO was issued by the Commission under authority granted it by the Legislature and the voters through the referendum process. That authority can be altered or repealed entirely by the Legislature and the Governor through the process for passage of a bill.[4]

---

[4] For example, the Legislature previously used its authority to override a firearms rule promulgated by the then Department of Natural Resources when it enacted 2004 PA 129 and 130. That law exempted persons licensed to carry concealed pistols or otherwise exempt from licensure under 1927 PA 372 from a rule that prohibited the possession of firearms while hunting deer during "bow and arrow" season. Editors Note, OAG, 2003-2004, No 7123, p 4, 7 (February 11, 2003).

It is my opinion, therefore, that the Legislature may, by statute, amend or repeal the firearm and ammunition restrictions set forth in Wildlife Conservation Order section 2.1 (3).

MIKE COX
Attorney General

Opinion No. 7260
September 2, 2011

FIREARMS: Possession of firearm silencers or mufflers

SILENCERS OR MUFFLERS:

MICHIGAN PENAL CODE:
The possession, manufacture, or sale of a firearm silencer is permitted in Michigan under MCL 750.224(1)(b) if the person is licensed or approved to possess, manufacture, or sell such a device by the federal Bureau of Alcohol, Tobacco, Firearms and Explosives, as required by MCL 750.224(3)(c). Possession, manufacture, or sale of a firearm silencer by an unlicensed or unapproved person is a felony, punishable by up to five years imprisonment under MCL 750.224(2).

Honorable Rick Jones
State Senator
The Capitol
Lansing, MI

Honorable Tonya Schuitmaker
State Senator
The Capitol
Lansing, MI

Honorable Mark Meadows
State Representative
The Capitol
Lansing, MI

Honorable Kevin Cotter
State Representative
The Capitol
Lansing,MI

In separate requests, you have asked whether, assuming the appropriate license or approval is obtained from the federal Bureau of Alcohol, Tobacco, Firearms and Explosives, a Michigan citizen may legally possess, manufacture, or sell a firearm silencer or muffler.[1]

Federal law imposes restrictions and taxes on the transfer or making of certain firearms, including devices such as silencers or mufflers. 28 USC 5845(a); 18 USC 921(a)(3).[2] The Department of Justice regulates firearms through the Bureau of Alcohol, Tobacco, Firearms and Explosives.[3] The federal licensing or approval process is set forth in the National Firearms Act, 26 USC 5811 *et seq* (transfers of firearms), and 26 USC 5821 *et seq* (making of firearms), and promulgated regulations. See 27 CFR Part 479. Both the transfer and the making of a silencer may be approved by the Bureau upon submitting the proper application forms.

In either case, the application process involves a detailed background check to ensure that the applicant complies with federal law, including a determination that the applicant has not been charged with or been convicted of a disqualifying crime; is a lawful resident and at least 21 years of age; does not use illegal substances; has not been adjudicated mentally defective or committed to a mental institution; and has not been convicted of a crime involving domestic violence. In addition, the applicant must undergo an identification verification process and secure a certification from a local law enforcement agency having juris-

---

[1] Section 224(4) of the Michigan Penal Code, MCL 750.224(4), defines "muffler" or "silencer" to mean one or more of the following:

(a) A device for muffling, silencing, or deadening the report of a firearm.

(b) A combination of parts, designed or redesigned, and intended for use in assembling or fabricating a muffler or silencer.

(c) A part, designed or redesigned, and intended only for use in assembling or fabricating a muffler or silencer.

[1]These devices are also often referred to as "sound suppressors." For convenience, reference to the term "silencer" or "silencers" throughout this opinion should be understood as referring to all the items listed in this definition.

[2] Federal law also requires that all firearms be registered and listed on the National Firearms Registration and Transfer Record. See 26 USC 5841 *et seq*.

[3] Historical responsibility of the Secretary of the Treasury of the United States to regulate firearms through the Bureau of Alcohol, Tobacco, Firearms and Explosives was transferred by Congress to the Department of Justice by Public Law No 107-296, Title XI, Subtitle B, § 1112(f)(4), (6), 116 Stat 2276 (codified at 18 USC 922 (2002)).

diction in the area of the applicant's residence that the device will be used for lawful purposes, and that its possession does not violate state or local law. See 27 CFR Part 479, Subparts E and F.[4]

Turning to your question, the analysis begins with section 224 of the Michigan Penal Code, MCL 750.224, found in Chapter 37 relating to firearms. Public Act 33 of 1991 reorganized the section into its present structure, including four subsections: prohibitions are stated in subsection (1)(a) through (e); the penalty for violating the section is stated in subsection (2); the exceptions are stated in subsection 3(a) through (c); and subsection (4) provides a definition of the term "muffler" or "silencer."[5] Section 224 thus provides, in part:

> (1) *A person shall not manufacture, sell, offer for sale, or possess any of the following*:
>
> a) A machine gun or firearm that shoots or is designed to shoot automatically more than 1 shot without manual reloading, by a single function of the trigger.
>
> (b) A *muffler or silencer*.
>
> (c) A bomb or bombshell.
>
> (d) A blackjack, slugshot, billy, metallic knuckles, sand club, sand bag, or bludgeon.
>
> (e) A device, weapon, cartridge, container, or contrivance designed to render a person temporarily or permanently disabled by the ejection, release, or emission of a gas or other substance.
>
> (2) A person who violates subsection (1) is guilty of a felony, punishable by imprisonment for not more than 5 years, or a fine of not more than $2,500.00, or both.
>
> (3) *Subsection (1) does not apply to any of the following*:
>
> (a) A self-defense spray or foam device as defined in section 224d.[6]
>
> (b) A person manufacturing firearms, explosives, or munitions of war by virtue of a contract with a department of the government of the United States.
>
> (c) A person licensed by the [Director of the Bureau of Alcohol, Tobacco, Firearms and Explosives] to manufacture, sell, or possess a machine gun, *or a device, weapon, cartridge, container, or contrivance described in subsection (1)*. [Emphasis added.]

The plain language of MCL 750.224(1) prohibits the possession, manufacture, or sale of silencers. But subsection 3 of section 224 states a number of exceptions to the general prohibition set forth in subsection (1). The question, therefore, is whether any of these exceptions apply to silencers. The first two subsections, (3)(a) and (b), do not relate to silencers. Thus, an exception to the prohibition against possessing silencers stated in subsection (1) may only be found in the language of subsection (3)(c).[7] When construing a statute, the foremost obligation is to discern and effectuate the intent of the Legislature as may reasonably be inferred from the words expressed in the statute. *Halloran v Bhan*, 470 Mich 572, 576-578; 683 NW2d 129 (2004); *Massey v Mandell*, 462 Mich 375, 380-381; 614 NW2d 70 (2000). Unless defined in the statute, every word or phrase of a statute should be accorded its plain and ordinary meaning, taking into account the context in which the words are used. MCL 8.3a; *Western Michigan Univ Bd of Control v Michigan*, 455 Mich 531, 539; 565 NW2d 828 (1997). Both the plain meaning of the critical word or phrase as well as its placement and purpose in the statutory scheme must be considered. *Sun Valley Foods Co v Ward*, 460 Mich 230, 237; 596 NW2d 119 (1999). Nothing may be read into an unambiguous statute that is not within the manifest intent of the Legislature as derived from the words of the statute itself. *Roberts v Mecosta County General Hosp*, 466 Mich 57, 63; 642 NW2d 663 (2002). But effect must be given to every word in a statute so as to avoid an interpretation that would render any part surplusage. *Jenkins v Patel*, 471 Mich 158, 167; 684 NW2d 346 (2004).

The language of subsection (3)(c) of section 224 must be analyzed with these guiding principles in mind. That language states that subsection (1) does not apply to: "A person licensed by" the Bureau of Alcohol, Tobacco, Firearms and Explosives "to manufacture, sell, or possess a machine gun, or a device, weapon, cartridge, container, or contrivance described in subsection (1)." The plain text applies to a person federally licensed "to manufacture, sell, or possess a machine gun." OAG, 2005-2006, No 7183, p 63 (December 27, 2005), examined this provision and the applicable federal licensing law and concluded that it authorized a person in Michigan to possess a machine gun if it was lawfully possessed before May 19, 1986, and was

---

[4] More detailed information regarding this process may be found on the Bureau of Alcohol, Tobacco, Firearms and Explosives website at <http://www.atf.gov> (accessed August 31, 2011).

[5] See the full text of the current definition quoted in n 1.

[6] MCL 750.224d defines a self-defense spray device to include those devices capable of carrying, and ejects, releases, or emits not more than 35 grams of any combination of orthochlorobenzalmalononitrile and inert ingredients or a solution containing not more than 10% oleoresin capsicum.

[7] But see MCL 750.231 for additional exceptions, not relevant to your questions, afforded to law enforcement, armed forces, and similar personnel.

properly registered under federal law. This language does not apply to silencers, however, leaving the balance of subsection (3)(c) for review.

The remaining part of subsection (3)(c) states that subsection (1) does not apply to a person federally licensed to manufacture, sell, or possess "a *device*, weapon, cartridge, container, or contrivance *described in subsection (1)*." MCL 750.224(3)(c) (emphasis added). Answering your question requires determining the meaning of this emphasized language, which is important in several respects.

First, the language refers to specific items mentioned in subsection (1) of section 224: a machine gun, as mentioned in subsection (1)(a), and the five items mentioned in subsection (1)(e) ("device, weapon, cartridge, container, or contrivance"). But it does not incorporate the same clause used in subsection (1)(e) to limit the items listed there ("designed to render a person temporarily or permanently disabled by the ejection, release, or emission of a gas or other substance").

Second, when qualifying the terms "device, weapon, cartridge, container, or contrivance," the exception refers to "subsection (1)" and not the more limiting subdivision (e) of subsection (1). The question therefore arises whether the Legislature intended to authorize possession of only federally-registered machine guns and certain gas-emitting devices or whether it intended to authorize possession of all the items listed in subsection (1) if federally registered.

Again, the foremost rule is to ascertain and effectuate the intent of the Legislature. *Halloran*, 470 Mich at 576-578. "[I]t is the court's duty to give effect to the intent of the Legislature as expressed in the actual language used in the statute. It is the role of the judiciary to interpret, not write the law. If the statutory language is clear and unambiguous, the statute is enforced as written. Judicial construction is neither necessary nor permitted because it is presumed that the Legislature intended the clear meaning it expressed." *People v Schaefer*, 473 Mich 418, 430-431; 703 NW2d 774 (2005) (footnotes omitted).

Here, the Legislature exempted from the prohibition set forth in subsection 224(1) any federally-licensed "device . . . described in subsection (1)." MCL 750.224(3)(c). A silencer is a "*device* for muffling, silencing, or deadening the report of a firearm." MCL 750.224(4)(a) (emphasis added). Had the Legislature intended to limit the exception in subsection (3)(c) of section 224 to machine guns and devices that eject, release, or emit gas or other substances, it would have limited the application of the exception to machine guns and those weapons and devices set out in subsection (1)(a) and (e). Instead, the Legislature chose neither option, electing to use statutory language indicating that any of the devices listed in "subsection (1)" qualify for the federal licensee exception to the state prohibition. Whether all of the devices listed in subsection (1) should fall within the exception for federally-registered devices is a policy determination for the Legislature alone to make; unambiguous statutes must be enforced as written. The wisdom of a statute is for the Legislature to determine and not the courts; the law must be enforced as written. *Smith v Cliffs on the Bay Condo Ass'n*, 463 Mich 420, 430; 617 NW2d 536 (2000).[8]

Moreover, since section 224 is part of the Penal Code and criminal penalties are provided for the illegal possession of a firearm silencer, specific rules of statutory construction involving criminal laws must also be considered. A fundamental rule of statutory construction is that criminal statutes must be strictly construed. *People v Carlson*, 466 Mich 130, 138; 644 NW2d 704 (2002). But see MCL 750.2 (requiring that the provisions of the Penal Code be construed according to the "fair import of their terms, to promote justice and to effect the objects of the law"). Any doubt whether conduct is criminal must be resolved in favor of the defendant. *People v Jahner*, 433 Mich 490; 446 NW2d 151 (1989). The fair and plain application of the exception set forth in MCL 750.224(3)(c) supports the conclusion that each of the devices or weapons "described in subsection (1)" of section 224 is exempted from the otherwise applicable prohibition of that subsection if possession is federally approved.

It could be argued that the Legislature's use of the phrases "machine gun" and "device, weapon, cartridge, container, or contrivance," which initially appear in subsection (1)(a) and (e), and then are repeated in subsection (3)(c), evidence its intent to restrict the exception to the enumerated items in (1)(a) and (e). Under this argument, the prohibition of subsection (1) would not apply based on the exception of subsection (3)(c) for a person licensed by the Department of Alcohol, Tobacco, Firearms and Explosives to possess, manufacture, or sell a "machine gun," see (1)(a), or for a "device, weapon, cartridge, container, or contrivance *designed to render a person temporarily or permanently disabled by the ejection, release, or emission of a gas or other substance*," see (1)(e) (emphasis added). A silencer does not fit either category, and thus, under this reading, would not be exempt from prohibition.

But this interpretation assumes that the Legislature mistakenly omitted from subsection 3(c) language it placed in subsection 1(e). Alternatively, it requires assuming that the Legislature intended "described in subsection (1)" to mean "described in subsection 1(e)." But under basic principles of statutory interpretation, language cannot be added to a statutory provision that the Legislature did not itself include. *Empire Iron Mining Partnership v Orhanen*, 455 Mich 410, 423; 565 NW2d 844 (1997); *Farrington v Total Petroleum, Inc*, 442 Mich 201, 210; 501 NW2d 76 (1993). Moreover, an interpretation that the Legislature intended to limit the "subsection (1)" exception to subsection 1(e) would require persons wishing to acquire any devices that disable a person through the ejection or release of a "gas or other substance" to secure a federal permit in order to qualify for

[8] In OAG, 1977-1978, No 5210, p 189 (August 10, 1977), the Attorney General opined that MCL 750.224 prohibited a person from possessing either an automatic weapon or a weapon equipped with a silencer. However, section 224 has undergone various amendments since that time, and these changes to the law supersede that opinion. See 1978 PA 564; 1980 PA 346; 1991 PA 33.

the exception, which is not possible since the National Firearms Act does not generally regulate such devices, unless they are in the form of a poison gas bomb, missile, grenade, etc. 28 USC 921 and 922. A fundamental rule of statutory construction is that the Legislature did not intend to do a useless thing. *Girard v Wagenmaker*, 437 Mich 231, 244; 470 NW2d 372 (1991). Accordingly, the better reasoned interpretation, and the interpretation consistent with the rules of statutory construction that guide this office and the courts, is that a silencer is a "device" exempt from the prohibition of subsection 1 under the plain language of subsection 3(c).

It is my opinion, therefore, that the possession, manufacture, or sale of a firearm silencer is permitted in Michigan under MCL 750.224(1)(b) if the person is licensed or approved to possess, manufacture, or sell such a device by the federal Bureau of Alcohol, Tobacco, Firearms and Explosives, as required by MCL 750.224(3)(c). Possession, manufacture, or sale of a firearm silencer by an unlicensed or unapproved person is a felony, punishable by up to five years imprisonment under MCL 750.224(2).

BILL SCHUETTE
Attorney General

CPSIA information can be obtained
at www.ICGtesting.com
Printed in the USA
BVHW091804070720
583169BV00002B/155

9 781640 020436